The Golden Yoke

The Golden Yoke

The Legal Cosmology of Buddhist Tibet

Rebecca Redwood French

CORNELL UNIVERSITY PRESS
Ithaca and London

THIS BOOK HAS BEEN SUPPORTED BY A GRANT FROM THE NATIONAL ENDOWMENT FOR THE HUMANITIES, AN INDEPENDENT FEDERAL AGENCY.

PUBLICATION OF THIS BOOK WAS AIDED BY SUBVENTIONS AWARDED TO THE AUTHOR BY THE GRADUATE COMMITTEE ON ARTS & HUMANITIES OF THE UNIVERSITY OF COLORADO AT BOULDER, THE EUGENE M. KAYDEN UNIVERSITY OF COLORADO ANNUAL FACULTY MANUSCRIPT AWARD, AND THE UNIVERSITY OF CHICAGO.

First published 1995 by Cornell University Press.

Library of Congress Cataloging-in-Publication Data

French, Rebecca Redwood.
    The golden yoke : the legal cosmology of Buddhist Tibet / Rebecca Redwood French.
        p.   cm.
    Includes bibliographical references and indexes.
    ISBN 0-8014-3084-4 (cloth : alk. paper)
    1. Law—China—Tibet.   2. Customary law—China—Tibet.   3. Ethnological jurisprudence.   4. Tibet (China)—Social life and customs.   I. Title.
    KNQ8708.F74   1995
    340'.115'09515—dc20   95-19360

Printed in the United States of America

Contents

Illustrations

Plates

❀

Illustrations

Preface

This book presents the "golden yoke" of Buddhist Tibet, the last medieval legal system in existence in the middle of the twentieth century. It is reconstructed as a series of layered narratives from the memories of people who participated in the daily operation of law in the houses and courtyards, the offices and courts of Tibet. The practice of law in this unique legal world, which lacked most of our familiar signposts, ranged from the fantastic use of oracles in the search for evidence to the more mundane presentation of cases in court.

Buddhism and law, two topics rarely intertwined in Western consciousness, are at the center of this work. The Tibetan legal system was based on Buddhist philosophy and reflected Buddhist thought in legal practice and decision-making. For Tibetans, law is a cosmology, a kaleidoscopic patterning of relations which is constantly changing, recycling, and re-forming even as it integrates the universe and the individual into a timeless mandalic whole.

This book also critiques our idea of legal culture. It argues that we conceal from ourselves the ways we do law by segregating things legal into a separate space with rigidly defined categories. The legal cosmology of Buddhist Tibet brings into question both this autonomous framework and most of the basic presumptions we have about the very nature of law, from precedent and *res judicata* to rule-formation and closure.

Over the course of ten years, the number of people who aided me in this research grew exponentially. E. Adam Hoebel was the first. He suggested that I study with Leopold Pospisil, who took me on as a student. At Yale, in both the graduate and law schools, I worked with Harold Conklin, Harold Scheffler, John Middleton, Stanley Weinstein, Michael Reisman, Mirjan Damaska, M. G. Smith, and Wesley

Needham. The LL.M. class of 1982 at Yale Law School was perhaps the most fun-loving and bright set of scholars I have ever encountered. Western scholars in Tibetan and Nepalese studies who provided invaluable instruction during this period include Robert Thurman, Geshe Sopa, Khamlung Tulku, Barbara Aziz, Nancy Levine, Beatrice and Robert Miller, Joe Elder, Geza Uray, Gene Smith, Josef Kolmas, Michael Aris, Krystyna Cech, David Gellner, and P. Richardus.

In Asia, the essential contributors to this work number in the hundreds. After our interviews, His Holiness the Dalai Lama of Tibet became interested and encouraged former officials to help in the reconstruction. The head of the Tibetan Library, Gyatsho Tsering, provided continuous encouragement and aid from the first time I proposed the project to him in the summer of 1981. Warmhearted Vijan Puliampet of the Berkeley Scholars in India fought many visa battles and provided constant encouragement. Particularly knowledgeable and patient with my questions in India and Nepal were Ngawang Thondup Narkyid, Tsewang Tamdin, Geshe Losang Gyatsho, Wangdu Dorjee, Phuntsok Tashi Takla, Drakton Jampa Gyaltsen, Kungo Shakabpa, Kungo Sampho, Lobsang Dolma, Lha Gyari Trichen, the Tarings, Trisi Tara, Sharpa Tulku, Thubten Dhoden, Lobsang Tenzin Thonzur, Sonam Wangchuk, Nyima Zangpo, Gelung Lobsang Dhonden, Thubten Nyingche, N. D. Gyalpo, Dhakpa Namgyal, Juchen Thubten Namgyla, and the Shelkar Lama. Lobsang Shastri and Karma Gyatso aided me in my research with infinite patience. I thank also the many other Tibetans I interviewed, both in India and the Tibetan Autonomous Region, who asked not to be listed by name.

It would have been impossible to present the depth of information given here without the daily instruction over three years of Kungola Thubten Sangye. His contribution was so profound that this book should be seen as a joint effort between the two of us. Working through the law codes line by obscure line, annotating every phrase with case examples from his own life, filling in points on Tibetan history and religion, he was a tutor whose broad knowledge and thoughtful understanding of the Tibetan law codes and legal system were unparalleled. Working with him has been one of the real gifts of my life, and his death was an immense loss both to me personally and to all of Tibetan scholarship.

The East Asian Legal Studies Center at Harvard Law School, where I wrote most of my conclusions, offers a unique atmosphere, with its research scholars and law professors from all over East Asia. I particularly thank Oliver Oldman, Bill Alford, Mary Moss Buck, Karen Turner, Susan Weld, Ta Van Tai, Reiko Nishakawa, and Miko Graffagna of EALS. Professor Nagatomi of Harvard was kind enough to give advice and to allow me to join him in Tibetan classes. Michael Aris, Jamyang Norbu, and Hugh Richardson reviewed the text while I was at Harvard. At the Institute for Advanced Study in Princeton, I converted the text into a book with the helpful comments of Clifford Geertz, Michael Walzer, Georgia Warnke, Gwen Mikell, Michael Meeker, Alan Ryan, Albrecht Funk, Paul Hyams, and Kristen Van Ausdall.

I owe a great debt to the individuals who have reviewed and edited various sections of this work, including Anila Karma Lekshe Tsomo, Leopold Pospisil, Catherine Jordan, Jerome Offner, Carolyn Jones, Jan Kristiansen, Don Brenneis, and the indomitable Pat Sterling. All the visual components, many of which do far more than the text in explaining my ideas, were conceived and designed by Peetie Van Etten and produced by Linda Nishio. At the University of Colorado School of Law, Bob Nagel, Dale Oesterle, and Pierre Schlag have offered useful comments; my research assistant Laura Teachout has been invaluable; and the staff, particularly Kim Clay, Marge Brunner, and Kay Wilkie have provided expert advice and typed innumerable drafts. Benpa Topgyal read a first draft of the book, reviewed my Tibetan, and assisted with the "pronounceable" transliteration. I also thank Mary and Jim French, all the Van Ettens, Michelle Nimrod, Melanie Romo, Susan De-Riemer, the one and only Quarrelsome Four, Suzanne LaFont, Michael Kaplan, Jeff Rogers, David Gellner, Maggie Rogers, Molly Teas, Linda Kilner, and my editor, Peter Agree.

Funding for this project has come from the National Science Foundation, Yale East Asian Concilium, Williams Fund of Yale, Wenner-Gren Foundation, Social Science Research Council, Berkeley Scholar in India Program, Woodrow Wilson Charlotte Newcomb Fund, American Association of University Women, and University of Colorado School of Law and Graduate School.

This book is dedicated to my husband, John Edward Hess, and my two daughters, Emilie and Clara Hess, whose love has sustained me from beginning to end.

REBECCA REDWOOD FRENCH

Boulder, Colorado

A Note on
Tibetan Translation,
Transliteration, and Citation

This text is based on taped interviews I conducted with Tibetans and materials translated from Tibetan. All quotations from Tibetan texts and interviews are my translations.

For the reader's convenience, Tibetan words in the text appear in a form approximating their pronunciation, followed in parentheses (the first time they are used) by the Wylie system's transliteration: for example, *timsa* (*khrims sa*). All Tibetan terms are indexed as well. (For more Tibetan terminology and Tibetan script, see French 1990a.)

References to Tibetan law codes throughout the text are based on my unpublished translation notebooks, cited by the following abbreviations with line numbers.

GP   the Ganden Podrang Code of the Dalai Lamas notebook, 1336 lines; translation of pp. 41–95 of *Tibetan Legal Materials* 1985

ND   the Neudong Law Code notebook, 459 lines; translation of chap. 3 of Sangye, "Handwritten Law Code Notes"

Ts   the Law Code of the Tsang Kings notebook, 696 lines; translation of chap. 5 of Sangye, "Handwritten Law Code Notes," and of "*Khrims yig zhal lce bcu gsum bzhugs so*"

Br   the Brown notebook, 723 lines (300–1023); translation of p. 25 to the end of *Bod kyi khrims yig chen mo zhal lce bcu drug gi'grel pa bzhugs so*

BrCC   the Brown notebook "Court Costs" section, 124 lines; translation of pp. 131–35 of *Tibetan Legal Materials* 1985

Gr   the Green notebook, 169 pages; analysis and partial translation by Lobsang Shastri, with Rebecca French, of Library of Tibetan Works and
Archives Documents

Note   LS   the Law Stories notebook (cited by page number); translation of sections
of Thubten Sangye's "Handwritten Law Code Notes"

The Golden Yoke

Plate 1. Mahro Monastery in western Tibet in the winter with estate lands below. 1976. (Syed Ali Shah, Leh, Ladakh)

Introduction

Religious law is smooth like a silken knot [around your neck],
State law controls like a golden yoke [on your neck].
                                            —Ganden Podrang Code of the Dalai Lamas

Standing in the middle of the field, the bald monk in faded maroon robes found that he was tired of the brilliant sun. The sky seemed all too bright around him, and he was sweating profusely, even though the cold autumn winds had already started. In his hands were sheets of paper with notes copied from a big book in the monastery, which described the lands in all seven villages of the monastery's estate. He had written down the description of two plots and now read from that paper to the two farmers who accompanied him as they began to look for boundary markers in the fields.

In the distance he saw out of the corner of his eye two horsemen on the road from Lhasa to Gyantse, coming south from the capital of this district of Nakartse. He stopped to watch them. They must find the day as bright as he did. Most of their three-day journey south had been, he knew, skirting the northern border of the incredible Lake Yardrok. It was impossible to describe its iridescent deep blueness to a person who was not from that district, how it sat like a mirrored plate sloping only slightly away from its sanded edge, almost slipping into itself. It was vast and many-armed, the most radiant and jewel-like lake in Tibet. Others had told him that the holy lake of Mount Sumeru in the west or the lake in which one can see visions of the future and the birthplace of incarnations was more radiant than Yardrok. He did not believe them. The travelers, very fortunate to have spent so many days near this lake, passed by and continued on the road.

The monastery of Dagon Tsanga Chokor Ling had been his assignment post for several years, and he rather liked it. As administrator and head of the small monastic community, he was pleased that this post allowed him to learn about compassion and life in a religious community. It suited his personality well and gave him enough time for chanting his daily prayers. Since childhood, he had been concerned with his future rebirth, which is why his parents had sent him to a monastery in his local town at a very early age. He contemplated this subject often and prayed to return as a human being in a propitious year, location, and body.

Still, as he stood there in the brilliant sun, he thought to himself that there had been too many disputes in this area in the last year. Was this a sign that merited watching? Before the birth of a great being into an area, there would often be a long period of droughts, ruined crops, and disharmony. But there was no important lama who had dissolved his body recently and would be taking rebirth; the last visitor from Lhasa had told them that His Holiness the Dalai Lama was in good health. Undoubtedly, the local protector gods disliked the proliferation of angry words and thoughts in this village, but would their displeasure take the form of sickness in children? Would the women stop bearing? Or was something else at work? He was determined to ask the senior monk about this and to schedule some rituals of appeasement for the local protectors.

With a call from one of the farmers, his thoughts returned to the fields. They decided to walk over the boundaries together. The description in the document in his hand stated that the first farmer's plot went "from the south of the hill to the bank of the river," then along the river and "over to the marker" (see Figure 1). He walked from the center of the field to the riverbank. Then, walking on what he thought might be a boundary line, he started from the river toward one of the farmers. Plots were rarely square in Tibet, and boundaries indicated by natural landmarks were common in the descriptions. But there was no large stone marker at the spot his notes specified. The three began to dig in the earth with a stick. One foot down, they uncovered a pile of white stones sitting in a bed of charcoal ash; this was always used to mark the placement of a stone in case it was subsequently moved. Neither farmer commented on how the stone had been moved, and so he said nothing about it. This was a fact for consideration. His investigation of the boundaries of the plot completed, he helped the farmers move a large stone into place as a new marker. The petitioner in this dispute had been correct that someone was tampering with the markers; who had been doing it and why were other matters.

As they set off for home, the monk Sonam chanted prayers again and again while counting one bead for each prayer with the rosary in his left hand.[1] He thought as he chanted that deciding this case would require a bit more effort, but the record book might have some answers. He needed greater detail as to the affairs of these farmers. If the southside farmer's plot had produced such a small crop, perhaps it was because he had mistaken the boundary and the northside farmer had taken advantage of this. Sonam needed to know how much grain the northside farmer had produced last year.

In the past, the monk had been asked to decide several different kinds of land disputes from this village. This dispute was over the corner of a plot that had not been indicated along a natural marker line, the river. The large marker that he and the farmers had put in position lay in the middle of the boundary line dividing the two plots, but there was no marker on the river's edge. The owner on the south side claimed that the boundary line's endpoint on the river was much farther upstream than the northside owner contended. Each owner's claim would increase his plot's size substantially. It was a perplexing case, particularly because it had not been solved by their investigation of the site together.

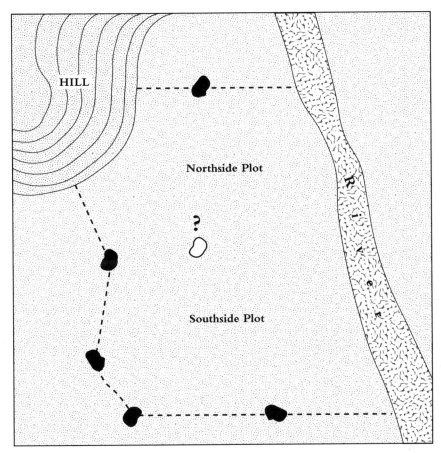

Figure 1. Sketch of the fields in the boundary dispute Sonam has been asked to conciliate. White circle is the location of the misplaced stone marker; black circles are other field marker stones.

The northside farmer, who first brought the problem up, had asked Sonam to be a conciliator, a *bardum pa (bar 'dum pa)*, not an adviser or a judge. This signaled that his was to be an "internal decision," not one that was part of his official monastic duties as a government administrator. Everyone knew that he had been chosen because he was the administrator; still, the request indicated that the disputants were not willing to go through official channels yet—they were reluctant to employ his expertise and weight in that capacity. So he accepted.

It was said that many years before, a land dispute between two owners of local fields had been taken to the district court in Nakartse, yet after several investigations and a costly procedure, it had still not been settled. Finally, a *bardum pa* had been asked to go to the district court, withdraw the case, and then settle it in the local village after paying high costs to the court and judges. Ever since, people in this area had been reluctant to turn to the district court. Saying that it would just end up in legal negotiation, they quoted the proverb, "Don't petition to the authorities; don't ask anyone for help"; the northside farmer had used this when asking Sonam to be a conciliator.

Sonam had learned in school that in the very early period, if one man killed another, then another man would be killed in revenge. Buddhism had changed that; procedures had been developed to avoid revenge killings, and now such matters were decided in light of the Ten Nonvirtuous Acts and the truth and untruth of the Law Code of the Dalai Lamas. Conciliation was even mentioned in the Great Law Code of the Fifth Dalai Lama. One passage he remembered had this to say:

> Moreover in cases of this type of fighting between two sides,
> If an elder man of that region or a thoughtful man, deciding a case,
> Issues a final decision document, it is said that
> "A conciliation made by a goat, should not be undone by a horse," and
> "A conciliation made by a beggar [should not be undone] by a mighty king."
> If an honest conciliation is made, whether the case is large or small,
> The judge should support that conciliation.
> As it is said in the old law texts, one should support the truth.[2]

Sonam found that his mind was wandering. He turned his head to the man walking next to him and asked if either field was rented. The southside farmer said that he had rented his out to a landless laborer for one growing season last year. The renter had not produced even forty-five *khel* (*khal*) of barley, a very poor harvest.[3] He had the rental document, drafted by a man in the village, at his house. The northside farmer added that he paid his taxes to the government, not the monastery, and that the farmers in this area all knew that the government taxpayers had the harshest burden.

There were more than enough complications here to think about. Seeing the monastery in the distance, Sonam turned, told both of them to come to his room the next afternoon, and started down the path toward the monastery. They both bowed slightly to him as he left the field.

On his own now, Sonam followed the edges of the estate fields until he came to a small irrigation stream and began to walk along its bank. The sun reflected brightly off the surface of the water. He could see the flat roof of the monastery's main building in the distance, and he raised his cloak to wipe the sweat from his eyes. Stopping for a moment, he took off his monastic cloak and folded it several times. Balancing the cloak on his head and the back of his neck, he felt the ease of shade for the first time that day and sighed with relief. Then he hurried on his way again.

Most of the fields he passed belonged to one of the seven villages of the monastery's estate, which had been arranged since earliest times in a collective pattern for taxation. Each village owed a certain amount of best-quality grain to his monastery, enough for eleven *khel* of barley for each monk each year—eight *khel* in raw grain and three in a roasted and ground form called *tsampa* (*rtsam pa*). This grain was collected yearly at harvest time by the storekeeper of the monastery. Fields in each of the seven villages were divided into two kinds: individual plots owned by a particular household, to be cultivated for personal use; and collective plots on which all members of the village had to work, the harvest of which went entirely to the monastery. Unlike those in other parts of Tibet, the peasants here were not taxed directly for grain by household, but each household was expected to contribute workers to the collective monastery fields for the entire summer season, a form of service-labor tax called *ulak* (*'u lag*).

As he walked, Sonam continued to review what he had learned from the land documents and his questions. The southside field was a "product of three *khel*" field, which meant that approximately three *khel* of barley could be expected for every one *khel* sown. It was part of the monastic estate and had no tax burden as it was owned individually by a household, not collectively by the village. The northside field was not part of the monastic estate; it had a tax burden in grain that went to pay government taxes. Sonam reflected that the tax assignments and grain production of the fields would not help him decide this particular case.

At last the door of the monastic temple room was in front of him, and he moved into the cool shade. On the porch he did three full prostrations to the image of the Buddha, touching his nose to the ground with his hands over his head, his legs stretched out. The cool stone beneath him felt wonderful. Rising slowly for the third time, he turned and walked around the small courtyard to see how the lessons of the young monks were coming this afternoon.

Approaching the group of students from the back as they sat in rows, swaying back and forth while they memorized texts, he caught the eye of the senior tutor, who rose and came to greet him. "We have just been practicing the prayers of Manjushri. The abbott has been away this afternoon on business. Will you give a lesson?"

This was not what Sonam wanted to hear, for he was expecting to return to his room and have a refreshing cup of hot tea. But the pupils should be instructed daily, and he went forward to give a lesson. Nothing came to his mind as he moved up the rows, nothing of the thousands of verses he had mastered in his own studies; he sat and everyone became silent, but still his mind would not bring up anything religious. And so he turned to the land dispute that was preoccupying him and decided to give instruction on that. When he had finished, Sonam began the chanting of the prayers and continued for several minutes. Then he motioned for the senior tutor to take his place and scurried off to his room. One student looked at him quizzically as he left.

A thermos of hot tea awaited him in his room. He took off his cloak and shook it out, placing it across the stretched rope on the wall. Sitting cross-legged on his mattress, he placed a cup in front of him and poured in the tea. After reciting a thanksgiving prayer for food, he drained the entire cup, refilled it, and drank again. Then he took out a small leather bag and, pulling the strings apart, took out some *tsampa* flour, which he ate in small handfuls. Eating and drinking in the quiet of his room was truly pleasurable. Perhaps he would not go to dinner tonight but remain in his room doing recitations.

Sonam arose and went to light the butter lamps on his small personal altar. Returning to his mattress and straightening his back, he began the recitations he had memorized years ago in the monastery near his home. It was dark before he finished, and his mind was finally very clear. Several other monks came by to talk or ask questions, but he was alone again in an hour or so, and his mind returned to the day's activities. Taking a small oil lamp with him, he went to consult the land record book for a second time.

It was a huge government record book, almost two and a half by one and a half feet, called the *jétha sherpang ('byed phra sher dpang)*, and it contained a record of every land plot in the area, giving—in this order—the name of the plot; a description of its boundaries; its seed requirement; the name of the owner; its category—monastic, private, or government land—and why; when it had been allocated; its tax burden on the land; and sometimes a map. There were also incidental descriptions and verifications of property ownership and some general tax regulations for the local villages.

This was the permanent official record. The government sent out officers from Lhasa to review and revise the land and tax allotments in the book, it was said, only once every fifty years or when a large dispute occurred. Revisers had come during the tenure of Sonam's predecessor at the monastery, and Sonam had learned a great deal from the older man's stories of their methods. Early in the day the government representatives had called the owners from a certain area and had gone with them to their fields. Comparing each owner's document with the description in the large record book, they had paced off together the boundaries of each field, following natural and stone markers. Standard natural markers used were the top of a hill, a riverbank, a stream, a tree, a path or road, an irrigation canal. Hand-placed stones— their location further indicated a foot underground with charcoal and white stones— served as markers where natural features did not suffice. As the government agents walked, they asked questions about the seed capacity of the land, its yield, the tax burden on it, and the status of the family that owned it, among other things.

Sonam had also been told by his relatives in the Gongkar District that when the value of the land and its fertility had to be assessed by the government, three experienced farmers were called, one from each type of estate or farm in the region. Since farmland was measured not by area but by seed capacity, the three men had provided the official with an accurate idea of how fertile the land actually was. Each of the three farmers was given a small bag of pebbles. Then, as he had walked around a field, he would take out a pebble for each unit of sown seeds it could hold. At the end of counting, all the pebbles from each of the farmers were put into a plate held by the secretary of the official, waiting at the edge of the field. Then the secretary had done the "taking the middle of the three": dividing the total number of pebbles by three and recording the quotient as the seed capacity of that plot. They had moved from plot to plot in this way. His relatives said that this system was used for many things and was quite accurate.

According to Sonam's predecessor, at the end of the officials' visit to the villages, they had sent revised assessments to the central government's Land Office in Lhasa. These were reviewed, and by return post the monastery received changes to be entered in the book kept in the local district. He said they had never seen the land assessment officials again.

Slowly, Sonam turned the large pages in the bound book and looked at the maps and descriptions. When he found the description of the monastic southside plot, he reread it, and compared it with the paper he had used in the fields that day. They were the same. Then he decided to check the description of the government lands, including the northside plot, but without a map the description proved unhelpful. He rose and put the record book back in its place.

Opening the wooden chest in the corner of the room, he began to take out cloth files of previous cases. Some of these he had read before, briefly; others he had never opened. The files were stacked chronologically and had an index. He searched for and found a boundary dispute case and unrolled the gray cloth file on the floor. The first document was the petition, and it bore a resemblance in hand and style to the one he had recently received. The last document in the file was what he wanted, the final decision and results.

Opening the large final decision paper on his knees, Sonam slowly read the contents of the entire dispute. The points made and presented were listed seriatim in the body of the document. In this case as in his case, a local headman had been the first person consulted. After that, the parties had approached Sonam's predecessor to make a formal decision instead of seeking a conciliator. Also in this case, there was a stone marking the edge of the plot.

As he read on, Sonam finally found something useful. The dispute in the file turned on a question of *bab* (*bab/babs*) payment: to avoid a dispute, the parties had written an agreement about the boundaries of the land in question and about cattle grazing as well; the agreement included a *bab* clause stating the amount to be paid if either party violated the agreement. His predecessor had decided that the old *bab* should be paid by the guilty party, and a new contract with a new *bab* amount should be drafted.

Sonam sat back and thought for a moment. If this was the first time that these two farmers had argued about the boundary, and if they both really wanted conciliation, why not ask them tomorrow to draft an agreement for the future? He would write a conciliation document containing an agreement on the location of the riverbank marker. It would also have a *bab* clause, and both sides would sign on the back, indicating that they agreed to the contents of the document. Afterward, he would make sure that both sides and perhaps their families met to exchange scarves and share some beer to indicate their good will toward one another—very important for the owners of adjoining fields. This gave him a plan for the next day, which had been the major impetus for his search through the record box. He replaced the documents in the cloth file, rolled it up, and put the whole file back in the box. Blowing out the lamps, he wrapped his cloak tightly around him and lay down on his mattress to sleep with a settled mind. His last thoughts were of the iridescent blue shimmer of beautiful Lake Yardrok.

Encountering the Narrator

I can remember my thoughts as I sat listening to this lama in 1986, the Sonam of the boundary dispute, sitting cross-legged before me on his bed in a dark, concrete-walled room with only a few lines of sunlight streaming through the small window behind him. Though my tape recorder kept failing and I was trying to finish the cup of tea his servant had brought me, I couldn't help wondering, "What is this monk doing running an estate and settling disputes? How does he come to know so much about land ownership and taxation?"

Our discussion traveled in and out of various worlds, the practical present, the known past, the karmic future; it dipped into the subject of spirits and angry protective deities and then came back to the style of the pages of the huge record book. In his monotonous singsong voice he spoke of the possibility of a great incarnation happening in his area, and I thought again, "Cosmic events are creating dissension, and yet, at the same time, dissension can create cosmic anger?" I had a feeling at once of surreal reality, of the sensical incomprehensible, of the mundane and fantastic coexisting in the everyday. His was a blended world of thought with interpenetrating cosmic realms existing and interacting, all in the present.

And yet his discussion of legal concepts and rules in the Western sense of those terms was so detailed and complex that it left me gasping.[4] Legal proverbs and phrases peppered every oral paragraph. The amount of grain used on fields, the niceties of rental agreements, percentages of tax payments—these particulars were all very much his concerns. He spent almost half an hour on the technique used by assessors for estimating the seed-planting and harvesting capacity of a field. His description of the enormous Domesday-like book of land ownership and taxation was almost poetic. I can remember shivering in the room at one point when I had lost my concentration and thinking, "How am I ever going to present all of this?"

Several years before this encounter, I had begun with a much smaller project than the depiction of the Tibetan legal system: a field study of dispute settlement in the Tibetan-speaking areas of Nepal. I had practiced law for several years only to find that more questions about the nature of social control and legal systems, not fewer, kept revolving in my head on a daily basis. So I quit practice and went back to school at Yale in law and anthropology, an act typified by my friends as a "crazy move to a ridiculous combination" which would result in a "vast hole" in my legal résumé. After studying for several years I received a grant and left for Nepal, where the problems began. Not only was it difficult to find the research site I had been imagining, but there was little doubt that Tibetans had, as an ever present backdrop to their conversation, a vast store of cultural ideas relating to dispute settlement and law. Elderly lamas talked of debating recitations used in court; former clerks spoke of the complexities of writing styles; one monastic scholar offered to read law codes with me.

I was torn. Here was a great project, a chance to work on what might truly be called the last, great unknown legal system of Asia: the ancient Tibetan legal system, replete with courts, judges, law codes, and a panoply of rituals and principles. That, I told myself as I lay in my bed in Kathmandu, eating a chocolate bar and staring at the ceiling for hours, was the project I should be doing. But putting on my hiking boots and taking off into the mountains to stay in a small Tibetan village was the project my heart was set on. The former would be longer and much more difficult to accomplish, particularly as a woman; it would be lonely, would involve traveling from one place to another interviewing and reconstructing, and would require learning classical written Tibetan, an appalling prospect. I spent two days in this posture, rising only to get more chocolate. At the end, I had decided to go with my intuition: the mountain village.

Before leaving, however, I had to pick up mail at the Fulbright House, and so I rode my crotchety bike through the chaotic streets of Tamel in Kathmandu. Waiting for me was a letter from my adviser at Yale, Leopold Pospisil, a strong-willed

Czechoslovakian lawyer-anthropologist, a Herculean figure in my area of study, saying that I was to take heart and do the more "important work." I think I cried for more than an hour. Emotionally, I saw the task as almost impossibly beyond my capabilities. His final words were something like "Remember, you are my student." Small comfort for my anxiety—but so much for the small village.

I began, then, with the rather simple goal of just finding out whatever I could, working primarily in India and Nepal. Two things became rapidly apparent: there was a vast amount of information, and I had no concrete system for collecting or organizing it—indeed, no idea of what was even important. There were other problems as well. Tibetans just do not think about law the way an American lawyer does, and my questions, mentally couched in American legal tropes—"*res judicata,*" "precedent," "evidence" (why had I fallen back on them so readily?)—resulted in answers I could not understand. Tibetans have their own specialized law terms, which no one could define for me. Most of those I spoke with were refugees from different parts of the Tibetan Plateau; they spoke strange dialects I couldn't understand and seemed to be using different legal vocabularies. Were these actually different legal concepts or the same concepts with different local labels? What was law to them anyway? I couldn't find the right term for it. What constituted an intelligent question within the context of the Tibetan legal system?

After stumbling for more than a year and returning to the United States to train in more spoken and written Tibetan, I relocated in the home of the government-in-exile of the Dalai Lama in Dharamsala in the state of Himachal Pradesh, India. Formerly a British hill station in the Himalayas, Dharamsala consisted of several thousand refugees living in small houses covering the mountainside; some small hotels, shops, and restaurants for visitors; the compound of His Holiness the Dalai Lama, in which I was privileged to live for a period of time; and other administration buildings, including the Library of Tibetan Works and Archives, which houses a collection of Tibetan manuscripts.

The director of the library, Gyatsho Tsering, whose continuing support of my project made it ultimately possible, offered one of the first real gifts in my research: the opportunity to work daily with an elderly resident, Kungola Thubten Sangye. Kungola, a very high-ranking official in the former government of Tibet, had been collecting and editing law codes in Tibetan for several years. He was in his seventies when I first met him in 1981 and had spent his life since 1920 in service to the Thirteenth and then the Fourteenth Dalai Lama, to whom he was completely devoted. Having joined the exodus from the Plateau in 1959, he spent his last years in Dharamsala, where he was assigned to various projects for the government-in-exile and received a small stipend and housing in return.[5]

He and I had a conflicted relationship at first; Kungola was hardly impressed by a young female who claimed to be a lawyer and scholar and yet asked questions that only confirmed how profoundly uninformed she was about everything in the Tibetan legal system. Soon, I took to dressing like a 1930s British missionary—in long shirts and skirts, my hair in a bun—to conform more readily to his image of a respectable, educated foreign female. For months at a time we met daily for three hours, translating and annotating copies of various law codes. When I was particularly stupid, he wadded up pieces of paper and threw them at me, shouting, or

Plate 2. Library of Tibetan Works and Archives, part of the Tibetan government-in-exile in Dharamsala, India. 1983.

banged his cane loudly on the table in disgust. His snuff habit made long breaks a necessity. When someone else was present, providing information or helping with the translation, Kungola often felt that he had an ally and would make derogatory comments under his breath in Tibetan.

After two years of work, however, our reluctance became attachment, and the daily sessions became the center of both our lives. He began to dream about my husband, who was working in the mountains. Kungola, having laboriously climbed the steps to our little office, would begin our session by announcing that he had dreamed John was coming on the four o'clock bus that day. We were therefore expected for dinner at six o'clock; he would make *momos*, the traditional Tibetan meat dumplings. And he would be right. Although Tibetan dreaming initially astonished me, in the absence of telephones or other communication I began to rely on him to let me know of John's whereabouts. For his part, Kungola began to defer to my judgment on some issues, to be reconciled to my ridiculous requests. He started to talk more fully of his own concerns, his daily mantra recitations, and his feelings about *bardo* (*bar ma do*), the forty-nine-day intermediate state after death before one is reborn.

When I left India, the parting was difficult for us both. Kungola was a brilliant, devout, unusual man of deep resonance, as well as a real character. His death in 1989 was a very great loss to me personally, an inestimable loss to Tibetan scholarship.

My daily work schedule was to rise around five o'clock and begin to transcribe the law codes. I had to copy each word onto a numbered line in a large notebook in a Tibetan script that I could read more readily than the bureaucratic script—called *duktsa* (*'bru tsha*)—in which the law code texts had been written. I worked on a translation through breakfast, developing questions and annotation requests on what would often be no more than half a page of the original text. Then I flew down the steep hill, sometimes in bright hot sunshine, sometimes in treacherous snow, to the tiny office on the third floor of the library, where Kungola and I met until lunchtime. In the afternoon I started on my interview schedule, which often lasted well through dinner and into the night. Throughout, Kungola was my guide, directing my interviews, correcting my mistaken presumptions, filling in unanswered questions in my research. He told me the background of everyone I interviewed who had been in the former government, the dates they had served, their family connections, and their place in history. His opinions and prejudices are the backbone of this work.

I spoke with several hundred Tibetans in Tibet, India, Nepal, England, and the United States over a total of four years (beginning in 1981) and conducted, both alone and with research assistants (Lobsang Shastri and Karma Gyatso of the library, and Anila Karma Lekshe Tsomo, all scholars of Tibet themselves), over two hundred in-depth interviews in Tibetan, many of twenty hours or more.[6] To do so, I traveled from our base in Dharamsala, for stretches of a few days to a few months, to the other hill stations of the Himalayas and into Ladakh, New Delhi, Nepal, and the central region of Tibet. Most of these interviews were taped and transcribed by me or a Tibetan.

The Tibetans interviewed ranged from former officials of the highest rank and most ancient nobility to local lamas in small villages in the far western region of the Plateau, nomad chieftains from the extreme northeast, and many former peasant farmers in the central region. I was lucky enough to interview several former magistrates from every level in the legal process and former petitioners, prisoners, district officers, clerks, and caretakers of courts. Although Tibet did not have attorneys as such, it did have "those knowledgeable about disputes," and one of my primary sources was a man who had been for many years the legal representative to the capital from the state of Sakya.

Tibetan law is part of a vast and complex Asian culture with fourteen centuries of written records, religious developments, and political vagaries. Traces and images of that culture are available in a wide variety of locations and sources throughout the world.

Thanks to the British presence in Lhasa in the initial decades of this century, there are collections and reproductions of diaries and papers from British consulates, old photographs, Tibetan texts, and other materials in the India Office Library in London and the Pitt Rivers Museum at Oxford. The photographs from the India Office

Library were particularly helpful, for I could use snapshots of courts, prisoners in stocks, posted edicts, and officials as a basis for asking questions. As the work with Kungola Thubten Sangye continued, I began to write to museums, libraries, and scholars around the world in an effort to amass several versions of the law codes. My present collection includes codes and legal documents—many kindly donated by Tibetan scholars—from sources in Manchester, Leiden, Prague, Munich, Tokyo, Kathmandu, New Delhi, and Dharamsala as well as Tibet. The Library of Tibetan Works and Archives staff obligingly microfilmed important legal and political documents in their collection. Tashi Tsering of the library, a well-known scholar in his own right, amassed secondary materials from Tibetan historical sources on the government and legal system for my later use. The collection of Tibetan books at the Yale library, covering every aspect of Tibetan literature, constituted another excellent source.

When I traveled into Tibet, I took with me a collection of maps and floor plans with which to access and photograph the old courts. Some of these were contained in published texts in Tibetan on buildings in Lhasa; some were maps recently commissioned by other scholars; some were drawings and sketches made by Tibetans when describing the legal system. In Tibet I collected more law codes and documents, schoolbooks, writing manuals, written accounts of myths and fairytales, religious texts, dictionaries, proverbs, and songs. Throughout, I kept personal journals and attempted to record my own daily observations of Tibetan life, ceremonies, and disputes.

My studies of the Tibetan Buddhist religion, an enormous subject of great philosophical and intellectual difficulty, commenced when I first began to learn the language in 1981 and have continued to the present. The Tibetans' religion is the foundation of all their culture, the source of their jurisprudence, the well-spring of their political history, the guiding principle in every Tibetan's life. Each narrator was first a Tibetan Buddhist and then, second, whatever designation the culture attached to her or him. The profundity of the Tibetan Buddhists' commitment and devotion to their religion is unfathomable to the modern Western mind; it constitutes a fundamentally different starting point for a Tibetan narrator.

Priests and Patrons

The nature of this study changed over time with the discovery of different sources and kinds of information. At first, I was simply pleased to demonstrate that a Tibetan legal system had existed prior to 1959. Most Asian scholars and all but a few Tibetologists had denied the possibility of a distinctive Tibetan legal culture, presuming that it was either a Chinese transplant or chiefly Indian Buddhist in nature. Tibet was viewed as overwhelmingly exotic, oriental and therefore consumingly "Other." Most assumed, in Max Weber's terms, that Tibet was a country controlled by "the hierarchic, rigidly organized Lamaistic monastic Buddhism with its boundless power over the laity."[7]

It is not surprising, then, that the first questions asked about my work by both academics and nonacademics concerned the religious nature of the legal system:

Plate 3. Sacred Tibetan Buddhist chortens, reliquary mounds of the Buddha, at Siling Monastery. 1942. (Ilya Tolstoy, Library, The Academy of Natural Sciences of Philadelphia)

"The Tibetans had a religious system of law, didn't they? Did those lamas administer the Buddhist canon? Did you primarily talk to monks?" Their questions were based on plausible assumptions, for not only were and are the Tibetans renowned for their intense religious devotion and quasi-theocracy, headed by a charismatic religious leader, but their religious canon itself includes a complete legal code laid out in extraordinary detail.

The paradoxical answer to such queries lies within the Tibetan understanding of Buddhism, which has never been simply a popular lay movement. Instead, it divides the world of social actors into two strictly defined groups: spiritual seekers or "priests," and spiritual supporters or "patrons."

The community of practicing spiritual seekers, on the one hand, consists of those who have adopted a monastic life and, often, celibacy as the basic conditions for the path to enlightenment. Monks in Tibetan Buddhism live primarily in separate, hierarchically delineated monastic environments that are governed by particular rules and requirements—rules about vows, rules about daily practices, rules about food, activities, and sexuality, rules about rituals, and rules about conduct—outlined in the Vinaya section of the Buddhist canon. It is the duty of these spiritual seekers to keep the religion alive, to perform rites correctly, and to secure the continuation of the religious lineage as it is handed down from teacher to novice. Tibetan Buddhism requires monasticism to survive.

The spiritual supporters, on the other hand, are the laypersons devoted to the continuation of the community of spiritual seekers. The lay population is crucial to the monastery for the provision of a continuous supply of recruits, for material necessities such as food, clothing, and money, and for political and social protection. They are patrons for the otherworldly priests.

This symbiotic dualism in the social structure of the Tibetan religion has been an unavoidable part of the social universe for each new leader of Tibet throughout its history. Thus, the Fifth Dalai Lama, who took over the Plateau in 1642 to establish the government that ruled until 1959, was too imbued with the cultural distinction between "priests" and "patrons" to conclude that these were anything but two separate worlds: the world of monks governed by the canonical rules of the Vinaya, and the world of laypersons governed by the laws of the ancient kings. The instructions of the Fifth Dalai Lama to his regent drafting the new law code were simple: take the secular law codes from the previous Tsang kingdoms and rework them. In every passage of the Dalai Lama text, the secular dynastic Tsang code was the paradigm from which the regent worked, altering, adjusting, or adding.

The paradox, then, is that even though the legal tradition was presumed to be wholly religious, the dualistic nature of Tibetan religious culture itself actually dictated that "secular" spiritual supporter laws were of necessity different from "religious" spiritual seeker laws. Although the Tibetan canon applies to all Tibetan Buddhists, it includes a legal code only for the spiritual seekers (unlike Islam's, for example), and thus the sacred realm incorporates the profane even as it defines its included distinctiveness. And although, as Peter Berger explains, the "entire society serve[d] as the plausibility structure for a religiously legitimated world,"[8] still the dichotomy between the religious community and the lay community required a separate and profane legal system—a golden yoke for those who were not taking on the silken thread.

Asian Antecedents

Given my conclusion after a year or two of research that secular, as opposed to religious, models of legal systems might offer better prototypes for organizing my study, I began to look at two additional sources: first, Tibetan political and historical studies; second, works on the structures of other East Asian legal systems.

Western works on Tibetan history, even well-documented recent studies, have focused on upper-level politics,[9] including the role of the important noble families[10] and international relations of the state,[11] often within a cultural (read "religious") context.[12] Melvyn Goldstein is the only one to deal with law or the legal system, and his recent book is particularly fascinating because Goldstein, as an anthropologist recreating the twentieth-century political history of Tibet through extensive interviews and document research, has painstakingly delineated the important corporate groups, their power bases, the economic stakes, and the detailed political interactions of the Tibetans at the national level which led to the Chinese takeover. He presents the *Sturm und Drang* of upper-level Tibetan politics—revolts, confiscations of property, treason, conspiracies, poisonings, blindings, international intrigues—in elaborate detail.

Goldstein sees law in general as an instrument of coercion for the current political power, a malleable tool for attaining and retaining economic prizes of offices and estates. His work adds to a growing literature on the asymmetrical relations of power and dominance between elites and other groups in Tibetan society. For example, scholars have argued in the past that monastic corporate groups were responsible for gross power plays and inequalities in the Tibetan system, thus preventing modernization;[13] that the Tibetan elites were arrogant, "irresponsible and pleasure-loving";[14] that the countryside was impoverished by repressive taxes owed to the central government;[15] and that the district officers possessed enormous arbitrary powers that they could use to inflict hardships on the local population.[16] Other scholars, Chinese and Americans using the Chinese perspective, have also pursued these themes.[17]

All these works pointed to what was missing in our understanding. What we did not know, and what I turned my attention toward, was the mundane perspective: the daily operation of the law in administrative offices and courts as understood by individual Tibetans—the average as opposed to the spectacular and influential. What, I asked myself, happened in Tibet when the average person had a conflict that led to a dispute settlement process not politically significant at the national level? How were such cases handled? My inquiry then began to move in the direction taken by some cultural historians, into the legal history of S. F. C. Milsom and the work of the later Annales school, Emmanuel Le Roy Ladurie and Pierre Goubert, Natalie Zemon Davis and Carlo Ginzburg.[18] I became interested in average citizens' reports of what they did, how they understood the legal system to operate, what they thought was right and wrong about it.

I also became interested in comparing the picture that I was beginning to develop of the Tibetan legal system with works on other East Asian legal systems. For example, John Haley has typified these systems as secular "public legal orders in which control over both the making and enforcing of legal rules is vested in the state and its bureaucracies," and he has stated that although law reflected norms, "legal commands were not in and of themselves moral commands." Like China, Korea, and Japan, Tibet had a bureaucracy that implemented its legal system. It had "magistrate judges [who were] neutral adjudicators, not policing or prosecuting officials," and petitioners who initiated and controlled the petitioning process: "Within parameters set by rules on pleading and forms of action, the parties themselves defined the issues, the facts to be proven, the evidence to be submitted."[19] The matched lay and religious official judges in most Tibetan courts resembled in part the "combined courts of the Yuan dynasty."[20] In Tibet, as in the rest of East Asia, no distinct set of professional legal actors had evolved. There were exams for entrance to the civil bureaucracy, and sets of regional district courts were staffed by government magistrates. In short, viewed from the legal institution perspective, Tibet was beginning to take the shape of a classical Asian state, all the more interesting because it had retained its essential form since medieval times.

As I continued to work with these models, however, I found—much to my dismay—that the differences were equally profound. Tibetan law codes were only prudential and, with the exception of payments for murder, did not link specific crimes with specific punishments—an essential feature in all other Asian law codes from Vietnam to China and Mongolia. The leader of the country was a charismatic religious figure, not someone who gained the attributes of power through his office alone. The civil bureaucracy was almost entirely based on a closed recruitment pool. The control of the state and its sanctioning ability in many areas was minimal. But the most intriguing differences were to be found in the reasons for and explanations of the legal system given by the Tibetans themselves. In short, although the external manifestations of the legal system made it look a lot like those of other Asian states or even some Western medieval legal systems, the whole legal cosmology in which it was couched—a system of thought and practice about how the world operates—was absolutely different. Nor did what was different about the Tibetan legal system seem to be covered by the idea of "legal culture."[21] Having collected information on the institutional and processual structures, on what existed in the way of substantive rules and doctrines, and, finally, on the legal attitudes and habits of the Tibetans, I still had only part of the picture. After researching for over two years, I began to ask about other concepts that mediated the reasoning processes and practices going on during a legal case.

Kaleidoscopic Cosmology of Law

What stops a person from going to court? How does a person understand where to stand in court? Why is there one result in one case, another result in another? What motivates someone to be a witness? How are certain situations rationalized by karma? What causes a conflict? What do the nature of reality and illusion, and their covering myths, have to do with legal cases? How does one determine the mutability of power in the process of talking? What is the emotive impact under varying circumstances of legal symbols? These are some of the questions I began to wonder about, but more simply, I realized that my framing of Tibetans' statements was hindered by a misunderstanding of how they framed law in general.[22]

Tibetans understand law, much as they understand the universe, as a kaleidoscopic cosmology: that is, as realigning sets of patterns and actions that are both constant and ever changing, integrating and disintegrating, coherent and incoherent. This stable state of complete destabilization is the interpretive framework used throughout the book to present Tibetan legal practices, concepts, and their interrelations before 1959. It is the underpinning for jurisprudential concepts such as the absolute uniqueness of each circumstance, the absence of precedent, the importance of karmic sanctions, and the legal structure of the country as a pulsating mandala. When the term "cosmology" is used in this book, it refers to this whirling, interpenetrating multiplicity, this atmosphere of interconnections and gaps, this determined indeterminacy. Each story in a chapter is only a frozen moment, a single frame in the moving kaleidoscopic cosmology.

Throughout this book, parts of the Tibetan legal cosmology are compared and contrasted with specific concepts and practices of law in the United States. For example, in Tibet there is no idea of secular law as an overarching construct of rules which fits every situation; indeed, secular law there is not particularly a matter of rules. Thus, a problem long addressed by U.S. legal scholars of the "gap in the law"—the notion that there are areas not covered by our blanket of rules which are therefore indeterminacies—is nonsensical in Tibet. Similarly, the mythic vision of an ideal legal system that is distinct and autonomous, neutral, rarified, and professional[23] has great cogency in the United States, but strikes Tibetans as naive. By the same token, a judge giving consideration to the karmic potential of a criminal—a very important part of Tibetan criminal law—would sound absurd in a U.S. courtroom.

This work, then, is a study of the cosmology of law in Buddhist Tibet in the first half of the twentieth century as reconstructed from interviews with Tibetans, both on the Plateau and in exile (most of those interviewed were from the nonmonastic, nonnomadic population of south central Tibet). As an exercise in historical perspective and imagination,[24] it is limited to the time period from 1940 to 1959. At various points during the analysis and writing of the book, I used the methods and theories of legal anthropology, comparative law, East Asian studies, religious studies, and cultural history.

Organization of the Book

The book is divided into five parts. Part One describes Tibet's major geographical divisions, the language, the various social groups, and Tibetan Buddhism (Chapter 1); offers a new look at Tibetan history through the eyes of the law codes, thus setting the tone both poetically and epistemologically for the rest of the book (Chapter 2); and briefly examines the government during the Dalai Lama period (1642–1959, most specifically 1940–59), the arrival of the Chinese Revolutionary Army, the division of the Tibetan population, and the current situation of the Tibetans in exile (Chapter 3).

Each part after the first is prefaced by a discussion of some theoretical points and a short introduction to the chapters that follow. Part Two presents the twelve major elements of the Tibetan cosmology of law—(1) concepts of reality, illusion, and nonduality, (2) cosmos and time, (3) inner morality, (4) myths and narratives, (5) language and discourses, (6) power and hierarchy, (7) ritual processes, (8) legal devices, (9) jurisprudence, (10) spaces and mental maps, (11) boundaries and units, and (12) symbols—and sets out the basic concepts and practices that informed the legal system.

The rest of the book provides its data backbone, constructed from hundreds of interviews. Each chapter is based on the exact wording of a single narrator and the corroboration of at least two other people who were there and knew the narrator. The cosmology of law is thus contextualized within the actual practice of the law, within the fighting, contesting, struggling, watching, ignoring, and rationalizing that constituted what went on in a dispute. If legal cosmology helps us with the "what," these narratives give us the "how, why, when, and where" of the practice and process of law in Tibet in the 1940s and 1950s. Legal cosmology can be elucidated only through such a series of instances of practice.

Cases are presented in five formats: (1) as brief summaries of the basic facts to illustrate a point; (2) as verbatim records of a narrator's rendition; (3) as narratives compiled from several Tibetans' accounts of a case from several angles, resulting in particularly rich, thick description; (4) as a combination of the facts of several cases to illustrate generally a single legal process; and (5) as a composite of some or all of these formats. Each case in this book was sent back to field researchers—often several times—for review, verification, and correction before being included.

Part Three presents four narratives from the countryside, the periphery, each concerned with a dispute and each chosen to show the practice of the law from the perspective of a different actor. Part Four moves to the capital city to examine the world of Lhasa, the Tibetan bureaucracy, the flow of legal cases through the upper levels of the government, and the functions and procedures of the major courts—again offering representative cases and exegesis. Part Five turns the kaleidoscope again to approach Tibetan law from two other angles: it considers Tibetan reasoning about crime and punishment and, finally, reorganizes all that has come before through the life history of one Tibetan official—told in his own words.

Several chapters are followed by excursions into substantive topics of interest ancillary to the main text—among them, land ownership and inheritance, documentary and accounting practice, taxation, marriage patterns, and ecclesiastical law.

Finally, the Conclusion reviews some intriguing aspects of the Tibetan legal system and asks what these features imply about the nature of legal systems in general.

PART ONE

The Context of Tibet

CHAPTER ONE

A Sketch of Tibet and Its People

If you want to please everyone,
It's not possible.
If you act honestly,
People will be pleased.
—Tibetan Proverb

Geography and Language

The high Plateau of Tibet protrudes like an enormous almond-shaped eye staring out into the heavens from the forehead of the earth. This vast region of approximately 1.5 million square miles averages more than 12,000 feet above sea level. Completely surrounded by mountains, the Plateau supports a desert-arctic environment mollified somewhat by its latitudinal location between the twenty-eighth and thirty-eighth parallels. High, isolated, and extreme in climate, this area called "the roof of the world" is the home of the Tibetan ethnic population.

The Tibetans' sense of geography, their mental map of their country, is determined by types of landscape—plateaus, ridges, pastures and valleys, mountain passes, rivers and lakes—and by regionalism. The country's five general regions, which have distinctive climates, are markers for differences among populations.

The northern half of the Plateau, the Jangthang or "northern plain," is divided into two latitudinal bands. The northern band—virtually uninhabited except for the occasional salt gatherer and hunter of wild yak, ass, antelope, or wolf—is a landscape of cold, desolate tracts, mountain peaks, internal drainage lakes, and pits of salt and borax. The climate is intensely cold and arid, with less than one inch of rain a year. East-west mountain chains run through this part of the plain, and a large mountainous barrier, the Karakorum range in the west and the Kunlun Mountains in the east, fences in the Plateau from the immense sand expanse of the Taklamakan Desert to the north. The southern band is a more hospitable, multi-leveled region of deep lakes and mountains with high plateaus of untillable soil. A thin layer of topsoil

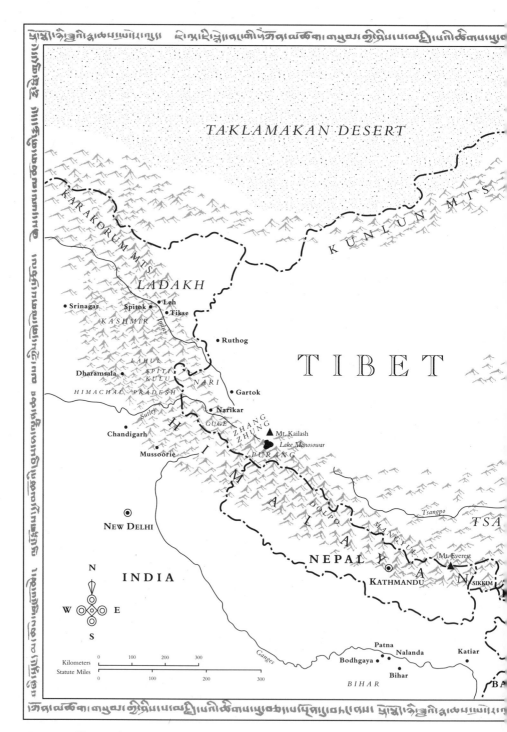

Figure 2. Tibetan Plateau circa 1950.

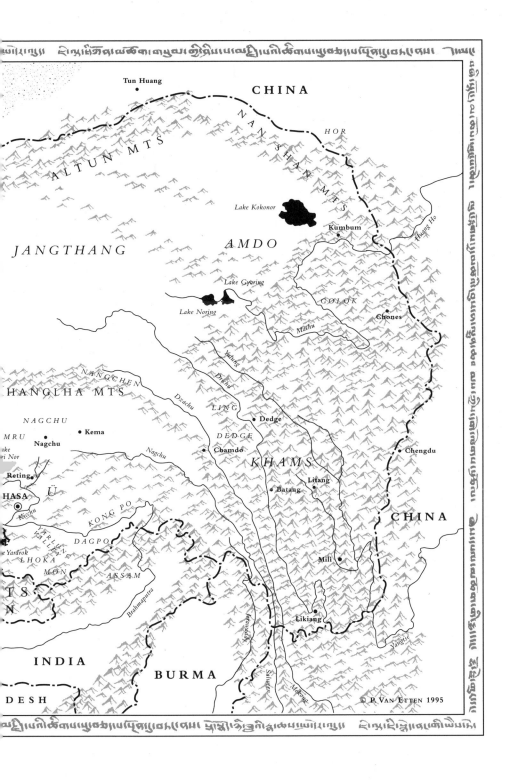

Plate 4. A wild yak. 1978. (Syed Ali Shah, Leh, Ladakh)

covered with "yak grass" supports herds of yak, wild blue sheep, and gazelle. Rainfall in this region is only six to ten inches annually, and the weather is quixotic: a clear morning in early July with a ninety-degree temperature can be followed by an afternoon of snow and hailstorms. This southern band of the Jangthang is only thinly populated by scattered nomadic groups herding yak, sheep, and goats.

The second regional area on the Plateau is the far western portion, distinguished as the site of several ancient Tibetan kingdoms: Nari, Lahul, Spiti, Purang, Guge, and Ladakh. A topographical combination of immense plains to the north and the deep mountain valleys of the greater Himalayas to the south, it is an arid zone with less than five inches of annual precipitation. Lacking an extensive agricultural base, these kingdoms, Ladakh in particular, existed largely as trade centers and experienced a greater mixture of population and cultural influences than other areas of the Plateau except the northeast. Ladakh, which was overrun in the nineteenth century by Muslims from the south, is now incorporated into the Indian state.

The southerly arc of the Plateau is the home of Tibetan civilization. Here in the river valleys just north of the Himalayas, in the central Tibetan floodplains where most of the population is still concentrated, agriculturists were able to make a rough beginning several thousand years ago. A wintertime visitor would find it surprisingly monochromatic, but the sparsely treed, rocky hillsides in sepias, browns, and grays are transformed in summer by brilliant green irrigated fields and deep blue lakes. From May to September, monsoon winds coming up over the Himalayas from the south shed approximately eighteen inches of precipitation per year. This, coupled with extensive stream and canal irrigation, provides sufficient water to grow high-altitude crops such as barley, wheat, peas, buckwheat, mustard, and some root vegetables. The rains supplying the southern arc of Tibet are also the source of several major rivers of southern Asia: the Indus and Sutlej in the west which irrigate western India and Pakistan; several branches of the Ganges; and the great *tsangpo* (*gtsang po*), later to become the Brahmaputra, which travels east and then south to northern India and Bangladesh. Lhasa, the religious, governmental, and cultural capital of Tibet, is in this southern region.

The fourth regional area, southeastern Tibet, is a land of north-south river valleys covered with rich temperate and subtropical forests of oak and conifer interspersed with poplars, shrubs, and fruit trees. Much of this region is encompassed by the former Tibetan province of Khams, known for its immense natural resources, excellent grazing, and tribal kingdoms. With rainfall varying from eighteen to forty inches per year, the scattered agricultural areas in Khams are planted with a wide variety of crops, including maize, rice, and grapes in addition to those prevalent in the southern arc. This region is also the source for most of the rivers of East Asia: the Irrawaddy River of Burma, the Salween, the lethargic Mekong of Southeast Asia, and the Yangtse River of southern China.

Amdo, the entryway for invaders, traders, and influences of all kinds, was the major province of the fifth region of the Tibetan Plateau, the far northeast; the silk route passed just to the north on its path to the cities of northern China. Like its counterpart in the far west, this area oscillated politically between incorporation and separation from central Tibet (understood as the southern arc) over a 1,300-year period. In this region, noted for its long, very cold winters and short but relatively mild summers, precipitation ranges from four to ten inches, and temperatures average sixty-four degrees. Amdo has a terrain of rolling grasslands dotted with northwest-southeast bands of mountains. The vicinity of Lake Kokonor, the largest lake in Tibet at fifty miles across, has long been a prized grazing spot for herders of several nationalities—Uighur, Tibetan, Mongolian, and Chinese. This is an area famous throughout history for its excellent horse, cattle, sheep, and camel breeding.

These five traditional regions of the Tibetan Plateau are currently divided into four separate Chinese provinces—Tsinghai, Szechwan, Yunnan, and Tibet—and one state of India. This, coupled with the fact that Chinese and Indians have moved in large numbers onto the Plateau, makes the calculation of the present size of the ethnic Tibetan population difficult. Until 1950 the entire Plateau was, as it had been for more than two thousand years, overwhelmingly ethnic Tibetan, with a population variously estimated at three to six million. The present Chinese figure for the total population of ethnic Tibetans in China is almost four million.

Tibetans refer to themselves as "people of Tibet," *bopa* (*bod pa*). This term traditionally identified persons who spoke Tibetan, lived on the Plateau, followed Tibetan Buddhism, read the Tibetan script, and employed Tibetan customs. It was used in opposition to the term, *chimi* (*phyi mi*), "outsiders." "Non-Buddhists" were called *chipa* (*phyi pa*), also translated as "outsiders." A Tibetan referring to other ethnic Tibetans, however, even today uses regional terms—for example, "the person from the Khams region," "the person from the U region [central Tibet]," or "the nomad"—not *bopa* or "Tibetans." Such usages suggest that Tibetans living on the Plateau in the first half of this century presumed a common regional ethnicity, using differences in life-styles and localities as markers to differentiate particular Tibetan groups. Indeed, for historians it is one of the confounding themes of Tibetan culture that so profound a sense of common ethnicity and nationality coexisted with a strong identification based on distinct regional dialects, histories, and economic patterns.

Although the oldest examples of writing date from the seventh century, Tibetan tradition alleges that the syllabary—an adaptation of a northern Indian script—was devised for the first historical king around 630 A.D. and associates the script with the introduction of the Buddhist religion into the country. The result has been a strong conservatism toward spelling changes and an emphasis on precision in calligraphy and the correct mental attitude when writing. Hence, phonetic shifts over the centuries, not mirrored in Tibetan spelling, have caused a large differentiation between the current pronunciation and the spelling of most syllables. Dialects on the Plateau vary greatly in the degree to which initial and final consonants are sounded, syllables dropped, or tones added.[1]

The theme of linguistic, geographical, and cultural isolation has been commonplace in literature about the Tibetan Plateau. Understandably, the Tibetans never speak of themselves as more or less introverted than other ethnic groups; most point to a strong readiness and ability to adapt to new conditions when pressed, as in the diaspora since 1959. Tibetan cultural isolation, although arguably no more or less than that of any other rural peasantry, may have been distinctive because of the conjunction of isolating circumstances developed over two thousand years: location on a high plateau that was not easily accessible; a harsh climate; separate language, customs, life-style, and material culture; a generally stable and static polity and economy; and engrossment of the population in a religion. Throughout Tibetan history, however, there were extensive cultural and economic exchanges with most of the societies bordering the Plateau.

Population

Before 1950, approximately 90 percent of the population of the Tibetan Plateau was made up of three basic social groups: peasants, nomads, and monks and nuns. The remaining 10 percent was distributed over a wide range of other life-styles and occupations: nobles, civil servants, soldiers, traders, itinerant bards, craftworkers, merchants, robber bandits, and religious mendicants. The extreme environment and the large proportion of celibate males tended to keep the birth rate and total population relatively low.

Tibetan peasants, farming small plots of land near waterways throughout the southern arc, made up the most important of the three groups for the Tibetan economy. They lived in both individual houses and clusters; the occasional solitary house was seen as commonly as groups of houses or larger villages. The basic social and economic unit for production, consumption, child rearing, and taxation was the ongoing household called a *kim tsang* (*khyim tshang*). The household unit controlled its own land and herds, was responsible for tax liability to the community and the government, and carried the name used by its members. The village, the next most important unit among agriculturists, was responsible for paying certain taxes, providing trainees to the monasteries, organizing labor for the repair of irrigation works and transport of supplies, assembling the resources for festivals, and providing the capital and produce for mutual trading ventures.

As the household unit handled many of the responsibilities of the family or individual, domestic and marriage patterns demonstrated considerable variety and flexibility in Tibet. There were seven different possible forms, ranging from the preferred marriage of a set of brothers to one woman (fraternal polyandry) to the unusual marriage of a widow and her daughters to one man (mother-daughter polygyny). A single household might cycle through several different marriage forms as family members moved in and out: some went on long trading ventures; others joined or left nunneries and monasteries, got divorced, or moved to other areas or into other households. Tibetans traditionally calculated the degree of relation allowable for marriage as five generations back on the mother's side (*ma,* the "flesh") and seven on the father's (*pha,* the "bone"), but several commented that it was difficult to count back so far, and they had not done so for their marriages.[2]

Tibetan peasant houses were rectangular, constructed of long walls of stone or sundried brick. They had small windows to avoid the sand-filled winds and were two-storied if the family was moderately well off. The flat roof of beaten earth served as the site for roasting barley to make flour and for drying and storing available wood. The ground floor provided space for livestock—cattle, yaks, a cow-yak crossbreed called a *zo (mdzo),* donkeys, and chickens—granaries, and storage for dried dung and tools. The family lived on the floor above.

In their daily routine the members of the household arose long before dawn to say prayers, and the head female made tea for all to drink before the departure of the men for the fields. At nine o'clock the women followed the men out to the fields, carrying their babies and bringing a breakfast of more tea, barley-meal bread, and cheese; they returned home before the men to do the milking and cook an evening meal of barley stew, meat, and tea over a peat or dung fire.

The chief crop of the southern Plateau was high-altitude barley, with wheat, buckwheat, peas, mustard, radishes, and potatoes following in importance. Extensive irrigation systems allocating water on a rotational basis to the various fields were operated by either the peasant farmers themselves or a local estate steward. Planting and harvest dates for the single growing season varied with the altitude, exposure, and precipitation of an area: from March through May for planting; from late August through early October for reaping. Tibetan harvests were constantly at risk because of poor soil, low precipitation levels, frost, hail, locusts, and rats—conditions that caused peasant farmers to supplicate local deities continually. Oracles and "hail protectors" advised the times for planting and harvesting and the propitiations necessary to ensure the good health of the crop.

The seasonal routine was punctuated by marriage feasts, dances, group work projects, and festivals at the local monasteries. On festival days enormous appliquéd hangings depicting religious figures were unfurled against the walls of the monastery to serve as a setting for operatic dances, while the clash of cymbals, beat of drums, and sounding of long horns created the music for a story presented as a dance

Plate 5. A young peasant farmer plowing in western Tibet. 1978. (Syed Ali Shah, Leh, Ladakh)

by monks in exquisite costumes and masks. Men came from throughout the region wearing new or clean clothes; women wrapped their hair in elaborate pillowed styles and donned silver, turquoise, and coral jewelry. All sounds and acts on these auspicious days worked as a whole to celebrate as well as increase the religious merit of the whole community.

Tibetan nomads and herders, the second social group, were scattered throughout the entire Plateau but predominated in the plains of the northern, northeastern, and western regions and in the forests of the southeastern region. The tribe—the overarching political unit for most nomadic groups—typically ranged from five to eighty tentholds when assembled. It functioned not for the purpose of pooling animals but for security, government, ceremonies, and assistance. The members of an individual tenthold, residing in a single tent of black, tightly woven yak hair, constituted the basic unit for livestock ownership, child rearing, inheritance, and other economic and political functions. The eldest male usually represented the tent and made the majority of the decisions affecting the group or family.

The life of the nomad centered on a bovine domesticated on the Plateau at least fifteen centuries ago: the yak, an animal particularly suited to the severe climate of the northern Plateau. Able to sustain exertion at an altitude of 20,000 feet, lick sparse grass off the surface of the soil, paddle through snow, withstand severe cold with its heavy pelt, and carry a pack or rider at a steady pace, the yak was the only animal useful to humans in all Tibetan environments. Other animals in various Tibetan

Plate 6. Traveling nomadic herdsmen from northeastern Tibet. 1920–21. (Pitt Rivers Museum, University of Oxford)

herds were sheep (which were the most plentiful and used for meat and wool), the *zo,* and, at lower altitudes, cattle and goats. Forced to be self-sufficient, the Tibetan nomad was trained early in life to protect the livestock from wild animals, disease, and other humans and to manage the herd according to the tenthold's needs and the conditions of the market. Pulling yak hair, shearing, calving, and butchering followed a seasonal schedule; milking, pasturing, and dung collecting were done on a daily basis.

The majority of marriages among the nomads were monogamous, though a considerable amount of sexual license existed, and all the forms of marriage available to the peasants were also practiced to some extent. As marriage was a union of herds, so divorce and tenthold separations resulted in a splitting of the herds, with males and females both retaining the animals they had brought into the union or inherited. There were gender-specific tasks in the tentholds—the females watched the children, curded the milk, and did the weaving, for example—but family members were able to exchange several roles in their operation as a self-sufficient entity.

In addition to herding, the nomads engaged in such economic activities as limited mining, collecting salt and borax from deposits, gathering roots, providing transportation for travelers, hunting wild game, and raiding other pastoralists. Annual grain-trading expeditions occurred in the late fall, with an encampment of tents functioning as a unit and each family contributing a member or supplies to the group traveling down to the lower regions. At the markets, they bartered animal products for the cereals, vegetables, and manufactured items available in agricultural areas. All the nomads I spoke with considered their pre-1959 life-style to have been far preferable to the sedentary lives of the peasant farmers with whom they traded.

The third major group, the monks and nuns living in sect-specific Buddhist monasteries and nunneries (some dating from as early as the eleventh century), made up an estimated 20 percent of the population in the first half of the twentieth century. Each monastery or nunnery was an economic household of its own, ranging in size from a small shelter to self-sufficient towns housing thousands of initiates. As the primary actors in the education of the public and the young, monks and nuns were the arbiters of the cultural traditions of Tibet. They produced almost all the Tibetan literature, performed many of the rituals at national and local holidays, trained doctors, artists, astrologers, and half of the government officials, and maintained economic control of large estates of land. Tibetan monasteries and nunneries were religious institutions in symbiosis with the secular population of peasants and nomads that maintained them.

A layperson older than seven could enter religious training at any point, provided that he or she was not crippled, blind, mute, or mentally retarded. Indeed, entering monastic life was viewed as a serious option for many of the individuals I interviewed, and neither age, sex, marital status, nor wealth were considered barriers to entry. After shaving the head and taking on burgundy robes, the initiate was questioned by the preceptor as to parentage, name, and background and then given the vows of the beginner on the religious path, *gelong* (*dge slong*). Although nunneries on the whole had smaller populations than monasteries, the following description applies generally to both.

Large monasteries employed monks in all the roles necessitated by a major institution, from carrying water and working in the kitchens to translating and printing scriptures, reciting religious texts, and painting ritual pictures. All ate together in the dining hall and worshipped together in the mornings and evenings in the central temple. A monk who was selected for higher religious training moved through a series of educational levels not unlike our college system.[3] After completing basic language and grammar courses, a monk trainee in a major *gelukpa* (*dge lugs pa*) sect monastery near Lhasa, for example, underwent five academic courses of study over a fourteen-year period: three years of logic, five years of the Perfection of Wisdom Sutra (Prajnaparamita), two years of Philosophy of Emptiness (Madhyamika), two years of the Canon Law (Vinaya), and two years of the Treasury of Philosophical Notions (Abhidharmakhosa). At the end of each section and after the final years of study, rigorous examinations were conducted in ritual debate style in the courtyards of the monasteries. The few successful students who achieved the highest academic degree, that of the *geshe* (*dge bshes*), were then qualified to become scholars and teachers in monastic colleges. Other than local schools teaching handwriting along with some basic skills, or government schools training students for the bureaucracy, monasteries and nunneries offered the only extensive formal education available in Tibet.

There were also many noninstitutional settings for a religious practitioner. The *nyingma pa* (*rnying ma pa*) sect of Tibetan Buddhism allowed its monks and nuns to marry and lead lives in the community. Hermit ascetics such as the famous Milarapa stayed in caves in the wilderness, and religious mendicants roamed the countryside

Plate 7. Woman from the Shachukol area of the northern plain of Tibet. 1976. (Syed Ali
Shah, Leh, Ladakh)

begging. A large section even of the lay Tibetan population spent several hours each
day in religious prayers, rituals, and offerings.

As monastic training was open to any male or female of normal ability, it became
an avenue for social mobility in Tibet. Many monks and nuns of lowly birth were
able to exert power as high-ranking members of their religious communities.
Monks also filled half the offices in the government and most of the skilled and
prestigious professions such as medicine and astrology. Thus a woman or man from
any level in society could enter a religious institution and distinguish herself or
himself, a fact that provided the society with greater internal flexibility than is
readily assumed.

The position of laywomen in Tibetan society, though better than that of their
counterparts in southern Asia, did not allow them to take part extensively in political
and legal spheres. With their first responsibilities always the care of their parents, the
rearing of children, the production and preparation of food, and the maintenance of

Plate 8. A husband and wife from the Golok area of Tibet who have come to Lhasa to trade salt and dried meat. 1920–21. (Pitt Rivers Museum, University of Oxford)

the family household, women were not as free as men to engage in political and income-producing activities. I did not interview a Tibetan judge, official, government caretaker, or clerk in the former government who was female, nor were women commonly either petitioners or defendants except in divorce and family separation cases. All the male and female Tibetans I interviewed saw the role of the female in their former political system as having been significant but indirect. The opinions, personality, and influence of particular women was commented upon, but except for the few who were petitioners in the legal process, their power was primarily exercised from the home, through a male, or behind the scenes in a public arena.

Nevertheless, women could be heads of households and as such maintain contracts and loans on land in their own names. Inheritance patterns allowed a woman to receive individual plots of real property from her family in most parts of Tibet, personal property from her mother, and the entire homestead from a mother without sons. Commonly, however, it was presumed that she would bring in a bridegroom *magpa* (*mag pa*), who would become the family's adopted son—a practice that occurred at all levels of society. As business owners and merchants, women could and did own shops, enter into trading contracts, and retain the profits for them-

Plate 9. Back view of a husband and wife from the Golok area of Tibet. On the woman's back are large engraved discs of silver, turquoise, and coral that are attached to her hair. 1920–21. (Pitt Rivers Museum, University of Oxford)

selves. It was more common, however, for them to be part of a business or trading family in which they had a significant voice. An important and necessary project for further research is the position and role of women in the legal system of pre-1959 Tibet.

Markets and Trade

Almost every conversation with a Tibetan peasant or nomad about conditions in the first half of the twentieth century eventually turns to considerations of markets, trade, and taxation. At regional centers throughout the Plateau, seasonal markets drew Tibetan producers to exchange their surplus for the necessities of the upcoming year. The agricultural produce of the farmers—barley, buckwheat, wheat, mustard oil, vegetables, and dried fruit—was bartered for the meat, hides, wool, butter, cheese, and salt of the nomads. Some exchanges at these local markets took place between individuals unknown to one another, but most involved representatives of particular groups of nomads and farmers who had established traditional exchange relationships over long periods of time. In the designated marketplaces of the larger cities, merchants, farmers, nomads, traders, and craftspeople could rent stalls to sell a wide range of goods of local and foreign origin; any individual could and did make purchases and sales at the market price, both in currency and in kind. Tibetans cited only three restrictions on their ability to purchase or sell available goods: a lack of purchasing power; the symbolic nature of some goods, such as the yellow brocade silk worn only by officials to indicate a certain rank; and government-awarded monopolies.

Silver and gold were employed as measures of exchange as early as the seventh century in Tibet; in the eighteenth century Nepalese coins were introduced in a limited form. The Tibetans issued their own coinage bearing the seal of the lion in the 1790s and paper money in 1890, but none of their currency was ever backed by reserves. Most taxes and other payments were made in produce and service rather than in currency.

There is historical evidence that the Tibetan people traded extensively both on and off the Plateau as early as the seventh century. External trade with other areas followed a general pattern of exporting raw materials and importing manufactured products. Christopher Beckwith points out that as early as the eighth century, Tibetans were engaged in large-scale export to China of animals, animal products (such as musk, yak tails, wool, and skins), honey, salt, borax, herbs, gemstones, and metal in exchange for silk, paper, ink, and tea; and to Muslim central Asia of musk, sheep, and cloth in exchange for manufactured iron and steel products, particularly chain mail and long swords.[4] During that early period, trade was controlled by government or monastic missions, with communities of Tibetans in the foreign countries and of foreigners in Lhasa arranging the missions and the sale of the items at each end. During the first half of the twentieth century, however, internal trade in most goods was available to anyone who had the capital. Any individual could join or start a private venture, provided it dealt in nonmonopolized goods.

The transport of goods was usually accomplished through private enterprise by the local population of a territorial segment. Each local area employed its own transport contractors with their teams of animals, a system that increased safety, as the local people were more likely to know the difficult mountain passes and crossings of a given area. Contractors picked up the goods at one end of a district and carried them on their pack animals through their own district. Payment came when they reached the other end and put the supplies on the backs of the animals of the next district. In the case of government transport, local districts provided this service as a form of tax.

The chief actors in large-scale international trade were professional merchants with extensive capital backing, political contacts, and foreign connections—wealthy Tibetans, Nepalese, Muslims, and Chinese—many of whom had exclusive trading monopolies granted by the government. Certain silks from China, horses from the Kokonor area, and metalwork for the Storage Office in Lhasa were exclusive monopolies in the 1950s. Transport over the mountains and into adjacent countries for these merchants was accomplished by caravans, but smaller traders with yak or camel teams and even individual porters made the trip for profit.

Tibetans are renowned throughout Asia for pious devotion to their particular brand of Buddhism, called Vajrayana or Tibetan Buddhism. Before 1959 the head of state was a religious figure, as were half the bureaucratic officials. Economic resources in the form of gifts, tithes, and taxes to pay for the support of monks flowed into the institutional practice of Buddhism: religious rituals, devotional tablets, butter lamps, statues of gods with their clothing and ornamentation, and the construction of religious buildings. For an individual Tibetan, a true belief in Vajrayana is considered to be the most precious attribute any human being can attain. Buddhism is an integral part of the Tibetan language and ideology; conversation switches easily from topics of dinner to conjectures on the past or future life of a relative and the karma of the Tibetan people as a whole. Tibetan families and individuals conduct religious rituals at household altars, chant through the beads of a rosary hundreds of times, circumambulate religious structures, and prostrate before religious figures as part of their daily routine.

Buddhism, which was brought into Tibet in an assortment of different forms beginning in approximately 550 A.D., did not achieve mass popularity until solitary ascetics such as the famous "cotton-clad yogi" Milarapa (1040–1123 A.D.) traveled and lived among the people, capturing their imaginations and hearts. The earlier local religion that Milarapa and other Buddhist ascetics encountered in the countryside had shamanistic, magical, and exorcistic elements, with a panoply of spirits, fiends, and demon gods inhabiting different parts of the landscape and other worlds. By conquering these local spirits with the higher mystical power of Tantric Buddhism and incorporating some of the local practices, popular Tibetan Buddhism began to develop in the eleventh century.

Vajrayana or Tantric Buddhism has four major sects and many minor ones: the Nyingma Pa, the foundations of which reach back into the period of the first propagation of the doctrine in the eighth century; the *sakya pa* (*sa skya pa*) school, which was the first to introduce Tibetan Buddhism to the Mongols; the *kadam pa* (*bka' gdams pa*) school, of which the Gelukpa sect of the Dalai Lamas is a later reform group; and the *kagyu pa* (*bka' brgyud pa*) school. Whereas the first of these was never a constituted religious order, the later three established large monasteries, developed particularized rituals, and emphasized certain texts and teachers that distinguished them as separate sects. Each sect had a powerful central monastery, plus satellite or branch monasteries throughout the Plateau from which it drew monk and nun trainees and resources. Indeed, allegiance to a particular sect was an important way in which Tibetans identified themselves to one another.

Ten core teachings of the renunciant tradition of early Mahayana Buddhism in India became central to Tibetan Buddhist philosophy: impermanence, suffering, denial of the soul, causality, transmigration, samsara, karma, the Four Noble Truths, the Eightfold Path, and nirvana. Faith in these core teachings from the words of the Buddha is an essential part of every Tibetan's view of the world:

Impermanence is the doctrine that nothing abides or remains, that all things change constantly, and thus that there is nothing a person can hold on to in this life. Humans can perceive only a small part of the world at one time, and that small flashing picture is always changing. *Suffering* is the nature of life. Our thirst for and attachment to things in this world, such as sense pleasures, wealth, power, ideas, and love, cause constant suffering because we want them to be permanent and they are not.

Denial of the soul is an idea unique to Buddhism. Because nothing in a person is permanent, everlasting, or absolute, there can be no constant individuality, no soul or self. A person is made of small pieces from five different elements, which are themselves impermanent and constantly changing. Humans have a false view because they see the combination of these five elements as one permanent unit, an ego. Yet Tibetan Buddhists often speak also of popular religious concepts of the soul, *la* (*bla*), which they held in addition, rather than in contradiction, to the core teaching of the denial of the soul.

Causality is not understood as a scientific principle in Vajrayana Buddhism; there is no supreme creator, no single cause, no accidentalism, but only a continuous and everlasting sequence of cause and effect. This principle is depicted for Tibetans as a wheel of suffering with twelve continuous steps, each depending on the one before it and causing the one after it. In essence, our ignorance (step one) of the effects of causality leads to desire and craving (steps two through eight), to grasping at things in this world (step nine), and finally to death (step twelve), which is immediately followed by rebirth into ignorance (step one).

Transmigration, or rebirth from step twelve back to step one, is the lot of all unenlightened sentient beings. It continues until a person is enlightened. All sentient beings have been reborn countless times before in many different forms and will be reborn again countless times unless they become enlightened. *Samsara* is the state of suffering in this world before a person is enlightened. *Karma* is the residue ("seeds") accumulated that conditions both the volitional present and the future lives of a human being. A person's acts produce karma, both good and bad, which affects his or her chances for enlightenment.

In his first discourse to his original five disciples, the Buddha taught that a person must follow the middle path of moderation and recognize the *Four Noble Truths:* (1) the existence of suffering, (2) its source as craving, (3) nirvana as the cessation of suffering, and (4) the Eightfold Path as the way to achieve nirvana. The *Eightfold Path* is a guide to an ethical life; it encompasses right view, right resolve, right speech, right conduct, right livelihood, right effort, right awareness, and right meditation.

Nirvana is an indescribable state of awareness that is not death, annihilation, or eternalism. It is completely separate and different from the entire cosmological sphere—hell, earth, and heaven—as humans know it. Sutras, or religious texts, often present nirvana in this fashion: begin by realizing that there is no self, develop equanimity, and then go to the highest of the meditative states. When the fire of ignorance and craving is gone, a person is fully "blown out" and henceforth has sensations but is not drawn to them. This is nirvana.

Scholars have argued over the sociological consequences for Tibet of these ten core doctrines. Buddhism's emphasis on acquiring merit for the next life through good deeds and accepting this life as due to past karma, some argue, encourages acceptance of the status quo and of one's own socioeconomic position in life, thus inhibiting change and stressing introversion. The emphasis on faith and obedience makes disapproval of the doctrines equivalent to an offense to the Buddha himself. Others have pointed to the essential importance of individual merit and effort, through the Eightfold Path to enlightenment, as promoting constant reflection, reassessment, and change. Both views are held by Tibetans I have spoken with as well.

Another aspect of Tibetan Buddhism is the system of succession by reincarnation, which allows authority, spiritual power, divine status, and even secular roles to be passed on through a method first expounded in the Kagyu Pa sect. Upon the death of a religious leader, it is presumed that he or she will be reborn in an infant human body, which can be located and therefore will actually succeed to the office of the previous religious leader as the next politically and religiously sanctioned leader. By the twentieth century several hundred persons throughout Tibet at all levels of society, from the high-ranking Dalai Lama to the heads of small local temples, had succeeded to their offices in this way.[5]

A system of succession by reincarnation requires both elaborate procedures for the discovery of the next human body—including the gathering of oracular and other mystical signs—and an extended period of training for the child during her or his minority. Even when these aspects of the Tibetan system operated smoothly, there was an inherent instability during the period of the search and the years of the child's minority, during which a chosen regent usually acted officially on behalf of the child. It is often presumed that a new incarnation such as a young Dalai Lama, free of political connections, court intrigue, and nepotism, was a symbol of political equality as well as an object of intense religious devotion for the population. But Tibetan historians have pointed out that some sects adopted the practice to gain prestige, while others continued it solely with political purposes in mind.[6] Furthermore, a reluctance to relinquish power by the political leader in control during the child's minority was a continuing problem—perhaps even accounting for the early deaths of the Ninth Dalai Lama through the Twelfth.

Tibetans in general either do not speak of the political or sociological aspects of succession by reincarnation or speak of it only in a future context, questioning what will happen to Tibetan policy when the Fourteenth Dalai Lama dies. The practical aspects, however, are a constant topic of conversation. During the years of my fieldwork two new and important incarnations, the junior and senior tutors of the Dalai Lama, were discovered. The process by which both children were recognized, the families they came from, and their special qualities were discussed at length by everyone throughout the Tibetan communities in India. Even though such a rebirth is an event of immense prestige for the family, several female friends expressed genuine relief once the incarnations were found in other families; they knew then that their child would not be taken away from them.

Excursus: Marriage Patterns

Marriage between a woman and a set of brothers, the Tibetan fraternal polyandrous household, formed a "stem family" with the wife producing one set of children who would then inherit the household property as an indivisible unit (Goldstein 1971a)—a wealth-conserving device in a society with scarce land resources and divisible inheritance. Other acceptable marriage patterns included father-son and unrelated male polyandry; sororal, mother-daughter, and unrelated female polygyny; and monogamy.

Tibetan households, depending upon the ages and life cycles of the inhabitants, often exhibited a sequence of these marriage styles rather than a permanent pattern established at one key point. Deaths, the addition or loss of economic holdings, the birth of children, individual desires, and the availability of in-laws or others as sexual partners all contributed to great fluidity in marriage and household arrangements.

Changing marriage patterns in the natal household of Kungola Thubten Sangye, for example (see Chapter 25), began with the monogamous marriage of his parents. Upon the death of his mother, his father began cohabiting in a fraternal polyandrous unit with his brother and brother's wife. Kungola was sent to live with his aunt in the house of his maternal grandmother. After the uncle died, leaving a monogamous marriage between the father and the uncle's wife, Thubten Sangye returned to his father's house, and a daughter was born to his father and stepmother. In an oral will, the father eventually left his household and land to this daughter and her children, because Thubten had joined government service as a monk.

Another example involved a woman called Amala, who was first married by arrangement to a *magpa,* or bridegroom, brought into her family household—an exception to the common pattern of patrilocality. After a few years he moved to another part of Tibet but remained married to her. His younger brother was then brought in as her *magpa,* creating a fraternal polyandrous unit that produced two children. When brother two left for a noncelibate monastery, stating that he would occasionally return to enjoy conjugal visits with Amala, the third brother came to live with her; by him she had three more children. As brother three traveled constantly, Amala openly entertained a local lover at her home when he was away. The five children grew up as siblings accustomed to viewing all three husbands and the lover as father figures.

In a third case, a woman named Sonam was married by parental arrangement to her first husband, Tashi. When Tashi died, she married an older, unrelated man, Dorje, who was already married to another woman, thereby moving from her original monogamous marriage into a polygynous marriage. After her second husband died, Sonam entered into a monogamous marriage with his son by the other wife and had children. When she became elderly, she left this third husband to be ordained as a nun and moved to Lhasa.

Descent groups were not strongly evident in Tibetan agricultural society except in the most important families. Although land ownership, occupational categories for sons, and membership in other social categories passed through patrilineal descent—as did some forms of outcaste stigma and spiritual power—there were no lineage gatherings except among certain nomadic tribes, no ancestor cults, no clans, and no marriages between moieties.

Marriage contracts and festivals were nonreligious in Tibet, yet the joining of two families or individuals was a serious subject of astrological and cosmological import, evidenced in the form of a legal contract between the parties. One Tibetan doctor spoke at length about marriage contracts:

> In my area of Kyidong we had the usual custom that we went to the girl's family and offered beer to ask the girl to come as a bride. Almost all the marriages in our area were arranged and involved marriage contracts by a very old tradition.
>
> Parents of the boy and girl first spent time investigating the other family and seeing to their character. The contract was called the "unchangeable document," which meant that they had to stay together for one lifetime, and it was made jointly by the four parents. Both sets of parents had to be happy, and the boy had to like the girl to have such a contract.
>
> There are eight sections to the contract. First there are the prostration words to the deities, especially Manjushri. There is a statement that both individuals and families have been matched astrologically with respect to fire, earth, water, and air according to their life spans, their bodies, power, and fortune. There is a statement that the son has gone to the girl's house to explain, in exact words, "the earth and the door," which is a recitation that allows him to enter into the house of the girl. Next, the contract states that all good things are invited into this marriage. Then it lists in eight categories all the valuables that the girl's side will receive during the ceremony, including ornaments, clothes, sleeping clothes, cooking articles, a ring on her right hand and later another on her left. There follows a statement that the boy and girl have been asked if they like each other.
>
> After this, the contract lists the rules and *bab* if anyone violates the marriage contract: if the boy violates it, double the value of those articles brought by the girl must be paid by the boy; and if the girl violates it, she is not given any property. Finally, they both have to sign the contract, and the parents sign it also.

CHAPTER TWO

Reading Law Codes
as Tibetan History

An official traveling to notify or collect due taxes
should procure his provisions locally per his official letter;
He should carry out his duties without a greedy mind
and administer to the people gently, for the benefit of self and others, according to
the law.

—Tsang Law Code

Although Tibetan kingdoms stretch back into the early part of the Christian era, Tibetan recorded history begins with the reign of the first historical king, Songtsen Gampo (*srong tsen gam po*), who in the year 632 A.D. sent scholars to Ghandhara (now northern India and Pakistan) to compose a script for the Tibetan language. He established the Yarlung royal dynasty that lasted for over two hundred years and built a Tibetan empire throughout much of central Asia. As numerous scholars have noted, with the advent of Tibetan writing many pieces of Buddhist literature could be accurately translated from the Indian languages into Tibetan. Of equal significance for the kingdom at that time was the possibility of accurately recording administrative matters, legal rules, financial records, and correspondence. Some examples of these very early records and even an early law code attributed to the reign of the first king were found among the documents recovered from the sealed Buddhist caves of Tun Huang in Chinese Turkestan. Now preserved in several libraries in Europe, these documents show the early formation of a secular rule of law in Tibet under the first dynasty of kings in the seventh century.

The first law code written in the Empire period (620–866 A.D.) comes to us in fragments from different documents.[1] The earliest has a beginning passage in which the king proclaims the granting of laws to Tibet, explains the purpose of the document, and enumerates the benefits it will bring to his subjects.[2]

At least three different types of rules were propounded during the first royal dynasty: (1) the Four Fundamental Laws prohibiting murder, thievery, lechery, and the bearing of false witness; (2) the Ten Nonvirtuous Acts; and (3) the Sixteen Moral

Principles. The lists of offenses were strongly based on Buddhist doctrine. The Four Fundamental Laws and the Ten Nonvirtuous Acts come directly from the Tibetan Buddhist canon.

Other sections of the code also revel in numerical lists—a style carried on into codes written over six hundred years later: for example, the first group of six institutions, the second group of thirty-six institutions including the six great principles, the six insignia of rank, the six seals, the six qualities, the six symbols of the heroes, excerpts from the six codes, and the four catalogues of different ranks.[3] Each of these lists stands as an outline for later elaboration, but all that is left of this enumeration style is the division of the code into sixteen sections and a reference to the previous codes in the title. The first code of the first kings does not appear to have been widely disseminated in Tibet in the twentieth century, but lists of sixteen moral principles said to have been formulated by Songtsen Gampo were very well known.[4]

After the murder of the last king in the Yarlung dynastic line and defeat by the Chinese in 866 A.D., 350 years of decentralization ensued. Several of the resulting small kingdoms throughout Tibet were established by relatives of the former royal family who preserved and adapted the administrative and legal rules of the former central government in their own localities.

In the thirteenth century the Sakya Pa sect of Tibetan Buddhism, with the help of Mongolian supporters, gained control of much of central Tibet and thereby began the first real Tibetan theocratic period. This hundred-year reign remains somewhat clouded with respect to legal administration and legal rules. Giuseppe Tucci has stated that the Sakya used Mongolian laws during this time: "probably at that time the Mongol penal code was introduced into Tibet, either the Yasa of Genghis Khan or more probably its successive elaborations and adaptments, incorporated into Yuan laws. . . . They were introduced into Tibet by the Yuan and found the *sa skya pa* ready to accept and enforce them."[5]

A knowledgeable Tibetan who worked in the Sakya region of Tibet and represented Sakya citizens in courts in Lhasa during the 1930s and 1940s told me several times that there was no Mongolian-Sakya law code and never had been; lamas from the Sakya sect now living in India and those living in Tibet responded in the same way. But two sons of the Sakya royal family, when interviewed extensively in 1960 after they fled the country, stated that a Sakya law code was used by government officials to provide standards and guidelines for judgments.[6] At this juncture, without examples of Sakya law codes, it is difficult to assess Tucci's statement that they followed Mongol law or to determine the degree to which Mongolian law codes influenced later codes.

In 1354 a young former Sakya monk overthrew the Sakya theocracy and established the first of three secular dynastic lines—known as the Three Kingdoms—that were to rule central Tibet for the next three hundred years. The reign of the first of these, the Phamogru dynasty, was a dynamic period in Tibetan history. The young former monk, Changchub Gyalsen, was a brilliant soldier, administrator, and organizer by all historical accounts. He has also been credited by several scholars with the drafting of a new legal code in his efforts to restore Tibet to the prominence of the early Empire period.[7] None of his law codes are known to exist today, however.[8]

The first extant law code composed during this dynasty is called the Phamogru or Neudong code.[9] It is a full-length code that represents the transition between the poetic numerical style of the early Empire and the codified rules of later periods. The code itself can be divided into two parts illustrating these separate modes of expression.

The lengthy introductory portion of this fourteenth-century code is divided into a short initial "general" statement followed by a long "specific" statement. Both appear to be compilations of accumulated wisdom and proverbs. Their subject matter ranges from the proper attributes of a good witness, judge, or guarantor to the proper and improper forms of speech in court and the best qualities for a party to a suit.[10] For example, a party to a suit who is distinguished by "high victorious speech" should display at least some of the Four Causes of Greatness (greatness in the heritage of paternal ancestors, greatness in acts for the country, learning, and great wealth); the Four Signs of Greatness (presenting tea and beer, wearing silk, lynx, or fox, using a *zo* and having important guests from a long distance); and the Four Qualities of Greatness (taking on a guru, taking care of one's parents, taking care of one's relatives and servants, and vanquishing enemies easily).[11]

The reader is often told directly which factors are positive and which negative in the consideration of a case; this method of giving the factors or criteria for consideration (but not how to rule in a case, given these criteria) shows up repeatedly in later codes. These signs of what might be called a prudential or admonitory style of writing distinguish parts of the later Tibetan codes as well.

The second part of the Neudong law code begins with a plain list of fifteen substantive laws and then proceeds to elaborate rather pedantically, one at a time, the factors and rules for each subject. The list covers murder, theft, oath-taking, adultery, family separation, selling and buying goods, accounts, loans of animals, rules for the chief of the army, rules for those who retreat, and rules regarding the payment of court costs. Gone is the whimsical, almost old-fashioned style of writing from the first part; these are rules for the operation of an official bureaucracy. This second part of the code is so sophisticated and so replete with exceptions and finely tuned distinctions that it suggests a long history of legal elaboration or borrowings from other cultures rather than the brilliance of a contemporaneous legal scholar.[12]

Unfortunately, nothing remains in the form of law codes from the succeeding Rinpung dynastic line that ruled the second of the Three Kingdoms, and little is known of its internal administrative structure or legal practices.

The third and last of these dynastic lines began with the overthrow of the Rinpung in the 1560s by a young farmer named Singsha Setan Dorje, who established the *tsang* (*gtsang*) kingdom. The fourth Tsang king, Karma Tenkyong Wangpo, who came to power around 1623, was keenly concerned with legal administration. Tibetan histories recount that he sent out edicts, called *tsasik* (*rtsa tshig*), to elicit responses and information for an official compilation of legal rules. He then appointed a compiler to write a code of laws for his kingdom from these responses.[13] The resulting code was stripped of the charming passages on the qualities of witnesses and the long enumerated lists of the previous codes. This was a true administrative code and our starting point for the modern Tibetan law codes.[14]

The Tsang code was the first to remain widely distributed throughout Tibet right up to the mid-twentieth century, and it is available in more forms than any of the other Tibetan law codes. Eight different versions, ranging from eleven to sixteen sections each, are in my present collection. Introductory historical passages often give a flavor of the legal system at that time. Following the introduction, a central core of twelve substantive law sections appears in almost every extant version of the Tsang or later codes, whether in full or abridged form. One or more of four additional sections in the various versions make up codes of thirteen, fifteen, and sixteen sections.[15] The format of the central twelve sections was standardized during the Tsang period and only added to or abridged by successive codes. Comparing a code of the later Dalai Lama period with a Tsang code leaves little doubt that the later codes used the Tsang as their template and added or subtracted paragraphs, often without making large changes in the rest of the text.

CHAPTER THREE

The Dalai Lamas and Recent History

Like the union of sun and moon, the priest and patron, together,
promulgated the legal system in the manner of the universal emperors of India
and led their subjects toward an age of peace and well-being,
bringing sunny days of happiness.
                                    —Ganden Podrang Code of the Dalai Lamas

The Gelukpa Period

In 1642, within a few decades of the compilation of the Tsang code, the Mongolian Gushri Khan swept into Tibet and put his religious sage, the Fifth Dalai Lama, in charge of the country. Secular rule under the Tsang kings gave way to the three-hundred-year rule of the Gelukpa sect—the second theocratic period in Tibet.

Based in the capital city of Lhasa, the government consisted of a charismatic religious head—the Dalai Lama or his representative—and his small administrative bureaucracy overseeing a loose federation of differentially incorporated regions of the Plateau.[1] The central southern region was directly under the control of the central government; the internal political systems of several other regions were not, though in some an appointed local district head was responsible to the central government for official business and taxes. The indirectly controlled territorial units used Tibetan administrative and legal procedures in their dealings with the central government.

His Holiness the Fifth Dalai Lama began his reign with the construction of a huge palace—the Potala—in the center of the plain of Lhasa, a functional symbol of the new magnificence of Gelukpa sovereignty. The Fifth and the regents who worked under him are credited with establishing a new bureaucratic administration and constructing a new law code. Their aim was a blending and balancing of "both religion and politics,"[2] as well as the unification of disparate political forces within the country. This goal would be achieved, over the course of the next three centuries, in several different ways.

First, it was embodied in the new law codes, which were compiled only a few years after the installation of the Fifth Dalai Lama and used without major changes for the rest of the three-hundred-year reign of the Gelukpa.[3] Despite their ostensible newness, the codes took their structure, form, and a large part of their content from the code of the Tsang kings. In every passage of these texts the Tsang code is the paradigm;[4] the regents simply altered, adjusted, or added to it. This represents a choice by the Fifth Dalai Lama to employ a secular rather than a canonical code, though a secular code based on and imbued with the spirit of Buddhism as practiced in their country. It appears that the codes written under the Fifth were never improved or substantially revised over the next three hundred years—a long time for an unrevised legal document to remain viable.[5]

The 1,336 lines of the first of the Ganden Podrang law codes[6] of the Dalai Lamas cover an enormous number of subjects and tell us a great deal about Tibetan administrative concerns and social structure in the sixteenth (and perhaps through to the twentieth) century. Among the specifics are the amount of pay to be given to government messengers on official journeys; the barter equivalents for measures of barley; what to do with a borrowed animal that dies the day after it is returned to its owner; the allocation of male and female children in a divorce; the proper interrogation method for a judge or mediator; and victim compensation and other payments for the murder of a monk. The result is a mosaic organized into fields of substantive rules with several underlying themes (such as judicial reasoning and legal procedure) and interspersed segments (historical comments, barter equivalents, proverbs), which makes for engrossing reading.[7]

Second, the balancing of religion and politics was achieved by dividing the bureaucracy of the new government into ecclesiastical and secular sections, the former residing in the palace of the Dalai Lama, the latter located in the old city at quite a distance from the palace, thus creating a literal and figurative separation of the two. Affairs of the monasteries and other religious issues were assigned to the ecclesiastic wing of the government headed by four Great Monk Secretaries. The secular wing was headed by a Cabinet with authority over secular administrative agencies including the secular courts. Both wings reported to the Office of His Holiness the Dalai Lama on all matters of importance.

Third, two separate avenues for entering civil service were established, one religious and one secular. Young monks who showed promise—from families of all social levels—were chosen, trained, and tested for government service; as monk officials they did not marry, but neither did they generally reside in monasteries. Secular officials were drawn from the families of government clerks and the traditional nobility.

Fourth, although the ecclesiastical wing was staffed only with monk officials, positions in the secular wing of the bureaucracy were filled by both monk and lay officials, commonly paired in each office. For example, the Storage Office in the 1950s had four senior officers, two of each type. Both monk and lay officers could hold any of the available secular positions open to persons of their rank, but they wore separate dress and were addressed by separate appellations: for example, Monk Officer, Fourth Rank and Lay Officer, Fourth Rank.[8]

To administer the vast territory over which it had sovereignty, the central government in Lhasa sent out monk and lay officials to act as resident district officers and governors in the provinces of the Plateau. Their duties were to collect taxes, keep records, arrange for transportation, receive and pass on commands or requests, deal with local issues, and decide local conflicts. There were seven directly controlled regional governors' offices, called *chikab* (*sbyi khyab*), in Tibet prior to 1959, and approximately 120 district subdivisions of these regions, called *dzong* (*rdzong*). The other, indirectly controlled regional areas operated under their own leaders and sent representatives to Lhasa. Many of these were small kingdoms and princely states that had been incorporated into the Tibetan nation, leaving the king or prince with the rank of a district officer or second-level governor. In these areas, the central government tended not to interfere with internal affairs unless serious problems were brought to the first-level governor's office by the administrators of that state.

Khams province in southeastern Tibet provides an example of how regional administration functioned in the 1940s. In this province, there were two headquarters: one at Chamdo, from which the governor exercised full civil, military, and judicial authority, and the other at Drachen. Several government district officers reported to each headquarters, in addition to local rulers of many indirectly controlled districts. The officials who reported to the office of the governor in Chamdo were monk and lay officials appointed by the central government to posts in directly controlled areas, plus local princes, tribal headmen, and abbots of monastic estates in indirectly controlled areas. Tibetans who had been government district officers in Khams in the 1940s stated that in their districts they were particularly concerned with the maintenance of authority and peace, dispute settlement, the collection of taxes, and the payments by the government to local entities such as monasteries or army patrols.

The rather small Tibetan bureaucracy was dominated in the twentieth century by two political factions. The first comprised the families of the nobility who had received grants of land in the form of estates throughout the thirteen hundred years of Tibetan history.[9] A few of these families developed into an upper class of official nobility: they maintained their estates through many generations, accumulating landholdings in exchange for providing as public servants one or more sons per generation, who were sent to secular schools and internships at secular offices.[10] The members of these families had enormous economic and political power and were treated with great deference.

The monasteries made up the second political bloc. With thousands of members organized in honeycomb buildings the size of cities, and with the head of their sect, the Dalai Lama, as the political head of state, the Gelukpa monasteries in the Lhasa Valley wielded great power. At the annual Mon Lam (Great Prayer) Festival held four days after Losar (the Tibetan New Year), the monks took over the capital both figuratively (for spiritual regeneration)[11] and literally, pouring in to engage in three weeks of mass rituals at the major sites of Buddhism within the city. During this period the monastery prefects acted as the legal officials of the city, observing and disciplining offenses. Monasteries controlled large estates of land as well. The impact of their political and spiritual power, evidenced both through individuals and through groups, was vast.

At the top, then, the Tibetan government was a bureaucracy with a supply of poli-

Plate 10. State Oracle at Nechung Monastery, near Lhasa. The Cabinet ministers (with their backs to the camera) await the Oracle's pronouncement of the future which he sees in the polished steel mirror held in front of him. 1942–43. (Ilya Tolstoy, Library, The Academy of Natural Sciences of Philadelphia)

tical goods delimited to the distribution of a few possible prizes to the members of the bureaucracy in the form of some political posts, landed prebendal estates, and resource monopolies. The economy was redistributive in nature, and no serious military was ever permanently established, which resulted historically in a variety of foreign states taking on the role of "patron" to control the foreign affairs of the "priest" who sat at the pinnacle of power.[12] This combination of inward-looking, internal jousting for political prizes and a compliance toward external states that intervened in Tibetan foreign affairs—and at times, such as the enthronement of the Fifth Dalai Lama, rearranged internal political alliances—typified Tibetan politics throughout the last three hundred years of the nation's history.[13]

One final and most unusual aspect of Gelukpa administration was the role played by the State Oracle, who exerted great influence as an adviser to the head of state. Tibetans have always used oracles to determine personal matters: the timing of marriage arrangements, business ventures, journeys. The State Oracle, a man chosen for his ability to receive the powerful protective deity Pehar while in trance, resided in the Nechung Monastery in the Lhasa valley and led a rigorously protected and devout life. Consultations for all important matters of state—such as the discovery of a new Dalai Lama, the political course of the country, the health of high-level officials, and even legal cases—were arranged with the oracle. After he had completed preparatory rituals and dressed in full costume, the body of the oracle was entered by the deity, sending him into a wild dance. During this possession the oracle answered many of the questions addressed to him, and a clerk took notes.

Tibetans often comment that it was the Nechung State Oracle who first predicted, in the early part of the twentieth century, an invasion from the east if the country did not reform. In the 1980s it was an occasion of very serious concern for the government-in-exile that upon the death of the Nechung Oracle—who had fled with the Fourteenth Dalai Lama in 1959—the deity did not return in trance form to another human body for several years (including the three years of my fieldwork).

The Coming of the Chinese

In the summer of 1950 inauspicious signs abounded throughout the Plateau: a devastating earthquake shook all of eastern and central Tibet; comets appeared that had never been seen before; and people told stories of a strange sulfurlike smell, the diffusion of red light in the east, and water pouring from the gargoyles on the main temple of Lhasa on a clear day. There were rumors throughout the country that the State Oracle's prediction of the state's imminent collapse after an incursion from the east was about to be fulfilled.

The Chinese army marched into the Tibetan Plateau from the east in the fall of 1950 in the wake of Mao's Great Revolution and began the process of incorporating the Plateau into the new Chinese state. Although most authorities agree that Tibet had controlled both its internal and foreign affairs for the forty years prior to this period Chinese leaders had long asserted that Tibet was historically a part of China. Tibetan government appeals to other nations and international entities failed, for the world was focused on the eastern border of China and General Douglas MacArthur in Korea. Thus the Chinese entry into Tibet was a swift blow at an opportune time, during an essential power vacuum.[14]

Between 1951 and 1959 the Dalai Lama attempted to work out a new arrangement with Mao Zedong while facing the difficulties of a large power differential and the Chinese concepts of manifest destiny and Communist reform. With some 20,000 Chinese troops stationed in Lhasa, famine became a serious problem because the fragile Tibetan agricultural economy was unable to support the tremendous increase in population. By 1958 the Tibetan resistance movement, called the National Volunteer Defense Army, had openly organized in the center of Tibet and began recapturing towns and fortifications from the People's Liberation Army.

In the midst of this explosive situation, the Chinese general stationed in Lhasa extended an invitation to the Dalai Lama to attend a theatrical performance, unaccompanied by other Tibetans—a gesture the people saw as a thinly veiled attempt to kidnap their leader. On March 10, 1959, the day of the performance, thousands of Tibetans filled the streets of Lhasa, securing the palace of the Dalai Lama and demanding the removal of the Chinese. The city was in a frenzy: resolutions calling for an independent Tibet were circulated and signed by important officials; mobs spread rumors and attacked Chinese in the streets. With even their collaborators in revolt, the Chinese built barricades, amassed armaments, and opened fire on the city. Chinese sources have claimed that more than 87,000 Tibetans were killed during this extended revolt.

The Tibetan diaspora began that very night. Determining that his own flight was the only method of preventing the complete slaughter of his people, the Dalai Lama fled in disguise toward the Indian border, accompanied by hundreds of Khams horsemen as guards. An exodus followed his path, and within a few years an estimated 100,000 Tibetans had crossed the Himalayas into Bhutan, Nepal, and India. The diaspora continues to the present day, with a flow of refugees and pilgrims making their way along known routes to Tibetan camps throughout southern Asia.

The Chinese government divided the Tibetan Plateau into the four People's Autonomous Republics of Tsinghai, Szechwan, Yunnan, and Tibet and installed Chinese regional governments. Military bases were built at several locations around the Plateau to secure the Chinese presence against possible incursions from India or Nepal. During the Cultural Revolution (1966–76), thousands of Tibetan monasteries, temples, and libraries—including one of the largest monasteries, Ganden, which had housed five thousand monks—were razed. Since 1980 the Lhasa valley and other major cities have been extensively developed with factories, hotels, and government buildings. The old Tibetan city of Lhasa is now primarily a tourist attraction for thousands of foreign visitors who stay at new hotels such as the Lhasa Hilton and take guided tours of Tibetan monasteries and other sites.

For the central government of China, the incorporation of Tibet has brought a vast increase in territory, accompanied by political problems. The Plateau remains an economic drain on its resources, despite tourism, logging projects in the mountain highlands of eastern Tibet, and several mining operations in western Tibet. The indigenous Tibetan population has not successfully intermarried with the Chinese and continues to resist most efforts to sinicize them; revolts and outbreaks continue to require military intervention. The Han Chinese who have been settled on the Plateau in the tens of thousands continue to demand hardship pay and complain about the conditions. Rapprochement efforts with the Dalai Lama, including several visits by envoys of the Tibetan government-in-exile in the 1980s, have not been concluded successfully. The current Chinese government remains steadfast in its historic political claim and its current political control of the Plateau.

Tibetans in Exile, 1959 to the Present

During the summer following the first exodus, the Dalai Lama began to set up a government-in-exile in India. At his request, an International Commission of Jurists investigated the situation in Tibet in 1959 and issued a preliminary report stating that the Chinese were engaged in a program of ethnic genocide in what had been an independent sovereign state.[15] With this report in hand, the Dalai Lama approached the United Nations, which subsequently issued three separate resolutions (in 1959, 1961, and 1965) reprimanding China for its treatment of the human rights of the Tibetans. None of the member nations recognized the new government-in-exile, however, and little came of the resolutions.

Covert aid and training for the Tibetan resistance was provided by the American

Plate 11. Street filled with the shops of Tibetan refugees near the compound of the Dalai Lama and the offices of the Tibetan government-in-exile, Dharamsala, India. 1986.

CIA from 1951 to 1971 as part of the Cold War struggle against Communism. With President Richard Nixon's overtures to the People's Republic of China, however, all American aid to the Tibetan guerrillas stopped. Chuzhi Gandrug, the group committed to a military struggle for the independence of Tibet, continued its efforts until 1974, when the Nepalese government placed strict limits on the Tibetan forces still using bases in Nepal to launch raids on the Plateau. All the remaining forces became stateless rebels and eventually either turned themselves in or were killed off.

The former British hill station of Dharamsala has been the site of the administrative headquarters of the Tibetan government-in-exile since the 1960s. Today, the compound of His Holiness the Fourteenth Dalai Lama straddles a ridge far above the town against a backdrop of the snowcapped lesser Himalayas. With his private quarters and staff at one end and the exquisitely painted Main Temple—his personal monastery—and the guest quarters at the other, this compound represents the executive and religious heart of the diasporic nation. On the hillside above to the east is the large brick Center for the Performing Arts, home of the Tibetan Drama Society; to the west is the complex of buildings that make up the Tibetan Children's Village, now a world-famous boarding school for Tibetan orphans and refugee children. Gangchen Kyishong—the administrative compound of the government, housing the Library of Tibetan Works and Archives, the Office of the Cabinet, other government offices, the Temple of the State Oracle, and staff living quarters and kitchen—lies down the road below His Holiness's residence. Standing among an array of Indian and Tibetan shops just above the town of Dharamsala are the Tibetan Medical Center and the Tibetan Printing Press.

The refugee government has taken as its goal the preservation of ancient arts, literature, and religion while working to modernize Tibetan political institutions. The Indian and Nepalese governments' acceptance of the refugees and their willingness to work with the government-in-exile to set aside special lands and schools for Tibetans have been key factors in the successful relocation of the refugees. By 1980, more than twenty segregated agricultural and handicraft settlements of varying sizes existed on the subcontinent, in ecological zones from the greater Himalayas of Solo-Kumbu to the hot and humid expanses of Mundgod in southern India. In addition, many communities of Tibetans living in Indian and Nepalese towns or cities had organized Tibetan schools and cooperative societies. And today, the Tibetan diaspora has spread not only throughout Asia but across North America, Australia, and Europe. Lamas traveling to Western nations have founded hundreds of centers for the practice and study of Tibetan Buddhism, creating further interest in the situation of the refugees and the preservation of Tibetan culture, particularly religious culture.[16]

The government-in-exile, which has been in existence for thirty-five years, is now facing several different issues. The Dalai Lama's own followers recognize that within another generation they may become a permanent government-*of*-exiles.[17] The position of the Dalai Lama internationally as the embodiment of the Tibetan people and nation, heightened by his acceptance of the Nobel Peace Prize in 1989, is threatened by his advancing age. Recently, there have been several anti-Tibetan riots in India.[18] Chinese and Tibetans continue to have opposing political agendas for the future of the Plateau; it remains to be seen whether some sort of political rapprochement will be reached, whether the refugees will realize a "free Tibet," or whether the political control of the Plateau will remain under the Chinese government with the refugees becoming a permanent diaspora culture.[19]

Excursus: Incorporation of Land

As explained by Tibetans, the incorporation of land into Tibet and the designation of areas fell into five different categories:

First, both before and during the historic period of the great Tibetan Empire in the eighth and ninth centuries A.D., enormous tracts of land were conquered by Tibetan armies. Most of these were incorporated into the Tibetan state as government lands. Throughout the history of the country and its successive centralized governments, various sections of the Plateau were reconquered and then occupied either by the Tibetans themselves or by Mongolians fighting in the name of a particular lama; these too were eventually incorporated into the contemporary Tibetan state as government-held lands. Most of the nomadic lands and the entire northern plain were considered to be held directly by the central government in this way, as was the Crystal Fortress area (Chapter 16) in the south.

Second, separate and rival kingdoms existed during the period of the Tibetan Empire, such as Dedge, Lingtsang, Chones, and Nangchen. It is said that their kings fought with the original Tibetan kings, were eventually subjugated or reconciled, and their kingdoms incorporated into the Tibetan nation. The head of such a state was granted the title of a high Tibetan government official and then allowed the freedom to administer his own internal affairs, using traditional titles, regulations, organization, and rules of succession. Government officers were rarely sent from the capital to interfere with the administration of these kingdoms.

Third, during the four-hundred-year period after the Tibetan Empire disintegrated (900 to 1200 A.D.), a series of small states were established, many headed by princes from the previous dynastic lineage who absorbed tracts of local land into their holdings. Some of the famous kingdoms that developed during this period of regionalism were Guge, Zhang Zhung, Tsang, and Rinpung. When later brought into the Tibetan state, they retained their regional names and titles acquired during this period.

Fourth, between 1247 and 1350, Tibet was controlled by the Sakya rulers associated with that sect of Tibetan Buddhism. After the decline of Sakya power the core of their lands and several satellite monasteries formed a separate state within Tibet proper, controlled by the Sakya Khon family, which paid only token taxes to the central government. Quite independent politically but remaining within the Tibetan state, Sakya cooperated with the central government when necessary but remained aloof and had its own administration, judicial process, and officials. It was, in effect, a Tibetan Vatican.

Fifth, some annexed areas maintained a status of semiautonomy, including Ladakh (which was at times a separate Tibetan kingdom), Amdo, and other outerlying but ethnically Tibetan areas.

The Tibetan nation, then, comprised lands incorporated as conquered territory, semiautonomous principalities and kingdoms, regions formed in the diffusion period, a separate Vatican-like state, and annexed territories—all loosely ruled by a small bureaucratic system operating out of Lhasa.

PART TWO

The Cosmology of Law

Introduction

Cosmological . . . categories are embedded in the rituals I shall describe; they chart the geography and define the architecture of . . . space and are expressed in the material symbols that are manipulated in the rituals. In the rituals, we see cosmology in action.

— Stanley J. Tambiah, *Buddhism and the Spirit Cults in Northeast Thailand*

An American law professor recently asked me, "So, Rebecca, what *was* the Tibetan law of torts?" His question makes sense in the context of legal treatises that discuss legal institutions, move on to substantive legal rules and procedures, describe appellate and Supreme Court cases of interest, and analyze the current state of a particular legal category—that is, in the way American lawyers typically construct and define what is important in their own and other legal systems. Indeed, they will say that this is what *constitutes* law.

What the law professor's question does not recognize are all the practical and conceptual assumptions that American lawyers already *know* about the world and about the law: the dimensions of space and time, the subtleties of legal myth and narrative, the legal rituals that define how actors act, speak, and move in a legal forum, social hierarchies that influence their decisions, the aspects of authority, power, and legitimation which they understand.

But what if most or all of these practical and conceptual assumptions were not only different from those that apply in Tibet but arranged in networks or sets of relations that were also entirely different? What if, when one first asked Tibetans about law, they said that no such category existed?

There is rarely a simple one-to-one correspondence whereby a legal category or activity in one society matches that of another society. Instead, the legal anthropologist must ask different sorts of questions: What activities result in disputes? What form do the disputes take? What conceptual assumptions inform the process? Who are the actors and what do they do? What do they tell you about what they are doing? How does this relate to other aspects of their social life?

"But surely," the American law professor countered upon hearing this explana-

Figure 3. Kalacakra Tantra Mandala.

tion, "this is all too complicated. Let me ask you a simple property question instead—what did a deed to land look like in Tibet?"

Since most Tibetans in pre-1959 Buddhist Tibet did have written deeds to their land, this question—unlike the one on torts—can be answered directly. But again, look at the assumptions that underwrite it. The professor assumes that Tibetans could sell or trade such deeds (they usually could not), that the deeds could be drafted privately (they could not), that land was valued by measured area (it was not), that a person was taxed for it (not necessarily), and that a living person owned it (not always; in Tibet, incarnations in the intermediate state between death and reincarnation remained the actual owners of their property). To respond, then, that Tibetans did have written deeds to land or even to list their contents, would result in an essentially incorrect answer because those deeds were *understood* inside a set of completely different assumptions. For the law professor to understand the Tibetan legal system would require that he come to appreciate not only the tacit assumptions that shape and motivate his own world-view but those that shape and motivate the Tibetan legal system. He would have to be conscious not only of his own legal cosmology but of Tibetan legal cosmology as well.

Explaining a cosmology of law begins with the aspects of a society that are least commonly assumed to be important to an understanding of the legal system: namely, the elements of the cultural backdrop that have an impact on the law. As Stanley Tambiah puts it in the epigraph above, "Cosmological . . . categories are embedded in the rituals."[1]

These cosmological categories, these conceptual and practical building blocks that structure legal reasoning and action, will vary from one group or society to another. Non-Western ideas of reality and illusion, karma, the cyclical nature of rebirth, nonduality, and multiple concepts of time and causation directly affect Tibetan understandings of the nature of law.[2] The practice of law in Tibet is also structured by the shape of the legal language, which is filled with proverbs and phrases from seventeenth-century law codes; by the ranked social categories and power dimensions of the actors; by the use of such legal devices as rolling dice, the general requirement of a "getting together" ceremony after a trial, and the belief that calming the mind and demonstrating inner morality are essential parts of the legal process. These are very different basic assumptions from those of an American law professor.

The chapters in this part are an attempt to map the basic cosmology of Tibetan law. Doing so entails not only setting out the basic concepts and practices but displaying their interrelated constellations, their historical location, their creative use, and then comparing them to concepts and practices with which we have some familiarity. The legal ethnographer tells what she does and does *not* know and presents the material from as many different angles and in as many different forms and voices as possible. The result is not a totalizing, glossy image or an ordered "cultural patterning" but an appreciation for the difference, the contradictions, the discontinuous nature of the space that law occupies in another society.[3]

Chapters 4 and 5 present karma, the cosmos, and time from the Tibetan point of view with case examples of their operation in the legal system. Chapter 6 charts some aspects of the moral universe of the culture and its relation to the legal system,[4] and examines the paradox that the sacred/moral and secular spheres were understood as interpenetrated yet divisible into the silken knot and the golden yoke. Chapter 7 discusses the role of Tibetan myths and stories that carry moral and legal messages. The image of the Buddha, as an immutable standard for human action, creates a particular resonance within this society quite distinct from the bargaining of the Muslim legal world[5] or the "reasonable man" standard of Anglo-American law.[6] Chapter 8 focuses on legal language, the influence of recitation and monastic debate on the law, and magical words.[7] Chapter 9, on power and hierarchy, presents new material for most Tibetologists in the law codes' social ranking system and its effect on positions within the legal system. Chapters 10 and 11 explain four different styles of ritual legal procedure in Tibet and the use of such non-Western legal devices as oracles and ordeals. The jurisprudential concepts that animated legal reasoning are the subject of Chapter 12.[8] Chapters 13 and 14 present Tibetan conceptions of legal space, access, appeals, boundaries, identities, and levels, following a fairly strict grammar of vertical, horizontal, and hierarchical relations. Chapter 15 addresses the differences between Tibetan and Western legal symbols and explains how the integrated symbol of the mandala—a multivalent representation that moves from the inner morality of the individual mind to the cosmic pattern of the universe—defines the Tibetan understanding of law.

CHAPTER FOUR

Reality, Karma, and Nonduality

A man is walking a narrow path in a sun-dappled forest. Before him on the path, amid the leaves and streaks of light, he suddenly sees a very large coiled snake. Shocked and afraid, he noiselessly turns to hide behind a tree and waits, anxiously aware of the great danger. In time, he ventures a look around the tree once more and refocuses his eyes. He focuses again. Then he comes back to the path and stares down at the snake. He sees that it is not a snake but a heavy, coiled rope in front of him. With a wave of relief, he bends down to pick it up and finds that the rope, worn with age, disintegrates in his hands into tiny strands of hemp.

—Tibetan Buddhist Parable

Among the basic Tibetan concepts that affect the law are those of reality and illusion, the role of karma and the nature of rebirth, radical particularity and nonduality. These concepts are interrelated; each builds upon and is structured by the others. For example, the tripartite nature of Buddhist reality is related to the level of "afflictions" of the individual perceiver, and these afflictions are affected by the cyclical path of karma. Similarly, the awareness of the illusory nature of the world leads one to see interrelatedness rather than opposition. The role of these basic ideas in the legal system of Tibet is illustrated in the Case of the Wandering Monk.

The Illusory Nature of Reality

For the Tibetan Buddhist, the parable in this chapter's epigraph demonstrates an essential, core truth of this life: everything we apprehend in the world is mere illusion. Like a delicious meal conjured up by a magician, our present observed reality is entirely an illusory feast; it has no substance. Appearances or "mental obscurations," as Tibetans call them, occur around us because we do not yet have the ability to see their insubstantiality. Because of our ignorance and grasping attitudes, we can see only the illusion.

The parable's images of the snake, the rope, and the hemp represent the three levels of reality available to a sentient being in this world. The first is an illusion that the man took to be real and responded to emotionally and physically. The snake is the level of appearance, the imagined aspect of reality, *kuntak pay* (*kun brtags pa'i*) in Tibetan.[1] The second level, represented by the coiled rope, is the functional or relative aspect of reality, *shengi wang* (*gshan gyi dbang*).[2] Finally, the tiny strands of hemp are the perfected aspect of reality, the essence of the composition of what lay before the man on the path, *yongsu dubpa* (*yongs su grub pa*).[3] To see the snake, therefore, is to see an illusion. A person who cannot see the hemp does not see the world as it truly is in its perfected aspect.

In Buddhist belief, we suffer from attributing significance to the dreamlike appearances resulting from the preconceived notions and categories that we carry with us and constantly use to interpret the world. These categories of data, acquired through our senses, keep us ignorant of the true nature of reality. A Buddha, seeing the world as it actually is, sits down at the magician's table but finds no meal before him, walks down the path but finds no snake before him—only tiny strands of hemp.

This notion of illusion is of profound importance in comprehending the Tibetan view of reality, including legal reality. These realities are states of awareness for individual minds. In essence, what we see and experience daily is only one type of "is," the type of "is" our minds are capable of perceiving. Even though Tibetan judges and petitioners often commented that they could deal with a legal problem only in terms of a this-worldly or apparent reality, at the same time there was a general recognition that this-worldly facts were not ultimate or perfected facts. Disputes were engendered by mental afflictions that hinder one from understanding the perfected aspect of the world. Any dispute was, therefore, comprehensible in an entirely different way by one with a more relative or a perfected vision, one not afflicted by certain mental contaminations.

It was not an uncommon move in a dispute to make reference to another frame of reality in which the same circumstances could be understood differently. The old man's argument, "You may think I am just a common beggar, but how do you know I am not an enlightened saint?" (Chapter 18) immediately shifted his beating of a small child from the this-worldly reality frame of child abuse to the perfected vision of an enlightened being helping a child to burn off bad karma from a previous life. Mitigation of punishment too was commonly argued with otherworldly reasoning.

Tibetans accept the presence of several simultaneously operating levels of reality, each giving clues to the next, each crafted of a degree of deceptive illusion except the last, each coexisting with the other in a non-nirvanic space. If all a person knows of the world, legal or otherwise, is illusion, one must attempt to operate within these limitations as a legal actor with the knowledge that there are other levels of Buddhist reality. As Clifford Geertz puts it: "The movement back and forth between the religious perspective and the common-sense perspective is actually one of the more obvious empirical occurrences on the social scene. . . . [Human beings move] more or less easily, and very frequently, between radically contrasting ways of looking at the world, ways which are not continuous with one another but separated by cultural gaps across which Kierkegaardian leaps must be made in both directions."[4]

In Buddhism, an individual experiences rebirth into this world and begins the volitional production of both good and bad karma, or *lay (las)*, which will determine his or her future rebirth and chances for enlightenment. Avoiding wrong action, seeing the world without mental afflictions, and taking part in religious activities produce good karma in this life. At death the individual goes into an intermediate state and then is reborn into one of six realms. Every human has had countless previous lives and will have innumerable future lives unless enlightenment is achieved. This is the cyclical nature of rebirth, a chain-of-lives connecting past, present, and future.

Thinking about their own and others' past and future lives comes very naturally to Tibetans; examples of this point of view abound in conversations. One Tibetan will tell you that the incarnation of his grandfather, who was a lama and is now a nineteen-year-old boy, is coming to visit him to ask for advice; an elderly Tibetan will say that he is going home to do his mantras so that he will be reborn in America; a third will talk about the future low rebirth of a man who is a known thief.

Tibetan law, both philosophically and cosmologically, is situated in a present that expands into otherworldly realms of the past and the future. Since every act done by anyone at any time is the result of both previous karma and the present possible exercise of will, a crime could have its cause in a previous life, its commission in this life, and its punishment in a future life in a lower or more difficult rebirth. In the refugee community in India, for example, when one Tibetan child made strange noises and threw a picture of the Dalai Lama on the ground, her behavior was taken as an indicator that she had been a dog in her previous life and would be reborn in a hell realm. A parable told by a Tibetan official illustrates the same idea:

> The throneholder of Ganden monastery was from Khams, and he was once asked by a layman, "Holiest one, why are all Westerners so very clever?"
>
> Then the monk said, "Why do you think that they are clever?" And the man replied, "Holiest one, they have so many things!"
>
> So the throneholder of Ganden replied, "Westerners are not clever at all. They are fools because they engage their entire lives in working very hard to make things now for themselves. What they produce is only for this life. What we produce is for the next life, which is much more important."

The impact of these views on the legal system was significant. In any dispute settlement proceeding, a good petitioner or witness was expected to be aware of future lives and their importance. Tibetans told stories of conciliators and judges asking parties about this directly, for such awareness indicated religious and moral depth. Judges were expected to consider the past and future lives of defendants when assigning penalties. Although self-responsibility for acts and choices in this life is an essential aspect of Buddhism, there is also a recognition that karma can dictate present circumstances. Thus, Tibetans would often comment that one did not always know the reasons for particular legal circumstances, because these were rooted in a past life. And if no punishment was forthcoming for a crime in this lifetime, the presumed repercussions of future karma served as a rationalization.

Cycling in and out of lives with not just one but infinite chances for enlightenment reduced the impact of death but increased the possibility of perpetual suffering. A meritorious life now would result in less suffering the next time around; an unmeritorious life now would result in more suffering, possibly even a rebirth in a vividly depicted hell realm. There are many stories of robbers and other criminals who, coming to the realization that they were destined for a future life of torture, converted and became religious mendicants.[5]

Radical Particularity and Nonduality

The Tibetan world view is radically particularistic. This means that it focuses on the small component parts as ultimately real rather than the larger entity, the pieces of hemp rather than the snake. Persons are made up of infinitesimal units which are themselves in constant flux, much like the tiny strands of hemp. At its most essential, everything is in constant movement, changing its composition continuously, never stable, combining and recombining into the various accumulations that we mistake for permanent objects and individuals. Rebirth is the total recombination of millions of these units and karmic seeds. One consequence of this view is that no "self" exists in any deep sense in Buddhist philosophy, no ego or actor, no constant or permanent individuality. Tibetans believe that it is one of our common illusions to see human beings as having permanence, when they are merely combinations of tiny elements. In law, however, these notions of radical particularity rarely surfaced as a part of the legal commentary except perhaps in recitations of religious verse.

Nonduality, one result of radical pluralism in the Buddhist world view, is difficult for Americans to grasp. Nonduality eliminates binary opposition—a cornerstone of Western thought in both everyday and scholarly reasoning. At this most fundamental level two orders of truth (absolute and relative), two types of worlds (supramundane and mundane), two phenomenal levels (nirvana and samsara) do not make sense within the nondualist bounds of Buddhist philosophy. There is no actual duality of subject and object, no independent existence of anything anywhere at any moment. Any duality is an illusion. Terms that present dualistic oppositions are used for explanatory purposes only.

An enlightened being in Buddhism, a Buddha without mental afflictions, is not subject to the duality viewpoint of lower states of consciousness, does not see subject and object, existence and nonexistence. All Buddhas, Bodhisattvas,[6] and deities with this higher consciousness also realize that they are one and the same. Everything is composed of the same small parts, which are constantly realigning, forming new identities and entities. Thus, real wisdom in Tibetan Buddhist philosophy consists of comprehending the radical particularity of all existence, the nonsubstantiality of things, and the ultimate union and interrelatedness of all persons and things.

Lay Tibetans and most Tibetan nuns and monks understand basic conceptions such as radical particularity and nonduality as a sort of story about the constitution and composition of the world. These ideas perfuse Tibetan thought and discourse; they are reiterated in liturgy, incorporated into proverbs, employed as idioms and jokes, used as rationalizations, explanations, and morals. Although apparently contradictory and difficult for the non–Tibetan to comprehend, they form the background for all Tibetan jurisprudential concepts and legal rituals.[7]

The Case of the Wandering Monk

How did notions of reality and illusion, karma and rebirth, radical particularity and nonduality operate in the legal system of Buddhist Tibet? Listen to the following narrative of a case that came before a local headman from the area of Sakya in the 1940s:

There was a headman of a region named Tseten which had a well-known monastery. One of the monks in that monastery, when his teacher died, began to leave the monastery and wander about the countryside. That monk often left during the day, and at night he came back to the monastery to steal food from the private rooms of the other monks. There were many complaints about this monk, and so a case was brought to the headman of the area by the complainants who had been burglarized.

Finally, the monk was caught and whipped and put in a jail cell in the main town of the area. The headman went to offer him food. Then, this first time, the monk returned the stolen articles and had another man pledge as a guarantor that he would not do it again, and he was freed.

But the monk continued to wander, and he returned many times to prison after this for stealing offenses. One time he escaped and went a long way away to Tsong Thopgyal, another time to the city of Gyantse, another time to Penam. He escaped several times when the jailers or guards slept and was recaptured. The first several times he was not chained in any way, and so he escaped easily. Then they put iron fetters on his legs during the night. These are the same fetters that we use on horses in the summer by putting the front and back leg together. No one knew how he escaped with the fetters on, but he did. The punishments of whipping and prison had no effect at all on him.

So the headman from that area had real pity for this monk because he was like an animal. Again, the headman had to make a decision about the wandering monk who had stolen once more, but the decision was hard for him. So the headman asked an old jailer in the prison to speak to the monk. He told him to ask the monk why he stole and how to keep him from stealing in the future. And so the monk told the jailer why he stole. He said that he was used to enjoying all the foods in all the monasteries and families that he visited, but after a little while they kicked him out. Then he didn't know how to get more food, and so he stole. After this investigation into the reasons why the monk stole, the headman asked others to see if what he said was true. People said what he said was true, and the wandering monk had never killed or stabbed anyone.

When the headman was told these reasons, he made up a new program for the wandering monk. He decided to send him home and told his father to take his son back and give him food and work to do. But his family came to see the headman and said that they didn't want the monk because it would create a bad name for their household. And so the headman had to think again, for this was a very big problem.

Finally, the headman went to see the monk. He told him that if he kept stealing, no one

Plate 12. A convict in city of Gyantse wearing iron fetters. Note that they are attached by two strings to his waist for support. 1920–21. (Pitt Rivers Museum, University of Oxford)

would like him or even want to see him. He said that he was creating very bad karma, and this karma would cause a bad rebirth. Then the headman told the monk that he was to stay in the headman's house from now on. Since he had a big family, there was enough food, and the monk was to have food, clothes, and a salary. The headman said that he hoped the monk would do this and remain good; if he didn't, both the headman and the monk were in serious trouble because many people were very upset.

And so the wandering monk came to live with the headman. He changed greatly then, and all the people were very surprised. Because he was a healthy monk and good at working, he was put in charge of all the cattle, yaks, and goats of the family. The monk stayed with the family and never stole again. In time, the wandering monk became so trusted in the area that during the irrigation supply time when water was distributed, he was asked to be the one to decide which farmer should receive the water first.

At the core of this legal case are the underlying notions of karma, radical particularity, and illusion. All the Tibetan participants considered the previous life of this monk and reasoned that he was acting like an animal because he perhaps *was* an animal in a previous life. The story even hints that the monk was in some way a different sort of being, since he could get out of leg fetters, escape prison, and remain unaffected by whipping. His current self was not a constant; he was obviously afflicted with several mental obscurations that caused his actions. The headman reasoned that the monk was not motivated to commit crimes; instead, raised in a communal environment, he had a view of the world which did not privatize food.

The headman did not deal with this case from a dualistic perspective of right or wrong, guilt or innocence, correct or incorrect rule application. Instead, with a keen awareness of the monk's nature and future life, he moved beyond determination of guilt to investigate the unique causes and circumstances of the case, reveal the illusory nature of the crime, and fashion a unique solution. Such a result is particularist and does not produce a general rule. In the words of one Tibetan commentator, it was as if the headman could look past the snakelike illusion of the crime to the ropelike, relative reality of the monk's nature.

CHAPTER FIVE

The Cosmos, Time, and the Nature of Conflict

The simultaneous, successive coming to this world of these Dalai Lamas . . . indicates that, owing to the ocean of compassion emanating from all the preceding and the All-Knowing, Victorious Fourth Dalai Lama to the Great Fifth Dalai Lama, whose compassionate deeds and white banner of fame rise high atop the three worlds, there has been an unbroken bridge of Dalai Lamas.

—Ganden Podrang Code of the Dalai Lamas

Each of the various realms of the Buddhist cosmos has its own time sequence, and yet they all simultaneously coexist in the present. The impact of these notions about the cosmos and time on the Tibetans' legal system and their view of conflict is reflected in the story of the monk Sonam's investigation of a land dispute (told in the Introduction).

The Everpresentness of Realms

At the center of the Tibetan Buddhist cosmos is the holy mountain, Mount Sumeru, surrounded by a succession of concentric mountain ranges and bodies of water. Above the mountain is the upper realm of the gods, divided into various cloud levels depending on the state of perfection. Many of the gods have the ability to see different aspects of reality and may live for several eons in this realm of "the world above."

Along the slopes of Mount Sumeru and on the earth below is "the middle world," comprising three realms: the realm of the demigods or *asura*, who are "not human, not gods"; the earth in which humans live, although—unlike the gods in their world—they rarely exist in this realm for more than ninety years; and, coexistent with the human world but at a lower level of spiritual existence, the animal realm, which is filled with sentient beings who are suffering from fear, poor food, and service to humans because they scorned the dharma (Buddhist doctrine and practice) in their last lives. These three realms of the middle world are filled with sentient beings most of whom can see only the illusory reality, the imagined appearance.

In "the world below" are two more realms. The first, the realm of hungry ghosts, is for those who were avaricious and envious in their previous lives. It is filled with beings who have long bodies, large heads, and enormous stomachs but tiny mouths; thus they constantly search for food and water but can never be satisfied. The second is the realm of hells, feared by all Tibetans, which contains the occasional, the cold, and the hot hells. Occasional hells are places of intermittent torture and rest. The eight cold hells are covered with ice, lashed by freezing winds and sleet, and plunged in complete darkness. Reborn into huge bodies with no protection from the cold, the miserable beings who inhabit the cold hells suffer sores, frozen joints, cracked skin, and self-disembowelment through lesions. People who during their life on earth believed in the wrong views and had cold, controlling personalities are reborn into this bleak, tormented realm. The hot hells, said to be located in the earth hundreds of miles below the place where the Buddha achieved enlightenment, are also eight in number and more Dantean, with physical punishment relating directly to the acts committed in the previous life.

The cycles of rebirth take place, from the Tibetan point of view, in a cosmos constructed from these six realms of existence,[1] often divided into the three (upper, middle, and lower) worlds, or *sipa sum* (*srid pa gsum*). None of these realms is part of the absolute other, nirvana; it is totally separate from the cosmos of heaven, earth, and hell. The six realms of existence in the non-nirvanic worlds of the Tibetan Buddhist cosmological universe all coexist simultaneously.

Every layperson in Tibet understood the Tibetan cosmos in part through a composite image called the "Wheel of Life," which was a popular wall mural and cloth painting throughout the Plateau. At the center of the Wheel of Life are three animals depicting the root afflictions of lust, craving, and ignorance. Next, the six realms of the universe—those of the gods, *asura,* humans, animals, hungry ghosts, and the creatures reborn into the hells—are depicted in their three respective worlds: the heavens above the sacred mountain, the earth, and the hells below the earth. Circling these images is a pictographic representation of the twelve steps of a human's life, from birth to death to the intermediate state of *bardo* or *barmado* (*bar ma do*) and then rebirth. (The term "three worlds" can also be used to denote the continuous cycling through birth, death, and *bardo* which typifies this samsaric, transmigratory existence.)

A visitor to the Plateau will see the mandala of the Wheel of Life painted on monastery walls, in chapels, in palaces, and in the altar rooms of private homes. Each representation is slightly different, but all convey the message that there is a direct link between a person's past life, the actions taken in this world, and the kind of heavenly rest, earthly existence, or hell to come in the next life. Itinerant mendicants and monks tour Tibet today with their Wheel of Life paintings as they have for centuries, expounding to any available passerby the meaning of the pictures and the karmic results of good or bad actions in this life.

Figure 4. Tibetan Wheel of Life.

Time within the Tibetan cosmos is understood as a range of different sequences, few of which have the pounding, progressional linearity of modern Western conceptions of time. Coexisting simultaneously within the Tibetan cosmology of law were notions of time in the cosmic realms, linear time, spiral-cyclical time, and non-time or static time. While each realm has, in a sense, its own time sequence, all the realms in the Tibetan cosmos are ever present: that is, they coexist simultaneously. Thus a Tibetan who is praying to a god in one of the heavens recognizes that the god currently exists in a separate, harmonious nether-world, has a lifetime of much greater length than a human's, and has a different perception of time.

Even linear time has a different quality in Tibet; it does not construct daily living into rigid units, and it is not punctuated by death in the same way as in the West, because each "individual" returns to the samsaric realms on a recurring basis. The process of rebirth is viewed by Tibetans as one that has been, is, and will be unending; it is the continuous spiral cycle of karmic seeds moving in and out of various human and other rebirths in the different realms. Barring an escape into the timeless emptiness of nirvana, all sentient entities remain on a cyclical wheel of rebirth, starting anew with each life.

Buddhist cosmology is ambivalent about the extent to which time requires motion and energy and demands measurement. The cosmic realms are both an arena of absolute nonmovement and nonchange and yet also an arena—given the core teaching of impermanence—of constant change. Nothing in them abides or remains. Thus time, because it is always both changing and unchanging, also has the quality of a static-state universal motion.[2] The empty timelessness of nirvana is a final cognition of time which must be both juxtaposed to and included in the Tibetan legal cosmology.

Tibetans' notions of time had a profound impact on their legal system. The verbatim case reports in Part Three reveal little discussion of when something happened, or whether it happened before or after other events. The time question so common in court dialogue in the United States—"and when did you notice that, Mr. Smith?"—was not a component of Tibetan interrogatory technique. The flow of a particular dispute was directly influenced by Tibetan notions of time: although procedural rules established a routine ordering of events, there was wide latitude with respect to completion dates; plaintiffs were not accosted for not having fulfilled requirements in a timely fashion; causation in the law did not require temporal proximity; the historical description of a case could include a larger range of facts uncoupled from their time markers; there were no statutes of limitation or arbitrary temporal markers to increase court efficiency; and a hiatus could occur in the process of a case for religious and other events.[3]

The Tibetans' understanding of legal time raises interesting questions about the construction and use of time in American legal culture. Their legal cosmology deemphasized rigid linear time as an important factor because so many different cognitions of time were incorporated into the legal cosmology. Given the simultaneous existence of many other realms and realities, each with its own time dimension, time in Tibet had a diffuse, multivariant, and ambiguous quality. In short,

Tibetan lawsuits emphasized "what" and "how" rather than "when." Although a multitude of time constructions undoubtedly exist in American culture as well, they are either held to a common legal standard or defined as "standard business practice" or the like.

The Nature of Conflict

The Tibetans' concept of time led perforce to certain complexities in their views of causation and, hence, of the nature of conflict. The introductory narrative of Sonam reveals some of these complexities.

> Still, as he stood there in the brilliant sun, he thought to himself that there had been too many disputes in this area in the last year. Was this a sign that merited watching? Before the birth of a great being into an area, there would often be a long period of drought, ruined crops, and disharmony. But there was no important lama who had dissolved his body recently and would be taking rebirth; the last visitor from Lhasa had told them that His Holiness the Dalai Lama was in good health. Undoubtedly, the local protector gods disliked the proliferation of angry words and thoughts in this village, but would their displeasure take the form of sickness in children? Would the women stop bearing? Or was something else at work? He was determined to ask the senior monk about this and to schedule some rituals of appeasement for the local protectors.

Cosmological balance, which was essential to maintain the well-being of the population and the harvest, was disturbed by conflict among humans, but conflict among humans could also be the result of past karmic occurrences or disequilibrium in the cosmos. Furthermore, as Sonam noted, all of this could be happening *at the same time*. Thus he asked questions from several different angles simultaneously. Did the increase in disputes in the area merit watching? Could they be the *result* of some great cosmological occurrence such as the rebirth of a great being into the area? Could they be the *cause* of angering the gods? Could this angering of the gods then be *resulting* in more disputes, sickness, barrenness? How could the cycle be stopped and the balance reharmonized?

To begin, conflict was definitely related to incorrect vision, to afflictions in the perceptual abilities of human sentient beings. In Buddhist philosophy there are six root afflictions and twenty related secondary afflictions that cause an individual to see the world in an illusory way and therefore to engage in conflict. The six root afflictions are desire, anger, pride, ignorance, doubt, and incorrect view; among the twenty secondary afflictions are belligerence, resentment, spite, jealousy, and deceit—all commonly attributed to the actions of litigants. Thus, a Tibetan who engaged in a legal case was presumptively acting both unmeritoriously and with mental afflictions. Likewise, engaging in conflict had a social cost, for it indicated a lack of religiosity and a projection of personal ego antithetical to Buddhist values. As a result, Tibetans were initially reluctant to talk about lawsuits, implying that their values inhibited them from describing circumstances of conflict. Plaintiffs and representatives preferred to speak of rectifying an error without anger.

As the cases in Part Three demonstrate, litigants often analyzed their involvement in a lawsuit, both before and after the fact, in terms of the religious—particularly karmic—consequences of conflict. As a monk who was involved in one lengthy dispute put it, "I thought to myself, 'from start to finish, we are accumulating sin and nonvirtuous actions [in this lawsuit], and if we die now, we are dying through hatred and anger.' So then I learned the nonvirtuous actions of fighting" (Chapter 22). Conflict in this life could be caused by bad karma from a previous life, or it could be the result of a volitional act to engage in conflict in this life, and it undoubtedly had karmic consequences in this and future lives.

Within the larger question of its relation to society and the cosmos, conflict was viewed as an inherent quality in all societies in samsaric existence—unavoidable until all humans reach nirvana. The range of consequences to society from acts of violence and conflict was potentially great, and Tibetans took every measure available to rectify the disharmony, from a secular legal proceeding to appeasement of the gods. The goal of a legal proceeding was to calm the minds and relieve the anger of the disputants and then—through catharsis, expiation, restitution, and appeasement—to rebalance the natural order (Chapters 23 and 25 describe this process at length). The jurisprudential concept of consensus and the ritual procedure of conciliation in Tibet were also thought to dispel anger and impede conflict.

The final question—whether or not the conceptualization of conflict as negative actually inhibited litigation—remains open.[4] Tibetans certainly did litigate. What is important is that their cosmology of law served to frame the issues in a manner that devalued the pursuit of open conflict.

CHAPTER SIX

Inner Morality and the Buddha

In Tibet it is said:
"If the wool is put outside, it will blow away;
if a stone is put on it, it will stay."
By this we mean, if you make your mind strong and stable,
you can accomplish great things.
—Quote from a Tibetan

Mind is one of the most important concepts in Tibetan legal reasoning, and there are many Tibetan sayings on the subject. Each conflict in Tibet was ultimately analyzed for its source in a particular mental affliction and its effect on the minds of the parties.

Inner morality and its outward manifestations were the core of both religion and law. In law, the individual who was governed by "self-law" or "self-regulation" was a person who was morally self-regulating, a person who followed the moral requirements of Buddhism in both the religious and secular spheres of his or her life. The Buddha stood as an immutable standard of reference, and canon law—codified in the Vinaya—provided a backdrop for all dispute settlement. Most frequently cited by Tibetans as the moral foundation of the secular legal system were two lists: the Ten Nonvirtuous Acts and the Sixteen Moral Principles of the First King.

Mind and Inner Morality

If there can be a core to a legal system, a center around which it operates, that core in Tibetan law was unquestionably the individual mind, *sem (sems)*.[1] In Tibetan Buddhism the mind, like a wild elephant racing through the jungle, must be tamed through ethical actions, meditation, understanding, and habitual calm, clear thought. The liberated mind achieves enlightenment; the afflicted mind creates conflict. It is the mind, not material possessions or relations with others, that brings happiness; it is the state of the mind that determines whether a being burns in hell or reaches nirvana. It is the mind that sees the snake, the rope, or the hemp, depending on its level of perfected vision. Only the mind can comprehend radical particularity, nonsubstantiality, and nonduality. The mind is the core of every sentient being, and every mind is capable of becoming enlightened, of becoming a Buddha-mind.

In Buddhism, one has the choice to act in a moral or immoral, positive or negative way. Individual morality is consequential: it can change the direction of one's present life and future karma. One is responsible for one's fate, and that fate will be determined largely by one's choices in moral dilemmas, general merit accumulation, and virtue. Choices therefore produce karma.

It is the mind that chooses and determines the karmic result of an individual's act. There are four karmic aspects to the accomplishment of an act in Buddhism. In the act of killing an insect, for example, the *object* is the insect; the *motivation* is to kill the insect; the *act* is slapping the insect; and the *completion* is the death of the insect. If any of these four are lacking, the act is not accomplished, but negative karma will still attach particularly to the second aspect: the intention or motivation to kill. The stronger the mental force of motivation, the heavier the negative karma. The karmic effect of actions, therefore, is determined largely by the character of the mind.

Mind, thought, intention, will, motivation—all these ideas are encapsulated in the word *sem,* which was simultaneously the source, the purpose, and the goal of the legal system. In most circumstances the source of conflicts and disputes was thought to lie in the mental afflictions of various actors. A primary purpose of trial procedure was to uncover mental states if possible, and punishment was understood in terms of its effect upon the mind of the defendant. In a profound way, Tibetans saw no possible resolution to a conflict without calming the mind to the point at which the individuals involved could sincerely agree to conclude the strife. Ultimately, unless each individual's conscience, or mind, eliminated its anger, no cessation of difficulty was feasible. Thus, the goal of the legal system was to calm the mind.

A mind or mental conscience that exercised moral self-regulation, *rongtim (rang khrims)*, was also the key to a peaceful, law-abiding society. *Rongtim* was defined in the law codes as "an examination of oneself according to one's attributes and abilities."[2] An individual with such a mind felt shame in wrong action, comprehended the weight of his or her actions, took responsibility for them, and agreed to compromises and correct action. In short, such an individual had inner morality based on proper motivation and a good character.

To act with bad intentions or a selfish motive was particularly significant in Tibetan law. Consequently, a party to a dispute who was seen as acting without good cause was questioned both in and out of court about her or his motivation: was the harm done knowingly or unknowingly? For example, a man had put up a fence to block traffic through a roadway into a common courtyard. His neighbors pointed out, both to one another and to him, that the courtyard and road were owned and used by everyone and that he should stop barring the way. Tibetans described his actions as "done with a bad intention" and "selfish." Similarly, as the dispute continued and was transformed into a legal case, this line of reasoning through attribution of bad intentions was used by both the conciliator and judge.

Other references to negative motivation in the law codes include "acting only for one's own benefit," "without respect," "without fault in mind," "without the ability to discriminate," "unintentionally," "with attachment," "with an intentionally bad mind."[3] The imputation of motivation was a very important rhetorical move in a legal case.[4]

In an attempt to externalize motivation, the law codes were rather specific in defining a person with inner morality. For example, "What type of person is necessary for one who takes an oath? A person who knows the purpose of both present and future lives, is stable in character, is honest, is considered to have measured judgment, is male, and is very polite."[5]

Good character, however, did not outweigh bad motivation. For example, if a man of good character dug a hole on his own land, it was the fault of the trespasser or guest if she or he fell into the hole. But if the same man dug the hole with the intention of causing people to fall in, then a resultant injury was his fault, and he could be sued and punished. Tibetans could shift the fault easily in such a situation, but proving the man's motivation was considered a more difficult matter. Their limited access to the actor's mental state created a profound tension in the Tibetan legal system (and perhaps in all legal systems): although the individual mind was unquestionably its core and moral self-regulation its standard, this core was often hidden and could be comprehended only through external manifestations such as actions.

The Buddha and the Vinaya

The ideal standard of moral self-regulation was anything but amorphous in non-pluralist, traditional Tibet. Stories, parables, and jataka tales (accounts of the Buddha's former lives) offered countless social examples of how the virtuous and the nonvirtuous actor operated in the daily world and provided Tibetans with a concrete understanding of proper action. Each Tibetan knew that the moral Buddhist cared more for the welfare of others than for his or her own welfare, gave to others rather than amassing a fortune, rigorously tried to prevent harm to others, never engaged in any of the nonvirtuous acts, had complete devotion to the Buddha and his path, worked to eliminate anger and desire for material goods, accepted problems with patience and endurance, and remained an enthusiastic perseverer in the quest for truth and enlightenment. As there was no confusion about this ideal, there was little ambiguity about how the moral actor would deal with a particular daily situation. Even though the average Tibetan may not have been any more likely to follow the moral path than a person in any other society, his or her understanding of that ideal path remained strong. Moreover, that understanding prevailed in reasoning about legal cases, even over reasoning connected with community standards.

These understandings of right action and of the ideal actor, for Tibetans today as in the first half of the twentieth century, are immutable and eternal. There is one path as revealed by the Buddha, one true moral universe, one core set of normative values. Stable and ideal, these moral rules are understood by Tibetans as unchanging, not subject to improvement or reevaluation. They may require interpretation but not revision. The Buddha outlined the planned program through which an individual consciousness may opt out of this-worldly suffering, and that plan is immutable. The individual can decide to follow it or not.

Plate 13. Image of the Buddha in the temple in the Dalai Lama's compound, Dharamsala, India. 1984.

The Buddha is credited in Tibetan tradition with having conceived and dictated orally the entire Vinaya, *duwa ('dul ba),* the book of canon law, to regulate followers of the religious life. As early as the third century B.C., monks living in established Buddhist communities in India were operating according to a Buddhist Sanscrit text called the *Pratimoksa*—part of the Vinaya—which outlined some 258 rules. These rules, still recited monthly in every established Buddhist religious community in the world, are extremely detailed and strictly enforced with elaborate ritual proceedings and strong sanctions.

The correct translation of the Tibetan term *duwa* is "discipline" or "taming." Inner morality was thought by the Buddha to be the product of practicing virtue, of disciplining one's thoughts and actions, of reading and memorizing religious texts and performing accordingly. Talal Asad suggests that these are difficult concepts for the modern Westerner to understand because our notion of religion, which has shifted since the Enlightenment, includes ideas of agency, improvisation, continual physical and moral improvement, teleological narratives, and self-creation. Religious practice has come to mean, for modern Westerners, repetitive acts in which they symbolically represent and communicate an image of virtue.[6] This is not how

Plate 14. Monk reading the Vinaya, canon law text, in Sera Monastery near Lhasa. In front of him are a tall tea churn and a tea thermos. 1986.

Tibetans understand the discipline of inner morality. Their "taming" is closer to the ritual practices of medieval Christian monasticism with its emphasis on developing a full moral self through strict discipline, intelligent practice of virtue, and calming of the mind.

The Vinaya, with its elaborations of the important factors in decision-making, the credibility of evidence, the faults of bad intentions, the appropriate circumstances under which to bring up a legal case, the correct speaking style of an accuser, and comprehensively delineated offenses with corresponding penalties, stood as the backdrop for the entire secular legal system. Even though secular actors operated from secular law codes and viewed themselves as distinct from religious actors, Tibet was a culture perfused with a religious mentality, and the moral standards of the Buddha and the Vinaya reverberated through every part of the legal system.

One important consequence of the influence of the immutable Buddha standard and the Vinaya on the Tibetan legal system was that the concept of reasonableness—

sometimes regarded elsewhere as a legal universal—was not considered particularly relevant, necessary, or appropriate. In the American legal tradition the notion of the "reasonable person" is the standard for determining liability for negligence, and "reasonableness" is judged in terms of a general understanding of action performed with reason: the moderate, suitable, rational act done with ordinary prudence. At law, for example, the question becomes "Would a reasonable person leave ice on the sidewalk and foresee harm to a passerby?" The court and the individuals are not expected to know or to ask the moral question "What would a correctly acting moral human have done under the same circumstances?"

There were three other repercussions from the religion's influence on secular law. First, legal decisions, according to Tibetans, were not calculated within a framework of balancing moral equivalences or bargaining from different Buddhist normative paradigms.[7] Second, Tibetan judges and individual petitioners *were* inclined to ask what a correctly acting moral human would have done under the circumstances; the standard was not the reasonable man but the moral man exercising moral self-regulation or *rongtim*. Third, as the choice to follow a moral path was entirely one's own, coercion was viewed as ineffective. Parties had to agree to work out their difficulties and to end conflict; otherwise a true solution could never be reached.

Nonvirtuous Acts and Moral Principles

The teachings embodied in the Ten Nonvirtuous Acts, *mége bacu* (*mi dge ba bcu*), were cited by Tibetans—either in story form or by listed elements—more frequently than any other Buddhist principles as the foundation of their secular legal system. The law codes too cite them as the source for all the laws of Tibet: "The Buddha preached the Ten Nonvirtuous Acts and their antidotes, the Ten Virtuous Acts. By relying on these, the ancient kings made the secular laws from the Ten Virtuous Acts."[8]

The Ten Nonvirtuous Acts are divided into three categories: (1) three acts of the body—killing, stealing, and sexual misconduct; (2) four acts of speech—lying, abuse, gossip, and slander; and (3) three acts of the mind—craving, ill-will, and wrong views. In religion, abstaining from the Ten Nonvirtuous Acts was a moral practice that allowed an individual the chance of a future human rebirth. It also laid the foundation for realizing ignorance and personal delusions, for meditation, and for the development of *bodhichitta*, or the wish to attain enlightenment for the welfare of all sentient beings. In Tibet, a good Buddhist was a good legal actor and vice versa.

Was there any distinction, then, between the moral universe and the legal universe? Or were they entirely one and the same? Tibetans had a very pragmatic response to this sort of question. All Tibetans agreed that the Ten Nonvirtuous Acts had negative karmic consequences. When asked if the same ten acts could be penalized in a legal forum, however, most responded that only killing, stealing, sexual misconduct (if disputed) and lying (if provable), could be punished by the secular courts—a view that correlates directly with sections of the later law codes. Moral (karmic) and legal consequences were two separate areas of consideration.

Tibetans explained that because they were limited in their access to the actor's mental state during a mental act or speech act, they could not judge it as legal or illegal. Therefore, these acts did not have legal consequences unless they resulted in physical acts or harm. The gods alone would know if a person had incorrect attitudes or speech. Even the law codes indicate that the official legal system was neither appropriate nor useful for judging "hidden" moral violations such as "Speech and Mind offenses, Lying, Covetousness, Evil Attitudes, and so forth; for these hidden sins, oaths with the deity protectors as witnesses were devised."9

This distinction is particularly interesting because the emphasis on speech in the Ten Nonvirtuous Acts demonstrates the importance of the spoken word in moral action for the Tibetan Buddhist. Reversing the famous English proverb "Sticks and stones may break my bones, but words will never hurt me," Tibetans expressed the sentiment that cruel words were truly hurtful—more so than minor beatings, even of children. Yet regardless of their importance, speech offenses were "hidden sins" unless they could be materially represented in court.

Tibetan officials also carved a clean line between religious views and secular legal views with respect to the practical outcome of a case. Disputes and crimes had to be handled and sanctioned in this world, without reliance on or presumption of karmic causes or effects in other worlds, which were unknowable.

Observance of community norms among the refugees in India—toleration of deviance, conflict avoidance, patience, nonconfrontationalism, family responsibility, and parental obligation—was often the source of praise; likewise, nonobservance brought derision. The phrasing of normative proscriptions resonated throughout legal and nonlegal Tibetan conversation: "He doesn't take care of his father"; "One should respect one's parents and repay their kindness." Tibetans attributed this language to two sources: Buddhist teachings, and the Sixteen Moral Principles, which were thought to encode all the major community and cultural norms. Though each Tibetan gave her or his own version of these principles, rarely arriving at the full sixteen and never providing a list entirely consistent with any other list, most used the phrasing identified with the ancient versions of these rules in the eighth-century law codes of the Tibetan Empire. For example, according to Benpa Topgyal, the Sixteen Moral Principles are these:

1. To worship with devotion, using the three jewels (the Buddha, the dharma teachings, and the sangha—community—of monks) as one's guide.
2. To practice the teachings of Buddhism for both this and the next life.
3. To repay the kindness of one's parents.
4. To honor and respect the learned, holding them above oneself.
5. To serve and revere the high and the elderly.
6. To shun novelty in friendship by maintaining sustained relationships with others.
7. To help the poor and one's neighbors as much as possible.
8. To be rational in analyzing the words of others and not be influenced by gossip.
9. To model one's behavior on that of a good person.
10. To avoid extremes and to exercise limits in one's life-style.

11. To repay kindness and generosity from others.
12. To avoid adulteration and false weights and measures in business deals.
13. To be fair in dealing with others and avoid envy of another's wealth.
14. To shun the company of bad friends and unreliable persons.
15. To be soft-spoken and polite in speaking with others.
16. To undertake spiritual and political ventures with strength.[10]

Unlike the Ten Nonvirtuous Acts, the Sixteen Moral Principles were never referred to in court hearings or dispute settlements as a set of legal rules; rather, they were cited individually for particular circumstances. For example, a Tibetan might use a phrase from these principles to take a normative stance in defending herself: "I fulfill my promises and pledges" or "in obedience to my parents' wishes" to explain why she married; "I do not want to interfere in the affairs of others" to avoid taking action. These ancient normative phrases are thus interchangeably employed as rationalizations, as sources of authority for one's actions, as ways of defining one's actions in a legal sphere, and as means of aligning oneself with the moral authority of the ancient kings.

CHAPTER SEVEN

Myth and Narrative

A long time ago there were two butchers, Karotse and Marotse, who lived in the same town. One day Marotse was trying to kill a sheep while Karotse was intent on killing a pig. Suddenly, the pig began screaming in fear while the sheep began bleating. Marotse put mud in the eyes of the sheep and finished killing it, but Karotse drew back at the sound of the pig and had no courage to kill it. So the pig ran away into the forest, and finding no pig food to eat, it ate some grass, which gave it the ability to fly. When one of the hunters in the forest saw the flying pig, he captured it and went to see the king of the region with the pig under his arm. The pig was presented to the king in his palace, who then asked the pig how it was that he could fly. The pig responded, "I am a pig. I have no education and so when I was hungry, I ate some grass and it made me fly." With this the king realized that this special pig had been set free by the butcher Karotse, and he called Karotse to him, who told the whole story. Upon hearing it, the king gave a very large present to Karotse and then he let the pig go. Years later upon their deaths, Karotse went to heaven and became a god, but Marotse went to hell. The Buddha has said, "If you are sinful, you will face the consequences of your acts. If you are good, you will also receive the consequences." This is the first law of Buddhism: *Do not kill*. These are not manmade laws but were here in the time before man came to this world.

—Thubten Sangye's Law Stories Notebook

Myth and law have a reciprocal relationship. Myths form the basis for law; they legitimate the authority of the legal system and its basic moral tenets such as "Do not kill." Myths teach how one should proceed in law, what to expect, and who can act in what way. Myths also contruct the place of the law in the world, explain the origin of law, and tell how aspects of the legal cosmology fit together. But law, in its turn, also forms myth. Law continuously shapes the mythic world as it represents and legitimates its acts, organizes and rearranges identities and possessions, and elevates individual legal stories into the status of mythic narratives.[1]

Every society and group has its own myths, often more or less closely allied with a religious system of belief. As collective representations of the elemental truths of a particular group, myths communicate the core ideas of the group to itself. They redefine the group and reconnect it to the world around them. As defined by

William Doty, myths are "culturally important . . . stories, conveying by means of metaphoric and symbolic diction, graphic imagery and emotional conviction . . . the foundational accounts of aspects of the real, experienced world and humankind's roles and relative statuses within it."[2] Within a cosmology of law, legal myths integrate the past with the present and the future, theorize about and explain the course of events, and act as templates or archetypes as well as coding mechanisms or practical guides for the conduct of everyday life.[3]

Every society also defines what "myths" mean to it, although the definition may or may not include its actual myths. For example, in the United States we understand myths chiefly as stories that the Greeks and Romans told about their origins and about their divinities, those superhuman actors who battled among themselves, engaged in amorous adventures, and dallied occasionally with humans. We also understand myths as fanciful origin tales told by "primitive peoples." Stories such as George Washington not lying when asked if he cut down a cherry tree are "history" (whether accurate or not), according to our formulations, rather than myth. This is because in our culture there is a persistent effort to insulate the mechanics of society, most particularly law, from ideas of myth; indeed myth is, in the legal context, a pejorative term. At the same time, however, our collective representation of the legal system is strongly mythic: we regard law as a form of rational science, a neutral procedural system independent of religion and the supernatural, agreed to by mutual consent, and codified in a document called the Constitution. Yet the legitimation of this mythic narrative depends on our seeing the process of the creation of law as real: that is, historical, factual, and true rather than mythic, which would imply that it was unreal and not scientific or rational.[4]

If pressed, many Tibetans will likewise claim that the life of the Buddha and the divine origin of the Dalai Lamas are "real," historical, factual, and true. A strong dichotomy between religion and politics, between mythic thought and rational thought, is not primary to their understanding of the world, however. Tibetans have a large assortment of forms of recounting: royal accounts, genealogies of kings or incarnations, tales of the origins of religious schools, biographies of saints, stories of those who have returned from the dead, legends of ancient times, explanations, expositions, archetypal illustrations, and others.[5] All these recountings have mythic dimensions in the sense that they are, as Doty says, culturally important stories, foundational accounts. Whether enacted in operatic performances, recited in monastic liturgy, or written as part of a religious text, myths in Tibet established origins, provided lineages, and encoded social behavior. Thus a legal concept could be understood through a myth of origin, a magical tale about a flying pig, a religious story in the life of the Buddha, a revelation of the culprit through the trance of an oracle or through the detailed rendering of the procedural steps of a particular court case. Although each of these was used in different settings and had different moral valence, they were all equally about legal truth.

The academic study of narratives has expanded in the past several decades to include issues of performance, meaning, emplotment, context, characteristic elements, and the role of the narrator and audience. A resurgence of the narrative style in history has been chronicled by Lawrence Stone, who cites the movement of the Annales school and the shifting style of such European historians as Le Roy Ladurie and Ginzberg. The key features of a historical narrative are that it is descriptive rather than analytical; its central focus is a person, not circumstances or a collectivity; and it has a theme, point, or argument.[6] Within the world of American legal academics, "legal narrative" has come to mean both a particular style of writing (usually, the telling of a personal story of subordination or exclusion)[7] and the analysis of story construction in and out of the courtroom.[8]

Narratives in the context of this book are stories—both those told in and about law and some that are not apparently about law at all—which encode social concepts, meanings, and structures in the legal cosmology. They may be dominant legal narratives—that is, significant stories that are told and retold through time—or they may be simple and particular. Narratives are often a strategy in the law, a way of presenting a contested paradigm that represents one party's point of view.[9] As such, they frame issues, name particular persons and acts, and locate the parties in moral fields. How these narratives are shaped, changed, and resolved is an important part of the understanding of legal stories.[10]

Tibetan myths offered here include the mythic origin and location of the components of the government of the Dalai Lamas according to the cardinal points of a mandala; a Tibetan culture hero myth, with instructions for decoding the legal information it contains; and traditional moral stories from the older law codes. Finally, the more recent tale of a corrupt governor shows how the narrative style of rendering a legal case packages both social and moral content.

Origin Myths

In Tibet the reciprocal relationship between myth and law was complicated by the country's extensive history and the introduction of Buddhism. For example, among the wide-ranging Tibetan myths of origin are accounts of the birth of the world from a cosmic egg or from the body parts of an underground waterworld female, and the origin of the Tibetan people from the sexual union of a monkey and a female demon. The myth of the first marriage has a goddess, the first to marry a man, playing dice with her brother over their inheritance and receiving her share of one-third.[11] Sacred origin and continous lineage were very important in Tibet, as they provided the legitimation for most of the secular dynasties and later Buddhist sects. In one version of the dynastic origin myth, the first king, a son of the Lord of Heaven, came down by a sky rope to become the ruler of the Tibetans.

Several former Tibetan officials recounted the origin of the offices of government under the Dalai Lamas in a myth that may be historically accurate, mapping directly as it does the actual locations of the offices in Lhasa until 1959. This rendering credits not the Fifth but the Seventh Dalai Lama, whose reign began in 1751, with interpreting the duality of the religious and secular spheres as a mandala, the sacred aspect providing the core for the necessarily temporal aspects of government administration that surround it. The government here is understood as a mandala with four sections arranged at the cardinal points around a central image of the Buddha—a religious cosmogram representing God, the universe, the state, and the individual all at the same time. A statement from one older Tibetan official is typical of the

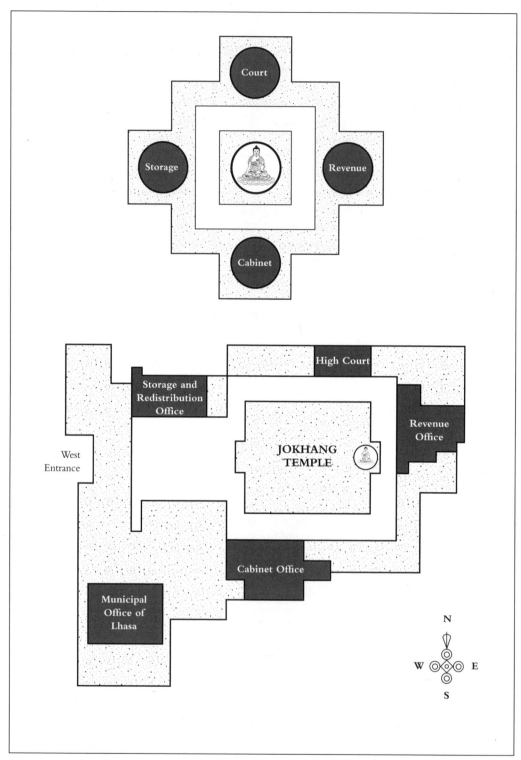

Figure 5. Schematic floor plans of the Cathedral Complex. Top: mandalic layout of the offices according to the origin myth of the government. Bottom: actual layout of the offices around the Jokhang Temple in 1950.

versions given. "The Seventh Dalai Lama rearranged the government as a four-part system," he began, drawing a perfect square and putting another square in the center as part of his explanation.

> Four offices are the foundation of the government, and they are the Court, the Revenue Office, the Storage Office, and the Cabinet. All of these sit at the cardinal points along the sides of the square around the central figure of the Buddha.
>
> On the south is the Cabinet, the "father of the house," which handles all of the home and outside affairs. On the east is the place of taking in goods, the Revenue Office, where all the taxes are recorded and collected. This office replaces the ancient office, called Babshi, that took in the government goods before it. Across from the Revenue Office is the office of supplies and redistribution, the Storage Office, which sits on the western wall. On the north side is the Law Court, the place of investigation and decision for all the conflicts in Tibet.
>
> This is how the government was arranged in four parts by the Seventh Dalai Lama.

As the official then pointed out, this symbolic understanding of the mythic origins of the bureaucracy—a central religious core with four major secular functions at the cardinal points around it—was mirrored in the physical layout of the central administration offices of the Tibetan government in Lhasa before 1959 (see Figure 5). As in the mandalic form described, the ancient temple called the *jokhang* (*jo khang*) is at the center of the Cathedral Complex and houses the Jowo Shakyamuni, the most sacred image of the Buddha in Tibet.[12] Said to have been brought to Lhasa by the Chinese wife of the first historical king, Songtsen Gampo, in the second quarter of the seventh century, this representation is the final destination point for all pilgrimages to the holy city. The Jokhang was ringed by an open-air walkway, the innermost circle of the ancient city. Together, the temple and the walkway surrounding it formed the religious center of the country for all Tibetan Buddhists, regardless of sect. It was, therefore, the perfect unifying core for the national government.

Around this temple and its walkway is a second building, like a square doughnut, said to have been constructed to house the ritual implements, jewels, and other accouterments of the statue in the central temple. Either before or during the reign of the Seventh Dalai Lama, the government offices took their respective places at the cardinal points within this outer administration building.[13] In the southern side were the two main rooms of the Cabinet, "the father of the house," plus an archival room, a waiting room, a kitchen, a toilet, a room for the secretaries, a treasury room, and storage for stationery and files. In the eastern side of the building was the large room of the Revenue Office,[14] or the "taking-in-goods" office, staffed by accountants and officers in training. The western side contained the main rooms of the Storage Office,[15] which recorded and stored all the supplies for the government. Finally, the northern side of this outer building housed the anterooms, storage rooms, and main area of the High Court,[16] where cases of conflict were investigated and decided.[17]

The original theory of Tibetan government encoded in the myth tells us that all government is based on the four functions of (1) administering, (2) collecting revenue, (3) storing and redistributing revenue, and (4) deciding cases according to the

Plate 15. The most famous image of the Buddha in Tibet, the Jowo, in the Jokhang
Temple in Lhasa. This central image of the Buddha was the sacred core around which the
offices of the former Tibetan administration were arranged at the cardinal points. 1986.

law. These four offices of secular authority remained the most prestigious in the secular wing of the government of Tibet throughout the rest of its history. When new offices were added, they were typically placed according to their relation to the original functions assigned to the cardinal points. It is not surprising, therefore, that the City Court of Lhasa resided in a structure along the outer north side—the law direction—of the administration building. Similarly, the Municipal Office of Lhasa, housing administrative caretakers for the city, was situated on the south side of the building, behind the Cabinet.[18]

Culture Hero Myths: Milarapa

Tibetans have several different forms of culture hero myths—such as the story of Gesar of Ling, the warrior king from eastern Tibet—and hagiographies of famous saints. Undoubtedly the most famous example of mythic hagiography—one Tibetans know almost by heart—is that of Milarapa, the ascetic, cotton-clad saint who is said to have lived in Tibet in the eleventh century (see Figure 6). We enter the story in his youth when Milarapa's father was dying:

When I was about seven years old, my father Mila, Banner of Wisdom, grew very ill, and the doctors and magicians believed that he would not get better. Our relatives and friends all knew that he would not live, and so my uncle and aunt and all our relatives, friends from near and far, gathered at our house. He was to appoint a person to take charge of the family and property, and finally, to secure the patrimony of his son, he dictated a written will which he read out loud for all to hear.

In this document it says: "This illness will not go away and therefore, because my son is now small, I entrust his care to his uncle and aunt, relatives and friends. In the higher grounds there are my cattle, horses, and sheep; in the valleys, several of my rich fields of which "Three Corners" is the best, so immense that you cannot see its limits; in the first-floor stables of the house, cows, goats, and asses; in the attic of the house, utensils, gold, silver, copper, iron, turquoise, and silk; in the storehouses, grain, etc. In short, my possessions are such that I have no need to envy the wealth of others. From the best of all of these, expenses for the arrangements after my death can be taken, and as to the rest, to all of you assembled here I entrust everything until such time as my own son can assume his role as a householder. In particular, I entrust his care to his uncle and aunt. When he is of age, Zessay, to whom he has been betrothed, should be welcomed as his wife. Let them both receive all my wealth without remainder. Make sure my son takes possession of his inheritance, and during this time the welfare of these three [wife, daughter, and son] should be watched by all relatives, particularly his aunt and uncle. Do not lead them into misery, for from the dead I will watch you."

Having said this, he died. After this, my father's funeral rites were done, and all the people there agreed on the remainder of the wealth, saying, "White Jewel of Nyangtsa (my mother), save these provisions yourself! Now everyone authorized by this agreement should receive according to their share and do what is good." But my aunt and uncle said, "Whoever is close is dependable, being relatives. We will not create problems for the mother and children but take care of the wealth according to the will."

Not listening to the speeches of my mother's brothers and the Zessay relatives, my uncle took all of the men's goods and my aunt all of the women's. All of the rest was divided in the middle.

Figure 6. Milarapa.

Then they said to us, "You, mother and children, will work to support us in turns." So the three of us did not have the control of the wealth.[19]

After being treated like a servant for many years, Milarapa reached majority, and at a party for the occasion his mother read the will in front of all the neighbors and demanded the return of his patrimony and status. Again, the assembled relatives and neighbors refused to protect the wronged widow and children against the aunt and uncle, who argued persuasively that the mother and children never had any wealth to begin with. Thus, Milarapa was sent on the path of revenge by his mother. But he later repented his black magic deeds and ultimately became a famous Buddhist ascetic known for composing 1,001 religious songs.

When asked about the legal aspects of this story, Tibetans, even former government officials, stated emphatically that there were none. It was understood as the true life history of a religious saint which instructed individuals on the path to enlightenment. But this culture hero myth does tell us several things about Tibetan law. For one thing, Milarapa's story describes the legal practice of nuncupative willmaking: that is, of creating a will at the deathbed of the testator to be enforced by the local relatives and the community. Forms of testamentary succession closely resembling Western succession—oral wills, testament *causa mortis*, testamentary gifts, holographic wills, wills creating a trust for a minor, and several other forms of testate inheritance—were common among landholding families in Tibet. Questions of inheritance were decided at a large meeting of the relatives, which provided a forum for discussions of family separation or household division as well.

The story also warns of the evil effects of not abiding by the terms of nuncupative wills: Milarapa, after learning black magic, destroys the family house and all the fields of the community. But notice that the government does not enter into this story. The mother is viewed as a subsidiary party to the transaction; the community and relatives are understood as the enforcing mechanism; and the government is not involved, either because it is just too distant or weak or because the issue is not deemed an appropriate one for official consideration.

Finally, this is a story about what is truly important in life. The mother's attachment to material possessions leads to the ruin of her life, the family house, and her son. By the end of the story, however, the entire family has returned to Buddhist values through the journey of the son, who calms his mind and becomes enlightened. Ultimately, then, it is not wealth or law that will redeem an individual or create harmony in a community; it is the practice of Buddhist values and the realization of the illusory nature of this world.

Legal Myths and Narratives

Legal myths and narratives encoded Buddhist values as well as providing instruction in correct ritual procedure and legal reasoning. Some of the older law codes contained stories—like the tale of the flying pig in this chapter's epigraph—to illustrate each of the Ten Nonvirtuous Acts. These remind the hearer of ancient

Indian origins and of the jataka tales, the mythic stories of the previous rebirths of the Buddha. Here are two examples that teach the evils of lying and slander.

The Story of the Lying Shepherd: Once upon a time there was a king named Charche who lived in India and had two servants, named Tamze Zumme and Zumbuche, which meant respectively, "the Brahmin who never lies" and "the liar." The first was very high caste, and the second was very low caste. The king sent both of them off to tend a thousand buffalo, and the lead buffalo was called Cucho Tagri because it had skin like a tiger. Cucho Tagri always got the best grass to eat and drank water first; he walked in front of the thousand buffalo in the morning and was the last one to come in at night. When other buffalo were eating, Cucho Tagri went up on the hill to look for predators. One day, Tamze Zumme and Zumbuche decided to kill Cucho Tagri and eat him because his meat would be very tasty. After this, Zumbuche said to Tamze Zumme, "We must tell the king that the leader fell down on his own." But Tamze Zumme said, "I have never told a lie so far, and this time I will not be able to either." The low-caste man said, "This time you must tell a lie or we will be killed." So the two agreed to lie, but when the high-caste man was practicing the lie, he found that he could not do it. Then the king met Tamze Zumme, and he said, "Do you have all the buffalo with you, even Tagri?" and he responded, "No, we killed him and ate him." The king lamented saying, "Ayi." Then he asked the other shepherd, who lied to him about Tagri, and the king had his tongue cut out. A god appeared, and he said, "You must abstain from telling lies and always tell the truth." When the liar died, he was reborn in hell, but Tamze Zumme was born in heaven. This is the fourth law: *Abandon lying and tell the truth*.[20]

The Story of the Close Friends: In a village named Magada in Bihar there was a king named Subchen Nyingbo and a head of the village named Baroyogun. They were both very rich and very friendly with each other. Also in the town was another man named Tamachen Timyik who went to the king and said, "Baro says that he is a better person than you and he is richer as well! He also says that he is better than you because he has more servants!" Then Tama went to see Baro and said to him, "The king said that you are under him, like a servant. He said that if you don't listen to him, he can kill you and have all your wealth taken away." Then the king and Baro started fighting with each other because of this man's words. At that time, a man named Tamze Tambala wanted to solve the problem of the fight and talked between the two men, bringing peace by showing them that it was a third person who had created the problem. Both the king and Baro apologized, saying that they were very sorry. Afterward the king had Tamachen Timyik's tongue cut out, and Tamze Tambala was rewarded one hundred gold coins by each of the two men. A god appeared and said, "Those who bring disharmony between friends will have their tongues cut out and be born in hell. Tamze Tambala was rewarded for the reconciliation!" From then on, it became the seventh law: *Abandon slander and reconcile hostile sides*.[21]

Like the mythic tales that embody legal principles, legal narratives—stories about a person and his or her circumstances, illustrating central themes—encode practices, roles, and truths about the legal system. A former Tibetan official recounted this case of a famous teacher of his who became a corrupt official and was punished:

There once was a man called Tuthobla who was an excellent teacher of Tibetan and had many students in Lhasa. He taught me Tibetan when I was a child. After many years, his influence became very strong, and he had many links with the aristocrats of Lhasa.

He was then given a post in the government and sent to western Tibet as acting governor

Plate 16. A monk from Drepung Monastery near Lhasa being punished for the offense of counterfeiting currency. He is required to wear a wooden cangue or collar called a *go* bearing a notice of his offense. In his lap are turnips that have been given to him as an offering. 1920–21. (Pitt Rivers Museum, University of Oxford)

in Ruthog in the very far west. While he was there, he was a very vicious governor, and he cheated the people of Nagari very badly by charging excessive taxes and other fines. Also, he conducted a lot of business and made a lot of money in this way.

The miscarriages of justice under Tuthobla reached the ears of the Dalai Lama through an "open appeal." On one of the Dalai Lama's trips to the Cathedral Complex a person shouted out to him about this case from the crowd, and he heard it. Then the Dalai Lama requested that the man who had shouted be brought to him and explain his case. After hearing the explanation of the man, who was a representative from this area of Ruthog, he ordered an investigation, and officers were sent to that area. From these officers it was found that Tuthobla had cheated the people of that area, and he was brought back to Lhasa.

For his punishment he was put in the prison in Zhol, underneath the palace of the Dalai Lama, and whipped. Day and night he had to wear a heavy wooden collar around his neck. During the day he was sent out of the prison and made to stand in different spots around this part of the city as a display. Separate from the Cathedral Complex, the Zhol part of Lhasa has its own jurisidiction system and different places where it displays its prisoners with the collars. His collar was three feet square and of heavy wood. When I saw him wearing it, he was standing at the foot of the palace near the Doring pillar, south of the Zhol wall. It was common for criminals who had to wear a wooden collar to stand in this place.

While wearing the collar, Tuthobla was able to stand up, which many others could not because of the weight. Sometimes the prisoners even had a stick to hold the collar up because it was so heavy. The description of his crime was printed on a paper and posted somewhere on the wall. Sometimes these descriptions were put right on the collar itself. People stood around and watched him, but most children didn't know what was going on. Sometimes people came up to taunt him or talk to him. One time Tuthobla told one of the aristocrats watching him: "It is not your knowledge or your intelligence that makes you aristocrats special; it is only your luck." Then the aristocrat cursed back at him.

The whole time he stood there, one soldier was watching him to make sure that he stood alone in one place. At night he went back to the Zhol prison. He was kept standing like this in front of the public for only seven days. During some of these seven days, his former students came to see him and brought a mattress for him to sit on and a table to place in front of him. He had been their teacher and they still revered him. I do not know what further punishment he received, for I did not hear about his case after this.

In this example, there are many themes that are central to Tibetan legal cosmology. First, prestige is accorded a literate and lettered person who is here given a special post and later, even when humiliated, is treated deferentially. The immorality of greed is emphasized: Tuthobla, although learned, suffered from the root affliction of craving. Another important theme is the openness, benevolence, and wisdom of the Dalai Lama as head of state; his bureaucracy responds effectively and efficiently to rectify its own mistakes. Imprisonment and public shaming are considered effective forms of punishment and social control. And last, the Buddhist public displays its compassion for the suffering of a criminal. As in this story of Tuthobla, each Tibetan myth and narrative constructs the place of the law in the social world, explaining, legitimizing, organizing, and realigning identities, possessions, and moral norms.

Excursus: More Mythic Stories

Chapter 7 told the law code stories illustrating the first, fourth, and seventh of the Ten Nonvirtuous Acts: killing, lying, and slander. Here are the other seven.

Two: The Story of the Laughing Thief

Once upon a time there was a thief named Gao, and one night he and many of his friends went into a house to burglarize it. Gao's friends quickly put all the gold, silver, and other valuables into bags and then they ran away. Gao went instead into the back altar room of the house, where he saw the splendid statues and offerings of gold and silver. Looking at the magnificent altar room, Gao thought to himself, "These people are very religious and I should not steal their belongings!" He began to laugh out loud when he thought of his friends stealing from people who were so religious, and this awakened everyone in the house. The entire family got up and saw Gao, but he was not caught as a thief because he had nothing in his hands. Instead, the family ran after his friends, who tried to blame him instead. Later, Gao was walking and a tree spoke to him, saying, "You didn't steal when you had the chance, so now I will make you rich! Dig here!" Gao dug near the tree and found so many gold coins that he became a very rich man. When Gao died, he went to heaven. But his friends who had been caught were once again very poor, and they went to hell at their death. One god has said, "See this. Gao did not want to steal, so he became rich and went to heaven, while his friends who took wealth from others became poor and went to hell. Stop stealing and make use of what you have in this life." This is the second law: *Do not steal: Abandon taking what is not yours and distribute gifts to others.* (LS:3–4)

Three: The Story of the Reluctant Whore

Once upon a time, there were two prostitutes, Gachin and Sewayo. Sewayo said to Gachin, "This is shameful, dirty, and sinful work, and one never gets any satisfaction from it." She regretted what she had done as a prostitute, and so she went to the Lord Buddha and took a vow to become a nun. When she died, she was reborn as the daughter of a goddess, and her name was Rinchen Yo.

But Gachin loved sex and thoroughly enjoyed her work. She used to make love all day and all night, and she even gave money to men sometimes to have sex with her. She thought, "Truly, the best life is to make love all the time." When she died, Gachin was reborn in the world of the Hungry Ghosts. Then the good prostitute was reborn as a boy, the son of a goddess. She looked down from the heavens at all the different rebirths and said, "This happened because I followed the steps of the Buddha. Therefore, one should lead a good life, take vows and do something good." After this, it became a law: *Do not engage in sexual misconduct, and accept vows of purity.* (LS:4–5)

Five: The Story of the Abusive Father

Once upon a time there was a king who ruled all the people. Two of them were Father Black Pile, who always used harsh words when he spoke, and the Brahmin called Softhearted Lotus, who was renowned for speaking to everyone politely. One day, Softhearted Lotus, upon hearing Black Pile speaking angrily, commented that his rough words would never heal, the way even a gunshot would. Black Pile replied, "Rough words are a sign of strength and power, and rough words stop people from gossiping. If I don't use them, I will be defeated." The people in the area did not like Black Pile, and one day they stole all his wealth and gave it to Softhearted Lotus. Then a goddess appeared and said to the people, "To use rough words is very bad. Father Black Pile lost his wealth because he was so abusive, and Softhearted Lotus won all his wealth because he never abused anyone." So this became the fifth law: *Abandon harsh words and speak with tender words.* (LS:6–7)

Six: The Story of the Two Blacksmiths

Once upon a time in Sergya in India, in the state of Bihar, there was a town in which there were two blacksmiths. One whose name was Mogyermawa always talked about other people, and the other, whose name was Barotsepasingee always talked facts and never gossiped behind people's backs. Now the king in this area had a monk with him called Gelung Nyima Yo, and one day the monk had to go to a blacksmith. The man he went to see, Mogyermawa, gossiped a lot with the monk. When Baro heard this, he came and said to the monk, "Please go back to your room in the castle. As a monk, you should not hear this gossip." One of the monk's daily activities was to perform a prayer ritual for the king, and because he had listened so long to the gossip, he was late and missed the ritual. The king was very angry because this monk had always been on time. When the good man Baro was called to the king, he told him that it was not the monk's fault. The king rewarded Baro and, calling for Mogyermawa, had his tongue cut out. Then, a goddess named Tangsonkatadom appeared and said, "Gossipers are mad people. Whoever gossips should be ready for the consequences. Baro never gossips." So gossiping was prohibited by law: *Do not gossip: Abandon foolish talk and speak sensibly.* (LS:7)

Eight: The Tale of the Miser

In a place called Sita in southern India there was a family head named Wo Tse, who was very rich. Wo Tse was a miser whose goal was to accumulate more money from other people. He was especially greedy for altar items, religious paintings and statues. Another man named Litsache, who was not desirous of wealth, went to Wo Tse and said, "You have enough wealth, so why do you still seek wealth for rituals or gods? I don't like that. If you continue, you will never have a prosperous time in this life and you will be reborn as a very poor man. Rich people do not need to go after others, whereas the poor may need to. You should be satisfied." The rich man said, "Poor people do not have wealth, so they are not greedy. If you don't have anything, you don't want much. Since I have wealth, I want to pile on more and more. There is not one person who is rich who will say he has enough. I even want God's wealth!" At that moment many people came into his house and took all his money away, causing him to have a heart attack and die. In the next life he was born as a Hungry Ghost. But the people in the area liked the goodness and personality of Litsache, and so they helped him and gave him many things. Then a god arrived and announced, "This Litsache was not after wealth but he became very rich. If you are greedy, you will die early of a heart attack." And so this became the eighth law: *Abandon covetousness and subdue desire.* (LS:8–9)

Nine: The Story of the Bully

In a place called Sinkala there was a porter named Dawa Sampo who was very strong. He was known for bullying, beating, and robbing people. There was a king named Sersung who was very kind to everyone and well trusted by the people. When Dawa Sampo died, he was taken down to hell, and Sersung went to heaven the day he died. A god appeared after this, and he said, "If you try to think evil of others, this is not good. Thus, this porter went to hell, while the king went to heaven." From that day forward, this became a law: *Abandon a destructive mind and act with a loving mind.* (LS:9–10)

Ten: The Story of the Disbeliever

There once was a Hindu teacher named Yotsum Gyokche who said, "There is no life after death nor is there sin. I do not believe in God nor do I believe in fate." He lived with these ideas for his whole life. At that time also there was a Buddhist monk called Sengye, who was a true believer in God, sin, fate, and life after death. He said to Yotsum, "We should all believe in these things." Then Yotsum died and was reborn in hell, but when the monk died, he was reborn in heaven. The god named Dorje Nyimbo then appeared and said to all, "The person who does not believe will die and be reborn in hell. I feel sorry for disbelievers. Sengye the monk was reborn in heaven in his next life." From that day forward, there was the law: *Abandon wrong views and take on the correct views.* (LS:10)

CHAPTER EIGHT

Language, Debate, and Magic

The Three Necessities:

1. Your speech should be more sweet than the bell.
2. It is necessary to do more than just blow out air.
3. In responding to the other party, whatever comes from your mouth should be as sharp as a thorn.

With the help of these three, judges should discuss among themselves the ways of the speech of the debate.

—Neudong Law Code

How did Tibetans talk about "law" and what space did it occupy in their language? What do their semantic categories tell us about the distinction between religious and secular law and what part did magical speech play? Many of the traditional words, phrases, and proverbs that Tibetans used in their legal proceedings derived from the ancient law codes, but the highly ceremonialized dance of monastic debate also profoundly influenced language and phrasing in the law.

A legal system's patterns of speech involve what Charles Frake calls "codes for talking, a linguistic code."[1] Americans tend to understand legal language as rarefied and separate, the exclusive and excluding linguistic code of professional actors who have studied it specifically. In Tibet, legal language was not professionalized; the language of the law codes was both read aloud to the public every year (as described in Chapter 17) and studied by a variety of laypersons (who acted occasionally as legal representatives) as well as by officials. Whether or not the language of proverbs, codes, conciliation proceedings, and courts constituted a "legal discourse" within related socially constituted institutions and practices[2] or a mode of power that legitimated inequality in Tibetan society[3] remains an open question. Although it is true that a noble from Lhasa could speak in a more educated and elegant dialect than a nomad from the western region, a monk from a small monastery in the west who had studied debate and ancient texts could probably factor a law case and use legal phrases better than the Lhasa noble.

For the Tibetan layperson before 1959 there were no clear divisions between religion and the state; indeed, there were inviolable connections, as both were based on the teachings of the Buddha. Tibetans saw religion, politics, administration, and law as an interpenetrated whole from which it was difficult to separate out "secular law" as a particular category in the Western sense. But although it was only loosely denoted by the term *gyatim* (*rgyal khrims*), "law of the kings" or "state law," the ambiguity of the general category did not prohibit an understanding of the particular. Individual Tibetans could always discuss the probable outcome of a case, describe the correct attitude of a judge, or supply the legal proverb that applied to a specific situation.

The general word for law in Tibetan, *tim* (*khrims*), is generally understood to mean "moral rules." Compounds create general categories: in addition to state law, *gyatim*, there is local law, *yultim* (*yul khrims*); religious law, *chutim* (*chos khrims*); commandments of law, *katim* (*bka' khrims*); moral law and monastic rules, *tsultim* (*tshul khrims*); and self-law or self-regulation, *rongtim*. Of these compounds, the law of the kings or state, local law, and commandments of law come closest to a Western notion of secular law. Many Tibetans described state laws as those rules and regulations pertaining to goverment that were based on Buddha's teachings and established at the time of the ancient kings, often echoing the wording of the law codes cited in Chapter 6: "By relying on these [Ten Virtuous Acts], the ancient kings made the secular laws."[4]

Compound words formed with *tim* first are used only to refer to the official government legal system. In Tibetan the term for court, *timkhang* (*khrims khang*) or *timsa* (*khrims sa*), refers exclusively to a governmental court or a hearing before a government official. A Tibetan who has never been to an official government court will say she has never seen "a court," even if she has attended hundreds of local dispute settlement proceedings. In the law codes as well as in colloquial Tibetan, the terms for court are tightly connected to the terms for the government bureaucracy, reflecting a sharp division between internal, private legal rituals and official, administrative procedures (Chapter 10).

Similarly, the words that mean judge, *timpon* (*khrims dpon*) and *timdak* (*khrims bdag*), apply only to a government official or representative appointed to a judgeship or one settling a dispute in the government manner.[5] These terms are not used for a person performing judgelike activities, such as a local headman asked to settle a dispute. Other particularized vocabulary designated the activities of judges in court. Thus, though secular law in Tibet was intimately associated with and understood by the layperson in the context of its religious underpinnings, it was referred to in specific terms and had a distinct operating vocabulary of its own for use in the governmental sphere.

Tibetans' ready phrases and proverbs about law cases relied on a core of repeated words uniquely their own. As one former legal representative commented:

> A person with a good knowledge of law will use many legal phrases, *timdem* (*khrims gtam*), and this will give him a great advantage. Even if the opponent has the truth on his side, without legal phrases he will be at a disadvantage.

For example, there was a case in which one man had lent another man some money, and the borrower had not repaid. This lender asked many times for the money. Then he filed a case in court, saying: "When the words of the document are not stable, when the record is not adhered to, what is left of our contract?"

The lender used this language in court to accuse the borrower's guarantor of not returning the money.

Some Tibetans considered legal proverbs different from legal phrases because they gave specific advice. For example, in a case of alleged theft by Sonam of the possessions of Dorje, the judge asked Dorje for proof. When Sonam was called into court, he did not agree to what Dorje had said, and until he did agree, Dorje's accusations were considered untruthful. Dorje's friends out of court and the judge in court both used the same legal proverb when speaking to Dorje. "Don't allow your things to be stolen; don't investigate for stolen articles. What happens when you call a man a thief? The thief will be empty-handed."

Some phrases or proverbs are poetry in seven metered lines; some are in colloquial language or in songs used as political commentary; others are traditional sayings.[6] All are legal epigrams that were used both in and out of court to accuse the other side, to argue for mitigation, to protest dishonesty, to demonstrate the burden of the risk, to comment on an injury, to promote truth-telling, to describe the character of a party, and generally to present the Tibetan point of view in a legal situation. In dispute settlement, these ritual legal phrasings reflected ancient norms, called on particular Tibetan meaning structures and contexts in the cosmology of law, and indicated both education in and respect for the legal process on the part of the speaker.

Many of the legal phrases and proverbs contained in the law codes of the fifteenth and seventeenth centuries were still being used by Tibetans on the Plateau in legal cases in the 1940s and 1950s. The language of the law codes (quoted at length in Chapter 2 and throughout this work), with its lyrical and archaic quality, carried legitimacy from both the authority of the ancient kings and the religious sovereignty of the Dalai Lamas. But law codes were not "interpreted" in the sense in which American lawyers use the term for rule formation or application to specific cases. Most of them were not meant to be exclusive instruments: they did not supersede all earlier laws; they did not have accompanying commentaries or sets of illustrative cases; and their language was often precatory and prudential rather than commanding and hortatory.

The law codes were instead treasurehouses of reliable suggestions, resources for advice on decision-making, and compendiums of traditional ideas. Their wealth of information about ways of doing things and points of view—ranked social hierarchies, marriage and divorce patterns, barter equivalencies, proverbs and sayings—give a new picture of Tibetan society for Tibetologists, anthropologists, and historians alike. The general population's absorption of ideas from the codes appears to have been extensive; most of the law cases collected for this work include concepts and language from these codes, which until 1959 could be found on the desks of district law courts, in the High Court of Tibet, in estate houses, and even in the tents of nomads.[7]

Plate 17. Monks in Sera Monastery outside of Lhasa. 1920. (Pitt Rivers Museum, University of Oxford)

Recitation, Debate, and Magic

The importance of ritual legal phrasing is related to the role of the memorization and recitation of religious texts in Tibetan Buddhism. Tibetan religious texts are commonly written in an outline form after a beginning sentence or paragraph of homage to a Buddha or Bodhisattva and to previous scholars. Often, the outline is presented first "in general" and then elaborated "in particular," with numbered sections divided into numerous subsections and sub-subsections. Respected teachers are expected to be able to recite thousands of pages of text and complete books of religious commentary. Bestowing karmic merit on both the repeater and the hearer, such recitations constituted the daily instruction in monasteries. They were an essential part of temple ceremonies for the layman and one of the decisive elements in the ranking of monks for the *geshe* degree.

All legal rituals in Tibet also took place against the background of formal monastic debate, *tsopa* (*rtsod pa*), a highly structured public dialogue between two religious practitioners. The format for debate in Tibetan Buddhism is an argument not before a third party (except during final examinations, when the debaters have an audience) but between two individuals. The first monk or nun stands and makes a verbal challenge, emphasizing each point with a thrusting, clapping gesture. The second monk or nun sits almost motionless and responds in turn to each verbal sortie. In

Plate 18. Monks in Sera Monastery relaxing after their afternoon debate session. 1986.

Tibetan refugee communities today, this ritual bilevel dance takes place daily between pairs of monks and nuns on the grounds of their religious institutions, and they follow the same daily debate schedule they had in Tibet. Each part of the exercise, each hand and foot movement by the challenger, has a symbolic meaning related to the life of the Buddha or aspects of Buddhism.

The point of monastic debate is to acquire the correct view and to persuade another, through reasoning by syllogisms and consequences, to abandon an ignorant viewpoint. It is also to memorize, internalize, and repeat orally the Buddhist doctrine as a technique for disciplining one's thoughts and actions in order to develop inner morality. A basic premise of debate is that the mind of each individual must come to its own understanding.

The vigorous questioning and response of judges and petitioners, analysis by factoring, outlining the arguments, truth by consonance, the uniqueness of a case—each of these aspects of the Tibetan legal system reflected monastic recitation and debate. Tibetans often spoke of debate training as the most important factor in their choice of a monk as a legal representative, conciliator, or judge, for debate sharpens mental skills, requires a quick wit, and trains one in logical analysis. In the monastery or the court, it ultimately led to, reflected and reinforced religious values and training. The purpose in both arenas was the same: enlightenment and truth through correct reasoning. Until the mind of the participant was satisfied, neither the case nor the debate could come to rest.[8]

The effectiveness of recitation and debate to discover truth was thought to be matched by the effectiveness of equally ritualistic magical words. In fact, secular legal rituals were commonly regarded throughout Tibet as adjuncts to magical practices (see Chapter 16).

The Tibetan language is filled with magical words and speech: mantras that have power, charms to invoke or coerce demons, spells to propitiate a god, sorcerers' formulas for producing hail or earthquakes.[9] Magical speech pervades both the Tantric and non-Tantric aspects of Tibetan Buddhism. As a rite performed by a specialized actor, it involves the recitation of ritual formulas, particularly archaic verbal formulas. It has power because it creates binding social relations and influences "uncontrollable agencies."[10]

Magic interacted with the Tibetan legal system in several ways—some of which were not entirely unlike Western practice. For example, the recitation of certain legal formulas, both orally and in writing, were understood as speech acts much as they are in Anglo-American law.[11] This is very much magical speech in that the recitation of a ritualized formula creates binding social relations and invokes multiple layers of religious, social, and personal sanctions, in both America and Tibet.

Furthermore, the magical rituals of oracles and oathtakers were formally employed in Tibetan lawsuits to find evidence and culprits and to prove the veracity of both parties and witnesses. Indeed, an entire section of the law code of the Dalai Lamas outlines the proper ritual performances and wording to be used by those taking a magical oath for official use (see Chapter 11).

On the other hand, powerful Tantric practitioners capable of performing astonishing magical feats were not allowed to be witnesses, parties, or oathtakers at trial. They were described metaphorically in the law codes as "poisonous black snakes" who lacked competency to testify because they had the power to project any illusion or undo any oath (see Chapter 14).

Sometimes secular law was understood as a possible procedure for counteracting negative magical acts such as sorcery; Chapter 11 recounts the case of a man's complaint that a woman has cast a spell on him. In other instances, the magical words of mediums, Tantric priests, and sorcerers permitted the Tibetan layperson to circumvent the legal system and achieve reprisal or restitution more directly—as in the following story told by a learned monk:

> In my time, there was a nun named Tating Wangmo journeying with other mendicants to northern Tibet to collect offerings, and as she was traveling through the Namru area, she met fifteen robbers all on horses. They were afraid to rob Sakya monks and nuns, but they stopped and argued for food and presents. The robbers asked for excessive amounts of food, and so the nun became afraid that they would all starve on their journey.
>
> With the nun there was an ascetic Tantric monk called Lama Yeshe Penba, who saw that she was worried and came to her saying, "Give all the food to them." Then he went to the side of the tent, put a robe over his head, and started to chant and meditate deeply. The nun offered the rest of the food to the robbers, who took it all and started to walk away from the tent. They climbed up on their saddles, and as their horses began to move, the robbers became fixed to their saddles and the horses stood completely still like statues. They were frozen like this for several days.
>
> After three days the nun asked the Tantric monk to stop because she was afraid that the

robbers would die. So he allowed the lowest-level robbers to go away. Then, one by one, he allowed them all to go. Later, the robbers came to their encampment, returned everything they had taken, and fully confessed to the lama. These monks are very useful because they have many mantras that can accomplish different things. That Tantric monk was from my area, and this happened when I was a very small monk, less than sixty years ago.

CHAPTER NINE

Power and Hierarchy

The ten powers of the Buddha are the ten kinds of knowledge possessed by the Buddha:

1. The power to know correctly what is real and what is not real.
2. The power to know the relationship between action and its retribution [consequences].
3. The power to know correctly the depth and progression of contemplative meditation.
4. The power to know correctly the depth of man's mental capacity and his potentiality.
5. The power to know correctly the limit of man's intellectual capacity.
6. The power to know correctly man's ability, personality, and action.
7. The power to know correctly which actions land one in which existence.
8. The power to recall past events correctly.
9. The power to know through divine eyes the time of one's death and the good and evil existences in the future.
10. The power to know that, when one's emotions are overcome [one's own afflications are destroyed], a future existence will not take place and to know that others will overcome their emotions [afflictions].

—Herbert V. Guenther and Leslie S. Kawamura, *Mind in Buddhist Philosophy*

Within both a society and its legal system, power is reflected in notions of reality and illusion, through myth and narrative, through boundaries, identities, and levels—indeed, through all the elements of the cosmology of law. In even the smallest of groups it is a complex matter requiring investigation and positioning in historical context. For example, Tibetans have at least six different words for power (some of which can be used interchangeably), depending upon whether one is talking about the power of rule, dominion, and authorized governance over subjects, *na (mnga')*;[1] inherent, efficacious powers such as magical power, *tu (mthu)*;[2] the power of physical, moral, and mental strength such as that of the Buddha, *tob (stobs)*;[3] power as a capability in intelligence or use of the sense organs, *wang (dbang)*; or power as ability and force, *nupa (nus pa)*; or power as strength and energy as in the power of love or faith, *shug* (*shugs*). Thus, Tibetans understand power both as a highly centralized, rigidly controlled, and hierarchically determined force and as a diffuse and multi-valent force. Michel Foucault's conceptualization of power as pervasive in social life—dispersed, productive, and formed through the knowledge of its techniques, strategies, discourses, and targets—is useful in discussing Tibet.[4]

The study of power within a legal cosmology—its qualities, movement, dispersion, exercise, loss, disciplines, and institutionalization—requires the examination of at least three different aspects. The first is the way in which power is understood within the society or group. What are the different meanings of the term? Which of these correlate with notions of hierarchy? Are the primary meanings physical, ideological, mystical, economic?[5] Does power flow from person to person? What is religious power and how is it different from other kinds?[6] What kind of knowledge shapes it? What reality shifts and karmic rationalizations avoid, enhance, relocate power?

The second is the operation of power within the social structure. How do different types categorize people? What forms and variations do they take? What kinds of power can be used in which settings, by whom, when? How does it structure and move through social institutions? What power do social institutions have?[7]

The third aspect of power has to do with its effects and movement in the legal (and illegal) segments of the society. Which types of power operate in which spheres? Why? Who can get into which forum? When and how? What do the naming, claiming, and blaming aspects of a dispute tell us about the movements of power through the system?[8] What kinds of sanctions are employed? How and why? What do legal symbols encode and how do they represent power? In what ways are sections of the society and individuals excluded, controlled, and dominated through the cosmology of law?[9]

Central to Tibetans' understanding of power are their pervasive and unique notions of hierarchy, which they encoded in their language and even their concepts of the body.[10] Hierarchies also defined the operation of power within the social system. For Tibetans, social power and most of the economic power belonged first to the old noble families and the monasteries (Chapters 19 and 20 illustrate the balancing of power between these two groups); next, to a wide variety of networks of relatives, guilds, persons with wealth or connections; and finally, to those from a particular religious sect or region. Cultural factors determined social rank, which in turn directly determined the relative power of an individual in the political and legal systems—that is, his or her access to legal forums, both informal and official. Legal power as discussed here is the power to lodge or to avoid a grievance. (Other agential aspects—persistence, oral and written verbal ability, investigatory skill, knowledge of the law codes and legal procedures, astuteness in negotiating legal channels—are illustrated in Parts Three and Four.) The forum in which one could wield that power varied with Tibetan notions of appropriate jurisdiction.

Hierarchy

The Tibetan world view has a pronounced concept of hierarchy, of levels and zones moving from the inferior to the superior and from the secular to the sacred.

These levels are primarily understood as the graduated steps of a mandala telescoped out into three dimensions.

Higher and lower levels appear in multifarious guises throughout the Tibetan cosmological and social world. The Buddhist cosmological universe consists of levels, from the heavens above Mount Sumeru—themselves graduated according to the degree of their inhabitants' spiritual development—to the spheres of the lesser gods, humans, and animals at its feet and various hells below it. Cyclical rebirth takes place on this cosmological stage as persons who collect good karmic seeds move up into better positions in the human and god realms and leave behind those who collect bad seeds.

Similarly, the human body comprises differentiated hierarchical zones, from the most pure and essential (the crown of the head) to the most filthy (the feet).[11] A Tibetan might be upset if the soles of your feet are turned toward her, or if she is touched by your foot. Tibetans might also tell you not to pat the heads of their children, an essentially sacred zone.

The use of honorifics in the Tibetan language is another example of hierarchical levels. Three or, on certain occasions, four levels of speech are used in direct address, depending upon the rank of the speaker, the hearer, and the subject matter. A person must choose the correct vocabulary and form of address in any given conversation. When speaking to a superior, one refers to oneself at the lowest appropriate level while at the same time exalting the other person. Language mirrors the levels of the social hierarchy, rigidly outlined in the law codes, which assigns a very specific rank to each individual in the society.

Social stratification also meant obedience to authority—parental, religious, political, and legal. Officials were viewed as having been born into their excellent situations as a result of karma, and this reinforced the legitimacy of their positions. Religious charismatic figures received unquestioned devotion from many Tibetans, and obedience to religious authority often seemed to carry over into obedience to authority in general. Finally, hierarchism was fueled by fear of the unknown upper levels—the more sacred, the more powerful, the more wealthy, and the more politically adept—and this fear spilled over into laypeople's attitudes toward the official courts.

Notions of hierarchy entered legal procedure through concepts such as *shuwa shulen* (*zhu ba zhu lan*), or the judge's questioning of both parties together. This practice was discouraged in the law codes. For one thing, it was thought to be unfair to have a less socially powerful person debate a more powerful one face to face; as the Ganden Podrang code comments: "People in the same category [may] debate face to face. If the persons are not of the same category, they [should] not debate face to face. They should be questioned privately, and so forth. However, generally, it is necessary [for the judges] to try to fulfill the wishes of the parties."

Moreover, it was thought that allowing both sides to be in court at the same time would greatly promote false testimony. Persons on one side, hearing the version of the other side, might change what they said they had seen, said, and done to promote their own interests rather than concentrating on giving an accurate and truthful accounting. This was generally called in the codes "speaking to benefit oneself," *rangnang gi dope* (*rang snang gi 'dod pas*) or *rangdo* (*rang 'dod*), and equated with "not knowing the real meaning of the law," *godon malon* (*go don ma lon*), which the codes considered antithetical to the legal process and punishable behavior in itself.

According to the law code, then, one purpose of the legal process is to encourage all persons concerned in a case to give a truthful accounting of what happened. This end is not promoted by ignoring hierarchy, by pitting the more socially powerful against the socially weaker. To do that allows self-interest to become an aim of the speaker and may encourage either side to change its story in response to the other.

Social Categories

In pre-1959 central Tibet, differences between individuals were based on a series of culturally determined categories: (1) region of affiliation; (2) occupation (nomadic, sedentary agriculturist, or monastic); (3) sect of Tibetan Buddhism; (4) position in the social stratification of the local and national society; (5) family lineage; (6) wealth; and (7) other personal attributes. These were delineated both separately and in patterns. The law codes added two more categories: (8) government office and (9) stigmatized attribute (outcaste status). All these factors affected the relative social rank of an individual or social unit, and social rank directly determined the relative power of the individual.

My collected interviews indicate that the layperson saw traditional social ranking in central Tibet from the top down, like this:

head of state
noble families of three upper levels
noble families of the lower level
landlords
landowning peasants
landless persons

It was the early Tibetan kings of the seventh century who stratified the noble families below the royal family, and by the nineteenth century the upper level of nobles comprised three strata: *yabshi* (*yab gzhis*), thought to be descendants of the Dalai Lamas; *depon* (*sde dpon*), said to be descended from ancient royal and noble lineages; and other nobles called *midak* (*mi drag*). The *kuma* (*dkyus ma*) formed the lower level of noble families and were largely petty officials in the government.[12] Many of the nomadic leaders I interviewed outlined a similar two-step nobility ranking for the attendants and officers of their pre-1959 regional administrations.

Locally, Tibetans from the southern agricultural countryside differentiated landlords further as noble, monastic, or government officers; and peasants as those directly owning government land and those holding land on an estate. Below these were landless persons (including hired workers and nonoutcaste craftspersons) and outcastes.[13]

These rankings do not account for certain powerful and wealthy religious figures both inside and outside the monasteries, monastic estates and *labrang* (*bla brang*),[14] nomadic groups and their leaders, traders, itinerants, yogis, and myriad other cate-

Plate 19. Noble ladies dressed for the Mon Lam Festival, followed by their maid, in Trapchi Thang outside of Lhasa. 1943. (Ilya Tolstoy, Library, The Academy of Natural Sciences of Philadelphia)

gories. Nevertheless, they provide a basic hierarchical model that most Tibetans would approve, at least in relation to the agricultural areas in the southern arc of the Plateau. Other attributes besides hereditary social category, however, could improve the power of a person or a family: the number of incarnations in a family, education with a particularly renowned teacher, control of a trading contract particularly favored by the Dalai Lama, or a highly unusual trait such as oracular powers.

At the bottom of the power hierarchy were persons with the outcaste stigma, a hereditary social trait. The stigma was usually acquired from the "bone," the line of a person's biological father, but it could also come from the mother. The category of outcastes, below all other social categories, was regarded as both polluted and polluting. It included fishermen, butchers, executioners, corpse carriers, some painters, blacksmiths, some metalworkers, and all their offspring. These impure people were not allowed to share food or cups with anyone outside their group, and they were expected to have sexual relations and to marry only within their group. Otherwise, they shared in the social and religious life of most communities. In the view of religious Tibetans, these stigmatized groups (which matched the Indian outcaste categories so precisely that their origins were not in question) were defiled because they had violated Tibetan Buddhist proscriptions (such as killing other sentient beings or violating the earth itself). Even extensive wealth could not improve the social rank of the socially polluted. In many sections of Tibet, outcastes were not even permitted to become monks.

When Tibetans were asked about people who never participated in the legal system, they often mentioned members of these outcaste categories. A man who had acted as a legal representative in Lhasa for many years explained:

> These *ragyab pa* (*rags gyab pa*), the Lhasa beggars, they did not come into the Lhasa City Court. They decided their own disputes among themselves with their headman. Also, the tailors had their own group and would not come in; so too, the goldsmiths, *tanka* (*thang ka*) painters, blacksmiths, and butchers. Some of these people would request representation if they had a big problem, and then the representative might go into official court. I don't think they weren't allowed; it's just that they didn't ever go, but I don't know this.
>
> In the case of the guilds, they needed to decide their own disputes quickly so that they could go on with their work, and I think that the government approved of them making their own decisions internally. The goldsmiths and painters were not as low castes as the butchers and corpse carriers; the people who killed animals or manufactured weapons to kill or dealt with the dead were the lowest castes.

This question of social stratification as a way of defining power and economic worth in the society interested the Tibetan government as early as the seventh century, when a social ranking system was included in the first law code's sections on murder payments.[15] Compensation payments for death were thought to depend on the social level of the victim, so the government matched social levels to payment amounts. Later law codes have a scheme that sounds very much like notions of class (upper-middle class, lower-upper class) to American ears. Everyone was divided into nine ranked categories from the highest of the high to the lowest of the low.[16] Figure 7 outlines this interesting social stratification for males as it appeared in the Tsang and Dalai Lama codes of the seventeenth century, undoubtedly influencing the later popular understanding of social rank throughout the entire Himalayan region. These categories were still used to assess victim compensation payments (see Chapter 23) in the courts of Lhasa as late as 1959.

Some social mobility was available in pre-1959 Tibetan society (except to outcastes) through monastic training, wealth accumulation in business or trade, marrying up (particularly if a group of brothers married a single woman of higher social status), government service during the reigns of the Thirteenth and Fourteenth Dalai Lamas, and education or skill in an occupation such as astrology or medicine. Stories of self-made men and women—such as that of an uneducated wood carrier in Lhasa who, through excellent business acumen, had become a very wealthy trader—were topics of conversation. The possibility of increased wealth was also linked by many to the number of sons in a household; each could be assigned a different income-

Plate 20. Outcaste beggars in the city of Gyantse. Notice the convict with iron fetters on the right. 1920–21. (Pitt Rivers Museum, University of Oxford)

producing task, while the basic farm paid the household taxes. Economic power augmented one's social rank. The accumulation of land, houses, and flocks in the southern countryside indicated increased local status, prestige, and power.

Difficulties in social mobility were encountered at the bottom, where the outcastes could not move from their category; at the top, where the upper levels of noble families guarded their privileges and prestige and government positions; and, in general, within the hereditary occupations. A male received his social position and occupation in Tibetan society from his father, a female received hers from both her father and mother. This fact, combined with a strong emphasis on obedience to parents and the expectation that children would continue in the family occupation barred change for many. Until the twentieth century the upper ranks of the secular government were reserved for the sons of noble families, a pattern altered in part by the meritocratic changes of the Thirteenth Dalai Lama. Peasants on noble and monastic estates were expected to marry into other families of those respective groups and to carry on the occupations of their parents; peasants who held land directly under the government had a bit more leeway.[17] Tibetans reported some cross-category marriages and cross-category land arrangements or purchases, but at the very least, such transactions involved getting permission from landlords and making special payments.

A final impediment to upward mobility or change in social rank and power was the tenuous nature of life and agriculture in Tibet, which caused families to be small, crops to die, trading ventures to fail, and landowners to accumulate debts as a result.

Category of Male	Tsang Law Code	Dalai Lama Law Code	*Tong* Amounts
❖ HIGH			
Highest of High	(empty: presumably the Dalai Lama)	(empty: presumably the Dalai Lama)	(no amount)
Middle of High	1) religious teacher of high rank	1) member of noble family	200 *sung*
	2) a regional head of Tibet	2) upper government officers	100 *sung*
	3) important lay officers of government	3) monk of pure conduct	100 *sung*
Lowest of High	1) mid-level lay officers	1) lower government officers including the staff of the Dalai Lama	80–90 *sung*
	2) monks of pure conduct	2) tax collectors	80–90 *sung*
❖ MIDDLE			
Highest of Middle	1) other lay officers	1) government messengers	60 *sung*
	2) security guards and old-time soldiers	2) government stablemen	60 *sung*
	3) other official government workers	3) other official government workers	60 *sung*
		4) landowners	60 *sung*
Middle of Middle	landowners of private government land	landowners of private government land	50 *sung*
Lowest of Middle	landowners of land on monastic or noble estates	1) small families (probably including landowners on monastic or noble estates)	40 *sung*
		2) bachelors	40 *sung*
		3) landless persons	40 *sung*
❖ LOW			
Highest of Low	(open)	blacksmiths	5–20 *sung*
Middle of Low	(open)	butchers	5–20 *sung*
Lowest of Low	bachelors, beggars, blacksmiths, executioners, hermaphrodites	executioners	5–20 *sung*

Figure 7. Social ranking systems from the Tsang and Dalai Lama law codes with matching *tong* monetary payments from the Dalai Lama law code (Ts:300–333 and GP:607–54).

A large debt load was considered by all Tibetans to be a very serious if not permanent obstacle to altering one's social position.

Power and Appropriateness in Tibetan Law

The idea of authority or power, *na og* (*mnga' 'og*), to decide a case and the idea of a forum as appropriate, *opo* (*'os po*), for deciding a given matter were two Tibetan notions that approximate rather closely the concept in English of "jurisdiction" as a set of rules governing which actors and cases have the power to access which forums. With the caveat that the word jurisdiction is a polyseme filled with legalese potential and requiring discriminate use, I employ it here in a limited way because of its usefulness and the similarities in meaning.

The Tibetan *na og*, literally "under the power (of)," was one of the terms applied to a forum or a person that had power over an issue, a place, a thing, or another person. This sense of jurisdiction carried with it the idea of a forum or person having power over disputes involving a particular group of persons or subject matter. Other uses of *na og* indicate that it was commonly understood in a hierarchical sense: that is, one was under the power of a superior in employment, of one's parents, of the landlord of an estate, and so forth.

Tibetans used the term *opo*, in general, to convey the concept of appropriateness, suitability, or competence in things legal and, in particular, to describe a forum for deciding a specific case. This second sense of jurisdiction relates to a very similar idea in English, that a case is within the powers of that forum to decide and therefore is appropriate and suitable. A forum that was the right place to file a particular suit was *opo*.

The English term "jurisdiction" is reflexive: that is, a forum is appropriate if it has power, and a forum that has the power is appropriate. In Tibetan, however, this is not true; the two words *opo* and *na og* are not viewed as linked or necessarily reflexive at all.

Nine types of jurisdiction, power plus appropriateness, can be abstracted from my collected cases, but it is important to remember that in Tibet these were *not* mutually exclusive. Jurisdiction could be based on (1) *territory*, for it was the first thought of a Tibetan to present a case in her or his local area, yet there was no requirement that this general propensity be followed. Most direct-access courts[18] had a territorial jurisdictional base—they could accept or refuse a local case—but had little power to compel civil cases or to refuse a directive from a higher level concerning their area.

(2) *Subject matter* might determine the forum in which a case was heard: murder and other very serious offenses were crimes involving the government over which the local district court had what amounted to compulsory power or jurisdiction.

When both parties came to a conciliator or court *and* the suit was accepted for consideration, jurisdiction was established by (3) *consent*. Consensual jurisdiction generally worked in conjunction with other forms as a secondary basis, and appearance was not equivalent to consent.

An office, person, or forum could acquire a case through (4) *referral* (surprisingly, consensual basis still operated in several such cases), but a referral down was not necessarily a remand for reconsideration. Also, the power over the case that a referral gave the new forum was not necessarily appropriate.

In some forums a possible basis for a case was (5) *kinship* between a member of the staff and the petitioner. The opponent, thought to be protected by his or her ability to refuse consent to the forum, nevertheless often agreed on the grounds that the petitioner was more likely to stand by a decision in which his or her relatives had participated.

Jurisdiction was influenced by (6) *social level*, particularly at the top and bottom of the scale. Conflicts concerning persons at the highest levels were frequently political and not legal affairs. When the father of the Thirteenth Dalai Lama created a ruckus in the streets of Lhasa in the 1920s by mercilessly beating another man, the regular police could not arrest him; a special panel of officials had to be convened to deal with the issue. When the King of Dedge and his brothers disputed the throne, petitions were given directly to the Dalai Lama himself. When the Dalai Lama became ill, the monks who were believed to have brought about the illness through black magic (Chapter 11) were treated in a political rather than a legal forum. Extremely sensitive cases such as that of Regent Reting were also handled in a political forum—the National Assembly or the Cabinet—in a political way with quasi-legal procedure. Most forums simply did not have jurisdiction over legal cases concerning very high-level affairs or persons of a very high social rank. One Tibetan stated that the police did not beat the drunken sons of the nobility or even take them to the police station but returned them to their family homes; other Tibetans denied this statement. Once jurisdiction was established, however, social rank did not affect certain aspects of legal procedure. For example, a land deed given to a member of the Dalai Lama's family had the same wording, general requirements, and efficacy as all other land deeds.

Persons of the three lowest ranks, including blacksmiths, butchers, and execu-tioners, seldom entered the legal system at all. None of the cases I collected con-cerned beggars or mendicants, but it is not clear whether they were excluded from the normal legal system or simply chose not to use it. Like the legal representative quoted above, Tibetans, when questioned about these groups, replied that they settled everything internally and never dealt with the government system. Unfor-tunately, jurisdictional bases at the lower end of the social scale remain cloudy.

Special forums existed for those of (7) *outsider* status. The Office for Nepalese (the most numerous foreigners in Tibet) handled all disputes in which citizens of Nepal were concerned, as well as their visas and other affairs. The Foreign Office handled all the remaining cases concerning foreigners, including Caucasians (a rare phenom-enon) and others residing in Lhasa. The exceptions were cases involving Chinese and other Asians in the provinces, which were dispatched by the district officers; and all cases concerning Muslims—both Tibetan and non-Tibetan—within the capital city, which were handled by the Lhasa Municipal Office.[19]

The monasteries and nunneries of Tibet had their own internal legal procedures, following the Vinaya, for the resolution of disputes involving parties of (8) *religious status*. Monks or nuns in disputes with other monks or nuns went first to their local units and then to higher monastic authority levels, culminating in the Ecclesiastical Office.[20] A religious actor or institution concerned in a secular civil dispute could

Plate 21. Some of the staff of the Lhasa British Mission in 1920. Disputes concerning outsiders were dealt with by the Foreign Office and the Office for Nepalese. 1920–21. (Pitt Rivers Museum, University of Oxford)

approach either a secular or a monastic forum but usually proceeded in the secular forum. For a criminal offense committed outside the monastery or considered too serious for the monastery to handle, such as a monk's murder of a layperson, the offender was turned over to the secular authorities. If a nun or a monk was the victim of a crime, the social standing and occupation of the other party was the most important factor in determining jurisdiction. If a member of the army killed a monk, for example, the case was sent first to the Cabinet, which received all murder cases, and then by referral to the Office of the Army.[21]

Members of the army operated under the Office of the Army, which dealt with all internal disputes as well as external disputes in which any actors were (9) *military personnel*. For example, all murder cases in Tibet were expected to go to the Cabinet and then to the High Court; however, if the defendant was in the army, the case would be heard instead at Army Headquarters.

Excursus: Land Ownership

The three levels of land ownership in Tibet, as evidenced in my interviews, were (1) government ownership, (2) peasant ownership, and (3) secondary or intermediate title ("estate") ownership.

The underlying right of ownership to all the land in Tibet (with the possible exception of a religious state such as Sakya or the independent outerlying kingdoms) lay in the person of the Dalai Lama and his government. Therefore, all land grants were conditioned on the continued good will of the government toward the grantee. In general, however, land grants were very stable, and most families and monasteries held their titles through many generations as long as they continued to pay their taxes and were not the subjects of political power plays.

The government was the source not only of all land grants but of all land documents demonstrating ownership. Every Tibetan landowner held a deed, *dantsik* (*gtan tshigs*), stating that he or she owned a particular piece of described land given in a specific year and on which taxes were due in such and such a kind and amount. A duplicate of each deed was inscribed in huge government record books, *jétha sherpang* (*'byed phra sher dpang*), with copies kept both in the Accounting Office in Lhasa and at local administrative headquarters. In the 1890s a compilation of landholdings called the Iron Tiger Land Survey Revenue Document was said to have recorded accurately all landholdings in Tibet at that time. Periodically, the government also issued a book called a Detailed List of Government Lands.

The second most important possessory interest, after that of the government, was that of the peasant. While the central government held land from the top, at the bottom the individual farmers held deeds to actual plots, which could not be alienated from them without sufficient cause. Peasant farmers occupied their land with reciprocal obligations: they had the generally inalienable right of ownership attested by a deed, but to maintain it they were bound to remit the required taxes determined by the government. (It is important to note here that it was an individual, commonly a male representing his sibling group, who was named in the deed as owner, even though the occupiers of the land as a household unit were responsible for the taxes.)

Peasant farmers could hold land whether or not there was an intervening secondary title: that is, directly under the government or within an intermediately titled monastic or private estate (see below). Dargyay (1982) has indicated that the direct title to land was more prestigious and often involved a reduced tax load. There was some agreement with this observation among the people I interviewed, but practices varied greatly across Tibet. It is true that some government landholders accumulated very large holdings—even larger than the local estates of petty government officers—and rented out their extra plots to laborers for a percentage of the produce.

These two primary levels of property ownership in Tibet—the peasant farmers from the bottom and the Dalai Lama at the top—were the most stable throughout history and were not changed by the secondary grants that formed an intermediate layer of property ownership. A secondary title to land gave the holder certain rights to the taxes paid by the peasants on that land (close to that of a "percentage usufruct" in Western civil law: that is, the right to draw a percentage of the profits of the land without altering it substantially).

The land granted under secondary ownership is referred to in this and other texts as an "estate," and there were seven basic ways in which such grants originated. First, both before and during the Empire period, palaces for the kings and their relatives, called *podrang* (*pho brang*), or royal residences, were built throughout the country, often with huge tracts of land attached. Some of these tracts remained for well over 1,300 years in the hands of the families that occupied them, such as the Lhagyari estate controlled by descendants of the first kings of Tibet (see Chapter 18). Second, ministers of the original kings were given land in exchange for their service. Descendants of these families formed some of the first-rank nobility in Tibet in the succeeding centuries.

Third, although each Dalai Lama acquired the base title to all Tibetan lands, individual relatives of the new incarnate became nobility and received tracts of land by intermediate title. Fourth, throughout the history of Tibet, lands were granted to monasteries and lamas for their support, or an individual might will his land to a monastery. These tracts became monastic estate lands; some remained so for 1,000 years or more and were considered difficult for the government to reassign (see the Introduction and Chapter 16). Fifth, to provide newly found incarnates with an income, lands called *labrang* (*bla brang*) were often granted to them. These remained with either the child found to be the lama's next incarnation or the lineal descendants, depending on the system of succession. The *labrang* of the most famous incarnate, the Dalai Lama, included the famous Potala Palace and the Summer Palace, as well as the base title to all Tibetan land.

Sixth, lands were commonly granted to an officer of the government for his livelihood, and these generally remained in the official's family, passing down to each generation from which a son was sent to serve as an officer (see Chapters 17 and 25). Officials could also apply for an additional estate on the basis of a special service or special need. Seventh, lands could be granted to an individual as a reward for a particular act of service to the government or an important member of it.

Secondary titles were rarely sold; they were normally transferred only to a lineal or designated heir as long as he was registered with the government. Or they could be rescinded and regranted by the government. For example, in a very famous political case before the National Assembly in the first half of this century, when it was determined that the former regent of Tibet had committed treasonous acts, the lands of his entire family were taken away. Similarly, a monastery found to have members who were conspiring to take the life of the Dalai Lama was stripped of its estates. In these situations the lands returned to the direct control of the central government and could be regranted elsewhere. There were ways to get around the restriction of transfer only by inheritance or regranting; if the land was used as security against a debt, a third party could assume the debt and take over the estate and its taxes, after requesting the issue of a new grant-deed by the government (Chapter 25 has an example).

Within this tripartite system of ownership, an individual, family, household, or monastery could hold lands granted in several different ways without contradiction. Moreover, incorporated and granted lands held by the same authority might be scattered throughout Tibet in patches. One old official family (described in Chapter 17) held eight tracts of land, four large and four small, each acquired under a different Dalai Lama. One of these had originally been granted to a relative of the Dalai Lama, then transferred to this family for service rendered. In another example of diffused property, the state of Sakya had not only a large central holding west of Lhasa but other monasteries and lands spread from western to eastern Tibet. The resulting mosaic of landholdings was actually a unifying factor for the state, since it was not to the advantage of landholders with interests in several regions to have areas of Tibet significantly alienated or conquered. Further, because these disparate units acted as one before the government, traded information, and shared supplies, they created useful interconnections between sections of the vast Plateau.

The organization of land into estates on which peasants worked has led several authors to compare Tibet with feudal Europe (Goldstein 1980; Li 1960). During the Middle Ages that system produced legal terms to describe the relationship between lords who granted land and their vassals who lived on the land and in turn served the lord. The vassal received livery of seisin of a freehold estate to the land after performing the rites of fealty and homage to the lord. A large body of law developed concerning the creation, granting, and prerequisites of such estates. At the bottom of the feudal system were serfs working the land as laborers for the vassals without any deeded rights to actual plots.

By contrast, Tibet was a state run by a governmental bureaucracy of officials who were paid in the profits of land instead of wages. Rather than two landholding levels (lords and vassals), there were three levels of titled ownership, the third vested in the peasant farmers who actually worked the land, paid taxes, enjoyed specific rights of ownership, and had recourse to the government in case of difficulties. There were no oaths of fealty or homage, no vassals with freehold estates, and few of the other necessary and sufficient conditions for an operating feudal system. As a consequence, feudal legal terms are not particularly appropriate to this three-tiered system of land ownership and are not employed here.

CHAPTER TEN

Rituals of the Golden Yoke

In brief,
A sewing needle (to stitch the story together),
A cutting knife (to make sharp distinctions),
Fingers clasped in the proper way (bringing the two sides together),
It is necessary for [a good judge or conciliator] to know these methods.
—Neudong Law Code

Tibetans described four different processes or legal rituals for settling their differences when a situation had become a serious and intractable problem. Because these processes were not mutually exclusive either temporally or spatially, they could occur simultaneously, flow from one type to another, or replace one another with great flexibility. The four—from least to most formal—were internal settlement, conciliation, visits to an official at home, and an official court proceeding. The first three were all regarded by Tibetans as "internal" rituals; the fourth involved forty-four formal steps divided into three basic stages: the initiation of a case, the transaction of a case, and the closing of a case.

Internal Rituals

Internal dispute settlements by means of discussions within families or between relatives, singing contests among the nomads, rolling dice, champion-style fights, negotiations, and consultation conferences with important people were all reported by Tibetans as having occurred regularly. The method employed depended on the area of Tibet, and this diversity caused many Tibetans to comment that their locality had procedures that were different from all other regions. These procedures, which took place outside the formal goverment bureaucracy, only rarely resulted in a written document but were undoubtedly the most common form of dispute settlement in the country. Chapter 11 discusses and illustrates some of the legal rituals involved.

A conciliation, a nonbureaucratic resolution of a controversy by a conciliator or middleman, was also considered a type of "internal settlement" by many Tibetans. In contrast to the court's operation in the public, official, and governmental sphere, conciliation was private, unofficial, and nongovernmental. It had its own distinct ritual vocabulary: a conciliation, *bardum* (*bar 'dum*), between two or more parties was arranged by a conciliator, *barmi* (*bar mi*), and often resulted in a written agreement called a *dumyik* (*'dum yig*).[1]

With its added degree of formality, a conciliation agreement took on increased legitimacy and protected the parties in case of a later contest or appeal. If a document was to be issued, the middleman chosen for such a proceeding was often either an educated person capable of composing and drafting documents in the government style or a respected but unlettered member of the community whose decision was then recorded in writing by someone who had those skills.

Conciliation in Tibet was a very common and very important form of dispute settlement. The distinction between judges and conciliators is an ancient one; the fourteenth-century Neudong law code, which antedates the Dalai Lama codes, repeatedly opposes terms for judges to terms for conciliators. For example, the Neudong code discusses the choice of a person to be a conciliator, compensation payments to the conciliator, the conciliation document, and the factors to be considered: "The conciliator should ask a learned person (about the case), think hard (about the case) for three days, look at the history of the dispute between the parties, and look to the root of the guilt."[2] Then, at the end of that section, a judge and a conciliator are represented in the same line. Having decided the case and made a document giving the punishment amounts, the conciliator asks "the first person who began the dispute, (as to) the amount of the punishment, 'Will you do this?' If this man says no, (he) must petition to a judge who will (then) make an investigation. So it is said."[3]

Another way to approach the distinction between a judge and a conciliator is to ask Tibetans their preference. Without question, they will say that it is much better to handle a case through internal conciliation than to take it into court. The advantages of this preferred form of dispute settlement were enumerated by Tibetans at length:

- It saved the reputation of the family or person involved.
- It reduced and confined conflict or its appearance "in the community."
- It allowed for flexibility and unusual compromises.
- It reinforced the value of consensus and agreement.
- It did not necessitate the point-by-point delineation of the issues required in court.
- It was much less expensive than presenting gifts to the authorities and paying final court costs.
- It did not result in the corporal punishment that could be inflicted by official authorities in court.

On the other hand, Tibetans were not blind to the disadvantages of internally conciliated decisions. They commonly admitted that these agreements did not have as much social weight as official decisions, that they could be difficult to carry out, and that they were only as good as the people who decided and agreed to them.

Showing respect by visiting a person at home was a Tibetan ritual that applied to the legal as well as the social sphere. Judges commonly received parties to a dispute, at home as well as at court, throughout the duration of a legal case. Such visits were understood by all parties to be not social but legal interactions intended to allow the judge to give advice, receive presents, and speak somewhat informally. It was a legal procedure that most Tibetans disliked, but many said that this was the only way to determine a judge's opinion of the case and how best to proceed. It is certain, however, that judges were visited primarily because they had authority in court, not because they were a source of advice. In fact, many judges told petitioners who visited them at home to seek forums elsewhere, to find a suitable conciliator, to employ a legal representative for the case, or to drop the suit entirely.

This legal process was the most difficult and controversial area of discussion with Tibetans. Although it was a procedure that allowed for flexibility and, in some situations, circumvention of the more formal court proceedings, it was also the arena in which present-giving, quasi-bribing, and actual bribing took place. It was hard to differentiate between a present and a bribe in some circumstances, but several Tibetans stated that visiting the judge who had jurisdiction in your formal case for the purpose of presenting more than a nominal gift was bribing—a very common, often expected, practice. All other gifts made to a judge at home were merely respectful presents.

Bribing and giving presents to officials at home were practices fraught with uncertainty. Although the practice was widespread, anything more than a white scarf was punishable if revealed to higher government officers. Moreover, regardless of the size or nature of the gift, a decision in one's favor could rarely be guaranteed because more was involved than the good opinion of one judge, and a petitioner could not visit and give presents to all the judges on a panel.[4] Tibetans also clearly stated that no judge was bound in court by anything he received or said at home.

Official Court Proceedings

The only form of legal ritual a Tibetan would not describe as "internal" was taking a case into the public, official, governmental sphere of the courts. A specific vocabulary demarcated these formal government procedures for a case or controversy, *kachu* (*kha mchu*).[5] The process was familiar to most Tibetans in at least its basic formulation; even those who disclaimed any knowledge whatsoever of legal procedure knew what to do—or they knew who would know what to do—and what would happen in the petitioning process because it constituted part of the basic social interaction routine.

The intricate forty-four steps outlined below in chronological order—two in the initiation stage, thirty-two in the transaction stage, and ten in the closing stage of a case—have been pieced together from hundreds of cases and interviews and extensively reviewed with several former judges and clerks. This was not a written

Plate 22. A view of the Zhol area from the steps of the Potala. Before 1959 the Zhol administrative offices, court, and prison were in the building on the far right. 1986.

pattern of procedure; it was learned by officials on the job and then transmitted through practice. Nor did all these steps, in this particular sequence, occur in every grievance brought before a government court. Formal legal procedure could be greatly contracted, the order rearranged, or many of the steps simply eliminated. Nevertheless, as any of them could and often did occur in a case, it is important to set out the various possible steps as a sequence. Every step and its relation to the other steps has been confirmed by both former officials and petitioners.[6] Each one is a recognized part of the legal procedure; they are combined and ordered here for the sake of clarity and analysis.

Because the *initiation of a case* in Tibet occurred only through a petition to a court or an office with judicial powers, the two steps involved were (1) presentation of a case to the formal court, and (2) the acceptance of the case by that court as appropriate. Both were necessary, though if the case had been referred from another office, its acceptance might by only pro forma.

The *transaction of a case* is best divided into four subsections: the statement, the questioning, the investigation and testing, and the decision. The *statement of the case* consisted of (1) the calling of the petitioner, (2) the presentation of the petition in court or the taking of the petitioner's initial statement, and (3) the initial questioning of the petitioner by the judges. The original petition set the framework and often limited the subject matter of the dispute to the series of points it presented.

The judges' *questioning* of each party and the witnesses could have as many as thirteen parts:

Plate 23. Three judges and their two clerks positioned for an official Zhol Court proceeding. Note the legal documents and files on the right pillar and hanging from the window on the left. Edicts and lists are posted on the wall behind the judges. The judges' tables hold tea cups and ink pots; counters and writing supplies are on the desk in front of the clerks. 1920. (Pitt Rivers Museum, University of Oxford)

1. calling the opponent named in the petition
2. presentation of the opponent's response petition or a response statement recorded by the clerk (or the refusal of the opponent to appear)
3. calling the petitioner
4. the petitioner's reply to the opponent's response
5. requestioning the petitioner
6. recalling the opponent
7. the opponent's response to the petitioner's reply
8. presentation of important documents or other evidence
9. recalling and requestioning both sides by turns
10. possible recall and requestioning of both sides at the same time (although this procedure was generally discouraged)
11. calling witnesses or other persons involved in the case
12. presentation or recording of each witness's statement
13. questioning the witness

It is important to notice that formal Tibetan legal procedure emphasized holding to the original points introduced as the substance of the case, and the purpose of this repeated questioning was to come to an agreed statement of the facts at issue.

The *investigation and testing* that could occur during a trial might include (1) an investigation ordered by the court, (2) the investigators' report to the court, (3) veracity testing of the petitioner, opponent, or witnesses, (4) a decision by the judge(s) on the veracity tests, and (5) the imposition of penalties for untruthfulness.

The *decision* process of the court then moved through eleven steps:

1. decision of the case by the judges (or through some other method)
2. drafting the final decision document
3. recalling both sides to court to hear the decision
4. presentation to both sides of a copy of the decision agreement
5. consideration of the document by both sides outside the court
6. recalling the parties to give their opinions of the decision
7. presentation to and acceptance by the court of any guarantors for the agreement
8. signing the agreement or refusal to sign by either side
9. signing the agreement clause or refusal to sign by any guarantor to either side
10. exchange of the copies of the decision document between the parties
11. final statement by the judge(s) or his (their) representative

And finally, the *closing of the case* in a formal Tibetan court had eight steps plus two other possibilities:

1. acceptance by the court of the signing or refusal to sign on the part of either side
2. remittance of any payments or articles due the court under the decision
3. remittance of court costs and any additional fees
4. return by the court of any articles or money held during the transaction of the case
5. payment by either side to the other of money or articles according to the decision
6. further punishment of either side carried out by the court as determined in the decision
7. drafting any other necessary documents
8. a formal reconciliation between the sides

Should no final acceptance and reconciliation prove possible, however, (9) the court might send the case to a higher administrative body, or (10) one or both sides might appeal the case to a higher authority.

This extensive list stands as a paradigm; it formed the backbone of formal procedure in court as Tibetans understood it. Parts of this process, sections of this mental map of how to proceed, were reiterated over and over by Tibetans at every level and station in society from every section of the Plateau. Rather than a set of substantive rules, this unwritten procedure was a Tibetan universal and the template for other, less formal proceedings, interactions, and even documents.

Excursus: Court Costs

Several Tibetan law codes have a section, not directly included in the legal texts but appended at the end, titled "Court Payments." It is usually an enumeration of types and amounts of articles and money considered appropriate for the payment of court costs following case decisions. Court costs in Tibet were customarily allocated to both parties, although this was a matter of judicial discretion. Conciliation procedures did not result in such payments (a conciliator was customarily given a gift), but for any case filed with a court—even if it was subsequently withdrawn by a conciliator—payment of some court costs was necessary.

Weights, coinage, and money varied greatly both through time and by area of the country, but for the purposes of figuring legal expenses, several sources agreed on the following basic equivalences:

1 *dotsé (rdo tshad)* = approximately four pounds of silver in bar form
1 *sung (srang)* = approximately one ounce of gold or silver, usually a coin
1 *zho (zho)* = approximately one-tenth ounce of gold or silver; 10 *zho* = 1 *sung*

The court costs owed the government could be determined in three ways. The first was to use the court cost tables that were appended to some law codes. Most of these had thirteen entries from very high payments (for "very big crimes and difficult cases") to very low (Tibetans stated that the largest and smallest levels were rarely assessed). For example, one of the law codes lists costs at the first level as

an excellent gold scarf worth 2 *sung*, 8 *zho*;
gold coins worth 9 *sung*, 6 *zho*;
one roll of silk brocade worth 41 *sung*, 4 *zho*;
ordinary silk in blue, red, and yellow worth 9 *sung*;
one roll of flower design silk worth 13 *sung*;
four rolls of cotton cloth worth 1 *sung*, 5 *zho*;
shan phab [unidentified] worth 3 *sung*; and
government tea worth 2 *sung*, 5 *zho*—for a total of 82 *sung*, 8 *zho*.
[Then] judge's payment is 20 *sung*; secretaries' fee of amount [illegible].
(BrCC:1–12)

These were the amounts owed by the parties in money and goods if the judge specified a court cost payment of level one in a final decision document. Several judges commented that this method was directly affected by inflation because the law code amounts had not been changed since the sixteenth century.

The second and most common method was to assess court costs as a percentage of the monetary compensation owed in the case: for example, they could be calculated from the *tong (stong)* amount in a murder case (Figure 7), or from the *bab* in a case of contract violation (Chapter 11).

The third method was for the judge to base the amount on his own evaluation of the circumstances. Confidence in his fairness was the primary criterion for the acceptance of his assessment by the parties, who could otherwise respond by requesting one of the other methods.

Tibetan officials and laypersons reported that even after the court costs that went to the government were figured, this was not the end of the matter: as the foregoing quotation from the law code indicates, the judges and secretaries were still to be paid. One former Tibetan official gave me an example: "Let us say that the court cost amount is 600. . . . The judge's separate payment is one-fourth of the court costs or, in this case, 150. The secretaries' payment is one-fourth of that or approximately 37. Thus the man actually owes 787 and not 600 by the time he leaves court."

The result was that there might be four kinds of expense involved in going to court. Three were official—the monetary compensation, such as the *tong*, decided in the law case itself; court costs; and fees to individual judges and secretaries for their services—and these were in addition to whatever unofficial payments had been made to judges visited at home. Tibetans often commented that they were dumbfounded by the total costs involved in this system.

CHAPTER ELEVEN

Of Oracles, Oaths, and Dice

Establishing Evidence of the Truth Through an Oath . . . The one who wins the dice can choose the order of the administration of the oath. Whatever the dice indicate, the judge or conciliator shall read into the ear of the oathtaker the oath document three times, explaining each term one by one in such a manner that it goes well into the realm of the oathtaker's mind.

—Tsang Law Code

European medievalists have argued that within the rubric of the "central beliefs of the age," institutions such as the judicial ordeal made sense and were intellectually coherent as a form of proof for hard cases.[1] Like their European counterparts, the various Tibetan ordeals, along with other forms of proof, were frequently used in official trials as means of establishing facts, discovering the truth, or settling a case when other techniques proved ineffective. Besides ordeals, other cultural practices that could be imported into the Tibetan legal process included casting lots, applying to an oracle or a Tantric priest, taking oaths, and rolling dice. When employed for an internal settlement between parties, such devices could constitute all or part of the proceeding. When brought into an official government proceeding, they were most commonly used to determine veracity, establish a difficult fact, find material evidence, or, when the parties could not agree, place the dispute in the hands of a deity.

Distinctive in the Tibetan approach were the variety and flexibility of these techniques, the continued insistence on agreement between the parties regarding the use of each device (even in an official setting), the clearly magical nature of many of these practices, and the number of mythic legal cases recounted to demonstrate their efficacy. Tibetans saw no difficulty in leaving the outcome of a dispute to what Americans would term "chance," as all results were karmically determined, and one could always appeal to the gods. These devices were viewed as legitimate instrumentalities (much like a lie detector or breath analyzer), particularly if they worked to the advantage of one's own side.

The casting of lots, *mo* (*mo*), by a lama or a fortuneteller or layperson took several forms. It could not be employed directly within the official Tibetan legal system, but it was extensively used to make decisions about whether to proceed with a legal case and where to find evidence. Private families did a *mo* or had one done for them to determine such matters as the identity of a thief or robber, the possibility of success in a case, or whether a judge liked them. Officials were more than willing to accept an object or person thus discovered *if* the result could be substantiated by other means. A *mo* was considered quite advantageous for a petitioner who was unclear as to how to proceed, as demonstrated in the following account of an incident in the 1940s:

> A family had several things stolen from their house when they were out and had no idea who the culprit was. The family did a *mo* privately, and the *mo* said that one Tashi had done it. So the family went to his house and found the stolen articles there. When they took him to the local district officer, they did not say that they had discovered them with a *mo* but instead presented the articles as evidence, which was accepted by the court.

The same reasoning applied to the use of oracles in dispute settlement, whether the oracular technique involved a trance in which a deity entered the oracle's body or divination with the use of the Melong mirror.[2] Considered extremely powerful predictors and recounters, oracles were nonetheless not appropriate to secular legal proceedings except as an aid to the discovery and proof of a central issue. The most famous example is surely the case involving the severe onset of an unexplained illness of the Thirteenth Dalai Lama. As treatment appeared ineffective and the Dalai Lama continued to sicken, the State Oracle was called in to reveal the cause of the illness. It was discovered through this medium's trance that one lama acting for an entire monastery had sewn a black magic charm into the left heel of a pair of boots presented as an offering to the ruler. Immediately opening the boot, government officials found the charm and sent representatives to investigate the monastery. Legal proceedings were initiated, the responsible monks and the monastery were severely punished, and the Dalai Lama completely recovered.

Another example (noted in Chapter 23) was the use of oracles by the High Court of Tibet, whose staff and officials regularly attended the local oracles, presumably to find out whether criminals had come to them requesting auspicious dates for committing crimes!

Ordeals and Oaths

The law codes from the seventeenth century have an entire section on the administration of oaths and ordeals. A section of the Dalai Lama code titled "Taking an Oath due to a Big Lie or Blaming" details the elaborate procedures to be followed, the expenses of which were to be born by the person being tested.

The basic purpose of either an oath or an ordeal was to verify an individual's story, as set out in these introductory lines:

> For the bad person who lies and blames others, a truthful and unbiased person as decision-maker should investigate and make a clean differentiation between truth and untruth using a suitable method such as:
> oath-taking with a friend,
> [hot] stone,
> [hot] oil,
> [hot] muddy water, and
> [hot] iron.[3]

Although these devices are described in the codes as part of a court proceeding, they were also used in unofficial internal dispute settlements.

In brief, taking an oath required that an individual perform several rituals, wearing particular items, and swear to the truth of his or her statements in front of a very powerful god, who was then presumed to take on the responsibility of rewarding or punishing the individual in this or another life. Ordeals—used after an inconclusive oath, in conjunction with an oath, or by themselves—varied in form. One required that the individual put a hand into boiling water or oil to draw out a black or white stone; another, that he or she hold a hot stone while taking seven steps, after which the hands were sealed and then examined the next day for incriminating blisters; a third, that the individual's tongue be touched to a hot iron. Unlike oaths, ordeals soon revealed the truth or falsity of the party's statements. The law codes described what would be seen on the tongue or hands if the person had told the truth or had lied, thereby allowing the court or conciliator to continue with the case.

Although only one actual instance of an ordeal was recorded—and it took place among the refugee community in northern India—most Tibetans interviewed knew about ordeal procedures. Oaths, however, were much more commonly used in recent times, as pointed out by one former Lhasa native:

> These ordeal procedures described in the codes are very old, and they were generally not used in this century in Tibet; however, oaths in front of a protective deity were used very commonly throughout all Tibet, including Lhasa up until the 1960s.
>
> The purpose of the oath is to test the truth of someone's words when the truth cannot be discerned otherwise. The person taking the oath does have to loosen his or her hair, take off amulets, religious strings, knives, and in some cases even shirts. This procedure can be used for any hearing, even a land law case. Sometimes it is for one aspect of the case only, and other times, it concludes the entire case.

A case said to have occurred in the 1930s is typical of the mythic legal style. It was recounted by a Tibetan as a legendary story demonstrating the efficacy, legitimacy, and power of oath-taking as a legal device:

> This was a big case in the area of Nagchu at that time which I observed. A nomad woman and a nomad man were in a fierce argument about casting spells. The man contended that

the woman had cast a spell on him, and the woman in turn accused the man of being a sorcerer. The man said that she did cast spells, but the woman said that she didn't.

So both of them were brought before the district officer, although he was reluctant to take the case. After hearing the arguments on both sides, the officer knew that it was a matter of truth. So he set a time for an oath-taking.

On that day, the district officer brought out his *tanka* [a cloth painting] of the fierce protective deity goddess Lhamo, and told both of them to come and prepare to take an oath before the deity. Then he went to his seat, and to the right and left of him were seated the representatives of all the four major nomadic tribal groups of the area and the village heads who had been called to be in attendance.

First, a ceremony was performed where the painting was hanging. Both the man and the woman presented white scarves to the deity, and then a ritual was performed to the goddess by the district officer, using tea and beer given by the man and woman. No special clothing was required of the parties, and neither of the parties read a document during the oath-taking as it says in the law codes.

Then the district officer sat on his seat while each of the parties in turn, the man and the woman, took oaths that they were telling the truth in front of all of them and the goddess. Both said in their oaths that they had never done any sorcery or cast any spells. With this, the law case was concluded.

After the oaths, both parties were finished and went out from the district officer's room. As the nomadic woman left the room, blood began to flow down from her nose in a solid stream, and she was unable to stop it. She went home, and her nose kept on bleeding for one week, no matter what help she was given. At the end of one week she had lost so much blood that she died.

Quite a while later, more evidence was discovered about this case and brought to my attention. A *bonpo* (*bon po*) lama in the area had sorcery powers, and this lama had asked the woman to do sorcery against that man's family. It was not known if she had done the sorcery or not, but she had defended herself and knowingly taken the oath. If one takes an oath in front of the Dharma Protectors, then they are in charge of all the punishment thereafter.[4] So since people of the area thought that she had done the act and had still knowingly taken the oath, she was considered very bad, and her death was attributed to the goddess.

Legal representatives from Lhasa and the southern countryside gave detailed explanations of the use of oaths in formal court proceedings, in conciliations, and in informal dispute settlement at every level in Tibet. Oaths were administered when there were persons who could not be whipped and from whom there was little hope of arriving at the truth by other means (for example, old or unhealthy people); when parties to a dispute were willing to take an oath to clear themselves; if the authorities determined that someone was lying; or if a case was unclear or stymied. As one proverb had it, "[If the case is] clear, [decide it] by law; [if the case is] unclear, [decide it] by oath."

If an oath needed to be taken on behalf of a group, such as a father for the entire household or a headman for the community, the other members of the group had to agree to the process beforehand. An equally elliptical proverb is used in this situation: "[If] the headman takes an oath, his region [should agree]; [if] the father takes an oath, the son [should agree]."[5]

After dressing or undressing as required, the oath-taker performed the ritual in the

Plate 24. Masked operatic dancer, representing a Dharma Protector god, performing at a monastic festival at Tikse Monastery in western Tibet. His apron is bordered with embroidered images of skulls and thunderbolts. 1976. (Syed Ali Shah, Leh, Ladakh)

courtroom, in a room with a religious picture, or in a temple near the court. In some cases, both parties were expected to stand in front of the protector god or goddess and to repeat wording decided on by the court or informal authority. An oath settled an issue or concluded a case because it was uniformly believed that the Dharma Protectors would severely punish a liar. Those interviewed cited general suffering, illness, death in the family, the decay of a good family over time, and general misfortunes as the results of a false oath.

Within the ambit of a particular case an oath-taking, to be effective, had to be agreed upon by both parties, whether one or both sides were participating. This allowed a party to reject the process if he or she believed that the other side would not take the oath seriously or would not do it without trickery. An agreement also had to be reached as to the outcome; usually the non-oath-taking side would agree to accept the truth of the oath-taker's statement, to make a payment called an "oath cushion," or to conclude the case—as a former Lhasa resident illustrated in two examples from the 1950s.

Thubten blamed Lobsang for stealing an article. This case was brought before an authority, and Lobsang denied it. Lobsang then asked Thubten what oath cushion he would give if Logsang agreed to take an oath. Thubten, the accuser, said that he would pay the price of the stolen article as compensation for a false accusation if Lobsang would take an oath. If it is a small matter, the oath will just be in court, but if it is a big matter, they will go to the temple of the protective deities for the oath, which is what they did here. Lobsang took the oath, [was given the payment], and the case was concluded.

In another case, Tsering blamed Lakpa for stealing an article, and Lakpa said that he would take an oath. Tsering said to Lakpa, "If you take the oath, I will drop this suit completely." No request for a cushion was made. This oath was done in front of a picture of His Holiness the Dalai Lama in the courtroom itself, and the case was over.

Rolling Dice

The general term for gambling with dice, *sho* (*sho*), was also the term used for throwing dice to settle a law case. As a legal device, it was used if the two parties were both unclear about the case or if there was insufficient evidence for any resolution satisfactory to both sides. *Sho* was viewed by Tibetans as an impartial form of decision-making and quite satisfactory, particularly if combined with religious sanctions. It could be done informally or within the context of a conciliation or court proceeding. The location of this exercise was determined by the parties, who, just before they rolled, were expected to say very loudly, "You are the Dharma Protector gods; you know the real truth. Please show the truth now." Although I collected only a small number of cases, no one had heard of an instance in which the parties, after agreeing to roll dice, had not accepted the result—possibly because they believed that the gods would punish an illicit winner or because they knew that the case could be reopened later if necessary.

The practice was common in villages and border areas, as two instances will demonstrate. First, a case from the 1930s was told by a former Lhasa native:

My relative had some land that had been handed down to him from a forefather many years ago. There had been an agreement written in a document many years before between the forefather and another family that I will call Wangchen, allowing them to use the land of the forefather. The document stated that the relatives of the forefather should be given particular articles and cash upon his death and that the payments for the use of the land by the Wangchen family should also go to my relative. Then my relative, some years later, informed the Wangchen family that he had decided to use the land himself, but the Wangchen family disagreed, saying that they had a document to show their right to use it and that their payments for the land were good, even excessive. A big quarrel ensued.

In the legal case, my relative argued that the document was invalid, while the Wangchen family said that it was valid and their payments good. The district officer, after questioning the parties, decided that both sides should throw dice in front of a protective deity. The exact question to be presented to the deity was whether or not the paper presented by the Wangchen family was a valid document from the forefather.

On the appointed day the parties appeared, and both sides rolled. The member of the Wangchen family got the highest number from the dice. So, my relative was required to pay the court costs and even to make large payments to the Wangchen family.

The second case was recounted by a layperson from the southwest:

When I was in the Shika [a farm estate] in the southwest, there was a Nepalese man who had married a local Tibetan woman, and he had thereafter made a false loan document stating that he had given money to four or five families. All the people of the area knew the loan was false, but he had good support from some important people, and he knew the government officer.

Finally, as this was becoming a big dispute, the families asked the man to play dice in front of the community. On the first roll, the person to roll first was determined. On the second roll, each family head rolled in turn and then [the man] rolled. All the other families got a higher number than he did, and the case was decided against him.

Every dice-rolling case recounted indicated that the populace of Tibet considered this form of decision-making effective, accurate, and true. Cases like the following one, which would elsewhere be classified as mythic legal stories, lent credence to this popular view:

In Shigatse, there was a large dispute over the ownership of a piece of land which could not be resolved after quite some time. The party from a nearby region and the party from Shigatse had even gone into the court at Shigatse without coming to any resolution. Finally, it was decided that the two parties would play dice to settle the case.

After doing the proper procedure, it was determined that the man from Shigatse should roll first. So the first man rolled the dice and came up with twelve *sho*. Everyone exclaimed, because it is not possible to beat this. The man from the nearby region called upon the gods, and then he played the dice. He rolled six and six, but with the strength of his throw one of the die was shattered and broke off a corner, making it thirteen in all. So the second man won because he had a higher number.

Bab

One further legal device was the *bab*. A clause intended to force parties to a contract to abide by its terms, the *bab* set fees to be paid if the agreement was violated—it was a "liquidated damages clause" in American law. (This form of payment clause set into a contract should be distinguished from *bab* used in the sense of income, taxes, or payments collected by a court.) *Bab* were commonly included in court decisions as well, to bind parties to their word. "In an ordinary decision document," said the law codes, "the amount of the *bab*, depending on the importance of the case, is written at the bottom."[6]

A case recounted by a former government official demonstrates the use of this legal device in Tibet:

> Tashi and Tsering were two businessmen who had a written loan contract between them that had been sealed to demonstrate their agreement and friendship. In it was a line that said, "If you go against this contract, then you destroy it, and you are committing a great wrong, so you must pay a *bab* of one thousand more." Tsering had borrowed money and agreed to pay on a particular date. If he did not pay on that date, he owed Tashi one thousand more.
>
> Tashi did not receive his money on time, and a quarrel broke out between the two. Tashi went to court, saying in a petition that he wanted both the [original] money and the *bab* payment. The court then sent out a representative to find Tsering and take his statement. So the representative had to get paid, too, and took as much as one-fourth more of the amount collected.

Even the very early codes are filled with phrases about the importance of such penalties. They condemn actions that breach contracts, thereby requiring payment of the *bab*, and they outline the factors to be considered "with a Bodhi [Buddha] mind" in the event of such a violation.[7] By the fourteenth century, taking a more realistic view of the excessively high *bab* amounts included in contracts, the codes no longer required automatic payment for any breach but suggested instead a reconsideration of the issues. Nonetheless, *bab* were regarded by Tibetans as a sort of secular amulet that both warned the parties and warded off future conflict.

CHAPTER TWELVE

The Jurisprudence of Truth

Oaths before Deities for the Substantiation of False Statements: Though truth is the principal object, yet the truth of the oath-taker may not be reflected in the oath because of karmic action or the wording of the oath. For example, if he inserts the phrase "It occurs to my mind" or "I think so," the oath will not reveal the truth.

—Ganden Podrang Code of the Dalai Lamas

Tibetan notions of honesty and truth, consensus, non-decay, flexibility, risk, responsibility, causation, factoring, proof, and uniqueness provided a range of assumptions that guided reasoning in cases of civil conflict.[1] Equally fascinating is the absence from the Tibetan legal system of such Western notions as *stare decisis*, *res judicata*, mutual exclusivity of jurisdiction, and precedent.

Truthfulness, *denpa* (*bden pa*), and honesty, *drungbo* (*drang po*), were the most universally employed terms for evaluating aspects of the legal system. The law codes ring with these words, and Tibetans used them frequently with reference to every part of a case, from the testimony of the parties and witnesses to the decision of the judge. They suffice to express the concepts denoted by a wide range of English terms in law, such as probity, due process, justice, fairness, veracity, factual consonance, even ability in speaking.[2] Falsehood and dishonesty were correspondingly negative assessments.

Whereas the American view is that legal truth emerges from the clash of opposing forces asserting their interests, Tibetans saw little value in weathering such a process with all its extremity, anger, and passion. Truth was understood in one of two ways: as an ideal and separate standard, or as consensus—that is, the result when disagreeing parties reach a similar view of what happened and what should be done. The idea that in agreement lies truth is reflected in the law codes' warning [if the parties return to arguing], "truth may turn to untruth."[3]

Truth as consensus meant factual consonance. The facts given by both sides had to agree, not with reality (in any correspondence sense) but with each other. Thus, if both parties agreed that the sky was red, factual consonance had been achieved. If the parties did not agree, then the decision procedure was stymied. Judges were often reluctant to go forward except to ask more questions and take more statements in an unending cycle, for no truth had been reached. From the perspective of Western philosophy, legal truth in Tibet was radically coherent: that is, the perceptions of only the two parties had to cohere or agree for a statement to become a legal fact. A mutually coherent reality was sufficient truth.

Truth also meant fairness in procedure: well-experienced, well-learned, intelligent, unbiased, and honest judges conducting cases with proper formal procedural steps that resulted in fair decisions. It meant not using phrases that were inconclusive or indefinite—such as "I think so," "maybe," or "probably"—in court. It meant using legal procedures and rules of evidence that encouraged parties and witnesses to be in an emotional and mental state allowing them to speak adequately.

Truth also meant maintaining a personal standard for honesty and fairness. One Tibetan told me that when he was called to repeat his testimony in court on a murder case, he was asked by the judge if he would tell the truth as he had before. He replied, "There is no difference between my two eyes. I will speak truthfully."

Tibetans further used the terms "honesty" and "truth" to describe acts falling within the large and amorphous American legal categories of fundamental fairness and due process. Tibetans have the idea that an individual is entitled to certain legal procedures before the government can act to his or her personal detriment. These procedures include notice, presence before an unbiased tribunal, the opportunity to be heard and to controvert evidence, and the right not to be prejudged under arbitrary laws. Of a person charged arbitrarily with an offense or given no chance to present his or her side, Tibetans said, "Truth has not been done in his case."

Consensus, Non-Decay, and Flexibility

Since truth meant factual consonance, the necessity of consent and consensus, *pentsun thunpa (phan tshun mthun pa)* and *loka zotap su dowa (blo kha rdzogs thabs su 'gro ba)*, permeated the entire Tibetan decision-making process. A civil suit could not be addressed in most forums without the consent of both parties. A case was not considered settled until there was agreement as to the facts, and a judicial decision (even in a murder case) had a subsequent requirement of consensus among all parties. Moreover, a signature or seal in the *chuyik (mchu yig)* section of every decision document was required from each of the important parties and their guarantors to signify their consent. Lack of agreement meant lack of permanency for a legal decision as well as lack of truth. Factual truth thus became defined by the court as "the agreed truth," or the facts that the parties no longer contested. Settlements were supported by the consensus of the parties and their belief that the conclusion aligned with the truth.[4]

The requirement of factual consonance often determined the amount of time a case spent in court—called the "thickness of the case," *kachu karlo (kha mchu gar los)*, by Tibetans. If the parties were unyielding or hard in their opinions, if the facts of a case remained inconsistent, a case was "very thick." It might take a long time to decide a thick case, because if the parties could not agree, truth could not be reached.

Consent and agreement were also understood to include the work of the parties to reharmonize themselves and the community after a bitter fight.[5] Tibetans stated that the jurisprudential concept of consensus and the ritual procedure of reharmonization helped dispel the parties' mental afflictions, such as anger or jealousy. The law codes specified the assessment of a "getting together payment" to finance a meeting at which all the parties could drink and eat together as equals,[6] thereby promoting catharsis and reconciliation following the disposition of the case. One Tibetan from the southwest described such an outcome: "Then, after all this, when the case is over, the petitioner and opponent feel happy because they have agreed, so they offer scarves to each other, and when they go out of the gates of the court, they do not show their displeasure anymore. They talk to each other and say, 'From now on, we shall be as relatives.' They smile and then wrap their scarves around the decision document that they have both received and return home. This is very important."

Even a decision agreed to by all parties could lose its finality at whatever moment the parties no longer agreed to it. The Tibetan idea of the "non-decay of an issue," *rulsubmé (rul sub med),* was related to the concept of consent because reconciliation was not always lasting. "Fighting and disputes, these two do not decay [with time]," says a Tibetan proverb. "Ill words spoken in the summer don't rot; ill words spoken in the winter don't freeze." In Anglo-American law the principles of *stare decisis* (a previous decision on similar facts is binding precedent) and *res judicata* (a judgment on the merits of a case is final and a bar to subsequent action) generally do not allow a decided case to be reopened. In Tibet, however, even after a signed document had been issued by a conciliator or court, the case could be reconsidered by the parties at any later date.

However astonishing from the Western point of view, this feature of the conciliation and judicial system was a source of pride for most Tibetans, who cited the freedom to disagree that it allowed. It was considered a beneficial aspect of the legal system which promoted harmony, catharsis, reconciliation, and truth. From the Tibetan perspective, if the parties continued or resumed fighting or exhibiting enmity, no true decision had been reached. Until they accepted a decision and stopped disputing, conflict could go on indefinitely.

Great flexibility in choice and level of forum and the type of legal procedure were combined in the Tibetan legal system with freedom of movement and the non-decay of issues. Tibetans could start a case at any of a wide variety of levels in any of the four different types of procedure (Chapter 10) and then move back and forth between levels, forums, and procedures. Indeed, the amount of leeway and play in the system was one of the key reasons that Asian scholars presumed for many years that no Tibetan legal system existed.

This case provides one example: Two peasant families got into a fight about a long-term land lease. The Sonam family stopped paying the yearly rent, and Lobsang, of the landowning family, got angry and pulled a stone out of the Sonam house foundation, causing the whole house to fall down. The local headman talked to both families and decided for Lobsang, but Sonam would not agree. Then Sonam petitioned the Cabinet in Lhasa (several legal levels above the headman). The Cabinet requested that the parties and the headman all come to Lhasa for a hearing and referred the case to the High Court. Sonam went to a noble family head in a different region and asked him to represent the Sonam family. Lobsang's representative and the headman went to the High Court in Lhasa, which stated that it could not proceed without an appearance by the petitioner, Sonam. The Cabinet sent a letter to the noble family requesting that Sonam come to Lhasa. In the end, however, Lobsang's representative and the local headman traveled to the noble's estate, which resulted in a decision letter from the noble family stating that Sonam should go back to his land.

Although this case, called *kachu mépa* (*kha mchu med pa*), "The Case That Never Happened," can be interpreted in many ways, it aptly demonstrates the practice of hopping from level to level, forum to forum, procedure to procedure. The strategies and manipulations of the two parties illuminate the dynamic, flexible characteristics of the legal system:

1. Cases could be started at any of a wide variety of levels and procedures and then move up or down.
2. Authorities and forums were not "legal level specific": that is, taking cases only after proper exhaustion of remedies and with appropriate subject matter. In the case just described, the High Court was an appropriate forum for a local squabble.
3. Except for the government courts, authorities and forums were not "legal procedure specific." Thus a High Court judge could handle family disputes brought to him at home and was not required to use just one kind of legal procedure at all times.
4. The choice of forum, authority, and procedure had to be agreed to by both the parties and the deciding authority, or the case would not go forward.
5. The factors affecting where a case was started were social status, occupation, social connections, attitude or orientation of an individual toward conflict, information availability, and the locus of the incident.
6. The Tibetan legal system was not of the "linear-chain" variety in which the subject matter of the dispute determined the level at which one entered the system, the forum, authority, procedures, and possible sanctions. (Americans have a distinct linear-chain model of legal processing such that if one commits a parking offense, one goes to parking court, not the Supreme Court; is processed expeditiously with parking court procedure; and gets a parking fine, not jail for ten years.)

Cases in Tibet, then, were very flexible, and did not decay, *rulsubmé*, until both parties to the dispute achieved true agreement, *loka zotap su dowa*. In the interim, most cases remained dynamically open and capable of being brought to the same forum repeatedly or to a mixture of forums, levels, and procedures in any sequence.[7]

Risk and Responsibility

From the Tibetan point of view, involvement in this world means acceptance of its risks and dangers, *nyenka* (*nyen ka*). The burden is on the actor to watch his or her actions and accept their consequences: a traveler on the road should look where he is going; a trespasser or guest is responsible for her actions; a purchaser must examine the quality of his purchase; an owner should safeguard her possessions. The rule

Plate 25. Bookseller's stall in Lhasa. 1920. (Pitt Rivers Museum, University of Oxford)

enunciated by a businessman from Shigatse was assuredly caveat emptor: "In business transactions, we say that people should look to the articles that they are buying or selling, and then there is no dispute. If they do not see the article, then this is different."

The relationship between acceptance of risk and karma was a subtle one. Karma was used both as a rationalization in cases in which the social sanctions were not strong and as a reason for accepting risk in other situations. The blind, crazy, or young Tibetan who was injured by falling into a hole on another's property did so "because of his karma"; the landowner had no responsibility, because such an action was "bound to happen." The victim had to accept the risks and consequences of the actions in which he or she was engaged unless it could be demonstrated that the other party had had a bad motivation in placing the hole there.

On the other hand, although an individual accepted risk for him- or herself, members of a community, village, neighborhood, or household recognized that they had responsibility, *ganjan ('gan can)*, for the other members of that group. In many cases, both their religious values and the government enforced their concern. Neighbors were expected to report a crime if the family affected had not done so; all members of a household were ultimately responsible for the household tax; everyone involved in a legal case could be held responsible if the key actors did not respond or were not apprehended.

This view provides an interesting contrast to the traditional American jurisprudential distinction between omission and commission, which places social responsibility only on a person who acts or commits, not on a person who omits or does not act. Such a distinction did not apply in Tibet, because there one had a general duty to act in a socially responsible fashion. Thus, an adult watching an unrelated child drown would be held liable for failing to aid another human under the general Buddhist duty to act in a moral and socially responsible fashion. Unless special circumstances pertain, such as a parental duty to a child, an American adult has no legal duty or responsibility to help. Tibetans find such an attitude repulsive and inhuman.

The much wider range of persons liable for the results of criminal acts in Tibet than in modern Western countries created a large net of social responsibility. A similarly wide range could make claims for compensation based on their relation to the victim. Tibetans viewed the reciprocal nature of social responsibility as a means of increasing the social harmony of the entire group. For example, anyone who bought stolen goods, whether a "fence" or an innocent person, could be called into court and punished under the Tibetan reasoning expressed in the proverb that the path of a thief and a black-bottomed pot were the same: both stained the hands of those who touched them. In a long chain of events that caused a final negative act (such as a fire that spread and killed animals on a distant farm), Tibetans would state that all the persons along the way had responsibility to watch for such circumstances and would in part be liable.

Causation

Two basic forms of causation were used for legal analysis: root cause, *tsa wa* (*rtsa ba*), and immediate cause, *ken* (*rkyen*), both derived from the Buddhist scriptures. A man from Sakya explained this distinction:

> In Tibet, all disputes were investigated from the root cause, or background of the fight, not just the particular incident. *Tsa wa*, or root cause, is the more important because it is the cause of their fight, whereas the secondary or immediate cause, *ken*, is what has happened now.
>
> So in one case I know, two men met on the road, and one was drunk, and the other accused the drunk of stealing from him a year before. The drunk got mad at the accusation, and they began to fight. Now the root cause of the argument is the year-old theft. On the spot, the immediate cause of the argument is the accusation of theft. There are only these two.

The concept of proximate cause in Anglo-American law looks for an unbroken link that joins cause to result without intervening causes: that is, for the primary or moving cause producing the injurious result. The Roman codes and their European successors echo this idea in the phrase *no remota causa sed proxima spectatur* (the immediate and not the remote cause is to be considered). These causational schemes would in most cases relegate the Tibetan notion of root cause to background information rather than consider it a key factor.

A divorce case serves as an example. A Tibetan husband and wife got into a large

argument about household property. After several serious physical fights had occurred, the two came to court for a divorce and division of property. When questioned about the history of their marriage, the husband related that he had been
cuckolded by a close friend many years earlier. The Tibetan judge deciding the case
called this previous act of adultery by the wife the root cause of the divorce proceedings; the current disagreement was called the immediate cause. The wife's guilt was
considered by the judge to be the greater, given that her acts in the past constituted
the root cause of the present suit. In an American divorce case (prior to no-fault
divorce), one spouse's act of adultery ten years earlier would be considered useful
only as background information or as one part in a permanent pattern of abuse; it
would not, contrary to the Tibetan case, establish that spouse as the primary guilty
party.

The law codes echo these two causal concepts at every turn. They cite adultery as a
very bad crime, largely because it is the root cause of many serious offenses such as
fighting and murder. A conciliator investigating a family separation suit was instructed to look for the *tsa wa*—the root cause for the separation—as well as the
types of agreements made by the parties.[8] The nature of a significant and appropriate
root cause was culturally determined: cuckolding for divorce and a prior theft for a
drunken argument were considered appropriate.

Even when a cause (whether root or immediate) and its effect were understood as
linked, guilt did not always lie with the causal agent. Attenuation of the circumstances and the motivation of the individuals were also important considerations. To
describe cases in this category, Tibetans used proverbs: for example, "If you don't
place a stone marker, a bird can't land on it. If the bird doesn't fly up, the horse
[going by] won't scare. If the horse doesn't scare, the rider won't fall." Although the
responsibility for having placed the stone marker did lie with the landowner, the
circumstances that led to the accident were so attenuated that he could not be blamed
for the rider's fall. It is also important to recall here the foregoing discussion of the
nature of conflict (Chapter 5), which pointed to the multidirectionality and simul-
taneity of cause-and-effect calculation in Tibet.

Factoring, Evidence, and the Uniqueness of Cases

In recounting suits from former years, Tibetans often listed the points or factors,
rig (*rigs*), brought forward by the parties and the court. This tendency undoubtedly
derived from analytical distinctions in Buddhism and Buddhist canon law, the Vinaya. Different factors were considered significant for different cases, and it was most
important to arrive at the correct factors for deciding the specific case at hand.

Nagarjuna, the great Indian Buddhist scholar of the second century, set out the
four factors for analyzing the Ten Nonvirtuous Acts: the object of the action, *shi*
(*gzhi*); the motivation of the actor, *sampa* (*bsam pa*); the action itself, *jorwa* (*sbyor ba*);
and the completion of the action, *thartuk* (*mthar thug*). The weight of the karma
attached to an act was determined by six factors: the nature of the karma; the force of
thought or mental strength with which the act was committed; the severity of the
action (killing invoked the heaviest karma, idle gossip the lightest); the type of object

(some objects, such as one's parents, would have greater karmic effect than others); whether there was constant commitment, continual repetition of an act; and the opponent forces or amount of virtuous action opposing the bad act.

When Tibetans were asked how a particular case would be decided, some cited as the basis for decision the four or six factors listed above. Others included the size of the injury, the social position of the individuals, the area of occurrence, mitigating circumstances such as self-defense, the fairness of the judge, or the truth-telling of the parties. Some mentioned the law code's use of the three necessary aspects of all cases: preparation for the act, its actual occurrence, and its conclusion or consequence—which is terminology also employed in Buddhist meditation.[9] This kind of factoral reasoning permeated every discussion of an individual case and is illustrated in the comments of a former legal representative in Lhasa:

> Even in a case of stealing, a decision cannot be the same for all people, so it can never be equal (in that sense).
>
> There are always many bases for investigation, such as the size of the action taken, the type and cost of property stolen, the owner of the property stolen, where the property was stolen, was it done in day or night, done secretly or not, breaking into a building, the thief himself as a person, the number of times he has stolen, where the thief comes from, why he stole the articles, his degree of contrition, and many other things.

Tibetan factoring did not necessarily result in skeletonization and decontextualization of the facts. Instead, the conciliator or judge took the points presented by the petitioner and factored or clarified them into a series of number positions, which were then placed before the opposition for agreement or rebuttal, refashioning, and response. In non-criminal and even in many criminal cases, the parties usually determined what was to be factored. Any details they left out were generally omitted from the record; there was no need to clarify them. By the same token, when the parties gave extensive contextualization, it was included in the record.

Whether or not there was enough proof, *kungkel* (*khungs skyel*), to support a case was a matter of investigation by the individual Tibetan before she or he brought it to a conciliator or judge. In the words of a former legal representative: "We had to investigate the case ourselves before we went to court to be sure. In court, a petitioner will always be asked for his proof from the judge, and then the judge will say to him, 'If you don't have enough proof for this case, it is better not to file it.' Moreover, since Tibetans really don't want to file in court if they can avoid it, because it is considered complicated and difficult, if they do actually go to court, they usually have sufficient proof."

Two types of evidence or "verified" proof, *rato* (*ra sprod*), were considered equally valuable: physical evidence and oral evidence.[10] For example, the petitioner in a case involving a physical injury was expected to produce physical evidence, such as the knife used by the other party (which was wrapped in a white cotton cloth and kept in court) and the wound on her arm. Her story of how she had been injured with the knife, if delivered without a document, was oral evidence. Witnesses could be called to give both kinds of evidence. Each petitioner was expected to have enough proof of the offense to substantiate his or her side of the case through witnesses and these two kinds of evidence. This also meant knowing the factors that established a case and the types of proof necessary for each of the various factors.

During the decision-making process, Tibetans very rarely cited previous legal situations as examples for their present circumstances, nor did they refer to decision documents from cases or even argue from example. They amassed no sets of previous cases into categories to create lines of precedent. Their reasoning patterns in legal matters displayed no strong sense of either the logic of antecedents or the logic of consequence: that is, relating the particular back to a set of prefigured cases or concepts, or relating it forward to the possible consequences of the outcome.[11] Instead, they used religious principles, proverbs, rhetoric, factors, and their understanding of the ancient legal rules.

When I presented Tibetans with a series of hypothetical repetitive circumstances (in an attempt to approach the question of precedent from a different angle), they responded uniformly that each case was unique, *daba metse* (*'dra ba mi tshad*). They said that the repetition of a single factor—say, the character of the individual—was more helpful than developing a general legal rule to encompass all the cases. The comments of one who had been clerk in a southwest regional district court in the 1940s reflect this idea:

> I heard a divorce case before the judge ten years back when the case was brought to court and decided. After ten years, the same man has found a new wife and is engaged in new fighting. The people at court will know this man's old case with his former wife, and his previous actions, and in our small area, everyone will know the case. In this second case, if the wife is completely wrong, she will be punished. Otherwise, he will receive a very heavy punishment because he has done it before and is repeating the same offense.

When asked about decision-making in two hypothetical cases that concerned different individuals but had exactly the same factors, Tibetans merely denied that this was possible. One legal representative responded that the two might, by chance, be decided similarly according to local area rules, but not because of common factors. "How could the cases be the same when some factors were sure to be different?" he asked. The same reasoning prevailed when Tibetans were confronted with actual cases that had had identical results. The possibility of precedent formation was further limited by the practice of storing court documents chronologically.[12] The Tibetan concept of equality, fundamentally rooted in radical particularism and the route to enlightenment, lay within this framework of factoring, uniqueness of circumstances, and an awareness of the social aspects of each case.[13]

In short, in most situations, parties, judges, and conciliators engaged in factoring, viewed each case as unique, did not cite previous legal situations as precedents, and therefore did not elaborate precedential chains of legal rules based on cases.

CHAPTER THIRTEEN

Legal Space and Movement

Again, if the case is mutually settled by conciliation outside of court after being filed in the court, half of the court fee is required to be paid according to the extent of the fault, and then the case may be withdrawn to be settled internally.
—Ganden Podrang Code of the Dalai Lamas

What were the basic components of legal space in Tibet and how were they arranged? How did the conciliators, clerks, and petitioners move through this legal space? What constituted a "court," and what offices—permanently or occasionally —served in that capacity? How could they be approached?

Ritual Legal Spaces

Like most rooms in Tibet, courtrooms and formal places of conciliation tended to be rectangular with a single entrance. The basic elements were (1) a sitting area for the conciliators or judges, (2) a place for a clerk, and (3) an area for a third person to stand or sit and speak. The floor space was divided into more-honored and less-honored zones: the area near a door was least honored; the area farthest from the entrance and preferably against a wall without windows was the most honored. Thus, the adjudicator or conciliator's mattress was placed farthest from the door, the clerk's mattress nearby but closer to the door. The area for the disputant or witness was always immediately adjacent to the door, allowing persons being questioned to enter and exit easily.

This pattern follows basic Tibetan ideas of social ideology in a spatial format (see Figures 8 and 9). The most honored object (altar, picture) or person is placed farthest from the door against a solid wall; beds and sitting areas—often the same pieces of furniture used interchangeably—are placed against the other walls, abutting one another; and the area near the door is reserved for storage or such activities as the entrance of guests. The most honored spot might shift somewhat according to the location of the most important person or object in the room, with that space becoming the most dignified and the spaces around it in concentric circles decreasingly

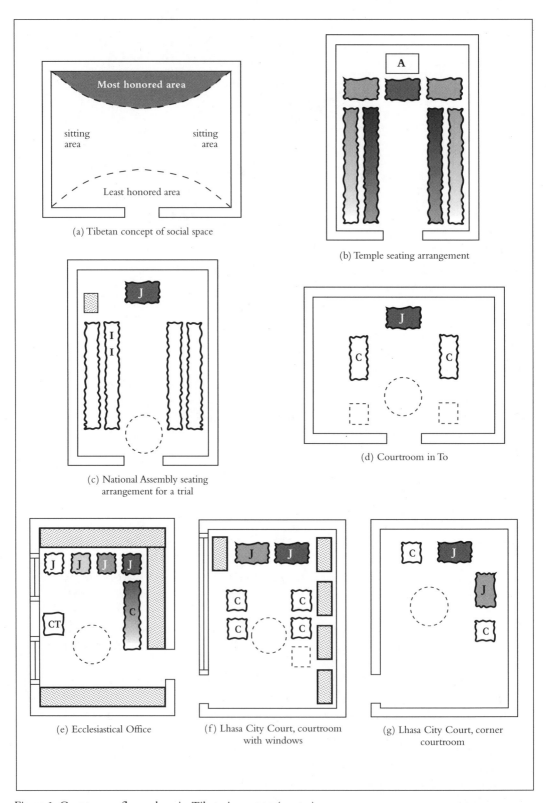

Figure 8. Courtroom floor plans in Tibet circa 1950 (part 1).

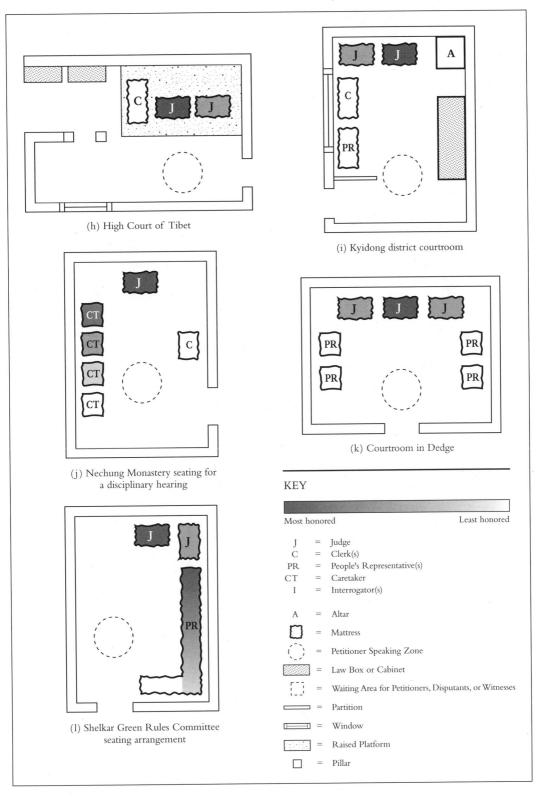

(h) High Court of Tibet

(i) Kyidong district courtroom

(j) Nechung Monastery seating for
a disciplinary hearing

(k) Courtroom in Dedge

(l) Shelkar Green Rules Committee
seating arrangement

KEY

Most honored   Least honored

J	=	Judge
C	=	Clerk(s)
PR	=	People's Representative(s)
CT	=	Caretaker
I	=	Interrogator(s)
A	=	Altar
	=	Mattress
	=	Petitioner Speaking Zone
	=	Law Box or Cabinet
	=	Waiting Area for Petitioners, Disputants, or Witnesses
	=	Partition
	=	Window
	=	Raised Platform
	=	Pillar

Figure 9. Courtroom floor plans in Tibet circa 1950 (part 2).

dignified. Also, a location to the right of this important person was more revered than one to the left, the spaces decreasing in intensity of importance along either side. If numerous persons of an official capacity were present, long rows of mattresses were placed on both sides of the room with positions of honor moving down the row toward the door.

Vertically as well as horizontally, legal space was arranged in a simple hierarchy. The most important persons and objects were expected to be the highest in the room, and each descending level was of decreasing importance. For example, in one courtroom a picture of the Dalai Lama hung on the wall above the backs of the judges in the most revered spot. The adjudicators or conciliators had the highest mattresses, followed by those of the clerks and then the caretaker of the room. The one exception was the disputant, who stood throughout most proceedings and therefore remained higher than the judges in some courtrooms—but only because standing was viewed as a less dignified posture socially than sitting. As one Tibetan stated, "They have argued and therefore don't deserve to sit."

The vertical hierarchical component seems to have been more important than floor position zones if these two came into conflict in a legal space. When it was not possible to seat an important person opposite the door, he or she would be accommodated near the door or in the middle of the room, but it was considered impossible to convey his or her dignity adequately if others in the room sat in higher seats. Thus, the most important indicator of the dignity of a legal actor was an elevated mattress or seat.

Even temporary places of conciliation or court proceedings, whether in the provinces or the city, inside or outside, retained this basic spatial format. When chieftains in the far western province of *to* (*stod*) convened to establish their list of governance rules and decide a few legal cases, they seated themselves according to the diagram in Figure 8d. When the National Assembly of Tibet was called to deliberate a case of malfeasance by a regent in the 1940s, the seating was arranged in a similar fashion (Figure 8c).

While the respective positions of a judge or conciliator, clerk, and disputant were the three basic components of every legal space, most had several other features: windows (if indoors), small writing tables (often individual ones for each adjudicator and clerk), huge storage boxes and cabinets for filing documents, open shelves and hanging devices for holding current documents, posted edicts and lists for reference, wood-fired urns for heating, and miscellaneous equipment for counting, safeguarding the premises (keys), and writing (ink, paper, pens, seals, wax, and knives).[1] On the whole, legal spaces were free of decoration, religious objects, altars, or pictures. Tibetans stated that upon entering they knew these rooms were not religious in nature. When empty of their actors, legal spaces looked like the interior of any administrative office.

The High Court of Tibet was a unique exception to this description of courtroom space because it was the first court and a continually sitting court. Instead of one room, the High Court consisted of five interconnected areas with a single entrance. In the main courtroom the judges and clerks sat on a raised platform separated from the disputants by a wooden divider screen some four feet high. Anyone approaching these judges to give a statement or to be questioned was immediately presented with

Plate 26. The seats and tables of the judges in the courtroom in Shigatse district. Charles Bell's comments: "In the front of the seats are the tables with pens, sealing wax, etc., on them. On back of each seat is painted on silk [the] three gems (*norbu*). Behind the seats on left side is a wooden screen, ornamented with circles painted red; surrounded by gold tracery." 1933–34. (Bell Collection, Mss Eur F 80/291, J286, Oriental and India Office Collections, The British Library)

a clear indication of the distance between his or her respective status and that of the court judges and clerks (Figure 8h).[2]

Because most legal spaces were single-entrance rooms, judges, conciliators, clerks, and bailiffs could not exit through side doors to discuss issues, eat, or relax while a case was in progress. Nor could they choose a time for their entrance after the other participants had arrived. Thus, with no alternative spaces for the actors, legal space was also divided temporally. It was not operable as a legal forum until the adjudicators arrived, and even though the clerks and caretakers could attend to business in their absence, no actual trial proceedings took place until the adjudicators were seated. Judges and conciliators of any rank could step over the mattresses of clerks who were working but never clerks over their superiors.

Once seated, the judges or conciliators engaged in legal business and did not move around the space; carrying out tasks in the rest of the room was the job of clerks, bailiffs, or helpers. It was an adjudicator's prerogative to regulate the affairs of the forum, but many left to a senior clerk or caretaker such tasks as keeping a list of the daily cases. If more than one person presided, they were customarily seated in descending order by general seniority or government rank, not seniority of tenure within that office or forum. In their own rows, both adjudicators and clerks were seated in descending order from the most to the least senior. There seems to have been some variation in the location of the clerks' mattresses with respect to the judges: in the Ecclesiastical Office the senior clerk sat closest to the senior judge, whereas the two clerks in the High Court both sat near the senior judge.

Former judges and conciliators stated that when working with others during a legal proceeding they operated as a unit, and all members were expected to participate equally in decisions. Although personality, energy, enthusiasm, competence, interest, and seniority in rank played essential roles in determining the weight of different actors in decision-making, these were balanced by the common view that shared responsibility for a decision substantially reduced the possibility of incorrect action and karmic responsibility.

No panel of government judges exceeded four members unless it was a specially constituted court, but other groups of decision-makers could be quite large. The number of clerks varied widely. In the Ecclesiastical Office there were at least twelve; in the High Court there were only two. Courts with few clerks often compensated with a large staff of caretakers or sweepers who handled clients, bags of evidence, and the delivery of documents and messages. Long-term storage was often in a separate room in these courts.

Official legal spaces in Tibet were not, in general, easily visible to the public but bounded and closed, with both movement and visibility highly regulated. There were no public viewing areas in the formal courts. Some legal forums had windows looking out onto courtyards or other open spaces, and one Tibetan recalled being asked with several others to observe a trial in the Lhasa City Court by looking through the windows (Figure 8f), but this was not a common practice. Rather, legal proceedings were generally private, in keeping with the notion that disputes were unhappy and undignified matters to be approached with contrition and regret. Some Tibetans from the provinces spoke of hearings that took place in front of others in the large courtyards of district buildings, but most reported that cases were heard in closed rooms where the official and the clerk were the only listeners. It was also thought that this closed style facilitated the Tibetan form of private, individual questioning of each disputant and so prevented the opposing parties from hearing the speaker's testimony.

Movement within the legal space itself by disputants and other actors was limited to the entranceway and the speaking area. One of four deferential postures was expected of disputants before the adjudicators; from least to most deferential they were sitting, standing, kneeling, and full prostration. Sitting, usually at the end of the clerk's bench or on the floor, without a mattress, was the most dignified position for a disputant either waiting to testify or testifying. This position was used in the provincial courts in civil cases. Standing with bent head to indicate respect for the person addressed was the accepted posture, however; most disputants remained standing during all their testimony and questioning. Kneeling was reserved for presumed criminals, as was prostration—the most severe and least dignified posture.

The zone of questioning in every legal forum was a liminal space in which only the disputant remained—uneasily—for long periods of time. Clerks and caretakers passed over and through this area, but none stayed there. For the majority of Tibetans it was a singularly lonely and vulnerable spot fraught with embarrassment, a place that required direct confrontation in a society that valued indirect suggestion. Clearness of thought and volubility were impeded in the weak-hearted who stood before a row of adjudicators. Since the zone of questioning had as its primary features two of the least dignified aspects of any room, the door and the floor, its occupant was at best marginal. Even though it was an area reserved for the disputant's use, the values of the society put those who entered it at a disadvantage, for voicing and explicating dissension were acts presumed to indicate a lack of Buddhist inner morality. So it was with great reservation that most Tibetans approached such an experience. The very difficulty of entering this zone was a curb for many who thought of initiating legal proceedings.

Court Categories

Tibetans made two important kinds of distinctions between types of legal forums. The first was between offices that only occasionally heard legal cases, and permanent courts that sat continually: that is, between administrative offices that sometimes switched from their regular duties to the consideration of disputes, and offices of the government that had almost exclusively courtlike functions. The Tibetan use of special reference terms for judges presents this distinction clearly; officials in chiefly administrative offices were not called judges unless a specific legal case was being tried before them. Almost all courts in Tibet were occasional except two: a district court in Lhasa (described in Chapter 21) and the High Court of Tibet (Chapter 23). These two permanent courts were by far the most famous and prestigious in the country.

The second distinction was between direct-access and referral forums: those one could approach directly as a petitioner, and those to which a petitioner was referred by another office. The difference was perceived to be significant in several ways. First, the judge in a referral court had to answer both to the parties and to the referring office, which increased his accountability and placed a heavier burden on him to comply with normal standards of decision-making. Second, many more officials were involved and aware of a referred case, which made visits to a judge at home and influence peddling more complex, difficult, and circuitous. Third, the possibilities for resolution in nonofficial forums—that is, taking the case to a conciliator or deciding among parties—were generally decreased once a case had been sent to a referral court. Fourth, Tibetans stated that the process of referral meant that the case would be protracted in length. And finally, most referral courts were part of an internal governmental circuit that could involve more than the initial referral. For example, a case sent to the High Court (the only continual referral court) traveled, at the very least, from the Cabinet to the High Court, back to the Cabinet, up to the Dalai Lama's Office, back to the Cabinet, and finally back to the High Court before it was completed. (See Figure 15 on page 266.)

The referral process inside the central government in Lhasa (described extensively in Part Four) did not simply follow the Western distinction between appellate and lower courts. An appellate court in the United States has jurisdiction to review and possibly amend cases already heard in an inferior court. A referral, as described here, was the process of sending a case on to another office or court for the purpose of having an advisory decision drafted which would then be reviewed by the referring office or court. Referral was not necessarily from an inferior to a superior court.

The issue of whether a forum was a direct-access or a referral court was complex: it could be both direct-access and referral, or exclusively one or the other. Certain forums functioned as referral courts for certain kinds of cases, as direct-access courts for others. In the provinces of Tibet the district offices all served as occasional, direct-access courts. Many of the occasional courts in the central government, such as the Accounting Office, were only indirectly accessible because petitions had first to travel to the Cabinet in Lhasa and then be referred to the Accounting Office for deliberation. Of the two permanent courts in Lhasa, the lower district court heard both direct-access and referral cases, whereas the High Court of Tibet could be reached by referral only.

Tibetan appeal procedure—unlike that of the United States—was a separate process involving both continual and occasional, direct and referral courts. For example, when a district officer in *kyidong* (*skyid grong*) was petitioned, the parties approached him directly, and he decided the issue in his office in its occasional function as a judicial court. If the parties did not agree with his decision, at their request the district officer appealed the case to the Cabinet Office of the central government. The Cabinet acted as a general clearinghouse for all nonecclesiastical government petitions; it could itself be an occasional, direct-access court or refer the case for an advisory decision to another appropriate office or court.

Excursus: Writing and Documents

As traditionally represented, the Tibetan writing system was introduced to preserve the words of the Buddha. This made the forming of letters an important, sacred, and meritorious act. Highly valued from very ancient times in Tibet, excellent handwriting and a knowledge of correct spelling and sentence formation were absolutely essential skills for a member of the government staff, and their acquisition often consumed a major part of a child's education and required instruction from several teachers.

There are numerous variations on the basic script, each of which had a different use. The most formal and most difficult script, *uchen* (*dbu chan*), meaning "with head," requires individual formation of each letter in exact stroke order, making it slow and laborious to produce. It was reserved for very formal documents and for the carved wood blocks used to print Buddhist and other texts. The fastest and easiest, *kug* (*'khyug*), or "running script," has informal, cursive letters that are stylistically freer.

Initially, however, students were instructed in a script of intermediate difficulty, the classic elongated form called *umé* (*dbu med*), "without head," and then several of its variations: *tsuring* (*tshugs ring*), *tsutun* (*tshugs thung*), *tsuchung* (*tshugs chung*), and *tsukug* (*tshugs 'khyug*). Though all these scripts are variations on the original *uchen,* each one has stylistic conventions that separate it from the others. There is also an official correspondence script called *duktsa,* also used for some law codes.

The script used in a legal or administrative document depended on the type of document and the issuing official's ability. A lower-level official in an outlying area might not have a government scribe available to him or know the necessary script style himself. Because even the uneducated Tibetan would rarely submit an official letter that was incorrectly spelled or in an unacceptable script, he or she would travel at length or pay to have it drafted correctly by a scribe.

Edicts from the Dalai Lama or the Cabinet, the documents that came from the central government in government script, were thought by many to be works of calligraphic art. The more formal edicts for important occasions were copied on a very expensive Tibetan paper with the upper portion backed in expensive cloth. Several of the oldest formal documents in Tibetan, such as a special document unfolded once a year at the Mon Lam Festival, were written entirely on yellow silk brocade. The script used for such an edict would be a very fine *umé* done in a large style.

An administrative clerk, seated on his low mattress, spent the day receiving, reading, copying, and correcting documents between sporadic conversations with visitors, drinking tea, instructing assistants, and checking the calligraphy of his pupils. Pupils were trained in administrative offices to write correspondence correctly, having already been through the basic school program of learning to write on slate or wooden boards with chalked lines.

Preparing a document correctly required a particular body posture: sitting cross-legged on the floor with the back strongly curved and the back of the left hand supported by the left knee, the paper held between the fingers of the left hand. In preparation for writing, a large sheet of paper was folded accordion style into a long, very narrow strip that showed only two or three lines of text at a time. As Tibetan script is written in horizontal lines from left to right, a scrivener held the pen in the right hand and used the middle three fingers of the left hand as a backing, feeding the strip smoothly to the left with his left little finger and thumb. When the strip was filled, the paper was refolded to uncover the next empty strip. This system may sound awkward to a Westerner, but clerks and officials managed to write very quickly in government script with only their hand for support. Most of the older Tibetans I met, given the choice of a table or their hand, still preferred this method for Tibetan writing, although for a particularly unwieldy document, a scrivener might rest his left hand against a table or mattress instead of his left knee.

Numerous varieties of paper were available in Tibet, their names usually a conjunction of their place of origin and the root of the word for paper. For example, *kongsho* (*kong shog*), a type of paper from the region of Kongpo, is a contraction of that place name and the word for paper, *shogu* (*shog bu*). Special papers, made of wood fibers from local trees, were sent as part of the produce taxes from that area to the central government. Once they reached Lhasa, the sheets from each paper-producing area were ranked according to quality, thinness, absorption, and other characteristics and kept in government storehouses. Writing supplies were highly regulated: the Office of the Dalai Lama ordered specific qualities of paper and inks that could be used only by that office; offices at the next highest level had their own exclusive paper and ink, and so on; offices at the lowest level were issued a few standard grades, from excellent to poor, on which to draft their missives.

Sheets of document paper came in many sizes, varying from eighteen to forty-eight inches in both width and length. Each government document was expected to be inscribed in its entirety on one continuous surface of paper no more than a yard wide but of unlimited length; thus, many sheets of paper might be glued together end to end, with an overlap of less than an inch, to complete one document. Each overlap was imprinted with the office seal to indicate that the next sheet had been officially added. As the scribe continued his writing, he glued on a new sheet, sealed it, filled that sheet, attached and sealed another one, and so on. In a long legal case the final decision document could extend fifteen feet or more; in Dharamsala, India, and also in the Bodleian Library in Oxford, England, I have personally unfolded several documents that stretched across an entire room.

At the bottom, the document was completed with a date, the inscription of the sender or sending office, and an inked seal stamp. The document was then folded up from the bottom, over and over, in strips no wider than four inches—usually along the original crease marks made by the scribe—and then from side to side in thirds or in half. The result was a two- or three-tiered package of perhaps twelve to eighteen inches by four to five inches, which was then marked as to its content in one corner on the outside.

Every Tibetan office, every Tibetan association, and every Tibetan family (or individual) of import had a seal of its own (made of wood or metal) for use in official documents. Many were formed from religious or personal symbols, regular Tibetan script, or the letters of an ornamental script called *lantsa* (*lan tshwa*). A seal was either kept in a locked box inside a cabinet or worn on the belt of the individual who was personally responsible for safeguarding it. Only the judge or a clerk appointed by the judge could use the official seal of a court.

Documents were stamped at every correction point in the document (with a half-seal mark) to indicate that only authorized alterations had been made in the text, at the joins between sheets, at the bottom (in the appropriate ink) by the drafting office, and at the bottom or on the back of a legal decision by all the parties and their guarantors. If the document was sent in an envelope, the envelope was closed with wax and impressed with the same office seal.

A large part of the training of both a clerk and an official was also devoted to the formalized, stylistic requirements of Tibetan correspondence. Form books, called *yigkur namshak* (*yig bskur rnam gzhag*), gave the prescribed words and sentence sequences for addressing different parties and conveying different messages. A student learned these standardized formats by copying letters with his tutor.

The real message of a Tibetan letter or document—text, subtext, and medium combined—was carried in several ways. The choice of paper, script, and ink indicated the status and possibly the wealth of the sender and the importance of the recipient. A document stamped with a seal indicated that the sealor had authorized and agreed to the contents (an unsealed document was perhaps an office copy or was meant to be informal in some way). The level of honorific language and formalized wording revealed the writer's education and training and degree of deference to the receiver. A well-trained official was able to recognize the correct format and wording for the various types of official documents and correspondence; indeed, many of the former Tibetan officials I interviewed could recognize the handwriting of other officials and clerks. The few paragraphs between the standardized opening and closing sections told the reader whatever factual message the writer intended to convey.

Cloth backing usually indicated that the subject matter was important, that the message was a weighty one (such as an official edict), or that the sending office was very high in the government (such as the Cabinet). If the document had real importance or would have long-term use, the top section of the first sheet was glued to a piece of cloth big enough to be folded over the top and sides of the folded document for protection. The fabric in this case could be patterned or plain cotton, silk, or even silk brocade, depending on the importance of the contents and the sending office.

Paper envelopes were another form of protection usually made by a separate staff of clerk-stationers to fit the folded documents being sent out. Taking measurements first, a stationer constructed an envelope according to the specifications, using a metal or wooden blank the size of the letter. (Outside of Lhasa, government clerks and other scribes generally performed this task themselves.)

All the folded documents pertinent to a particular administrative or legal case— witness statements, land records, petitions, final decision—were kept in that case's file—sometimes, but not ordinarily, in envelopes. Files were made of white cotton cloth and constructed to order by tailors. First, a white cotton cloth was laid out on a flat surface, and the various documents of the case were placed down the middle of the cloth in the correct sequence, from the index at the top to the final decision at the bottom. Strings run from top to bottom on both sides were marked to be stitched to the cloth between the documents to hold them in. From right, left, and bottom, the cloth was folded over the documents, measured to cover them completely, cut and hemmed. At the top, a long piece of cloth was left and also hemmed.

Filling the file was simple. After being stitched, it was again laid on a flat surface, and the documents were inserted under the strings. The overlaps of cotton cloth were folded over; the whole file was rolled up from the bottom; and the extra band of cloth at the top was wrapped around and around for protection and tucked in to secure the bundle. Finally, a small paper label was glued on the outside for reference.

Documents and files were stored in four ways: on open shelves, hanging from strings or held behind a strap against a wall or pillar (as shown in Plate 23), in stacked cupboards or cabinets, and in large wooden boxes. Officials mentioned the last as the most common permanent storage system, describing large wooden boxes that opened at the top and were filled with cases filed in chronological order. Boxes used only for law cases had a special name, *timgam* (*khrims sgam*), or "law box." The chests were labeled alphabetically, and a short description on the outside indicated their contents; inside was a much more detailed index. In the High Court of Tibet, chests of this sort were also used to store sacks of evidence, robes for the prisoners, and various supplies. A special room in the Cathedral Complex building called the *ganjokang* (*'gan 'jog khang*), or document locker, stored only government documents; its title was probably derived from the word for written contract or document, *gangya* (*'gan rgya*).

In the Office of the Thirteenth Dalai Lama, files and copies of correspondence were kept in rectangular, two-doored cabinets about three feet in height, stacked to form a wall of cupboards. In the cabinet reserved for copies of short correspondence, unfolded letter copies were piled flat with blank sheets between to protect them. Other cabinets held folded documents and cotton-wrapped files.

Each office of the government retained most of its own files, all stored chronologically. Thus, a clerk sent from one office to another for information about a previous case needed its name and approximate date. As there appears to have been no cross-referencing by subject matter or name, the memories of older clerks were the chief repositories of information about the location and contents of files. Many offices did have large record books listing landowners, tax accounts, supplies received, loans made, and other aspects of government administration, and in some instances the time and location of a particular file could be gleaned from these records. Also, parties to a suit who were reintroducing the matter could often supply the dates of their previous legal problems or dated copies of the original documents.

CHAPTER FOURTEEN

Boundaries, Identities, and Levels

When one is called upon to take an oath for the purpose of verification of truth and untruth in the presence of the protecting deities possessing true eyes of wisdom and power to know the unforeseen, the early law texts state thus:

> Do not trap the golden swan.
> Do not let the black venomous snake wriggle downhill.
> Do not aim to hit the black crow.
> Do not beat a pregnant dog.
> Do not string up the tiny red turquoise.
>
> —Tsang Law Code

By the nineteenth century, European lawyers, sociologists, and anthropologists were beginning to question the idea of law as the function and province of the state alone. Eugen Ehrlich, an Austrian legal scholar often cited as the founder of the sociology of law, and Otto von Gierke, a German legal philosopher who wrote on the role of voluntary associations in the law, both noted the difference between two legal levels: the *folk tradition* (Ehrlich called it "living law"), and the *state*.[1] (In the twentieth century, this distinction was discovered anew by American legal academics.[2]) Max Weber wrote of legal systems "guaranteed by authorities other than the state," and pioneers of legal anthropology Karl Llewellyn and E. A. Hoebel stated in their study of the Cheyenne Indians that "there may be found utterly and radically different bodies of 'law' prevailing among these small units."[3]

In the 1960s, Leopold Pospisil's expansion of these ideas into the "theory of the multiplicity of legal levels" had a strong influence on the sociology and anthropology of law. For Pospisil, every society is composed of overlapping subgroups of varying types. Each of these functioning subgroups, including the family, has its own legal system, which operates to maintain social control within that group but may differ greatly from that of other subgroups. Since an individual is commonly a member of several subgroups at the same time (family, school, town, state), it is a matter for investigation which legal level is strongest for that individual.[4] For example, a member of a juvenile gang in the United States may be more concerned about the rules and sanctions of his group than about those of his family or the state; a nun in Tibet may feel more threatened by the loss of robes than by the loss of her family inheritance. Sally Falk Moore has redefined the idea of legal levels into "semi-autonomous social fields" to blur the hard edges of the boundaries and allow for movement between them.[5] Although I use the term "level" here, following the Tibetan terminology, rather than "field," Moore's greater emphasis on the process and on the malleable and multivalent nature of these boundaries fits the Tibetan understanding.

I suggest that identities, units, and levels in the law have multivalent boundaries: that is, their various meanings or values of sameness, uniqueness, or representativeness depend on the context. First, an individual's identity in the law depends on the reference point taken: a member of a family, a member of a household, a member of an association or occupation, a member of a social category, a member of a town. Second, Tibetan society added several different legal units (monasteries, guilds) and many different legal levels or fields where conflicts could be addressed (local conciliators, district officers, courts within the government). Third, identities, units, and levels were all ways of thinking about the same issue in Tibet, given its tax structure and notions of responsibility. For example, a household was (a) an identity for a family member—"I am from the Tsering family/household"; (b) a legal unit with responsibility to the government for taxes and to the local town for participation in certain activities; and (c) a legal level for dispute settlement. This multivalence of boundaries—a level also being a unit and an identity—is one of the most interesting aspects of the Tibetan legal system and perhaps of other legal systems as well. What constitutes an identity, unit, or level and how these boundaries are produced, relate to one another, change, and are maintained are among the most important, and least researched, aspects of the cosmology of law.[6]

A Human Sentient Being

The first key boundary in the radically particularistic cosmology of Tibetan law was a human sentient being (animals were also sentient beings in Tibet). The relationship of this boundary to ideas of reality, karma, and equality provide the foundation for the following discussion.

In Tibetan philosophy, human sentient beings—what we might term "persons," "identities," or "individuals"—are momentary accretions or accumulations of elements that have combined to constitute individual persons with mental consciousness. The doctrine of nonduality reminds us that an accumulation of elements forming an "I" is not "real" in a perfected sense. A Buddha with perfected vision who recognizes the nonexistence of the "I" is simultaneously able to understand that people see her or him as just that, an "I." As Robert Thurman explains: "The rigorous nonduality here is . . . noteworthy. . . . There is no artificial goal set for the philosopher-yogi, such as that he must 'attain ego-loss,' wipe out his naughty 'I' and so forth. Rather he is encouraged to accept as incontrovertible the everyday conventional sense of 'I,' while attaining simultaneously the rational certitude of its intrinsic nonreality."[7] Thus, while the average person may see you as another human, a Buddha or philosopher-yogi sees the everyday conventional "you" but is simultaneously aware that this identity, person, individual, this "you," has no intrinsic reality.

At the same time that the "you" and the "I" have no ultimate reality, in Buddhist philosophy they are also the only entities capable of achieving the ultimate goal of all beings—liberation through enlightenment. With enlightenment, cognition of all types of reality is achieved. As this was the ultimate goal of the Tibetan society as well, the individual was allowed essential freedom to pursue a religious life and religious activities—even if doing so meant disregarding important social and legal commitments. A miscreant who recognized her actions and then took the vows of a religious life as a nun received a lighter penalty. A householder who left his land and tax requirements for life in a monastery was neither arrested nor faulted for not paying his taxes.

Human sentient beings could not avoid the karmic consequences of any of their actions. A judge took on the karmic results of his actions as a judge, regardless of the cloak of governmental office. There were no fictitious legal entities in Tibet, no corporate veils screening individuals from legal and karmic liability.

For a Tibetan thinking in Buddhist terms, the Western idea of the "individual" as a hollow shell, a sort of mask equal to any other regardless of what entity occupies it, is incomprehensible. It is exactly the unique conjunction of circumstances, elements, and karmic seeds that constitutes a human individual, not its absence. If every individual is truly singular, then every action and indeed every misaction of that individual is unique and unlike any other. There may be categories of acts, but no act is actually *like* another for a Tibetan in the sense that it should be treated in exactly the same way.[8]

The legal consequences of these views were innumerable: the absence of extensive categorization in law, factoring as opposed to the categorization of legal events, minimal rule formation, and the lack of precedent. Predictability in the law, an ideological pillar of Western legal systems, was not an issue for Tibetans rooted in Buddhist philosophy.

Identity and Competency in the Law

In Tibet, the qualifications of someone who could be questioned in a conflict were described by the phrase "a mind that can be burdened,"[9] which also meant "worthy of confidence" and "responsible." Certain categories of human sentient beings were not allowed to give evidence in disputes because of particular attributes attached to their cultural identities. American lawyers would call these issues of "capacity" and "competency" rather than identity.

For example, evidence of an age limit showed up in cases concerning children. Eight years appeared to be the significant age at which mental volition was regarded as such that an individual could be held legally responsible for his or her physical acts. When asked about a hypothetical murder by a child, Tibetans responded that the child would be responsible for killing only when she or he was over the age of eight years. If a child under eight hurt someone of any age in Tibet, the act was viewed as innocent and attributable to the karmic background of the person who was injured. In effect, the victim was responsible for the act, and the child was merely an innocent agent working out that person's karma. By nine years of age, however, the child had become a knowing agent and was legally responsible for acts done to another person.

When the child committed an act of impiety or social offense against the mores of the whole community, however, the *karmic* responsibility lay with the child. For example, in 1986 in a refugee community, a child of five years who was staying with one of the nuns took the picture of His Holiness the Dalai Lama, spat on it, threw it on the floor, and stamped on it with her foot. This was viewed as such an outrage that it was considered in a special meeting called by the local head of the nunnery. The decision was that the child should not be punished because—not having reached the age of capacity—she lacked an understanding of what she had done, and her act was due to karma in her previous life. Nevertheless, stigmatization of the child did occur through the final statement by one of the heads of the nunnery: it was obvious from this act, she said, that the child had been no better than a dog in her previous life.

Rationalization in the face of an act that cannot be dealt with socially is one possible interpretation of the attribution of karmic history in these cases of capacity. It is one way of discussing a case that cannot move through a regular social-legal process within the community. Most Tibetans, however, did understand and interpret acts in terms of their karmic causes and effects, regardless of their legal effects, so the difference is primarily a matter of emphasis. Perhaps it is best to say that in the Tibetan view all acts were due to karma, but those acts by children under eight years of age were primarily understood by the community in terms of karmic *causes* as opposed to karmic and legal *consequences*. Age at the other end of the scale—for example, an old person who was infirm of mind and body—was never an issue in any collected case, nor was it discussed.

When questioned about diminished capacity due to mental illness, all Tibetans commented that there were few insane people in Tibet and attributed this variously to life-style, religion, or other factors. Generally, it was said that one should not talk to a crazy person; continuing to do so was itself a sign of craziness. People did not interfere with the insane unless they became dangerous to themselves or others. A competent person who willingly engaged in conversation or interacted with an insane individual was taking on the risks involved; it was not possible for such a person to petition in court against the insane individual or seek compensation for any injury incurred. The mentally ill were simply not competent to sue or be sued, to stand witness, or to act as guarantors.

Those who were simpleminded (which included "dumb" in the physical sense, as well as moronic) were thought of not as separate from normal individuals but rather as "stupid persons." This same word, "stupid," was also used in conjunction with the word for mouth—"mouth-stupid"—to describe a mute person. There is little question that the slow-witted person had a harder time in a courtroom than the verbally clever. On the other hand, simplicity and honesty were viewed as important characteristics in a human being, and judges reported giving weight to the testimony of a man who repeated the same circumstances over and over in a simple way and maintained his version of the case.

Still, business dealings by and with the truly simpleminded seem to have been approached by the courts and others with the recognition that the simpleton did not have full competence. Anyone who chose to deal with such a person (for example, grant an inheritance, lend money, or make a contract) was presumed to have taken the responsibility and accepted the risks. A Tibetan mother with assets to pass on would not allow an idiot son to inherit the estate but would make other arrangements before her death. Cases in this area are few, however, and I collected no actual cases of criminal offenses involving simpletons, but the impression gleaned from conversations with Tibetans was that a simpleton would be punished as a normal person under two conditions: if the offense was serious, and if punishment would prevent him or her from repeating it.

The law codes identify several additional classes of people on the basis of their capacity to participate in legal procedures. The Neudong law code of the fourteenth century has few direct comments on the competency of women and children but does put them in distinct categories. It states, for example, that a child below the age of eight is not responsible for killing a person and need not give victim compensation payment but only make the payments for religious rituals for the dead.

The later Tsang and Dalai Lama codes use metaphorical language to talk at length about the competency of lamas, Tantric practitioners, poor people, women, and small children to take oaths:

In the old legal texts it says:

> Don't catch the trapped golden swan.
> Don't run down the poisonous black snake.
> Don't throw stones at the black crow.
> Don't beat a pregnant dog with a stick.
> Don't try to thread the small, red turquoise.[10]

As to the first three categories above: a religious person (golden swan), a Tantric priest (poisonous black snake), and a poor person (black crow) are all inappropriate as witnesses—the first, because she should not be called; the second, because nothing he says is necessarily true; the third, because she can be paid to say anything. The text then continues:

> The meaning of the "pregnant dog" is: A women who takes an oath, for the sake of her own husband and children, should not be included as an oathtaker.
>   The meaning of the "small, square, red turquoise" is: Small children, being innocent, can't differentiate between good and bad; being foolish, they do not understand.[11]

A women was seen as too compassionate and nurturing toward her family to give accurate testimony or take a serious religious oath when a family member was concerned. This was understood as a profound compliment, given the high value Tibetan Buddhism placed on compassion and selfless giving to others.

The child, on the other hand, was seen as innocent and foolish because he or she could not differentiate good from bad. In Tibet the ability to make such a distinction was, in fact, a general way of thinking about the competency of all possible witnesses, including children, women, lamas, and others: if they understood the difference between right and wrong and the consequences of their acts, they were responsible for them. It should be noted that this is exactly the same basis for competency as that of the M'Naughton Rule, under which sanity is determined by whether the defendant in a criminal case knows and understands the difference between right and wrong.[12] Established in Britain more than two hundred years later than the Tibetan code, this rule is used in the United States today.

Legal Units and Legal Levels

Notions of hierarchy and identity in Tibet, combined into a graduated series of legal units and levels, are outlined here—up to the level of regional governor—with a few illustrative cases. (Chapter 15 discusses these distinctions in their symbolic forms; Part Three provides more detailed narratives and verbatim cases. Part Four completes the picture by presenting the upper three levels of the central government.)[13]

The first level was that of the *individual,* who was governed by self-law or self-regulation. *Rongtim,* "an examination of oneself according to one's attributes and abilities,"[14] was understood by Tibetans as moral self-regulation or the effort to follow the moral requirements of Buddhism in both the religious and secular spheres of one's life.

The second level of Tibetan law, but the first in which disputes arose and were settled, was that of the *household* or family, *khim tsang rimpa (khyim tshang rim pa).* Disputes there were described as occurring "in the family" or "in the household" and as being decided "among themselves," "by the father," "by a friend," or "by a neighbor." Typical areas of conflict included domestic arrangements, land ownership, conjugal rights, and inheritance of land and personal property. The punishment of servants and disputes between servants or between servants and outsiders also appear to have been handled entirely within the domain of the household.[15] It was generally considered best not to expose the household's problems to the outside if at all possible but to keep them "internal," as the following proverb implies: "A wound in the mouth is better cured inside the mouth."

The household legal level was assigned a special section in the early law codes; "The Separation of Relatives" discusses in detail, for example, cases of divorce in which the husband was at fault for a previous adultery. Obedience to one's parents was also an important cultural norm informing household disputes. The Ten Virtues were the primary standards for behavior in disputes, and the Buddha was often presented as an ideal figure for comparison.

Decisions made at the household level could employ any of the four ritual procedures (Chapter 10), including the variety of internal settlement processes and legal devices. But whether a member of the household itself, a neighbor, a friend, a local lama, or a high government official[16] decided the dispute, a case inside the house was still considered to have occurred on the household level. The role of the helpful neighbor was considered a particularly important one in Tibet,[17] as this personal recollection of a family quarrel demonstrates:

> One time my sister lost some jewelry. She got angry and blamed me. The neighbors discussed it with her and with me, but still she remained angry. Finally they bought new jewelry and gave it to my sister to solve the problem. This was considered very good, and it brings much religious merit to the neighbor who did it. Later, we apologized to the neighbor and did something in return to thank him.

Moving outside the household, the next level was that of disputes settled "in the village," "in the community," "by the headman of the village," or "by a knowledge-able older man." A *community, dong rimpa* (*grong rim pa*), could refer in the Tibetan context either to a rural village; a series of spread-out households that were associated in some way, such as to allocate corvée taxes, control irrigation or grazing, or exchange marriage partners; within a city, a block of houses that had one watchman or headman in charge; or a small unit of nomadic tent households associated through shared grazing lands, marital relations, a common headman, or other ties.[18]

Like the individual within the household, the household was the primary legal unit at the community level. Official government legal procedures were employed less often than conciliation procedures for settling disputes at the community level— most often interhousehold disputes or problems with activities organized by the community as a whole, such as the regulation of irrigation.

Within the city, the neighborhood block or in-facing courtyard was a collection of households that organized to elect a headman, report crimes, initiate safety patrols, decide neighborhood disputes, and coordinate various mutual adventures such as commercial trips and prayer sessions. Because the chosen headman was the legal authority in his neighborhood community, he was the first person to call the police when trouble arose, to notify the district court of major crimes such as burglaries, robberies, or murder, or to be called to conciliate a case in his block.

Landowning households both in Lhasa and throughout much of Tibet were personally responsible for acts committed and disputes arising on their premises, which made it very important to eliminate problem persons and settle minor difficulties by banding together into larger neighborhood units. An example of the severe ramifications of this form of household liability is a case that occurred in the late 1930s concerning three city landowners who were not organized into the same block group:

> In Lhasa, there was an internal courtyard onto which none of the three houses that adjoined it faced. The house of Tashi on the left owned half the courtyard; the house of Dorje on the right owned the other half. The third house did not own any of the courtyard.
> A murder took place on the land in this courtyard, and the one who did the murder ran away. The two owners, Tashi and Dorje, and the local neighborhood headman were supposed to report to the court if something happened on their land. Also, Tashi and Dorje were supposed to tell the court formally that they would pay the compensation for the murder if the murderer was not found.
> But Tashi and Dorje never reported the murder and never appeared in court. So the

Plate 27. An association of Nepalese businessmen and traders picnicking next to a Tibetan tent near Lhasa. 1920–21. (Pitt Rivers Museum, University of Oxford)

family of the victim went to court with a petition. Then the court staff came to the neighborhood to investigate the murder, and they asked all the adjoining landowners, "Does this land belong to you?" Dorje and Tashi both responded, "This land does not belong to us," thinking that they would have to pay high fees to the court if they spoke up. They both signed papers saying that the murder did not take place on their land.

Then the family in the third house said that they would pay the compensation and went to court. After this case was over, the family in the third house requested of the court that the land be registered in their name with a deed to them, and so it was. When Dorje and Tashi found out, they were very angry, but there was nothing they could do because they had not taken responsibility for their land. No one in the neighborhood could help them because they had not been good neighbors.

Perhaps the most important interstitial and interconnecting networks of individuals in Tibet were *associations, kyiduk dang tsokpa (skyid sdug dang tshogs pa)*. As the fourth level, they constituted bounded social units that played an essential role in solving the disputes of their members and acted on behalf of their members in disputes with outsiders. Associations could be based on ethnic, religious, occupational, or social similarities or formed around mutual-aid and special-purpose commonalities. Former Nepalese-Tibetan traders called "kasara," for example, spoke of the immense influence of their association in Lhasa in establishing business practices, protecting members, and dealing with the Tibetan officials through the Nepalese Foreign Office, *gorship lékhung (gor zhib las khungs)*. Guildlike associations such as the Committee of Stone Masons and Carpenters, *doshing chipa (rdo shing spyi pa)*, regulated the affairs of their own craft, arranged tax payments and loans as a group, and provided conciliators or representation in court for disputes between members and between members and outsiders. "Happiness-sadness" associations, *kyiduk* (*skyid sdug*), a name describing the range of emotional states to be shared by members, were also very common. They coordinated activities such as performances and weddings; solicited funds for funeral expenses, large trading ventures, and loans; organized pilgrimages, temple ceremonies, and prayer groups (*mani* associations). Even the beggars of Lhasa—called *ragyab pa*, which meant "behind the embankment" of the river, where most of them slept at night—formed a community association. It was reported by three different Tibetans from Lhasa that the beggars not only settled their disputes among themselves but assumed group tasks such as the daily raising of the flag at one of the Lhasa monasteries.[19]

Little is known about the internal dispute settlement procedures of these associations, even in the new forms that they have taken among the Tibetan refugees.[20] A few of the cases I collected, however, involved association members and outsiders, such as the Muslim businessman and the Buddhist in the following narrative. Tibetan Muslims, a distinct ethnic group in Lhasa, had their own association with its own procedures for settling internal disputes. But because this dispute also involved a Buddhist, jurisdiction shifted to an official from the special office in the government with authority over Muslim matters (members of associations placed a high value on finding an official or conciliator knowledgeable about their group to handle an insider-outsider problem).[21] Notice the use of shaming, the call to the internal morality of the Buddhist when the government official pressures him for compliance, and the details of commercial record-keeping practices. This case was recounted by a former judge of the Municipal Court who demonstrated his own insider-outsider categorization by referring to the Muslim Tibetan as "the Muslim" and the Buddhist Tibetan as "the Tibetan."

There once was a Muslim businessman in Lhasa who sold a great deal of cloth. Like most Muslim businessmen, he kept daily records of all his transactions in Arabic, Parsi writing. The Muslim people in Lhasa had their own schools and separate names from other Buddhist Tibetans.

One time, a Tibetan, who was Tibetan Buddhist and not Muslim, came to this Muslim and asked if he could take some of the Muslim's material out to the villages to sell. Because he was a friend, the Muslim agreed, and he wrote an entry into his record book and then had the friend sign a "receiving receipt" for the goods he was taking. There was no signature or stamp on the receipt, but it was done by the Tibetan in his handwriting and then given to the Muslim. Then the Tibetan took the cloth material from the Muslim and went out to the villages to sell it.

Two years later the same Tibetan came back to Lhasa, but he never looked up the Muslim businessman. Finally, the Muslim heard that he was in town and went to see him, asking for the money. The Tibetan said that he could not remember what he took and so would not give the money.

So the Muslim came to see me, because I was one of the officials of the Lhasa Municipal Office, which handles Muslim affairs and problems between Muslims and non-Muslims in Lhasa. At first, he came to see me at my home and explained the problem. And I said to him, "What shall I do? There is nothing that I can do unless you have a receipt. Do you have a receipt?" and he said, "Yes, I will bring the receipt tomorrow."

Plate 28. Cloth seller's store and its outside stall on a street in Lhasa. The bolts of textiles on the left are from India, the cups on the right from China. 1920–21. (Pitt Rivers Museum, University of Oxford)

So the next day he came in the morning to my home with the record book and the receipt. Seeing this, I said, "First, don't come to the office, because you are a friend. Don't go to see the other officers at their homes, because they will expect presents. Next, tell the Tibetan that you have the receipts for what he took and you are friends, so he should pay. Tell him that if not, you will have to go to the Lhasa Municipal Office." Then the Muslim went to him and told him this.

A while later, the Tibetan came to me at my home, and I received him. Then he said to me that he could not remember what he had taken. I told him, "Do you remember writing a receipt?" and he said, "Yes." Then I said, "Why do you cheat a Muslim when you are a Buddhist? I feel very ashamed."

The Tibetan knew my father's teacher very well, and he mentioned his name when he came to see me. So I told him to visit the old gentleman who was my father's teacher and ask him how to solve this problem. I also said to him, "I am young and inexperienced, so you should ask this teacher. But do not go to the office."

Early the next day I went to see Pola, my father's teacher, and told him the story and the whole truth of this case. But the Tibetan did not go to Pola as he was instructed. So then I told Pola to call the Tibetan to his house. Then I sent a clerk to the Muslim's home with instructions for the Muslim to take the book and the receipt with him to Pola's house, and the message "Pola will solve the problem. Do not go to the office." The clerk came back to me asking directions to Pola's house. Then he went back to the Muslim, and the Muslim went to Pola's house also.

In this way, the case was solved. Pola talked to the Tibetan, and he finally agreed to pay back the money slowly. Then Pola wrote out a money agreement, and it was signed by both men. So the decision was made by Pola, in this case, as conciliator.

The fifth level in Tibet was the larger *township, dongkir rimpa* (*grong khyer rim pa*), encompassing several villages or communities. Disputes at this level were decided by "the wealthy man in town," "the steward of the estate," "the regional headman or council," or "a knowledgeable person of the region." Fights over the irrigation of fields in a series of communities serviced by the same river, robberies committed by a member of one community in another community, land disputes over boundaries between adjoining villages, and cases not settled at the community or association level were commonly brought to the township level—where many, but by no means all, cases ended.

Monastic and noble estates that covered several villages, as well as government-designated townships, were legal units that operated as townships for dispute settlement. Examples of decisions made at this level abound. Sonam, as administrator of a monastic estate (see the Introduction), was in charge of its seven disparate villages as well as the monastery. Similarly, in the Case of the Wandering Monk (Chapter 4), the decision-maker was the headman of the township in which the monastery was located.

As the cases reported in Chapters 16, 17, and 18 indicate, not only did townships devise their own local rules, but the headman or council having jurisdiction often had wide discretion in deciding cases and fixing punishments. In a small town the facilities often included a one-cell jail and hired workers who could act as guards or as representatives of the headman. Townships were also in regular contact with the district office and central government and had specific responsibilities for collecting taxes and supervising corvée labor. In Lhasa and the larger cities, the neighborhood block units served as both community and township levels.

Central Government Levels

Tibetan territory governed directly by the central government from Lhasa was divided into *districts* or *dzong*, each administered by a district officer. The word *dzong* means fortress or castle, and many of the towns that served as district centers were built on or near the hills originally occupied by the fortified castles of ancient Tibet. A district could encompass any number of townships or local areas. Some districts were rather small and had only six or seven areas under their jurisdiction; others had many, sometimes including several large estates which themselves encompassed twenty or thirty more local areas.

The district office was the first of the five basic administrative levels of the Dalai Lama's government; above it were the state or provincial governor's office, the central departments, the Cabinet or Ecclesiastical Office, and the Office of the Dalai Lama (see Chapter 20). Most Tibetans' only contact with the central government was through the district officer in their area. Chapters 19, 20, and 21 detail the context and proceedings of district courts in the provinces and in the capital city, for even Lhasa was divided into two districts with separate administrators and courts.

Collecting taxes and dealing with disputes and crimes were the two most important aspects of a district officer's job. The following case told by a man from the town of Gongkar, near Lhasa, demonstrates the importance of the role of the district officer as a government representative in a criminal case:

> In Gongkar, my birth district, when I was a boy, we heard of a big group of night thieves. They were very famous, but the district officer could not trace them. They had murdered people and stolen many things.
>
> In our village there was a very rich family. One night this group came, and one man stayed at the gate while another entered and killed two or three people and stole necklaces, clothes, altar articles. One person who came from outside the village was sleeping in the house, and he was stabbed by the thieves. He did not die but pretended to die, and then watched them. He recognized the thieves. The next morning he woke up and told all his neighbors. He said, "I know the thief but I will only tell in front of the district commissioner."
>
> Then the witness told the district officer his story, and the officer sent his representative to the home of the thief. The thief was from Tamolong, more than twenty miles away, at least a day away. The representative went to his home and asked of the members of the household, "Where did your father go last night?" They said, "He was out last night, he usually goes out after some beer." And so they caught him, and he told them all the names of the other thieves.

Most districts in Tibet were parts of a larger region coordinated by an overarching governor's office. For example, the district of Kyidong, described in Chapter 19, was originally in the larger *state* of Nari and overseen by the Nari governor. Later, the district was transferred to the state of To which had two levels of governors: minor governors for Lower To and Upper To reported to an overgovernor in the town of Shigatse.

The degree of power exercised by the governors and their staffs varied. In Khams and Amdo, huge states in eastern Tibet, the governors had extensive control and independence, whereas regions close to Lhasa were often administered by lower-level officials with much less independent power. A case from the 1940s in the region of Khams illustrates how governors in certain regions had autonomy even in a matter of murder. Notice that the district officer who told the story was well aware of the dimensions of power and social hierarchy of the two families. He employed formal ritual procedure, factored the case according to its unique elements, and finally fashioned a solution that he thought fit the circumstances:

> There was a man from a very good family in this region who went out and stole a *zo* from the home of another family. The son of the owner saw him and pursued the thief, finally killing him. The case went to our office, and the son was brought before us in court and whipped when he first came. After investigating, I decided the case, had him whipped again, and then circulated a final decision document. The governor agreed to my decision, and the matter was not sent to Lhasa as would be necessary for murders committed in other areas.

In the decision document, I did not give him a blood (physical) punishment because the thief had come into his home. Depending on the size of the crime, whether or not he can prove self-defense, the actions of the person killed, and other justifications, blood and other punishments are assessed. In the written document, I said that the son must pay the *tong* (*stong*) monetary amount for this man's life and all the other costs for the murder, including the court costs for our office. The man was allowed to stay in his home and continue to live, but he had to make the payments. No one complained about this decision.

Excursus: Inheritance

Tibetans distinguished between real and personal property for the purpose of inheritance. Personal property, *nor* (*nor*), consisted of all the movable material wealth of a person or family, including animals. This was contrasted to "family fields," expressed by a compound word *pashi* (*pha gzhis*), which comprises the two sememes "father" and "fields" and means both (a) the lands owned through time by one's forefathers and (b) an inherited farm. Two other sememes meaning "father" and "the place left by" combined to form the compound *pashul* (*pha shul*), which means the property of a deceased person: that is, a paternal inheritance or patrimony.

The most common Tibetan aphorism about inheritance is "the son inherits the father's place," *pashul budzin* (*pha shul bus 'dzin*). In one sense, this meant that at least one son would follow in his father's occupation. Unless he took monastic vows, a farmer's son was expected to become a farmer, a butcher's son a butcher, a tailor's son a tailor, and a nomad's son a nomad. In the other sense of "place," it mean that the sons would inherit the possessions, specifically the land and house, of the father.

The word for ancestors, *yabmay* (*yab mes*), and descendants, *butsa* (*bu tsha*), are male terms in Tibetan, as is the ancient concept of one's stock consisting of descent through the "bone" of the male side to which is added the "flesh" of the mother's side. Patrilineal inheritance, patrilocal residence, and primogeniture were the approved ancient norms (see also Stein 1981). In actual practice, however, intestate inheritance was more flexible, given the many forms of marriage permitted, the various occupations available, and other factors. Moreover, it should be noted that the occupation and management of the land was coordinated through a central household, the members of which could vary widely over generations. It was the household that was responsible for the taxes and that provided landholding continuity, whether or not it was headed by a male member of the patriline. Consequently, the general pattern of intestate inheritance of the main family lands in the southern central arc of the Plateau was as follows:

1. If there was a nonmonastic eldest brother who would stay on the land, with or without his younger male siblings, he took the lands *in toto* and replaced the father in ownership and family authority (an adopted son was considered a blood relative for the purposes of inheritance). This was the preferred pattern, particularly if he and his brothers formed a polyandrous union with one female, all of whose children were then presumed to be his. Although younger brothers and sisters might be given sections of the property if they left home after their father's death, these gifts were ultimately the prerogative of the eldest brother.

2. If the eldest brother, for whatever reason, did not take the inheritance, then a nonmonastic son (normally next in order of seniority) willing to take over the land, house, and taxes had the right to do so and thereby assume the position of his father. This was preferably done in cooperation with his brothers, especially in a polyandrous union with the remaining brothers, the eldest of whom represented the entire group. If the younger brothers could not agree, preference was given to the oldest or to the one most capable of maintaining the paternal lands as a unit.

3. If a nonmonastic son did not take the inheritance, the next choice was the son of a daughter of the deceased father if that grandson was available to occupy the house and work the lands. If a number of such sons of daughters were available, a younger son who was not eligible to inherit other lands and did not want to join his elder brother in their paternal lands was favored.

4. If a capable grandson did not take responsibility, the lands fell to the eldest daughter who had not joined a nunnery. If she was unwilling to marry, however, a daughter who would marry and remain in the house on the land took precedence. A daughter who inherited from her father retained possession of the land; it did not go to the husband she brought into the household but would pass from her to her eldest son. Alternatively, an uncle of the daughter, part of the male sibling group of the father, could make a claim to the land at this point.

5. If no daughter or male sibling of the father would occupy the land and take the inheritance, then any of the father's sons and daughters who would not occupy the house or land could inherit, starting with the eldest male through to the youngest daughter. This nonoccupying member of the sibling group would either keep the title to the land and rent it out to tenants or neighbors, or dispose of it in some other way.

6. If there were no clear heirs and no other relatives who could make a claim to the property, the land of a peasant returned to the local government unit with the provision that it be regranted within its secondary title unit: that is, monastic estate land had to be regranted to a monastic estate peasant, government land to a government peasant, and privately held land to a private peasant. If the unclaimed lands were secondary title lands such as a private estate held by a government official who had no descendants, the land reverted to the state with no restrictions.

The origins of this sequence in intestate inheritance in southern Tibet are very ancient; some parts were recorded as early as the Empire period in the eighth century. As cases from the twentieth century indicate, the many forms of marriage and recoupling that might occur throughout the life cycles of members of the household occupying the land could complicate intestate inheritance.

A will, of course, could alter the inheritance. The story of Milarapa (Chapter 7) is perhaps the most famous example. Tibetan wills superseded the general intestate inheritance pattern unless they completely disowned obvious male heirs without good cause; in that situation the male heir could protest the will in court. In Thubten Sangye's case (Chapter 25), his father's oral deathbed will gave the land and house to the younger half-sister, who had sons. Thubten, the older sibling, was by then a monastic government official and did not inherit because he had taken religious vows.

Drafting a will *causa mortis* was a practice that continued in Tibet through the 1950s, as a Tibetan woman from a town south of Lhasa explained:

Sometimes the lands were divided up long before the parent's death, but normally it happened that the parent—say, the father—would make his will when he realized that he was terminally ill. He would call together three to five of his closest friends. Then he would choose the one most trusted to act as his executor: that is, to see that the provisions of his will were carried out equitably. In the presence of these friends he would divide up his lands and properties. The house and surrounding lands would be given to the eldest son if he was willing to remain and oversee them. If he was not—if, for example, the eldest son had settled in town or at some distance—the best lands and the main house would fall to the second son.

The provisions of the father's will were then committed to writing by the appointed executor, or scribe, and copies given to all those present. Those who acted as witnesses to the will all signed it and were responsible, out of their sense of friendship and regard, to see that its provisions were carried out.

This woman's eldest brother had been given his share of the estate several years before her father's death. (In this form of *inter vivos* deed transfer, common throughout Tibet, the eldest son took over the management of the lands before the death of his elderly parents, allowing them to devote their energy to prayers in preparation for the next life.) Then, on his deathbed in 1958, her father dictated a nuncupative will distributing the remaining properties among his daughters, second wife, and second son, with "certain things of value" being allocated to the executor and friends present. In richer families, wives often received the jewels and the lands that they had brought into the marriage, and the daughters were allotted their jewels and small pieces of lands from the father as well. Under some circumstances, inheritance taxes were also assessed.

In short, although patterns varied somewhat, the preference for inheritance of the main family lands by a male and for continuing ownership of the land by someone within the descent group of the father was very strong throughout Tibet. Subsidiary land plots and personal property might be left as gifts to younger sons and daughters. Even monks and nuns could inherit land but usually not the primary family lands unless they renounced their vows. In the case of incarnates, of course, this discussion does not apply; the new body is presumed to be a complete replacement for the old and takes full possession of all real and personal property without exception.

CHAPTER FIFTEEN

Legal Symbols and Representations

When, then, . . . the Tibetan artist designs a *mandala,* he is not obeying the arbitrary command of caprice. He is following a definite tradition which teaches him how to represent, in a particular manner, the very drama of his soul. He does not depict on a *mandala* the cold images of an iconographical text, but he pours out upon it the phantasms of his subconscious ego and thus knows them and liberates himself from them. He gives form to that world he feels surging within him and he sees it spread out before his eyes, no longer the invisible and unrestrainable master of his soul, but a serene symbolic representation which reveals to him the secrets of things and of himself. This complicated juxtaposition of images, their symmetrical arrangement, this alternation of calm and of menacing figures, is the open book of the world and of Man's own spirit.

— Guiseppe Tucci, *The Theory and Practice of the Mandala*

Tibetan Buddhists have a prefigured, complex, interpenetrating, and "overdetermined"[1] symbolic world view. Indeed, the terms "sign" and "symbol" are inadequate in the sense that they *underdescribe* the way Tibetans understand what they are looking at or representing. Images, clothing, colors, a pantheon of deities, cardinal directions, hand movements, implements are all part of a rich interrelated network of symbolic meaning that has enormous religious and social import. Tibetans' initial understanding of the world is one of integration, of all realms and all times and all beings as interrelated, with each person, symbol, thought, action, and color having a place within the mandalic whole. In their notion of the One, each level or unit of the whole both actually is and also reflects the All. This rather different starting point for a cosmology of law is embedded in their legal symbols and representations.

A "symbol" in Western culture is a term of reference used by a whole school of thought—which has developed from the work of European medievalists, using the terms *signans* and *signatum,* to that of modern linguists[2]—to represent the way in which a particular mark or sound conveys meaning to a receiver. This line of thought is based on a one-to-one correspondence between a particular *signifier* mark or sound (the written or spoken word "pig") and the particular *signified* concept it denotes (the actual pig in a field), and the complexities related to this formulation in context.[3] Pragmatics and code theory look at the conditions, context-dependent and context-independent, under which messages get conveyed through signs or symbols. Signs can be strung together by rules of use into long sets of signs or compound signs, as in a sentence.

Working from this base, anthropologists developed the idea of culture as a system or code of manmade symbols which provides and creates meaning in particular contexts. Claude Lévi-Strauss analyzed myths and found binary opposition as a human universal: he posited that cultures are always resolving basic dualities, mediating polarities, and, through a dialectical process, synthesizing the structural oppositions inherent in the human state.[4] While others emphasized the symbolic nature of rituals[5] or metaphor,[6] Clifford Geertz produced the idea of culture as "meanings embodied in symbols."[7] An approach to the study of law as symbols involves the interrelation of smaller projects (the symbolic analysis of a particular ritual or object of legal life) with the larger project of the constitution of the symbolic order and meaning of these analyses within a society.[8]

Still, modern scholars considering complex, integrated, All-One symbols such as the Tibetan mandala face the original problem of this limited conceptualization of symbols, the one-to-one relationship of signifier to signified. They must also confront the modern tendency to divide symbols and reasoning—that is, to state that there are two different *mentalities*: the cosmologically integrated, mystical, symbolic world view based on belief (of the primitive), and the scientific world view based on rationality and logic (of the modern). Lucien Lévy-Bruhl first posited these contrasting modes of thought, typifying the first, beliefs, by the "mystical participation" of similar forces in a wide range of objects, words, and phenomena.[9] In a famous series of arguments, philosophers and anthropologists have discussed and disputed the validity of this dichotomy and the nature of rationality and the scientific paradigm.[10]

What is important for consideration here is that this dichotomy not only posits rational, nonintegrative thought as different from and better than "primitive" thought but also labels as "scholastic" and rudimentary any rational thought within a mystical cosmological framework—such as medieval Christian scholasticism.[11] Noting that Tibetan Buddhist reasoning fits within his definition, José Cabezón has identified scholasticism's key features as "[its] formal nature, its systematicity, its preoccupation with scriptures and their exegesis in commentaries, its rationalism and its reliance on logic and dialectic in defense of its tenets, its penchant for lists, classification and categorization and its tendency toward abstraction."[12] Such definitions, though useful and illuminating, are based on the traditional division of modern and premodern. It would perhaps be more fruitful to compare reasoning patterns for their relative "scholasticism." The American legal system, for example, with its "scripture" (the Constitution), has many of the foregoing characteristics and has been described by several modern theorists as a closed, self-referential system of communication.[13]

Marshall Sahlins, in discussing the link between symbolism in traditional and modern societies, has pointed out that modern Western symbolism is dualistic: it divides the world into oppositions such as nature/culture, work/play, expressive/practical, religious/secular, and belief/knowledge. This implies that modern Western culture will frame arguments in terms of such dualisms, and it explains the attraction of theories such as that of Lévi-Strauss. Sahlins's thesis is that modern production for a consumer market requires symbolic differentiation.[14] Jacques Le Goff and other Western medieval scholars, however, see dualistic oppositions such as up/down and inside/outside as central to the ideology of the Middle Ages.[15] One can argue whether the complexity and abstraction of the medieval Christian world or ancient Chinese thought[16] or the phantasms of American MTV are similar or parallel to those of the integrated mandalic symbols of Tibet. What is certain is that one should describe specifically the meanings and the use in legal contexts of each, looking both for one-to-one symbolic codes (such as the "law poles" that indicated a court or place of legal authority, in contrast to other spaces) and for the much more integrated All-One symbols. Avoiding dualisms that label certain forms of thought and symbols as irrational or scholastic (hence, inferior) is an important caveat.[17]

From the Tibetan point of view, the all-encompassing interrelatedness of the world and every being in it is a central idea represented in the symbol of the mandala. Guiseppe Tucci has applied the term "psycho-cosmogrammata" to the Indo-Tibetan mandala archetype that represents reintegration from the level of the individual consciousness, the One, to that of the universe, the All.[18] It is a symbol within which every idea, person, entity, and lesser symbol has a place. It is an image of the world as both unchanging, timeless, and eternal (in the sense that it is the ultimate reality) and ever changing, time-filled, and present (in the sense that its very nature involves impermanence and cycling human rebirth). It is a structure that incorporates the diffuse, the arbitrary, the ambiguous and contested, the known and unknown, disorder and coherence, everyone and everything.

Mysticism, rational thought, magic, and analysis of illusion are all ways of understanding this integrated Buddhist world. In Tibet, rational thought with its linear, dualistic, agential foundation is not primary; it is only one of several techniques for understanding the world. This does not mean that all Tibetans have a singular, logical system of thought or an outlook that can be reduced to one core idea, or that types of explanations did not vary within the society, or that they did not ever use binary oppositions. Tibetans simply had a different symbolic starting point, an initial view of the world as All-One. Understanding that starting point is an essential part of understanding their cosmology of law.

Indeed, the mandala represented all the basic ideas of Buddhism: karma, the everpresentness of realms, radical particularity, the cyclical nature of existence, the Buddha core (see Figure 10). The government of Tibet itself was understood as a multilayered mandala with successive levels of periphery leading to a core in Lhasa, the home of the Buddha. Hierarchy, social categories, power relations, legal levels from the household to the High Court, all accorded with this representation (Chapters 9, 13, and 14).

The individual mind at the center of the personal mandala was also understood as the center of the legal universe, and the mandala reiterated in symbolic form the movement of the legal system. Just as Buddhas emanated from the core and aspirants in meditation, moved from the outer to the inner doors of the mandala, so the legal system was understood as flexible, allowing movement up and down and between different procedures, forums, and levels. Moreover, the mandala was a spatial organizing device used in both religious and secular architecture, to map out

The Individual	**The Building**

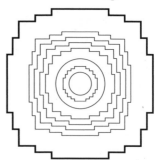

The individual mind at the center of the personal mandala is the center of the legal universe in Tibet. Like the Buddha, any individual mind can learn to become enlightened.

The basic mandalic shape is also a floor plan for Tibetan structures and buildings. Note it is oriented according to the four cardinal points.

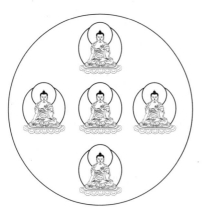

In one of its simpler formulations, the mandala is a diagram of five deities: one in the center, four more placed at the cardinal points around the center.

Tibetan chortens range in size and represent the funeral mound of the Buddha, the cosmic mountain and the state of enlightenment all in one. Large chortens are circumambulated clockwise.

A complex mandala can have hundreds of deities. The Buddha, or deity, at the center emanates from the core of the mandala and is transformed, manifested and multiplied into other Buddhas.

The Kumbum at Gyantse is the largest chorten in mandalic form in Tibet. Built in the 15th century by the Prince of Gyantse, it contains over 100,000 images in hundreds of chapels arranged along several levels.

Figure 10. The mandala as an encompassing mental model in Tibet. From left to right, the vertical columns demonstrate the individual, the building, the country, and the cosmos as mandalic representations.

The Country

This mandala depicts the land and government of Tibet with its central core in Lhasa. While it demonstrates hierarchy, power relations and legal levels, the mandala ceaselessly pulsates with movement up, down and between its different parts.

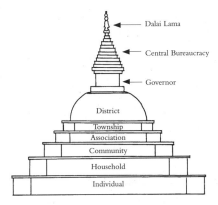

The legal units and levels of Tibet can also be understood as a three-dimensional mandala in the form of a chorten.

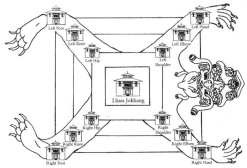

In one Tibetan myth of origin, the high plateau of Tibet is an enormous ogress beast who causes earthquakes when she moves. The Jokhang Temple pins down her body while other Buddhist temples secure her limbs.

The Cosmos

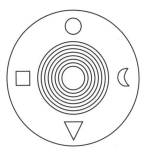

The Buddhist cosmos is a mandala with Mt. Sumeru at the center, seven rings of mountains and oceans and four continents at the cardinal points. This axis mundi (hub of the world) model of the universe was widespread in Vedic India and came with Buddhism to Tibet.

The Wheel of Life represents the Buddhist cosmos. The cosmic mountain is the center. The concentric circles depict the Buddhist heavens, earth, hells and the life cycle of an individual.

Older Tibetans drew maps of the modern world like this one which is based on a drawing by Kungola Thubten Sangye. It is a picture of Mt. Sumeru at the center, seven rings of mountains and oceans, the heavens above and fire hells below.

the rooms in an administration building (see Chapter 7) and the legal jurisdictions of the capital city.

It is important to note that there are at least two ways to use the mandala as a symbolic metaphor for a government: as a descriptive device derived from Tibetans' explanations; or as a label for an ideal type of state, as in the literature on southeast Asia.[19] I employ it here as a descriptive device; I do not directly address the debate over the nature of the Tibetan state and whether it was centralized or fragmentary.[20] The fact that Tibetan legal and administrative procedures were used throughout the Plateau on all different levels, however, may point to the need for a reformulation of those arguments. The political glue uniting the regions of Tibet was not simply military might, or a civil bureaucracy, or the charisma of a leader, or ritualized "theatre drama."[21] It was a mode of practice based on ritual ways of thinking and proceeding at every level of the political mandala.

The Law Poles: Symbols of Legal Authority

Tibetans cited many visual clues to their official legal system, such as posted edicts, the sealed documents carried by messengers, the fetters worn by prisoners. Some repeated the proverb about the golden yoke of government and the silken knot of religion. Each of these was a one-to-one symbol in which the image or phrase directly denoted an official government process. But the most interesting—and least known outside Tibet—were the various government "law poles."

Several words for these legal symbols kept recurring in interviews: *timjuk* (*khrims 'jug*), *chakjuk* (*lcags 'jug*), *timchak* (*khrims lchag*), *gyuktha*, (*rgyug khra*), *bochak* (*bo lchag*). All these words referred to poles that were sometimes carried but more often placed on either side of a doorway to indicate a place of political authority or legal function. Since no legal and few political symbols of this kind remain in Tibet today, the multiplicity and ambiguity of the references made exact determination of the poles' physical shape and symbolic importance difficult.

By separating out the use of the various terms, however, one can identify three basic categories of symbolic reference.

First, among primarily political symbols, the most important were the *bochak* symbols of royal authority derived from the ancient Tibetan kings. The *bochak,* still in evidence in the palace of the Dalai Lama today, were large straw-filled cylinders wrapped in rugs woven in a tiger-skin pattern with borders and fringe at the top and bottom. Hung on either side of the door of rooms occupied by the Dalai Lama and the Cabinet, these were instantly recognized by laypersons as symbols of government authority.

Second, symbols of monastic authority, iron or silver poles called *chakjuk,* were tied to a pillar near the door or carried by a servant following the head prefect of a monastery. Several Tibetans described such a pole as looking "like the British scepter" or an "iron stick" carried by monks during the Mon Lam Festival to indicate that monastic, not secular, government had temporary authority. One specimen from Lhasa is located in the Museum of Oxford University. Monks in Tibet indicated to me in the late 1980s that most had either been stolen or were hidden away in their monasteries.

Plate 29. Door to the private quarters of the Dalai Lama showing the *bochak,* ancient symbols of political authority, on either side. 1986.

Third, for the poles that hung outside the doorways of secular courts when they were in session the terms used were *timjuk, timchak,* and *gyuktha* ("many-colored stick"). Tibetans from every corner of the Plateau reported having seen these law poles and recognized their import. Most described them as wooden poles up to seven feet in length with spiral markings. Some said that they were trees with the bark cut off in a spiral; others described something like traditional Western-style barber poles in white and black or brown; still others spoke of a white spiral with a contrasting painted design in brown.

Except for the mandala, no other common Buddhist symbol was mentioned in reference to the law. No Tibetan ever reported the Wheel of the Law, a Buddhist symbol in the shape of an eight-spoked wheel, as a symbol of courts or legal activity; although thought to be derived from the chariot wheel of the ancient world-conquering chakravartin (ideal or universal) Buddhist kings, it was a strictly religious symbol.

Plate 30. Simple cloth mandala used during religious rituals in Dharamsala, India. Note the four color fields. Candles and bowls of rice and water surround it on the table. 1984.

The Mandala: An Encompassing Mental Model

In its simplest Tibetan formulation the mandala, *kyilkor* (*dkyil 'khor*), is a diagram representing five deities or Buddhas, one in the center and one at each of the four cardinal points around the center. Whether very simple or extremely complex, mandalas arranged in various concentric combinations of circles, squares, and triangles always represent sacred space. As a two-dimensional design on a floor or table or wall, the mandala is a location for ritual offerings or meditation. The Buddhist canon is filled with texts on the ritual preparation of these designs and the offerings and prayers that should accompany the proper worship of a particular deity. The center of a simple mandala may have the figure of a hand, while the four surrounding areas are merely fields of color in which various objects are placed as the ritual proceeds.[22]

In a complex design the degree of prefigured iconography and ritual is enormous. The Buddhas of the center and the four directions are flanked by several attendants and goddesses, each in a particular color, with ritual leg positions (*asanas*) and hand postures (*mudras*). Each may be accompanied by specific animals and ritual objects, planets, and gems and may represent a different element, sense, emotional hindrance, and part of the human body. For example, the center of the mandala used in part of the Kalacakra Tantra ritual (see Figure 3) is occupied by the Buddha Vairocana, called the "Brilliant Illuminator," whose color is blue, emblem is the wheel, sense is sight, element is space. To the east is the Buddha Akshobhya, the "Imperturbable," in white with a thunderbolt; his sense is sound and his element water. To the north is the Buddha Amoghasiddhu, the "Infallible," in dark green, holding a sword, with the sense of taste and element of wind. To the west in red is the Buddha Amitabha, "Boundless Light," holding the stalk of a lotus, with the sense of smell and the element of fire; to the south in yellow is the Buddha Ratnasambhara, the "Jewel-born," holding a jewel, with the sense of touch and the related element of earth.[23] This symbolic system is predetermined, complex, and interrelated.

The mandala may also be a three-dimensional design; as such it is the palace of the god, with the deity at the center and a gate at each of the cardinal points along the outside walls. Here the various circles or squares are telescoped upward to form platforms of successively decreasing size. In the Kalacakra Tantra meditation, an initiate *visualizes* entering the mandala (see Figure 10) at the lowest level and working her or his way up, often through successive doors at the cardinal points, until, on the final levels, spiritual union is achieved with the central deity. Similar social and spatial hierarchy are reified in actual architectural construction as the zones move from inferior to superior, from powerless to powerful space in a graduated series of steps. Temples in Tibet were often built on this mandalic plan, just as medieval (and modern) Christian churches were built in the shape of a cross. The *samye* (*bsam yas*) Monastery, constructed in Tibet in the eighth century, is a perfect example: its three-storied central temple is surrounded by a square wall with round funerary mounds on each side.

Guiseppe Tucci describes a further meaning of this symbol:

A mandala is much more than just a consecrated area that must be kept pure for ritual and liturgical ends. It is, above all, a map of the cosmos. It is the whole universe in its essential plan, in its process of emanation and of reabsorption. The universe . . . rotates round a central axis, Mount [Su]meru, the axis of the world on which the sky rests. . . .

The same concept of adaptation of a space to or of its conformity with the cosmos is one that . . . dictated the plan of royal palaces in the East, . . . and not only royal palaces, but ordinary dwellings were . . . transformed into a centre . . . and so put the inhabitants in contact with the three spheres, . . . the inferior, the atmospheric and the celestial. . . . It is the geometric projection of the world reduced to an essential pattern.[24]

Each mandala, then, is also a representation of the three spheres of the cosmos with Mount Sumeru at the center, the heavens of the gods above the earth, and the hells below. As a map of the cosmos it is understood as the "Wheel of Life" (also a mandala) described in Chapter 5 (see Figure 4) and gains the valence of most of the important ideas in Buddhism through that composite image: (1) the root afflictions

Plate 31. A chorten or reliquary mound of the Buddha constructed by the Tibetan refugee community in Dharamsala, India. The three spheres of the cosmos are represented by the base, the center, and the spire. 1986.

of lust, craving, and ignorance, (2) the twelve steps of a human's life from birth to death and then rebirth, (3) the cycle of samsaric existence, (4) the suffering of this samsaric world, (5) the possible karmic results of current actions, (6) otherworldly reality and nondualism, and (7) impermanence, the constant movement and change of this worldly existence.

As well as the macrocosm, the All, each mandala is further understood as a model of One, of the individual person, the microcosm. As David Gellner confirms: "The mandala model applies equally to the universe as a whole, to the country, . . . to each city, to each temple and shrine, and, tantrically, to the worshipper's own body. The realization of one's own identity with these larger designs is the attainment of salvation."[25] The body of the Tibetan Buddhist, then, is itself a microcosmic diagram of the mandala of the macrocosm. The cosmos, the government, the legal system, the city, the temple, and the individual in Tibet were each separate mandalas and, at the same time, one and the same mandala. What the individual felt and thought affected the entire cosmos; every act within the legal system affected every other part of the cosmos.

The Mandala of the Mind/Body: Meditating on Tara

In Tibet, the body was simultaneously understood in several ways: as merely a momentary congerie of particulars, as the repository of the powerful mind, as an entity that could be transformed into a deity and reach enlightenment, as the center of the individual mandala of self, and as a legal actor within the society. As Jean Comaroff has put it, the body was part of the "critical dimension of consciousness" in Tibet.[26] Because the boundaries of the body are not fixed, the mind can transform the body entirely. Through religious meditation, an individual can learn to absorb, transform, generate, and become a deity at the center of the primordial cosmos.

The goddess Tara is an example of the mind/body at the center of the mandala. Tara, or *dolma* (*sgrol ma*), one of the multitude of deities in the Tibetan pantheon, is a peaceful protective deity. She is the emblem of compassion and can be called upon for protection in difficult times. Not associated with any particular sect of Tibetan Buddhism, Tara was introduced into Tibet by the famous Indian master Atisha in the middle of the eleventh century. His personal devotion to the goddess, as well as his own importance in the development of Tibetan Buddhism, led to the diffusion of the cult of Tara throughout the Plateau. His disciple Taranatha contributed to the rise of the image of Tara as the Compassionate Mother of Tibet.

Tara's mythic connections are numerous. She has been incorporated into the Buddhist origin myth as the rock ogress with whom the god Avalokitesvara (incarnated as a monkey Bodhisattva) engendered the Tibetan people. Another tradition depicts the first king as an incarnation of Avalokitesvara, his Nepalese wife as an incarnation of the Green Tara, and his Chinese wife of the White Tara. Tara has also been identified with the mother of the Buddha.

In the Tibetan Buddhist pantheon, the acts and states of mind of a Buddha can result in instances of deification: that is, an emanation from the Buddha can result in the manifestation of a deity. Much as Pallas Athena, the goddess of wisdom in the Greek pantheon, sprang fully armed from Zeus's brain, a compassionate look of the Buddha (the aspect of the Buddha which is thought to redeem suffering creatures from pain by showing pity) resulted in the Buddha Avalokitesvara. Tara is thought to have come from a compassionate look of Avalokitesvara and is therefore an emanation of an emanation. As a Bodhisattva (an enlightened one who has chosen out of compassion for sentient beings to remain in this world as a guide), Tara is capable of many different forms and manifestations. Different iconographical representations abound—the four-armed White Tara, the eight-armed Tara, the famous Green Tara, the Yellow Tara, the Red Tara, and the Blue Tara—each with its different seated position and number of eyes, arms, heads, and ornaments.

Tara is more often adopted by an individual than by a sect of Buddhism. As a savioress, she is the feminine divinity who protects women and men from physical dangers such as the Eight Deadly Perils (fire, water, thieves, demons, elephants, and the like) and the Sixteen Great Terrors (the Eight Perils plus lust, doubt, avarice, envy, false views, hatred, delusion, and pride). Tibetans enjoy recounting stories of the efficacy of reciting her mantra or calling her name to produce her manifestation. In one story, after a woman calls her name a great wind dispels sword-carrying demons. In another, a man who is starving in the northern plains comes to a nomadic tent in which a beautiful young woman cares for him and supplies him with enough food for the rest of his journey to Lhasa; the woman is actually Tara in disguise. A mother who calls out to Tara as her house burns sees a green woman appear above the house, and rain begins to fall. A Green Tara appears above the head of an old man devoted to her worship as he circumambulates the holy city.

Tara is also a common vehicle for Tantric meditation, which is distinguished from other forms of meditation by the identification of the individual self with that of the chosen divine object.[27] In Tibetan Buddhism, an aspirant who is conversant with the faculties of mind necessary to be fully released from the sufferings of samsara in this world is then ready to receive instruction into meditation on a deity. During meditation, the initiate concentrates with such intensity on recreating the physical aspects of the deity that she or he is able to reproduce them within her or his own body. In this process of absorption, transformation, and generation, the aspirant takes on all the characteristics—physical, emotional, spiritual—of the deity. During a Tara meditation, one acquires the power of the goddess and becomes the essence of true compassion and inner morality.

Aspirants memorize texts that give a detailed description of the deity; they receive instruction from monks or Tantric meditators; and they stare for extensive periods of time at paintings of the deity. The purpose is to be able to remember every detail and recreate it in the mind so that the deity can enter one's body. Stephan Beyer's book on the cult of Tara gives part of the ritual language of the self-generation formula:

> All becomes Emptiness. From the realm of Emptiness is [comes the syllable] PAM and from that a lotus; from A is the circle of the moon, above which my own innate mind is a white syllable, TAM. Light radiates forth therefrom, makes offerings to the Noble Ones, serves the aim of beings and is gathered back in, whereupon my mind, the syllable, is transformed and I myself become the holy Cintacakra [the goddess Tara]; her body is colored white as an autumn moon, clear as a stainless crystal gem, radiating light; she has one face, two hands, three eyes; she has the youth of sixteen years; her right hand makes the gift-bestowing gesture and with the thumb and ring finger of her left hand she holds over her heart the stalk of a lotus flower, . . . her gesture symbolizing the Buddhas of the three times, . . . her hair is dark blue, bound up at the back of her neck with long tresses hanging down, . . . her breasts are full; she is adorned with diverse precious ornaments, . . . the palms of her hands and the soles of her feet each have an eye, making up the seven eyes of knowledge; she sits straight and firm upon the circle of the moon, her legs crossed in the diamond posture.[28]

In Tibet it was the mind that could transform the body at the center of the microcosmic mandala into the goddess Tara, the essence of compassion. It was the

Plate 32. Mural of the female deity Tara from the Potala. She is holding the stem of a lotus
in her left hand and touching the earth with her right hand. 1986.

mind that generated conflict or calm by leading an ethical life with inner morality. It
was the mind that constituted the core of both religion and law.

The Mandala as Legal Space: Districts in Lhasa

When any former or present inhabitant of Lhasa is asked about the districts of the
city before 1959, the response follows an ancient litany. Several former judges and
officials commented that they had been taught this litany at the government schools:

Lhasa City is composed of three concentric walkways like the rings of a mandala: the outer
ring, *lingkor* (*gling skor*); the middle ring, *barkor* (*bar skor*); and the inner ring, *nangkor*

Plate 33. A pilgrim doing the entire Lingkor in full prostrations, one after another—customary for those who believed they would have no other chance in this lifetime to make the holy pilgrimage around the city. Many Lhasa residents walked the outer ring daily. Undated. (Brooke Dolan Collection, The Academy of Natural Sciences of Philadelphia)

(*nang skor*), a promenade inside the major temple. The city itself is contained within the arms of the outer ring. The city is divided into two sections, east and west, at the famous Turquoise Roof Bridge, *yuthok sampa* (*gyu thog zam pa*), which spans a small river. The western half of the city is called *zhol* (*zhol*), or "below," for the area below the Potala Palace. The eastern half has the middle ring around the Cathedral Complex, and inside the Cathedral Complex is the inner ring.

In the early twentieth century, stories and reports from foreigners substantiated this mental geography. The maps of Lhasa and the surrounding area done by the British military expedition in 1904 under Sir Francis Younghusband show the city resting against the washes of the Kicchu River to its south, inside a large ring road, with a darkened clump of houses in the west and another in the northeast. Indeed, in the reconstructed maps of the city done from memory by an architect and former Tibetan official, Zasak Taring, the same basic layout is apparent.[29]

Although this is a clear and basic rendition of the districts of the city as understood by its occupants and visitors, it obscures somewhat the real complex of legal zones (see Figure 11). Cases and interviews reveal that a more detailed arrangement had developed by mid-twentieth century to handle the increasing diversity of interests in the city. Lhasa proper had extended in several directions to areas outside the outer ring roadway, a fact that officials and laypersons explained with the typical comment, "It is still Lhasa; if it is near the outer ring, it is attached to the city."

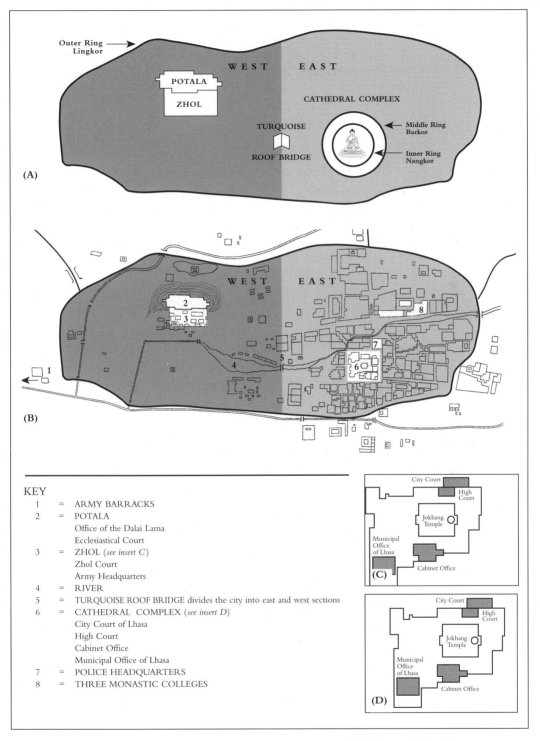

Figure 11. Legal districts and courts of Lhasa circa 1950. (A): mandalic layout of the city showing the outer, middle, and inner rings. (B): actual layout of the city showing location of courtrooms (based on drawings by Tibetans, maps and photos of Lhasa in the Pitt Rivers Museum, and the reconstructed maps of Zasak Taring).

In the western section of the city there were at least three separate legal zones. In the Zhol area, a clump of houses and offices just south of the Potala, a district-level court, the *zhol lékhung* (*zhol las khung*), handled both the legal affairs and the administration of the western half of the city. To the winter and summer palaces of the Dalai Lama went all the cases, on several different levels, involving any of the hundreds of members of His Holiness's personal and government staff and of the monasteries.[30] Barracks for the troops and their families were located near Army Headquarters, which had separate authority over disputes—even murders—that concerned military personnel.

To the east of the bridge, the situation was also more complex. The monastic colleges in the eastern section of Lhasa handled their own legal disputes under monastic law (unless they chose or were required to hand a monk over to civilian authorities). Police returning with petty criminals to the Police Headquarters located in this section dealt with minor infractions independently. The area of the Cathedral Complex was a separate legal zone. The walkway of the middle ring encircled a melange of private houses, shops, the ancient Jokhang Temple, and the government administration offices. Analysis of legal cases shows that both criminal and civil cases occurring within this walkway were dealt with by the Municipal Office of Lhasa. Most district-level criminal cases occurring outside the Cathedral Complex but inside or adjacent to the outer ring were handled by the City Court of Lhasa, which was the eastern equivalent of the western Zhol Court. Noncriminal cases from the eastern section could go either to the City Court or to the Municipal Office of Lhasa.

Outside the city and its surrounding arrondisements, the legal zones changed once again. All legal cases, except murder, that occurred within the valley but completely outside the city went first to their local level and then, if necessary, to the district office of the Zhol in the western half. All murder cases from the same area were sent first to the Cabinet and then to the High Court of Tibet.

In short, the district-level legal system in Lhasa, equivalent to the district offices in the provinces, comprised three courts. The Zhol Court, located in the buildings below the Potala, was the district court of the western area and had its own staff and the largest jail in Lhasa, with space for up to fifty prisoners. The City Court of Lhasa was a special direct-access court located inside the middle ring along the northern wall of the Cathedral Complex, housed in a three-story building with imposing front steps. This eastern district court was used primarily for criminal offenses: theft, robbery, personal injury (such as knifings), fighting, and drunkenness. Some noncriminal cases, particularly those of a contractual nature, were also handled there. The Municipal Office of Lhasa, inside the Cathedral Complex building, had jurisdiction over issues of land and housing, sewage, construction, renovation and improvement of land, water drainage, public access, and leases for the entire city. It handled any problem arising in the administration offices or family houses inside the middle ring and it was a direct-access court for all noncriminal complaints within the eastern half of Lhasa, and all cases concerning Muslims as well. The Municipal Office was also a referral court for cases from the Cabinet.

As this jurisdictional geography reveals, the mandala was the central spatial metaphor for the country, the city, the government offices within the Cathedral Complex, and the legal jurisdictions of the capital city. It was an organizing device memorized in the form of a litany by officials and laypersons. The realities of city growth and legal complexities were accommodated to the pattern. At the same time, each mandala construct repeated the mythic map as it reflected every level of the cosmos from the initiate meditating on the mandala of the mind/body to the mandalic legal districts of Lhasa in an integrated All-One symbol.

PART THREE

Reports from the Countryside

Introduction

In each region of the country, a learned person should decide [after considering local prices,] the system of value equivalents [for articles] in terms of *zho* [coins] for payment [in legal cases].

—Ganden Podrang Code of the Dalai Lamas

Like the introductory narrative about the monk Sonam, this and the next two parts of the book present the legal system of Tibet through detailed pictures of the actual practice of law by particular individuals.

The focus of Part Three is on the peripheral areas of the southern arc (Figure 12), the villages, smaller towns, estates, and districts of the Tibetan countryside. What constituted a legal problem for a Tibetan living far from the capital city? How was law practiced "locally," and did the rules vary by area? When did the government concern itself with local issues? Who were the local dispute settlers and what did they do? What were the strategies, resources, and approaches of the actors?

Each chapter sets the scene with a description of the countryside and the local social practices, then presents a situation of dispute from the point of view of its narrator(s). If a Tibetan talked at length about his or her reactions and attitudes, these are included, but no details have been presumed or added. The exegesis that follows gives what the narrators said they understood the case to mean and how I think it fits into their cosmology of law.

Each chapter reports from a different locality in the countryside of the southern arc. Chapter 16 describes a district in southwestern Tibet called the Crystal Fortress and uncovers the connection between ritual hail protection and the local legal system. Chapter 17 portrays a new steward who, arriving at a small country estate, is asked to review an old dispute. Chapter 18 concerns a property dispute that is taken to the great house of a very large noble estate in the southeast. Chapter 19 recounts the routine assignment of a Tibetan official to a district post and his handling of a case. These are images of local knowledge and local history from the lower levels of the legal hierarchy.

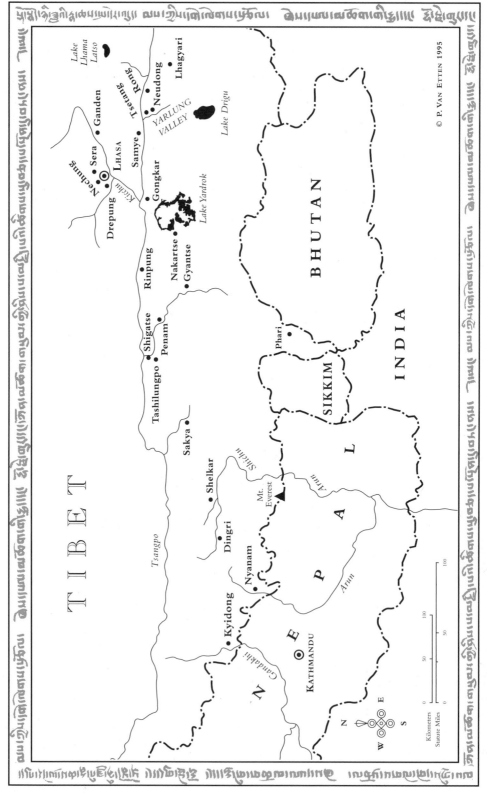

Figure 12. South-central region of the Tibetan Plateau circa 1950.

CHAPTER SIXTEEN

The Hail Protector
of the Crystal Fortress

To take a case to court without reason
only turns to dust one's small measure of wealth.
—Neudong Law Code

From a distance, one sees first the massive hill of brown stone and dirt rising from the plain. On its ridge, highlighted against the brilliant sky, are the ancient fortifications said by the local population to have been made after the period of the king called Ralpacan or Thidzug Détsen (*khri gtsug lde brtsan*), the third of the great religious kings of Tibet. Crumbling now, the towers of Shelkar, *shelkar dzong* (*shel dkar rdzong*), the "Crystal Fortress," and their connecting walls form a chain from the top of the hill halfway down its slope, each tower positioned to provide a view of the plains in every direction. Tibet proper was secured from earliest times with a series of such fortresses and towers, linking the country together within a network of defensive strongholds.

Below the fortress itself, in a saddle on the ridge of the hill, rests the House of the Protector Deities, a temple with statues of the local deities and the *dharmapalas,* or protectors of religion. No permanent caretaker lives there. Farther down the southeastern side of the hill stands the large monastery of the Gelukpa sect, said to have been built in the time of the Great Fifth Dalai Lama. In the center of the hill, facing due south and predating the Gelukpa Monastery by hundreds of years, is the Mendur Monastery of the Nyingma Pa sect. Until 1950 this monastery was surrounded by the homes of the monks and their families, and on the plain below, at the edge of the hill, were the homes of the people of Shelkar district, some five hundred dwellings in all.

Protecting the Harvest

As a regional center before 1950, Shelkar commanded the jurisdiction of seven adjoining regions and had its own *dzong pun* (*rdzong dpon*), or local district officer.

Plate 34. The ruin of an ancient fortress atop a hill in southwestern Tibet. The Tibetan countryside is dotted with such ruins, and many towns and monasteries are still located on nearby hillsides. The modern structure on the road below is a recent addition. 1986.

This small district lay within a larger region administered by a governor, *chikab*. Looking south over the valley of the Shichu River, Shelkar proper was primarily a farming area; the other six regions had mixed farming and grazing. The fields of Shelkar were situated at a distance from the town at the bottom of the hill, close to the local water source and the irrigation channels. As in all Tibet, clouds bringing moisture to feed the fields originated south of the Himalayan mountain chain in India and had to travel up over the peaks to reach this region. The people of Shelkar, which had a low annual precipitation rate of eleven inches and the unruly weather patterns characteristic of a perilously high mountain chain affecting even that, lived in a quixotic environment given to dramatic shifts in temperature and moisture. As a consequence, careful preservation of the harvest was essential. Sowing barley in the fifth Tibetan month in fields of only a few *kung* (*rkang*)[1] each, the farmers of the seven regions under the jurisdiction of the Crystal Fortress all relied very heavily on the official hail protector to keep them safe from the ravages of nature during the growing period.

The head of the Mendur Monastery in the center of the hill was called "the lama from below the Crystal Fort" or, simply, the Shelkar lama. His father had been the head of this old monastery, as had his grandfather and great-grandfather, for the position could be inherited only by the eldest male in the family. His entire life had been spent in Shelkar, where it was also the particularly consuming job of the head Nyingma Pa lama to be the hail protector of the entire area. He had entered the monastery at the age of eight to begin his training and by twenty-two had replaced his father and begun the annual cycle of rituals necessary to keep hail and other inclement elements from visiting the precarious crops of the entire district. In keeping with the traditions of his particular sect and his position, his hair was kept long, he did not wear monastic robes, and he had taken a wife and produced children. Part of his income was the yearly hail protection tax, *ser tel* (*ser khral*), from the people of the district.

The Shelkar lama, aided by an abbot, managed the Mendur Monastery, coordinating all its rituals and the lives of its eight other members, their families, and their fields. The monastery itself was provisioned from four sources: the work of the nine monks and their families and relatives in the separate fields assigned to the monastery, grain allocations from the fields of the surrounding population, funds from the local district officer, and funds from the local Gelukpa Monastery. Most of these provisions were used for rituals in the monastery, not as supplies for the nine monks; they provided their own living necessities from a yearly salary paid to them directly by the government and from working their own fields.

At the beginning of every growing season a small house was built in the middle of the fields by the Mendur monks, and there the Shelkar lama would begin his three-month period of daily rituals to secure the fields from the wrath of the regional deities. In his area the most important of six local protector gods was the Great Black One, Mahakala, whose statue stood in the House of the Protector Deities on the hill. The lama's rituals consisted primarily of obeisances to this deity.

Mahakala appears in over seventy different forms. In his form as one of the main protective deities of Tibetan Buddhism, he wears a tiger-skin loincloth and stands on a conquered demon. His skin is black, and his round face, savagely snarling at the viewer, boasts three wild eyes and a snake curling through his hair. Bedecked with ornaments and earrings, he is surrounded by an aura of brilliant yellow flames. The image of Mahakala in Shelkar showed garlands of freshly severed heads and human skulls around his neck and waist, and in his six hands he carried a chopper, a blood-filled skull cup, a trident, and thunderbolts.

Dharmapalas such as Mahakala—the masters of hail, the masters of lightning, the water spirits, and other demon gods—exert a great effect upon weather conditions. Only a person with the profound training of the Tantric practitioner, *ngakpa* (*sngags pa*), such as the Shelkar lama and his father (who had initiated him), knew the mystical prayers and chants that could properly effect propitiation. The lama sat throughout the summer in his hut in the fields, channeling and concentrating his energy into ritual ceremonies involving the five important instruments of the hail protector—the scepter, bell, dagger, thighbone trumpet, and drum—and chants and meditations to the deity. Only when he was called to the house of the head irrigator to adjudicate a violation of the "Green Rules" did the lama leave the fields.

The Green Rules

To secure the fields against the harm that would result from the acts of humans, rather than gods, required different steps. One of the headmen of the district, always a literate man, called a yearly meeting of ten to thirteen monastic and secular representatives from the region in the early spring to draft a long agreement document.[2]

Plate 35. Mural of Mahakala, a *dharmapala* or Dharma Protector, from the walls of Tashilungpo Monastery. In this version Mahakala has only two hands. He holds a *vajra* in his extended right hand and is surrounded by an aura of flames. 1986.

The final document was read to all present, stamped with a seal by each representative, and then related by them to most of the farmers of the seven regions of the district; it was presumed to be understood by and apply to all. These Green Rules, *ngotim* (*sngo khrims*) as they were called, prohibited the following actions during the growing season:

- crying or yelling in the fields;
- fighting or arguing anywhere in the district but particularly in the fields or between women;
- women loosening their hair in the fields;
- wandering naked in the fields;
- taking red meat into the fields;
- taking a red clay pot, a black animal, a black tent, or a yak into the fields;
- digging in the ground;
- constructing a building anywhere in the area.

Plate 36. Ritual implements for an exorcism in Dharamsala, India: two bells and two *vajras,* a polished mirror, a bowl of rice, and a ritual ablution vessel with peacock feathers to wash away the stains left by bad actions. Other implements used but not shown here included a dagger, a thighbone trumpet, a human skull cup, and drums. Two covered teacups sit behind the implements. 1984.

During the tenure of the last Shelkar lama, the members of an important family that owned a large amount of land in the area began to argue publicly. As it was during the summer months of the growing season, their arguments violated the Green Rules, and a servant of the family was sent to a servant of the headman of their region to discuss the problem. Fearful of getting involved, the headman's servant said that he could not help them. Next, one family member visited the headman himself and requested his advice. The response was deemed inappropriate by the whole family, and the fighting escalated.

Consequently, within a day or two a meeting of the Green Rules committee was called to consider this violation, and the Shelkar lama was brought from the field.

The meeting took place in the house of the Shelkar head irrigator, *nédan* (*gnas rten*), who was in charge of both the irrigation system and the allocation of water in the entire region. A farmer himself, he had inherited this position from his father; succession passed automatically to the eldest lineal male of the next generation. Each of the seven regions had its own irrigator in charge of water allocation, but the irrigator of Shelkar was considered the head irrigator.

Seating arrangements for the Green Rules committee (see Figure 9l), whether drafting the rules or hearing cases, followed a strict order by rank: the most honored cushions were placed farthest from the door with tables in front of them. From the highest position by the back wall to the lowest position near the door, the thirteen committee members assembled in the house of the Shelkar irrigator to hear this case in the 1950s were seated as follows: (1) the representative from the Gelukpa Monastery, (2) the Shelkar lama, (3) the head irrigator for Shelkar, (4–5) the head irrigators from the Dorgye and Phule areas, (6) the abbot of the Mendur Monastery, (7) the representative from the farmers of government land, (8–10) the headmen of the Moyel, Gayshin, and Yangshi areas, (11) an irrigation worker from the Mendur Monastery, and (12–13) two additional irrigation workers.

First, beer was offered to the assembly by the embattled family. After this, the committee heard testimony from both sides. Then, item by item, they allocated the property, servants, money, and land of the family so that a separation could take place. At the conclusion of the settlement the family was charged a prescribed amount of roasted barley flour and incense to be used for ritual offerings to the deities. This decision, reached and agreed to by all thirteen members of the committee, was accepted by the family, and the fighting ceased. No hail or inclement weather was reported as a result of the dispute, and residents of the Shelkar district concluded that the problem had been solved before damage could be done.

In another case, a member of the community reported that he had seen two people allow a black *zo* to wander into the fields. Three of the lowest-ranking members of the committee of thirteen—one headman and two irrigation workers—were sent out as investigators to find the two individuals and bring them, along with the witness, to a meeting of the committee the next day.

The seating followed that of the previous case. All three parties were called into the room at the same time, and the witness was asked to relate the incident. As the other two did not accept her story, the Shelkar lama and the other twelve members asked them questions until the two did agree with the witness's version. Once all parties were in agreement, no more questions were asked. After a brief consultation among themselves to determine the root cause, a punishment was announced, based on the "size of the violation." The penalty in this case included cash payments and ritual offerings of food to appease the deities. The offending parties and the witness were instructed to exchange white scarves and apologies after the proceeding.

Exegesis

In villages and estates throughout Tibet, just as in the house of the head irrigator of Shelkar at the foot of the massive stone hill, groups of local representatives met yearly to compose and enforce local versions of the Green Rules. These regulations were a secular means of discouraging human behavior that could violate the cosmological balance by offending the gods and thereby had an enormous potential effect upon the entire community. Just as the local hail protector provided proper obeisance to the guardian deities through his profound rituals in the fields, the correct behavior of the occupants of the area secured the community against the wrath of destructive forces. The Green Rules defined socially impermissible actions and provided guidelines for the whole community.

Perhaps the most distinctive and typically Tibetan feature of these rules was the limited nature of the jurisdiction of the decision-making body. Temporally, the committee of thirteen constituted a legal body only in the months of the growing season and for offenses directly related to the cosmological safety of the fields. The same offense occurring at another time was understood in a completely different way: that is, as socially incorrect behavior without cosmological consequences. The former Shelkar lama stated that a similar case of family separation in the winter months was *not* dealt with by these thirteen. Disputes over the ownership of land which occurred during the growing season but did not involve serious arguments between the parties appear not to have gone before the Green Rules committee either. And whereas an animal in the fields during growing season was the committee's concern, the borrowing and lending of animals in that period was not.

Although the dates of the growing season and some of the rules might vary, this form of agreement among local farmers was common in farming communities throughout Tibet. In Lhoka, more than three hundred miles east of Shelkar, the rules were much the same, although they did not include violations by animals. The Lhoka Green Rules were in force from the fifteenth day of the fourth Tibetan month, when the crops came up "as green as grass," to the fifteenth day of the eighth month, when they were harvested. During these four months the Green Rules of Lhoka, like the Green Rules of Shelkar, applied to the entire district population.

In the Tibetan world view of the everpresentness of realms, this-worldly and otherworldly realms coexist simultaneously, with immediate repercussions passing from one to the other. Discord in this world may cause repercussions in the next and project harm directly back on this world. These Tibetan cosmological conceptions were basic to the legal process itself and formed part of the legal cosmology. As a consequence, local nongovernmental units organized themselves into drafting and sanctioning bodies for their own protection against otherworldly reactions. The legal ritual employed used a legal spatial format and Tibetan jurisprudential concepts such as consensus, root cause, and reharmonization. Conflict in this world had to be avoided to protect the crops; local tribunals were the answer.

Excursus: Nomadic Legal Process

Nomadic legal processes on the Plateau are not covered in this book, but two nomads—one from the far west, the other from the northeast—offer a taste of their attitudes toward law. According to the son of a nomadic leader in a western area north of Mount Kailash,

> we nomads had our own legal system. So when the head of our people wanted all his people to meet, he didn't send out a paper, like the farmers, but passed the word around from family to family tent. If a man did not come on time to the known meeting place, he would be fined by the day for his absence. The rules of our group were known to every family head; they were written down in a folding document, which the headman kept. These were the local rules which we made for ourselves and not the government rules, which we also had to obey.
>
> Decisions in our group were made by the headman and four others in a meeting in the special tent that we had for this purpose called the headquarters tent. When they could not decide a case, it was sent to the district officer of our area, and from there it was supposed to be sent to Lhasa, but this was very rare. This was the way it was handled in our area of Nari.

In the comments of a nomadic headman from the Nangchen Kingdom in the northeast, south of Lake Kokonor, his tribe's access to several law codes is of particular interest.

> My father had over 3,000 families under him, all nomads, and also twelve monasteries within our grazing area. He was a big prince under the king of our area, and the king was under the central government in Lhasa, though he had no government officers stationed with him because he operated it like an independent territory.
>
> My father used to read all the Tibetan legal documents, and he understood all the meanings of the texts because he had been taught this from his father and from his father's father, and so on, and so he taught me. In our tent he kept three different law books. One was Chinese, and it was a book with a blue cloth and had been made by a Chinese man who came to our area once. He had copied it down. The second was Mongolian, and we got this from the Mongolians when they came through our area a long time ago with Gushri Khan. The third was a Tibetan law book, which was red, and it was called the Neudong code, which was written during the Phamogru period.
>
> My father taught me that the Chinese law book was all physical punishments, the Mongolian book talked of gold and article payments, and the Tibetan law book spoke of religious articles, moral rules, the making of Buddhist statues, and so on. This was the difference. My father said that our tribe used the Tibetan law, so I was taught this text.

CHAPTER SEVENTEEN

A Small Private Estate

In one of his previous lives, the Buddha was one of five hundred businessmen who were sailing across the ocean on a trip to sell sheep. He could foresee that one of the other businessmen was going to kill the sailor steering the boat and that this would cause all five hundred to die. So to save the five hundred, the Buddha turned and killed this man by stabbing him with a knife. Here

> (1) the *object* is the man trying to kill the sailor,
> (2) the *motivation* is to save the lives of five hundred people,
> (3) the *action* is to stab with a knife, and
> (4) the *completion* is the death of the businessman.

In the sense of *dharma,* this has a profound meaning, and [we assess this situation in *dharma* and] in law with these four [factors].

—Former Tibetan official

Private estates in Tibet, usually held as grants by private individuals for their service as government officials, ranged from enormous landholdings to single farms, from lands held by the same family for over five centuries to those recently acquired.[1] The typical private estate was of moderate size and included several peasant villages; an appointed steward ran the agricultural and administrative operations from the large estate house. Although a steward for a monastic estate might be a monk, a government official, or a layperson, the private estate steward was almost invariably a male servant of the family that held the estate. He was responsible for collecting taxes, organizing work, and handling legal disputes. Most disputes concerned property and taxes, but minor criminal matters, which had to be forwarded to the local district officer, arose as well. An estate steward could also accept cases brought to him with a request for conciliation or internal settlement.

The usual route for a legal case on a private estate began at the local community level—often a peasant village headman or council—and then went to the local estate steward. If the case was still not settled, two routes were available: it could be taken either to the secretary of the family and then the family head (usually located either on the major family estate or in the capital city), or to the government court of the local district officer. The former route was followed consistently in civil cases, the latter almost always in serious criminal cases, but both were available for either type of case. The steward's office in the estate house also served as the courtroom and storage room for documents, legal files, and record books.

The long case that follows, compiled from three narratives, starts with the arrival of a new family steward in the late 1940s at a small private estate of the Surkhang family in the Yarlung Valley southeast of Lhasa.

The New Steward

The ferry across the Tsangpo River disgorged its assorted contents onto the southern riverbank, and the new young steward, his attendant, and their horses disembarked. Karma Tesering and his attendant mounted their horses at the top of the bank. As they rode southeast, a strong, sharp wind came down the side valley that unfolded slowly before them. Distant ridges were only spotted with snow, for it was the third Tibetan month and the beginning of the end of winter.

Karma had traveled a hundred kilometers southeast of Lhasa and crossed the Tsangpo by ferry to reach the Neudong district on the banks of a southern tibutary of the river. This part of the district, called the Yarlung Valley, stretched fifty kilometers to the southeast of the river and was the seat of the royal lineage of the ancient Tibetan Empire. The famous Tsetang Monastery, founded in 1390, was located here. This valley remained one of the most sacred places on the Plateau.

Karma had been appointed estate steward, called a *shidu* (*gzhis sdod*), to manage *kesum shika* (*mkhas gsum gzhis ka*), one of the eight private farms held by the Surkhang family. This would not be a vast kingdom to oversee: he had been told that it was a small estate with an estate house overlooking two villages that comprised forty households altogether.

While staying in his employer's family house in Lhasa over the previous months, Karma had received his formal instructions, been given some provisions, and collected information from other servants who had been to the estate. He would be managing a seven-hundred-*khel* farm[2] watered by melting mountain snow that was supplied to the fields through irrigation channels. The irrigator on this estate, known as the *légyap pa* (*las rgyab pa*), was one of the first people he would contact. As every private estate had a central house from which it was administered, Karma knew he would be given the steward's quarters there; the family rooms would remain empty unless any members should visit this estate. He hoped the family would recall him to Lhasa after a few years and then reassign him—perhaps to a bigger estate, perhaps to a more important post in the city. Although he felt assured of a lifelong position with the Surkhang family, he knew his performance at this post would be significant in determining his next assignment.

His father had died when Karma was still very small, leaving the family without an income. From the age of eleven he had begged his mother to send him to Lhasa to be trained in reading and writing and from fifteen to eighteen he had indeed attended the Lhasa Narang Sha School for training that enabled him to enter the service of the Surkhangs at the age of nineteen as a personal servant. A lifetime position with a noble family meant a permanent income for his mother. Most of the other servants and managers of the Surkhangs had been capable children from the estates who had been schooled and trained at the family's expense.

Managerial skills, discretion, skills in writing and reading documents and correspondence, and the ability to win the good will of the villagers were the attributes of a good estate steward. Most important, he had to be able to operate entirely on his own but with a true sense of his employer's wishes and directives, particularly in the day-to-day aspects of running the estate. He would prostrate daily at the family altar and do a ritual when he arrived so that the goddess Tara would help him in this task.

The Surkhang family, Karma had learned from his teacher, was not considered a truly big landowner, despite its eight different estates throughout Tibet, four of which—in the Tsang area—were large. And even though highly ranked, the Surkhangs had received their land through government service; they were not descended from any of the original kings of Tibet or their ministers.[3]

Once, when traveling to the city of Gyantse, Karma had seen a truly large Tibetan estate. Its irrigation canals, he remembered, stretched as far as the eye could see. The estate house, where the travelers had stopped for water, had a very large courtyard containing outbuildings, and the main house had whitewashed walls, big windows outlined in black bands of paint, and a main door approached by wide stairs on which were perched pots of flowers in greeting. The household staff alone had seemed to him large enough for a small town: weavers, copiers of manuscripts, cooks, carpenters, and blacksmiths were working in the courtyard and surrounding buildings. The estate manager there must have been a very regal man because he had not come out to greet them when they arrived; instead, they were given water by a female servant. After chatting a bit with her, they had left, traveling for the rest of the day on roads through estate lands. Kesum farm would be nothing like that.[4]

Karma stopped twice on his journey from the ferry through this valley of monasteries, temples, and fortresses of ancient origin.[5] First, he made the requisite visit to the local district officer and his wife, staying for three cups of Tibetan tea. The district officer gave him a copy of a government document and the responsibility of carrying it to his area. Next, Karma stopped at a well-known monastery and, after making an offering, asked that a hundred butter lamps be lit in his father's name. Then he hurried on, anxious to reach the estate.

Asking the way from two or three peasants beside the road, Karma and his attendant finally turned up a small path leading toward the hills. The estate house he saw in the distance was quite small, really no bigger than a large peasant house. The caretaker took the horses to be watered, and he was led inside by a house servant. From the kitchen, he was taken into the main room and seated with considerable respect on a mattress on the floor. A small wooden table was placed in front of him, and sitting cross-legged on the mattress, he sipped Tibetan tea from a porcelain cup with a delicate lid and ate the meal prepared for him. After offering greetings, some of the estate servants engaged him in polite conversation and listened to the news of Lhasa with keen interest. Later he was shown to the steward's quarters.

Karma decided to open the government document before resting and immediately recognized that he had been given the famous Mountain Valley Decree, *rilung tsatsik* (*ri klung rtsa tshig*). He closed it, returned it to the table before him, then gently lifted the document from both ends and pressed the middle to his forehead in reverence. He said a quiet prayer for the long life of His Holiness the Dalai Lama. Then he carefully unrolled the document again on the table before him. It was indeed an honor to be entrusted with one of the copies of this decree, he thought, as awe tinged with pride washed over him.

When he was a child, everyone had been called to appear at the district office the day after the decree arrived in town each year. In the morning, the district officer came out and announced that he had received the Mountain Valley Decree; in a loud voice he said that all the laws of the country were contained in this document, which showed the basis of good behavior for all people. He then read the entire decree. It talked of the snowbound lands of Tibet, a place of few conflicts and strong religion, where the manifestation of the Buddha Chenresi lived in a human incarnation in the form of His Holiness the Thirteenth Dalai Lama. It listed the Ten Virtues of Buddhism, stating that all Tibetans should abide by them. Hunting of wild animals, overloading pack animals, and all fishing were prohibited. No hunting or killing of animals should take place on the eighth, tenth, or twenty-fifth day of the month. Young people were instructed to respect their elders, the blind, and the infirm. Countless other rules followed, including even such details as the interest allowed on government loans, private loans, and contracts.

Finally, the district officer finished with the closing lines, the full name of the Thirteenth Dalai Lama, the Tibetan year and date, and the official seal. Then he said in a very loud voice, "In the future, if anyone in this area violates this decree, you will be punished, because you have heard it read to you." With these words, he turned and hung the document under the eaves of the district house on a wooden board with the auspicious pot of flowers symbols, *bumpa* (*bum pa*), carved on either side. Once the officer had gone inside, everyone gathered around the board.

The decree, always written on the finest paper, unrolled to almost a yard in width and two yards in length. The writing was exquisite; even those who could not read would marvel at the elegant shapes of the finest government *duktsa* script. At the top was a large red seal of the Dalai Lama's Office; it was followed by exactly forty-five lines of even script, all perfectly spaced. The villagers went up to receive the blessing of the even larger red seal of His Holiness at the bottom, which was placed near his many-worded full name.

The decree on the table before Karma in the small estate house was just such a document. Hundreds of copies were drafted each year by the clerks in the Private Office of His Holiness and then stamped by that office with both seals. That the documents came directly from the Private Office pleased everyone who saw them. Karma had seen copies in other villages and around Lhasa, but he had not been impressed in the same way as when he was a child. Each year the basic content of the document was the same, but small changes were made by the Dalai Lama himself, usually concerning days for special offerings to certain images of the Buddhas and

Plate 37. An official edict, possibly the Mountain Valley Decree, posted in a covered area in Lhasa. 1920–21. (Pitt Rivers Museum, University of Oxford)

Bodhisattvas during that year. Sometimes there were comments about secular affairs, such as a statement that violations by the people should be treated through the government and headmen of the villages, or that monasteries should not avoid giving salaries to individual monks.[6]

The people in Karma's birth area said that copies of the decree were sent out by His Holiness to be read to all the people of the country to promote peace and prosperity, to remind Tibetans of the words of the Buddha, to reiterate the legal rules, and to caution them to avoid conflicts. Every villager knew that violation of the Mountain Valley Decree provisions meant punishment by the district officers. Karma wondered how the people in this area understood the decree and where he was supposed to hang it. He rolled up the document, covered it, blew out his mustard oil lamp, and retired for the night.

Reopening the Donkey Tax Case

More than a week later, while awaiting visits from the village headmen, Karma sat with a cup of tea before him, thinking of his mother. He came out of his reverie when a man called out a respectful title of address from the next room and then entered his room with an older woman in tow. They both wore the clothing of peasant farmers and had weathered faces and arms. The woman carried a bundle under her left arm, which she placed on the floor after Karma invited them in. Standing in a bowed position, the man introduced himself as Thobgyal Tsering, the headman of one of the two villages of the estate, and the woman as his elder wife, one of two sisters to whom he was married. Karma recognized him as one of the men who had previously come to give greetings. He beckoned for them to sit down and called for a servant to bring tea. Karma remained silent as the tea was served and watched very carefully the face of the man serving them. The best-quality cups had not been used, he noticed; apparently the servant considered the visitors somewhat lacking in manners and status. As the servant shuffled out of the room, Karma reminded himself to be cautious in initial encounters with subordinates.

Pleasantries about his health were exchanged, and then Thobgyal began in his best elegant speech: "Honored gentleman from Lhasa who has nobly come to our area to be the honorable estate steward, we are pleased to know that you will be guiding us in our business and farming. As peasants of the estate, we have been good subjects to the Surkhang family for countless years. We are happy that you have come." As he spoke, the woman came forward and placed a middle-quality white scarf and a small package on the table in front of him. "We hope, therefore, that you will listen to our humble petition to you. We bring it to you informally at home to ask for your advice."

The man then embarked on what was almost a lecture,[7] albeit in honorific language, which sounded as if he were addressing an important child:

As you know, tax cases in every area of Tibet are not really disputes. If a man does not pay his taxes, which is very rare indeed, in any case, he will eventually be persuaded by officials from the Department of Accounting of the central government to pay. The department will investigate his reasons for nonpayment, whether he is really unable to pay or just shameless, and so forth.

Then the man will be asked to pay the back taxes in a certain amount of time, and he must bring a guarantor. When he appears in front of the government official, the guarantor will be asked by the department to realize that he now also has full responsibility if the first man doesn't pay. The official says, "You must now pay if he cannot." All of this is then written in the debt document.

If the man still does not pay in the next year, the guarantor is called in and asked to tell the delinquent man to pay. Then the official says to the guarantor, "If the delinquent man has nothing, you will have to pay." The delinquent man, if he still does not pay, may be whipped or imprisoned, and the guarantor will be fined for the amount.

Thobgyal stopped to get his breath and take a sip of tea. Karma had remained absolutely impassive in his expression. He noticed, however, that the servant was listening from the doorway and that several people who had arrived to speak with the estate steward were gathered in the kitchen, also listening to this man's talk and whispering periodically among themselves. What did they all make of this, he wondered? The man continued as before:

Now if the guarantor is forced to pay and all he owns is his land, then this information is sent to the office in Lhasa. In the decision document, which comes from Lhasa, regarding the forfeiture of land of the guarantor, it says the way in which the land must be handed over: "In front of the village headman and the district officer, this piece of property described as being owned by the guarantor and called this name must be handed over." This is what it says.

Also, the central government will send a separate letter with the full instructions for implementing the debt punishment. Such a document, as you know, cannot be disobeyed. If it is, the person who disobeys will be severely punished. All this is known by a person who is educated, as you are.

"The man is becoming ponderous," Karma thought, "and I am tired of his speech. I hope that this is not the customary way of speaking in this area, because it seems rather insulting." Still he sat impassively and occasionally sipped his tea. As the woman got up and put a plain folded document on the table in front of Karma, her husband added: "Our petition to you, sir, which is written in correct form, shows that this has occurred just as I have described."

Karma looked down at the document and unrolled it. It was a formal, well-written petition, and the first point after the introductory section stated that a man named Wangchen Tsermo had been one donkey short of the corvée transport tax requirement for his area.

Karma, struggling to maintain his composure, asked, "You mean that the delinquent tax you propose to address to the Accounting Office of the government is for one donkey load?" He heard several people suppressing their laughter in the next room and realized that they had all been eagerly waiting for his response. Then he said in a calm voice, "When did this case take place?" Thobgyal Tsering responded:

Yes, it is for one donkey load, sir, but one donkey load is just that, one required donkey load. The sending of horses and other animals to carry the government taxes in produce to the district office is also a tax that we all must bear. In this part of the district, the private estates, which have their lands measured in *don* units, have approximately thirty *don,* the monastic estate has twenty-five *don,* and the government areas, with measurements called *kung,* have forty-five *kung.* This makes one hundred units for our area.

Now, ten years ago, a letter came directly from the Cabinet of the government of His Holiness the Dalai Lama to this district office saying, "This year we need five thousand *khel* for army food plus corvée animals in transport." To us, this means a prorated calculation [of 2,500 *khel* for our half of the district]. Each five-*khel* load takes one animal for transport, which means five hundred animals. One *don* or *kung* measurement equals five *khel* also. Therefore, to carry the *khel* of grain, the animals were divided up as follows; 150 animals due in tax from the private estates, 125 from the monastic estate peasants, and 225 animals from the government subjects.

Again the man stopped for breath and a sip of tea.

Now this is only one of the private estates in this area, and we owe a small part of the tax. But Wangchen Tsermo did not bring his donkey for loading of the tax and transport as required. My donkey was used instead, and the use has never been returned to me. For this reason, I petitioned to your predecessor and then to the head secretary of the Surkhang family in Lhasa that the Accounting Office be informed and that his land be taken away as a debt. You will see that in the document also.

Karma then said, "And why do you bring this case to me now, when it was decided against you ten years ago by the Surkhang secretary?"

The man responded, "Sir, there are still many problems between Wangchen Tsermo and me, and he still has not paid his tax. If a dispute is not settled correctly, it always causes disharmony in the future. We ask you to reconsider this case."

Karma asked, "And where is the piece of land you want in compensation for the debt in relation to your land in the village?" He hear loud stirrings in the next room.

The man replied without shame, "It is next to my piece of land in the village." With this, Karma looked at him squarely and said in a firm but low voice:

I have received your petition and have heard your side of this case. I understand the root cause of the dispute and will now consider the immediate cause. I will call the other party for questioning. In law, it is said that ordinary laypeople should not act for their own benefit, for if they do, they do not see the truth and they do not know the meaning of the law. Please return to me only when I send a servant to call you to discuss the case again. Otherwise, you need not come to discuss this dispute further.

He paused and then asked, "Do you as the headman have anything to report to me as the new steward about the households in your village?"

Thobgyal Tsering rose perfunctorily and bowed, as did the woman. "Our village lives harmoniously," he responded and gave the customary farewell in honorific but not elegant speech. The two exited amid hushed whispers, and as they left the house through the kitchen door, Karma heard the man shout back to one of the others something about never giving up his important case.

Several other men entered the room together and approached Karma respectfully.

As they sat, Karma noticed their good manners and friendliness to him, which he appreciated. Tea was served again, and introductory questions about health and travel were exchanged. Karma saw that his day would be long but relaxing. As he chatted, he remembered that he must ask which lama in the area would be appropriate for determining the most auspicious day for the reading of the Mountain Valley Decree.

Exegesis

Karma was given the Mountain Valley Decree, a formal legal decree that was read orally to the entire population once a year during the third month. Right after the new year, clerks in the office of His Holiness the Dalai Lama began making copies in elegant script, to be sent out to every part of Tibet. Although no copy of the edict has ever been obtained, many Tibetans recalled hearing it read aloud and seeing it posted, including a former clerk in the Private Office of the Dalai Lama who had himself copied it hundreds of times over several years. He confirmed that the decree was forty-five lines long and done in the best script on the best paper with large seals in red ink at the top and the bottom. He and several others stated that the decree began by describing the country of Tibet as a snowbound land over which the incarnation of the Buddha, the Dalai Lama, reigned in peace, a country of few conflicts and great devotion to religion. The fact that it came directly from the highest authority gave it great significance in the minds of the people, and given this traditional process of dissemination, many Tibetans knew of its contents. The document was understood to be a means of informing the population annually of their legal rights and duties and emphasizing the importance of Buddhism as the basic standard for all government procedures and all cases of law.

In the matter of the donkey tax, Karma, the estate steward, had no intention of pursuing the case but did not directly insult the petitioner. The case had already traveled extensively through the Tibetan legal system; it had been heard several years earlier by Karma's predecessor and also by the head secretary of the estate owners in Lhasa. Nevertheless, the petitioner presumed that with a change of authority, he could again approach the original forum level.

An important point here is the appropriateness of an issue for a suit. In speaking of what could be called a "frivolous" suit at law, Tibetans used words meaning not reckless or hasty action but crafty and deceitful behavior, implying the existence of a bad motivation: the frivolous petitioner was "acting for his own benefit" in filing the suit. Tibetans had a strong concept of appropriate subject matter at law, and they dealt with frivolous suits in several different ways: the judge could politely acknowledge the case but never go forward with it (which is what happened in this example); he could use backhanded ridicule of the petitioner, thereby causing the eventual dissolution of the suit; or, in formal government courts, he could order corporal punishment for the petitioner bringing a frivolous suit.

The concept of *res judicata* (the matter has been decided) in Western legal cosmology states that once a claim based on the facts in a particular case has been adequately and competently adjudged by a court with jurisdiction, and the positions of the parties with respect to those facts affixed, the decision by that court is a complete bar to any further claims by those parties in that or any other court. Such a concept was absent in Tibet, as the foregoing case illustrates. For Tibetans, unless both sides were in true agreement about the decision, or unless one party was so much more power-ful than the other that the case could not be reconsidered (as in criminal matters), or unless the Dalai Lama had decided the case, closure never occurred. This case could remain permanently open. Time was no bar, going to a judge was no bar, that both parties had signed and sealed a decision and stated that they would not reopen the case was no bar, and even payments and final settlement were no bar to reopening a case if one of the parties continued to feel injured. The locus of decision-making was the individual mind. Many Tibetans cited this as one of the fairest and most advan-tageous aspects of the Tibetan legal system; they would say, "It is not necessary to agree with the decision." Cases, like human lives, always had a new chance to improve in their next rebirth.

Ironically, even though Tibetans considered tax cases to be administrative rather than legal matters, this was a legal case based on an unpaid tax. The petitioner was suing for compensation for the services of an animal that he had provided to cover the animal tax debt of another, however, so it was actually a private, as opposed to a government, tax suit. Still, it should be noted that taxes, when paid by others, could be the subject of such suits between persons of the village, rather than between the government and the delinquent taxpayer. The explanation in this case of the process by which delinquent tax matters were handled was accurate for south-central Tibet.[8]

Three final small points of interest are the formal nature of this style of internal settlement ritual, the way in which deference by servants in Tibet gave clues as to the social position of various people, and the importance of levels of honorific address and language in Tibetan for judging the intended meaning and attitude of a speaker.

Excursus: Taxation

The standard Tibetan land tax was adopted from the ancient Indian system and called, "a sixth part of the field," meaning that one-sixth or approximately 16 percent of the produce of every field was due to the government. The tax on a newly cultivated field was a less onerous "tenth profit." An assessment of tax was computed when the land was granted to a person and written into the deed document. Every land deed held by a Tibetan peasant in the central area of the southern arc and recorded in the land book for the area included the name of the property ("white part" or "Dorje's plot"), a description of its boundaries, its seed requirements, the family name of the owner, its designation as monastic, private, or government land, and the kind and amount of taxes due from it.

Previous authors have stated that every agriculturist was connected to a village, a monastic estate, or a private estate to which he or she was expected to pay taxes and from the last two of which the peasant could not depart without permission and payment of a "man tax." According to Eva Dargyay (1982:9), the "state of dependency" was even more binding: it "began at birth; within a single family it was inherited unilaterally; when the father was subjected to landlord A, all his sons would belong as tenants to landlord A though the daughters followed their mother's dependency. Thus among the members of each family, theoretically, the male and female members belonged to different landlords. The tenant was incapable of canceling the dependency during his lifetime and the landlord, in turn, was not permitted to dismiss any tenant."

My data indicate that an inherited "dependency relationship" did obtain between the family and the estate landlord when a single family continued to maintain the land and household, did not cancel its tax liability through a man tax, and did not contract marriages with farmers of different landlords, thus allowing for the daughters and sons to have different landlords. Cancellation of tax liability certainly was difficult—involving permission, payment of the man tax, and the redeeding of the property—but it is important to remember that the household with its shifting membership, not particular dependent family members, owed the tax. The household occupying the land, the *kim tsang*, which could include an assortment of people, was viewed as the unit working and reaping the benefits from the land. If a daughter, her husband, and two laborers ate together, lived in the house, and worked the fields, it was this unit that was responsible for the taxes, not the brothers away in monasteries or on trading adventures. As a consequence, the more workers in a household unit, or tenants who paid an amount of their yield to the landowner for the privilege of cultivating the field, the easier the tax burden on the house. Thus, the household (or tenthold)—not the nuclear or extended family, the lineage, or the village—retained the primary asset for economic production (usually land or herds), the tax liability, responsibility to the community, and the name used by its members. Among agriculturists, the village—made up of households—constituted the next inclusive unit, not a lineage or clan. The village was responsible for organizing certain taxes, providing young boys to the monasteries as trainees, and supplying labor for the repair of irrigation works or transport of government supplies.

There were six basic forms of taxation in Tibet (for Tibetan terms, see French 1990a). First, agricultural taxes were paid in produce, labor, or manufactured products, as in grain (measured by volume), rice, field labor, roasted barley, braided ropes, mustard oil.

Second, animal taxes were paid in whole animals, their products, or manufactured items: for example, meat (measured by part and whole animals), butter (measured by volume), wool (measured in hides or by weight), and a "butcher tax" (paid in skins or their equivalent).

Third, tea, salt, and commodities taxes on collected or manufactured items were assessed in areas famous for their production; these included tea, salt, borax, paper, wood, gold, silver, and bamboo (for the construction of pens). Special government offices such as the Tea and Salt Office sent out inspectors and collected these taxes.

Fourth, requisitioned work (or corvée labor) taxes were paid in days of labor or specific jobs performed by individuals or by their animals; these taxes were usually apportioned by village and often performed in rotation by farmers. They might involve transporting produce to the next government checkpoint; providing animals for use in transport or carrier service for letters; constructing irrigation ditches, roads, and the like; reaping grass for horse fodder; providing porter service for luggage or carrying banners for the Dalai Lama in Lhasa; provisioning travelers who carried an official road pass; serving temporarily or full time in the military or police or as bodyguard to His Holiness.

Fifth, there were occupational taxes (such as those paid annually by craftsmen), income taxes (paid by traders, for example, on the goods they sold), and customs duties at the border.

Sixth, other assorted taxes and fees included an oracle tax (paid to the State Oracle by lesser mediums and others), a hail protection tax (paid by a village to its hail protector each year), a boat tax (paid annually by a village for ferry service), and some inheritance taxes.

An average Tibetan farming household, then, paid an agricultural tax, in grain or in labor, on its fields; if it had animals, it might owe a relatively small butter tax to the local monastery for use in butter sculptures at the time of the great festival; and it would send members of the household several times a year for government-requisitioned work such as transporting grain or repairing a local bridge. The grain taxes were collected by the local administrative unit—monastery, village headman, private estate office, or district officer; the butter went to the monastery directly; the requisitioned labor was rotated among the farmers of a village, each household's allotted number of days and animals proportionate to its grain tax assessment.

This is an example of an *average* taxpaying household, but in fact, a wide variety of tax patterns existed throughout Tibet. Within one village some peasant households might pay part of their proceeds to monasteries, others to private estates, and still others directly to the government—or the whole village could be entirely of one type. Alternatively, the peasants could have private plots that they worked for themselves and other plots that they worked—alone or with others—for the benefit of a monastery or private family. One household unit could pay government and monastic taxes (although rarely monastic *estate* taxes) at the same time: it could owe jute ropes, perhaps, to the government and butter to the monastery. A region famous for a particular product—such as the southeast was for the bamboo used to make writing pens—could owe its entire tax in its special produce.

Whatever the pattern, taxes could be a burden. Complaints varied considerably among my sources, depending upon the particular area they came from. Understandably, peasants who felt they had been overburdened with taxes disliked the government administration as a whole, while peasants who had had a great deal of autonomy and a light tax load were more likely to have appreciated it.

Some relief was available. The peasant landowner could request to quit the land temporarily or permanently, making a monetary payment for release in lieu of taxes for a number of years; this process, if permanent, could cancel the land deed as well. Peasants of an area could petition together for relief from their tax load, either because it was too burdensome or because of special circumstances such as a flood, fire, or bad harvest. A tax officer or local official who was dishonest or thought to be wringing excessive taxes from the peasantry could be the subject of a petition by local peasants to the Cabinet in Lhasa. Several of the documents I collected are responses by the Cabinet to an area's petition for tax reductions.

To Tibetans, taxation was an administrative issue, not a subject for the courts; as they understood it the legal system was involved in all other aspects of property and land ownership but not in the taxation aspect. In point of fact, however, a separate but similar legal process existed for handling tax cases, with the difference that petitions went to the Cabinet and the Accounting Office rather than to an official court. Shortages or delinquencies in taxes were noted by the local administrative head. If the household in question could not arrange a loan or other remedy, a serious case of delinquency was forwarded to the Accounting Office in Lhasa, which then requested additional information about the nonpayment. If the household had not paid its taxes for a considerable length of time and could offer no extenuating circumstances, a representative, usually the head male, was called to the district office and asked to bring a guarantor with him. Both signed a debt document that described in full the tax debt and the reason for nonpayment. If the person continued to be delinquent after he and his guarantor had been summoned and payment requested, the district official could whip or imprison the delinquent man and fine the guarantor. If both taxpayer and guarantor had only land as their assets, this information was sent to the Accounting Office. After a final investigation, the standard reply from Lhasa was a decision document stating that the land of the debtor or the guarantor should be formally handed over to the government in front of the village headman and the district officer. A separate letter specified the amount of the debt punishment.

CHAPTER EIGHTEEN

A Large Private Estate

The four corners of the human body are the origin of all happiness and misery.
[As] good and bad both come to man, it is necessary not to commit faults.
—Neudong Law Code

Of the many different types of provincial subunits within Tibet, several had an almost independent status. Among these were the two Vatican-like states of Sakya and Tashilungpo, the Kingdom of Dedge, and the ancient palace and lands of the lineage of the first kings, the Lhagyari. Their historic origins allowed them to be incorporated into the Tibetan nation as distinct entities.[1]

In 1940 the Lhagyari lands included twenty-three personal estates and twenty-seven regions that the family managed for the government. It took five days to travel by horse from the northernmost point of these holdings at Rong on the Tsangpo River to the southernmost point, and two days from east to west. There were estimated to be over 50,000 peasants on these lands, supporting nine large monasteries as well as the Lhagyari compound.

The compound of the central estate house—said to have "one hundred pillars," an extremely large structure by Tibetan standards—operated like a small city, storing and producing all the necessities for the family and the surrounding areas. Space was allocated in the compound for all such basic crafts as blacksmithing, weaving, and tailoring, as well as for the three major offices of estate administration, each with at least six staff members: the steward's office, called the *chanzo lékhung* (*phyag mdzod las khung*); the storage office, called the *nokang* (*dngos khang*), which kept the accounts; and the borrowing and lending office. Many of the estate functions took place in the family house itself. On the ground floor were several major storerooms for grain and other commodities. The second floor held the administrative offices, some rooms for visitors, a small chapel, and storage space. The third floor housed guestrooms, special chapels, and receiving rooms. On the fourth floor were the family rooms, quarters for all the personal family servants, and accommodations for very important guests. On the fifth floor were two very large chapels called the Lhakhang and the Gonkhang.

Letters from the central government went to the head steward of the Lhagyari estate, a man chosen through a nomination process by which representatives from the nine monasteries, the twenty-seven regions, and the thirty family servants each proposed a name, one of which was approved by the family. The approved man was then appointed by the central government as the district officer, although he was also expected to act as steward and discuss the administration of the estate daily with the head of the family.

Until the time of the Seventh Dalai Lama in the mid-eighteenth century, these lands had been an entirely separate state. The head of the family at that time accepted affiliation with the central government, and he assumed the third rank for government officials. Thereafter, the family had paid taxes to the government from the twenty-seven regions but never from its own personal estates. Instead, at each New Year, the head of the family took five *tolas* of "middle quality" gold (from the one hundred *tolas* panned annually on the estates) to His Holiness in Lhasa as a present.[2]

The Tibetans who related the following narrative were peasants and servants from the Lhagyari estate and the son of the family lineage holder, who grew up on the estate in the 1930s and 1940s.

Sitting on His Father's Throne

The young son of the Lhagyari family sat rather nervously on his father's seat awaiting the afternoon visits. Lobsang was dressed in a full robe of resplendent yellow Chinese silk with long sleeves turned back at the cuffs, a white silk shirt cut in a more Western style underneath, and a silk sash at his waist. His nails were not long enough or elegant, he thought, as he glanced down at his hands. But the rosary he had wrapped around his left wrist was of precious stones, and a servant had put a long jeweled earring around his right ear for the occasion.

Through the high windows on the fourth floor, he could see out into the courtyard of the palace where some of the headmen from the various regions were arriving on their horses. In the background he could hear the deep wail of the long horns of the seven hundred monks from the Dagpo Shethubling Monastery, who came for twenty days every year during this fourth Tibetan month, the month celebrating the birth, enlightenment, and final passing away from this earth of the Buddha Sakyamuni.

The monks had arrived yesterday afternoon, a vast, red stream pouring into the little village of Risgo Zhol near the palace. What excitement this brought! All the people of the surrounding villages came to see them and returned later to attend the rituals. The same monks also came for a whole month every year to celebrate the Mon Lam Festival at the New Year.

Lobsang's father, accompanied by several servants, had left a week before to travel west to the Yarlung Valley to visit the governor of Neudong district. He was worried about the news of the Chinese that he had heard from the capital and had decided to go himself to learn more. The chief steward of the estate would run everything in his absence, but it seemed more appropriate for his son to speak to visitors, and so Lobsang had been dressed formally this afternoon.

A servant entered, crossed the deeply colored carpets, and, bowing at the waist,

Plate 38. Monks arriving at Spitok Monastery in western Tibet for a festival, wearing the ceremonial yellow hat of the Gelukpa sect and carrying ritual drums. 1976. (Syed Ali Shah, Leh, Ladakh)

placed a silver-covered cup of Tibetan tea on the carved wooden table. Lobsang, sitting cross-legged on two high mattresses at the far end of the room, tried to feel the dignity of his lineage. His was the oldest family in Tibet, tracing back its ancestry through more than a hundred generations to the first historic king and back even further to the original deities who had descended from the sky to found the race of Tibetans.

As the eldest son of the family, Lobsang had already begun instruction in the administration of the estate, its taxes, and its landholdings. All the taxes in butter and barley from their twenty-three private estates went to the family storehouses and were kept there for distribution. The family offices dispensed supplies to the nine monasteries to meet their living requirements, as well as providing for ceremonies and festivals such as the one taking place right now. This estate, perhaps the largest in southern Tibet, had a complex operating and allocating system that required many record books and clerks.

It was Lobsang's job this afternoon to receive the chief steward and a few visitors from the region and to listen to their business for the day. The procedure was one that Lobsang had seen several times. Usually, the chief steward came to his father's rooms after office hours with a list of matters for discussion and would go through each one individually. His father would listen and then approve or make a decision for each subject on the list, and his choice was always the one that was implemented.

Plate 39. A Tibetan cobbler sewing a boot on the streets of Lhasa. 1920–21. (Pitt Rivers Museum, University of Oxford)

Hearing a flurry of activity below, Lobsang decided to see what was going on and stood up on his mattress. Then—not used to the heavy clothing—he gathered up his robes around him and waddled to the window. The courtyard below—ringed by large storage buildings and offices, workshops for craftsmen such as cobblers, and sheds for roasting barley and the like—was filled with people. It was the noise from the edge of the courtyard that held his attention. A large crowd of people had gathered in the corner near a shed, and at the center a monk seemed to be arguing with one of the craftsmen.

As Lobsang watched, however, he realized that it was not one of his family servants but a man from the village whom he had seen only once or twice, a traveling beggar with glasses and a cane who always kept a young boy with him. Together, the two traveled through the countryside begging. They slept wherever the night found them and cooked whatever people gave them, and although the man always wore moderately respectable clothing, the child was covered only in rags. No one knew much about them. The man often beat the young child with a stick and constantly complained about him to anyone who was within earshot. One time when Lobsang and his father had chanced to meet them, the old man sat on a rock by the side of the road while the child approached their horses asking for alms. Lobsang's father had given them a piece of cheese from their supplies but told the old man to take better care of the child.

Now, as Lobsang listened to the loud argument, he realized that the child was the subject of dispute. The old man had been sitting outside waiting for alms during the arrival of the monks, and when he had become disgruntled, he had taken to beating the boy harshly with a stick. One of the women servants had objected, a crowd had formed around them, and finally a monk had taken the stick away from the man. Now everyone stood around the two, listening to them and talking to one another at the same time. Several women came out of the doors to the courtyard, wiping their hands on their wool aprons, and then stood in the crowd with their arms crossed in front of them, children holding on to their skirts.

The monk had stopped the beating out of compassionate feelings for the boy, but now he seemed to be enjoying the argument as a demonstration of his debating prowess. Most of the educated monks had been trained for years in logical analysis. They had learned techniques for debating, using stylized movements that involved stepping forward and slapping their hands before they made a point for the other side to answer. It seemed that the old man would be no match for a monk. But after initially yelling and telling the onlookers it was none of their business, the old man had begun to answer quite well, and the two were engaged. The onlookers drew back from the argument as they saw that the opponents were equally matched and that the old man was using reason.

The old man stated that the child was with him because of the boy's actions in a previous life and that severe beating was the only way to make him behave. Besides, the monk had surely been beaten often at the monastery when he misbehaved; in fact, all children were beaten like this, so there was nothing unusual in it. The monk responded that the man was no religious saint with special knowledge of previous lives and kept the child only for selfish reasons. The old man, who sat on the ground looking up only sporadically, asked the monk how he knew that a beggar was not a famous religious saint. This caused everyone in the crowd to wonder; it was apparent that they had all begun to suspect something of the kind themselves. If the old man was a religious ascetic, the beatings could be a way of helping the child to burn off bad karma. Clearly now, no one would interfere, and although the monk kept questioning, he had lost the force of his argument.

Suddenly Lobsang heard the sound of voices in the corridor, and he leaped back from the window toward his seat. Just then the chief steward came in, accompanied by his secretary and four other men Lobsang did not know. He quickly decided to remain standing on the mattresses and bowed once after they began to bow to him. He thought that he had handled this all very nicely, given the distance he had had to sprint from the window. Sitting down, placing his hands on his lap and beginning to count rosary beads with his left hand, Lobsang waited for the chief steward to handle the meeting. He would say as little as possible; this was the best course.

Tea was served to all present. Everyone asked about his health in elegant terms, and he inquired about their names and their health in nonhonorific terms. It was immensely pleasing to be addressed in this elegant style, Lobsang thought. Although most of those present knew the stylized pleasantries in this exalted speech, they could not have continued in this way for the whole conversation. They spent their lives conversing primarily in ordinary speech and honorifics but were not as familiar with the elegant, highest level of speech.

The chief steward brought up the timing for the religious ceremonies that day and informed Lobsang of the schedule of meals and teas for the monks. Huge metal urns of Tibetan tea, as tall and round as a man, were cooking over fires in the courtyard below. In the large assembly hall in front of the palace the monks were now chanting the Heart of Wisdom Sutra. At night, the monks would sleep on the floor of this temple, while the abbot and his servants stayed in accommodations above the hall. The chief steward reported that the hall had been cleaned and prepared before the arrival of the monks and that the supplies of butter to fill the devotional lamps for the evening ritual were adequate.

Lobsang knew this ritual well and loved to watch it. The monks set up a huge altar in the assembly hall and filled it with offerings of all kinds, giving prayers five times for each of the twenty-one aspects of Tara. Then the monks sat together and, led by the chanting master, intoned the entire Heart of Wisdom Sutra from memory. It was a beautiful speech that had been given by the Lord Avalokitesvara, a Bodhisattva, when he was with the Buddha on Vulture's Peak in India. It contained the essence of the Perfection of Wisdom teachings, the heart of all Buddha's teachings in one, the concept of the emptiness of all things: "In emptiness itself, there are no forms, no feelings, no consciousness, no mental impulses, no perceptions; there are no senses of the eye, the ear, the nose, the tongue, the body, or the mind; there are no forms for the eye, no sounds for the ear, no smells, no tastes, no things to touch, and no objects of the mind."

The sonorous chanting sounded beautiful to Lobsang. At the end of the sutra the Buddha praises Avalokitesvara for his excellent understanding saying, "It is excellent, it is excellent." He loved to think of the Buddha praising his pupils, and he loved the mesmerizing rhythm of the chant. Even to hear it was to gain merit. He knew he would miss it today because of this meeting. At one time his father had thought that Lobsang should become a monk because of his interest in Buddhism, but the family had later decided against it.

The Quarreling Father and Son

Lobsang brought his mind back to the chief steward and the gathering before him. The next point brought up concerned a family dispute. This was exciting, for he had been learning the law codes in his studies, and he might have something to say about this issue. The chief steward outlined what had happened between a father and son who wanted to divide their lands. Lobsang knew that such a case was unusual, because an eldest son, who was expected to inherit the full lands and resources of the father, normally waited until he could take control. But disagreements between these two had led to continual quarreling, and finally a local headman had been called in to conciliate the case; the chief steward used a term meaning "conciliator," *barshu* (*bar gzu*), to refer to him. As the family was very large, the division had been complicated, but the *barshu* had tried to make it equitable. Now, the chief steward said, the *barshu* himself would speak, and he turned to one of the seated men.

The conciliator continued the story. After talking with everyone and achieving a consensual agreement to a division of the property, he said that he had drawn up a conciliation paper, *dumyik,* which was signed by both the father and the son, as well as by the conciliator himself. For several months everything had remained tranquil, but the division agreed to by the family was not made. Then more quarreling had started, and there were charges by both sides of theft of family property. At this point the *barshu* had sent a man to the chief steward, who returned with one of the steward's underlings (here he nodded to one of the seated men). This investigator, *timme (khrims mi)*, had brought back a report to the chief steward which included some written statements from members of the family. This matter was becoming a large dispute in the area.

The *barshu* finished speaking, and the secretary of the chief steward, whom Lobsang knew quite well, picked up the story. At this point, he said, the office of the steward had received a petition from the father requesting further consideration of the case because everyone in the family was dissatisfied. The secretary immediately recognized the handwriting of a well-educated man from that area who had written the petition. The secretary used an ancient phrase, "dispute adviser," *kachu bogmar lenken (kha mchu bogs mar len mkhan)*, to refer to this man, rather than the more common "law-doer," *timsopa (khrims bzo pa)*. The secretary said that the dispute adviser had done an excellent job of drafting the petition, presenting every issue carefully, and that he accompanied the father to present the case personally. At this point the other two men sitting with the *barshu* stood and bowed to Lobsang, coming forward with white scarves and a small, wrapped package. This was becoming more complicated than Lobsang had expected and was taking more time than he had hoped. He accepted the scarves, which were placed around his neck, and put the package on the table in front of him.

As the men reseated themselves, Lobsang thought of what his father had said about government law officials. Many of them could be bribed, and people in some areas repeatedly brought large gifts to officials in an attempt to influence their attitudes. It was said of district officers, who were changed every few years by the central government, that they manipulated justice for their own economic gain. This was not true with the Lhagyari family, his father explained, because they were very rich and could not be influenced by gifts. They did not change jobs every few years and would always be here, as they had always been, since the very beginning of time. So in a dispute they sought the truth, followed the law codes, and applied the law solidly because this made for better administration. Still, people did not usually come from this region with disputes, Lobsang thought. He would be interested in what the package contained when he opened it later.

Now the dispute adviser and the father had begun to talk, but Lobsang found that his mind wandered to the religious ceremonies, and his eyes strayed for a moment to the window. How could he make this case end quickly? He could say that it was not for him but for his father to decide, but that would mean a long wait until his father returned. He knew that a correct proceeding involved listening to both sides in great detail, and he was not interested in doing this. They were saying that this was a very large family with many assets and many children disputing the division of property. He decided to interrupt. As soon as he spoke, the other two were silent and listened, stopping in the middle of their stories. He spoke softly and directly as his father would: "The chief steward or his secretary was the next person to whom this case was addressed after the headman. Has a decision been rendered by that office?"

Immediately, the secretary confirmed that the father with his dispute adviser, the son, and even some other important people from that area had come to pursue their concerns in the office of the chief steward at the palace. Lobsang was relieved that this question had been the correct one, his father would not be embarrassed. He said, "And what was that decision, and why are these people now presenting this case once again?"

The secretary then began to relate all the points of the decision made by the office of the chief steward. He unwrapped a long document, which he referred to as "the decision," *kacé* (*bka' bcad*), and went through it point by point. The secretary referred to the father of the disputing family as a *shusho* (*zhu zho*) and his petition as a *shuway yigay* (*zhu ba'i yi ge*). The petition had a large space open at the top, a formal introductory section or *gochu* (*'go brjod*), in florid language, and then the name of the office addressed, the person addressed, and other formal statements.

By now, Lobsang knew that he would have to do something extraordinary to cut this discussion short. He had an idea and said, "Please bring me the law code. It is best decided in this way." The secretary rose and left the room to fulfill Lobsang's request. At this, the dispute adviser said to the boy on the high mattress, "And do you know the Tibetan Code of Sixteen Sections, sir?"

Although it appeared that he was being challenged, Lobsang ignored the implication and responded, "Yes, I have studied several of the law texts. The Thirteen Codes of the Fifth Dalai Lama are the most commonly used, but I have studied the Sixteen Codes, the Fifteen, and the Thirteen." This ended all discussion in the room.

When the secretary returned, he bowed to the boy on the mattress and put the book on the table before him. Leaning forward over the book, Lobsang opened it slowly to the tenth section and read the title aloud, "The Separation of Relatives." After reading the four poetic verses that came before the text, he scanned the rest of the section to find the pertinent parts. This was not a case of husband and wife separating but of father and son, so there were no questions of payments of consortium rights, of child custody, or of adultery. Finally Lobsang found the right passage and began again to read out loud:

> When the time comes to divide a fighting family,
> it is necessary to thoroughly investigate,
> what the two sides did,
> male and female differences, and so forth, and
> then decide suitably and honestly,
> according to the legal system. . . .

Moreover, in the case of a separation of family, splitting of father and son, splitting among relatives, this is done according to the number of persons in the house. The share of a woman is one quarter of the share of the man for this accounting. After determining the total number of shares in the house [with each man getting four and each woman getting one], the land, house, [cattle], jewels, [and other possessions] are distributed equally among the total shares for all the persons in the house. Each person should get some of each type. Parents and grandparents may decide which side they want to go with according to their own wish, but they still get their same share. Whatever others [such as servants] are left can be decided through a throw of dice. . . . If non–blood relatives living as a family have assembled to separate, it is necessary to decide the division through investigation of the truth and the size of their individual wealth when each of them joined [the household].[3]

When he had finished reading, Lobsang announced, "This is the law of the Fifth Dalai Lama formulated by his First Regent, Sonam Choephel, and his Mongolian benefactor, Gushri Khan. This is the law of Tibet and we should follow this. Please report to me when you have all considered this and come to a new decision which you will all accept." All the men in the room appeared impressed with his speech, and the chief steward was obviously pleased. Everyone stood and bowed to him and then left the room.

Once they were gone, Lobsang sighed with relief and went immediately to the window to see how far the religious services had progressed. The monks seemed to be coming out of the assembly hall and heading for various other duties, and Lobsang knew he had missed the afternoon ceremonies. His old servant, entering the room to take away the teacups, quoted a proverb about education, meaning that the boy had shown himself to be a good student. Lobsang smiled with pleasure at the compliment and its implication that he had comported himself well during the audience. He walked awkwardly from the room to take off his heavy robes so that he could go outside.

Exegesis

This case occurred on the Lhagyari estate in the 1940s and is presented here from the point of view of a young son of the family. A full conciliation process had taken place and failed, and in his father's absence he was asked to make a decision employing formal legal ritual.

The role of monks in the life of the estate and the dominance of religion and ritual in the lives of everyone are highlighted in this narrative. The family maintained a large Tibetan Buddhist temple in the estate compound, and support of the huge monastic population consumed a substantial part of the surplus revenues of this estate, as it did of the Tibetan people in general. The young heir is understandably taken with the excitement of the glorious annual ceremonies.

A monk is also the central figure in the dispute that takes place in the courtyard, a typical forum for public disputation, with a crowd gathered to listen and assess the arguments of both sides. The monk was using the situation as a stage for practicing his debating techniques; indeed, many monks acted as advocates for others throughout Tibet because of their skills in writing, debate, and Buddhist reasoning. The dispute adviser role could be taken on by any person in Tibet learned in debate or document writing, whether monastic or lay.

The concept of karma took on an important role in the child-beating disagreement. This powerful argument—whether karma was used as a rationalization or presented as the actual causal agent—forced others to pause when it was included in any law case. It pushed causes into previous lives and reconfigured possible legal violations in this life (such as severe public child-beating) as penalties for actions in a previous life. Here, a reality shift occurs from the imagined aspect (a man beating a boy) to the relative aspect (a saint helping another to burn off bad karma). The listeners are immediately reminded of the illusory nature of their perceptions and stop judging the incident for what it might only appear to be.

Other points of note include the dignity with which a very old family is approached and the pertinence of the law codes to many familiar situations. As a member of one of the oldest families in Tibet, the son is addressed in elegant language of the highest level, while speaking himself in honorific or normal language. He is clothed in silk, has long nails, and exhibits many other attributes of the very rich in Tibet. His knowledge of the law codes is respected despite his youth. The case itself touches on the inheritance pattern in southern Tibet.[4] Finally, note that rolling dice, one of the legal devices often inserted into formal proceedings, is presented in the law codes as a technique for the allocation of servants.

Excursus: Singing-Counting

The invention of what is termed "the second system" of Tibetan accounting is attributed to the period of the reign of the Fifth Dalai Lama. A man named Duchungpa is said to have developed it alone in his room and refined the method by practicing it over and over. There was a wall painting of Manjushri—the Wisdom manifestation of the Buddha—in his room, and he prayed to the god often. For many years, Duchungpa continued to work on the system until at last Manjushri spoke to him and said, "You are done." Hearing this, Duchungpa wrote a book on the "second system," the best known of several different systems of Tibetan accounting and the one employed in the courts and offices of Tibet until 1959.

An important part of Duchungpa's system is a unique form of singing-counting, most easily demonstrated with simple numbers. For example, to add 123, 456, and 789, one would sing out very rapidly as follows (the equivalent operations in the Western decimal system are in brackets to the right):

I have 1, 2, and 3,
and then I have 4, 5, and 6.
When I add these two, I get 9.　　　[add the ones column]
I add and get 7.　　　[add the tens column]
I add and get 5.　　　[add the hundreds column]
This equals 579.　　　[total of first two numbers, to be added
　　　to the third number]

Then I have 7, 8, and 9.
When I add I get 18,　　　[add the ones column]
which makes 1 and 8.
I add this to the 8 and get 9.　　　[carry over 1 to the tens column]
I add and get 16,　　　[add the tens column]
which makes 1 and 6.
I add this to the 7 and get 8.　　　[carry over 1 to the hundreds column]
I add and get 13,　　　[add hundreds column]
which makes 1368.　　　[total of all three numbers]

Arithmetic skill was essential for all government clerks and a compulsory part of the official examination for lay officers (it was optional for monk officers, but they often learned these skills as well). Given the necessity to keep tax records and other accounts, clerks in all government offices from local districts to the Cathedral Complex sat at their desks all day singing out sums, which were checked and recorded by other clerks. Many Tibetans told me they could hear this singing-counting as they walked by the windows. Throughout the countryside as well, the singing-counting system was used—to record harvests of grain, to determine the amounts of produce for taxes, and for any other counting task.

Since so many taxes were paid in produce and their measurements were based not on a decimally graded system but on traditional volumes—such as "the equivalent of two handfuls"—singing-counting was in common use where units of different sizes had to be added. Counters such as stones or beans represented the various units; thus, if 6 of unit A = 1 of unit B, then when six A counters were in the pile, they were replaced by one B counter. This versatility allowed almost any range of measurement equivalences to be accommodated.

Grain measurement, for example, was done with boxes of varying sizes in different parts of Tibet, but standard government measures and equivalences were as follows:

1 *pul (phul)*		(often described as a "handful")
6 *pul*	= 1 *dé (bre)*	(described variously as a "hand-sized bowl," "equal to 2 quarts," "about 2 pints," or "the size of a cow's hoof print")
20 *dé*	= 1 *bo ('bo)*	(a wooden box approximately 10 by 10 by 6 inches)
1 *khel (khal)*	= the grain in 1 *bo*	(said to be approximately 30 pounds)
1 *gyakhel (brgya khal)*	= 100 *khel*	

As in the number example above, only two amounts were added together at the same time, then the third was added to the sum of those two, and so forth, always working from the smallest units to the largest. Each time a unit was sung out, an equivalent number of counters was placed or moved from one pile to another as necessary: small black stones might be used for *pul*, beans for *dé*, pebbles for *khel*, and wood chips for *gyakhel*.

A recorded example of a Tibetan doing singing-counting addition starts with the following amounts of grain:

6 *khel*, 15 *dé*, and 3 *pul;* added to
15 *khel*, 7 *dé*, and 3 *pul;* added to
90 *khel*, 12 *dé*, and 0 *pul*.

The English translation of the Tibetan song used to do this sum goes something like this (the words in brackets have been added for clarification only):

I have 6 [*khel*], 15 [*dé*], and 3 [*pul*],
and then I have 15 [*khel*], 7 [*dé*], and 3 [*pul*].
When I add these [smallest two] I get
[3 plus 3 equals] 6 *pul*
[which] equals 1 *dé* [and add it to the 7 *dé*]
which makes 8.
I add *dé* and get 23 [15 + 8]
[which] equals 1 *khel* and 3 *dé*.
I add [this 1 *khel* to the 15] and get 16 [*khel*].
Add 6 [*khel* and 16]
equals 22 *khel*, 3 *dé*, [0 *pul*]. [end of first addition]
Then I have 90 [*khel*], 12 [*dé*], and 0 [*pul*].
When I add [the *pul*] I get 0.
I add *dé* and get 15.
I add *khel* and get 112 [90 + 22]
[which] equals 1 *gyakhel*, 12 *khel*, [and] 15 *dé*.

The final sum sitting before the singer in this example, therefore, would be represented by 1 wood chip indicating 1 *gyakhel* of grain, 12 pebbles for the 12 *khel*, 15 bean markers for the 15 *dé*, and no small black stones for zero *pul*.

This style of counting was employed not only by peasants in recording the carrying capacity of their fields and their grain harvests but also by clerks and others for keeping track of payments, in money or goods, as required by decisions made in courts and internal settlement rituals. Tibetans also mentioned that abacuses were used in some offices and storehouses for adding sums and keeping accounts but were not acceptable for demonstrating counting ability at the official examinations.

CHAPTER NINETEEN

The District Court of Kyidong

Judges and conciliators should:

> stitch the case together, as with a needle,
> cut promptly to make decisions, as with a knife,
> clasp together the two sides like the fingers on two hands.
> —Neudong Law Code

Most of the territory of the Tibetan nation, excluding the vast northern plains and some of the separate principalities and kingdoms, was divided into districts, each with its own appointed district headquarters and administrative staff.[1] District administration was not elaborate; officers often had only a small staff to deal with a very large area. They were usually ranked officials on assignment from the Cabinet in Lhasa for a period of years, although in some areas the government assigned a local person without official rank.

The Duties of a District Officer

Although the problems that arose and the roles to be fulfilled were often area-specific, the duties, functions, and professional lives of all district officers were similar, according to an edict posted in the district office of Shigatse during the first decade of the twentieth century. This text is from the private journals of Sir Charles Bell, a British Officer in Tibet in the 1920s, who stated that this edict was annually sent to and posted in every district office throughout Tibet (he did not give its relation to the famous Mountain Valley Decree).[2]

Because it was issued prior to the complete independence of Tibet in 1912, the text opens with a reference to the Chinese emperor:

General Rules of Conduct

Under the direction of the great Chinese Emperor, the precious and virtuous Dalai Lama, who lives to the west of China, is the master of all the religions of the world. He who knows all, Vajra Dhara, Dalai Lama, possesses the following powers. . . .

Plate 40. Courtroom in the Shigatse district. The edict describing the duties of district officers was posted on the wall. Charles Bell's comments: "[The courtroom] faces to a central . . . open space, which is surrounded by this and other rooms. Right centre background are the [judges'] seats facing to the left, i.e. towards the open space. Right foreground, the clerks' [mattress] seats . . . to the right of these, chests for records and other papers. Other records can be seen hanging from the pillars." 1933–34. (Bell Collection, Mss Eur F 80/291, J285, Oriental and India Office Collections, The British Library)

The people of the Thirteen provinces of Tibet of ten thousand each, the lamas, officers, the middle classes and the lower classes are hereby informed that the real benefit of the world proceeds from religion alone and religion entirely depends on the lamas. The three chief monasteries and the other sub-monasteries in different places should bear in mind that to observe religion, the religious law is to be carried out; namely to hear, to mind and to pray and thereby to give instruction from time to time to the Head Lamas of the monasteries.

The District Officers are to treat the subjects under them impartially and not to favour any one and not to give the subjects unnecessary trouble. Except for public purposes and for other purposes prescribed by the Government, no one is to be supplied with animals for riding or carrying loads, grass or corn for private ponies, porters, grooms, cooks or provisions. The District Officers are to see to this and to examine carefully the passports authorized by the Cabinet (lamyiks), and the Dalai Lama (tamkas), and to endorse them. At the end of every six months, a statement of the things supplied is to be carefully prepared and to be submitted to the Government. If any one comes without a passport obtained either from the Cabinet or the Dalai Lama and forcibly beats the people for non-supply the District Officer must submit his report on the matter immediately to the Government at Lhasa by mounted postman (tasam).

If any of the landlords or managers of the monastic estates punish their tenants by life-imprisonment or mutilation of the person, the District Officer must submit a detailed report immediately to the Government and he is warned against failing to report such matters.

If the District Officer receives a complaint to the effect that the property of a traveler or pilgrim has been purloined or snatched away or that such person has been beaten or killed or if an adult has ill-treated his old parents, an immediate report must be submitted to the government. The owners of images of Buddhas, religious monuments, places where religious emblems and golden scriptures are kept must take great care of their properties and prevent other persons from injuring them. Bankers are not allowed to charge compound interest nor to take the landed property, the cattle, ponies or donkey of the debtor. The District Officer, landlords and managers of monastic estates are forbidden to take by force the children or servants of their tenants into their own service. No one is allowed to charge for any article a higher rate than that prevailing in the village.

The District Officers must try to punish their subjects reasonably for any crime but must not fine heavily in an illegal way simply to benefit their own pockets. The District Officers are informed that they must not demand anything from their subjects in the way that a large insect devours a small one [a common Tibetan saying at this time was "the large insect (Britain) is devouring the small one (Tibet)"]. Even for a slight crime committed by any one, the subordinates of the District Officer will not punish the criminal without the order of the District Officer himself.

From the first day of the first month to the last day of the seventh month, no one is allowed to kill, except foxes and rats, any creatures, i.e., birds, deer, wild sheep, wild goats, fishes, otters and other animals or eggs which have no human owner. The District Officer must not be too lenient and his subordinate must not do illegal actions. The people are to observe the festivals by reading the scriptures, especially: the Kangyur, Bum, Sung-du, Getongpa, and Kesang, and to observe the fasting ceremony on the eighth, fifteenth and thirtieth of every month, which will bring prosperity. Accordingly, the District Officer and landlords will see that these festivals are observed without oppressing the subjects. During that portion of the summer in which there is scarcity of rain no one is allowed to construct buildings [May and June].

The Emperors from generation to generation and the world-protectors [Dalai Lamas] have issued this proclamation in order to keep the subjects in Tibet in peace, therefore all must obey this decree. If anybody transgresses it, the District Officer will at once enquire into the matter and the accused person will be imprisoned in a frontier District [far from friends and family] and his family punished by attaching his land and his other property. On receipt of this proclamation the District Officer must publish it at once in different villages under his jurisdiction through the village headmen and take receipts from them and submit the receipts to the Government.

Dated the Potala [Palace of Dalai Lama],
the Wood-Dragon Year [1905–]
[Seal of the Government]

An example of a particular district is *kyidong dzong* (*skyid grong rdzong*), in south-western Tibet, to which a government officer named Jampa was commissioned in the 1940s.

The town of Kyidong, "happy place," capital of the ancient land of Mangyul, perches on the Nepalese border in a northwest-southeast-oriented river valley surrounded by high mountains on three sides. The area has a famous history. It was the hiding place of the famous monk Santaraksita in the eighth century, when Buddhism had not yet been fully accepted in Tibet; it was the birthplace of the poet-saint Milarapa (see Chapter 7); and during the period of decentralization it was the location of several distinct kingdoms such as Mangyul, Purang, and Guge. Residents of Kyidong attributed the general good health and well-being of the population to the visit in the eleventh century of the famous Buddhist teacher and scholar Atisha, who is said to have left his footprints and implements there when he gave his first teachings.

Most important was Kyidong's position on one of the two major trading routes leading south along the Gandakhi River through the Himalayas into the lowlands of Nepal and then India. Pilgrims from all over Tibet made their way to this town before descending over the mountains to the sacred sites of the Kathmandu Valley or the holy places of pilgrimage for the Buddha in India and Nepal. Hundreds of traders and porters traveled up the long stone-laid path by the river to Kyidong, carrying grain and foreign goods for Tibetan markets.

Kyidong was more than one month by horse from Lhasa in 1944 when a district officer named Jampa was appointed for a four-year term. The journey was usually accomplished by traveling through the province of Tsang and then following rivers west and south. Previously, most of western Tibet had been under the administration of one large state called Nari, with its capital at Narikar, but in the early part of this century the towns of eastern Nari were consolidated into Upper and Lower To. The governor of Upper To, who supervised district officers from Shelkar, Dingri, Nyanam, Kyidong, and others, reported to an overgovernor whose office was located in the ancient capital of Shigatse.

Jampa was a civil bureaucrat who made his living from a very small estate—encompassing one small peasant village in Tsang province—allotted him as compensation for his government service. The peasants who worked these lands provided his family with their daily necessities, and his wife and children lived on the farm occasionally. When Jampa first received his assignment to Kyidong, a replacement was sent for the first year, as Jampa had several concerns to attend to before taking up his tour of duty. He had to provide for the education of his eldest son, who would normally have been training at a government school in Lhasa from age sixteen to twenty. After considering the option of having his son stay in their house in Lhasa, however, he and his wife decided to take the boy with them. In Kyidong a famous meditator and renowned scholar in Tibetan astrology, poetry, and grammar, Pelbar Geshe Rinpoche, lived in a cave in a hill called the Ru Pelbar (from which his name derived), and Jampa planned to send his son to this meditator for higher studies. Arrangements also had to be made for the care of the family's house in Lhasa and the farm in Tsang during their absence.

Jampa had to receive his orders and special instructions from the government, as well. In 1944, leaders in the central government of Tibet, nervous about the "outsiders' war" and changes in China and India, had been placing older, experienced officials in positions along the borders. The regent running the country during the minority of the Fourteenth Dalai Lama had been cautioning many of the district officials being sent to the provinces. At his death eleven years before, His Holiness the Thirteenth Dalai Lama had left a grave letter warning of incursions and predicting the loss of the country.

Once their affairs were finally in order, the family's move to Kyidong with numerous servants and animals took more than a month because they stopped along the way at several major temples. As Kyidong was an important but moderate-sized district, two district officers—one layman, Jampa, and one monk named Palbar—had been assigned to it without special secretaries or clerks. The officials were expected to use their own servants in these capacities.

The district office of Kyidong when Jampa arrived in 1945 had several rooms. There were eleven occupants daily: the two district officers, two representatives of the people called *tsodag* (*gtso drag*), two secretary-clerks for each of the district officers, two helpers, and one caretaker. One *tsodag* came from the peasants of the government and one from the peasants under landlords, either private or monastic, and each served a very long term of ten or fifteen years. They had been selected by the government (rather then elected) because they were the headmen of their villages. This system of people's representatives had been instituted in the time of the Thirteenth Dalai Lama (1876–1933), also known for such reforms as eliminating the cutting of limbs and the death sentence for criminals. With the advent of the representative system, however, administration had become more difficult for the district officers because they were required to ask the opinion of the *tsodag,* who usually knew a great deal more about the area then the district officer did. The caretaker of the office acted as policeman, postman, clerk, messenger, and housekeeper; he was also in charge of the key to the office. The key for the large documents cabinet in the office was kept by one of the secretaries; the seal box for the district, for which a district officer held the key, was locked inside the cabinet.[3]

The district office of Kyidong was utilized for both administrative and legal activities in 1945. It was open daily except for holidays, religious days, and times when the district officers were both out of town. There were several rooms for storage and other activities, but one central room, shown in Figure 13, was used for administration.[4] This main room was approximately square with the only door on the east wall in the north corner, allowing entrance by a set of stairs from the floor below. A narrow wooden partition hid the doorway from the rest of the room.

On low cushions in front of a window against the eastern wall, with low tables in front of them, sat the two *tsodag* and the clerks of the district officers. On a raised mattress against the south wall sat the monk officer and Jampa, the lay officer, with a larger table in front of them. Before the reforms there had been a small altar, with water bowls and butter lamps, in the southwest corner of the room. Against the

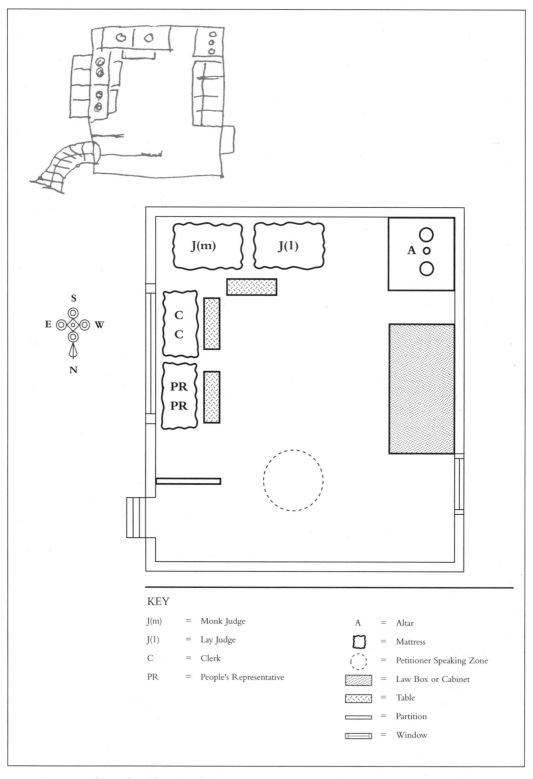

KEY

J(m) = Monk Judge
J(l) = Lay Judge
C = Clerk
PR = People's Representative

A = Altar
= Mattress
= Petitioner Speaking Zone
= Law Box or Cabinet
= Table
= Partition
= Window

Figure 13. Floor plan of Kyidong district court circa 1949. Top: original sketch by former clerk in the office. Bottom: schematic based on the sketch.

west wall was a very large cabinet for the storage of documents. At the top of the west wall was another small window. Petitioners and prisoners who addressed the court stood in the back center of the room—unless they had committed a major offense such as robbery, in which case they had to kneel before the court.

District officers in Kyidong were entirely responsible for the affairs of their area and viewed the primary function of their administration to be the smooth, efficient, and harmonious transaction of all government matters without the necessity of reporting back to Lhasa. Among Jampa's several duties was the collection of taxes. In Kyidong the people paid the traditional grain tax (one-sixth of their produce) to the district officer at the annual collection time. In 1945 the district paid taxes to the central government in the amount of two hundred *dékhel* (*bre khal*)[5] of grain and two *dé* of *wanglang,* a special herb grown in the area. Additionally, every three years a Nepalese metalworker named Payulten Shenpa came from Nepal to Lhasa to supply goods and metalwork to the Storage Office of the Dalai Lama; on his trip through Kyidong the district officers were expected to provide all the necessities for his workmen and the animals needed to carry the thousands of sacks of goods they brought with them. This and other government-required hauling by animals was assigned to peasants in the area proportionate to their tax load.[6]

Besides managing the collection and allocation of these tax burdens, the district officers were expected to call all the people of Kyidong together for eating and dancing during the first and second day of the New Year. The meal and entertainment were arranged and paid for by the officers themselves.

During Jampa's tenure, he received a letter from the central government directing the district office to increase the "border army" at Kyidong. After some deliberation, he and the monk official appointed seven local people to act as border police and gave them government salaries to buy tea, butter, and some grain. The district office was reimbursed for these costs.

Customs regulation was another duty specific to border districts. Tibetans were taxed when traveling out of their country, and all other nationalities except Nepalese were taxed coming into Tibet. Porters from different Nepalese groups (Gurung, Tamang, Rai, and Brahman), carrying wooden baskets filled with enormous loads of rice destined for the Lhasa markets, traveled up through the mountains to Kyidong. Before the advent of the British, Kyidong had also been an important animal trading center through which thousands of sheep were brought every year, bound for the Nepalese and Indian markets.

Where did the district officers get the money to pay for their servants, the required feasts, and general office management? Most Tibetans who had worked in district offices did not discuss this question, but a few said that the district officers held back large amounts of grain and other items collected as taxes for these as well as their own expenses, and used supplies from their own estates as well. A district officer was in a position to offer unusual privileges and monopolies on certain items for trade; in addition, he could receive large gifts when he was acting as a judge in a legal case.

What was considered an official legal case in Kyidong? During Jampa's tenure, matters he regarded as serious and worthy of official court procedure were those involving large land disputes (particularly if a big family attempted to seize the

Plate 41. Weighing wool for customs duty at the Tibetan border town of Phari. 1920–21.
(Pitt Rivers Museum, University of Oxford)

property of a small family), inheritance of property, monastic disputes over real and
personal property, land disputes between the monastery and the peasants, theft
involving substantial property, and robbery of any kind. Jampa heard cases from
monastic and private estates and from any associations in his area as well.[7]

He was particularly concerned with the correct handling of murders and other
major criminal offenses. As the first line of administration for the central government, district officers were expected to apprehend and arrest the criminal, investigate, and perform the initial punishment of the offender in a serious crime. Any
incorrect execution of these tasks would be glaringly exposed in Lhasa, to which all
such offenses had to be forwarded.

Minor disputes brought to the district officer in Kyidong were decided "according
to the rules of the area," using the customary traditions of the substantive local law.
Each case had to be investigated and decided according to its nature and the factors
relevant to that dispute. The time needed to reach a settlement depended largely on
the "thickness or hardness of the dispute." If both sides defended their positions very
strongly, then the dispute was thick and conciliation unlikely. A thick dispute could
go on for many months or a year without resolution because the parties did not want
to agree. It could continue until the parties said, "More than this, I have nothing
more to petition," or the district officer decided to stop the case. Punishments were
understood by Jampa to be of two kinds, physical (primarily whipping) and material, and they were awarded according to the type and size of the offense, either in
conjunction or separately.

Among the cases heard by district officer Jampa was a monastic dispute brought to the district court of Kyidong in 1945. It is recounted by a court clerk who witnessed the entire suit:

I can remember that the Samdeling Monastery dispute was fought during my time in the Kyidong district. The founder of this monastery was a tutor of the Eighth Dalai Lama [1758–1805].

In that monastery there was a layman who was the steward or treasurer of the monastery, named Tashi, from the Suru family. His family was a very powerful and rich family, and the people of the area liked Tashi very much. He was a layman with many children, which was unusual for a monastic treasurer. Tashi had worked for years as the treasurer running the monastery operations, with control of all the monastic lands and the substantial revenues from those lands. The monks of this monastery were all from local villages, very simple, and they always listened to what the treasurer said.

After many years, his term of office was over. As all the treasurers of this and other related monasteries were appointed by the Tsecholing Monastery in Lhasa, a letter came from the head office of that monastery appointing a new treasurer in Kyidong. It also stated that Suru Tashi should be the assistant to the new treasurer. So the new treasurer came to take up his position.

But Tashi refused to give up any of his powers, duties, or control of the monastery lands and houses. With both treasurers now working in the monastery, the monks didn't like the situation and complained that they didn't know whom to follow because they had two masters. The monks then wrote to the Tsecholing and told them about the situation. The result was that the Lhasa office appointed a third treasurer to run the monastery in Kyidong. At the same time, they sent a letter to the Cabinet and to the district officer in Kyidong apprising them of the problem in their area.

The Tsecholing office and the government in Lhasa, after further deliberation, both wrote again to the district officer stating that he was to be a formal witness to the handing over of the position of treasurer to the new appointee, the third treasurer. The district officer was to go, they said, not as a legal representative but as "a watcher, an observer," to see what happened at the required reassignment and to report to them. So the district officer went to observe.

When the three men came together in the office in the monastery at the appointed time for the handing over of the position, Tashi stated that he would not hand over the land and property of the monastery. The new treasurer responded that he must hand over control, and so a dispute started. The district officer then left the monastery.

After this, the monks came to the office of the new district officer and complained bitterly, submitting a formal petition to him. And so the dispute became a legal case. The monks were told to send a representative to court, and the new district officer began an investigation. With acceptance of the petition, he was required to start the standard procedure in court.

After this, the representative of the monks and the new treasurer both petitioned with written documents to the district court. After the petitions were read, a clerk was sent with a written order to call Suru Tashi to court. The order said that the court had received a petition from the monastery with these particular points and that Suru Tashi should come to court on a specific date "to justify his side."

So Suru Tashi, the opponent, arrived at court, and he came alone before the district officer and was asked to answer the first point of the petition from the monks. His response was that he need not hand over any property to the monastery. This was his only response. Then he was told by the district officer that he should bring a written reply to that and other points.

From the first day of the case, the district officer as judge said to each person called to testify, "From now on, you may not at any time show a black face in public; you may not fight; you may not create a disturbance either in or near the court. If you do any of these things, you will be given a double punishment by this court." This is what the district officer said to Tashi when he was called this first time.

The case went on for two months. The district officer read all the petitions and Tashi's reply statement. Then he called in either side one by one to ask them questions about the points in their petitions. If one side was called to speak alone (which is the usual procedure), then it was called "private cleansing," but if both sides were called to speak, it was called "face-to-face testimony."

During these questioning periods the person was not allowed to use any harsh words or street language such as "eater of your father's corpse" or "you dog." A person who did so would be whipped, but no one said such things in this case, so there was no whipping. Also, during these interrogations, it was possible that one side or the other would not meet the point or "not accept the viewpoint of the other side," in which case the district officer would stop questioning on that point and go to the next one. For points on which the two sides did not meet or give valid reasons, the district officer would do an investigation and try to help them agree or would decide the matter for himself. If the district officer came to know that one person or both sides had lied to the court or if there continued to be a big difference between the sides and a dispute broke out between the two in court, the district officer could place the two, head to head, face down on the courtroom floor, and have them whipped. But during this dispute, this did not happen.

So after submitting his written reply statement, Tashi was called again to answer questions about the petition of the monks. The district officer sat in the front of the room as judge with his clerk. After cautioning Tashi, he once again read the first point in the monks' petition to Tashi, who was standing before him, and then he said, "In the first point in their petition, they said that you claim to own the monastery lands but that you do not actually own these lands. In your written reply statement, you responded to their first point by saying that you do own the monastery lands. Is that right?"

Tashi said, "That is right."

And then the district officer said, "Why do you say that the lands are your lands? What is your reason?"

Then Tashi gave a full response as to why he thought that the lands were his. After he was through, the district officer went on to the second point of the monks' petition and Tashi's reply to this point, soliciting his reasons and so forth on every point. All this was recorded by the clerk in the court. After this, the district officer asked some questions of his own, and then Tashi was dismissed. This kind of questioning took place several times for both sides, with the district officer calling one, then the other party back for questioning.

The district officer also did his own out-of-court investigation. In this case, he first read through the petitions and then went to the land records to determine the actual ownership according to the government record books. After going through these documents, he sent out a servant to survey and measure the lands of the monastery. The district officer received other people who wanted to speak about the case and listened to them; he also called people to answer questions who had information about the case. In this district court any relative of a party was permitted to come forward to speak on behalf of that side, and a party who was a weak speaker was allowed to have another person come to speak for him.

After two months of questioning and investigation, the district officer came to a decision. Then he sent out a message through the clerk to both parties saying that they were to appear in court for the final decision in ten days. Before they appeared, the district officer would draft a document. To do this, he sat down and dictated to his clerk the final decision *chésam ki tama* (*bcad mtshams kyi khra ma*), which represented the final stage of the matter and was then recopied several times to be presented to all the parties. After reviewing all the petitions, statements, evidence, and investigation reports before him, the district officer began dictating to the clerk:

"First you must write the opening prostration words of devotion to the Buddha to begin the document." [The clerk did this and began the document formally:]

"By invoking the name of His Holiness the Dalai Lama and king of Tibet, to whom we prostrate, and by the power of the national law and also the strictness of the decision of the law, this document has been made. Under such strict rule in every place, people are very peaceful, but today you both have created a dispute, and that is not appropriate. This is a great violation of the law of the country and very bad.

"The amount of small punishment for filing this case in court [court costs] is ——. For studying your case in court until the end, the secretary, servants, and other staff deserve their pen, ink, and paper charge, which comes to ——. Both parties have to pay this amount.

"Regarding the first point, the first petitioner, the monks' representative, stated that the ex-treasurer of the monastery, Suru Tashi, claims to own the monastery lands but that he does not actually own these lands. Instead, they are the property of the monastery. In the written reply statement, Suru Tashi responded to their first point by saying that he did own these lands, and he gave for his reason the long term of service that he has given to the monastery. He stated that for this service, the lands have become his. The investigation of the court into the record books showed that the land deeds were in the name of the monastery only. The court clerk measured the lands listed in the monastery deed and found that they were accurate. The court's decision on this first point is that the lands belong to the monastery, and the monastery has the truth on this point.

"As to the second point . . ."

The district officer continued in this way, going point by point through the position of each side, presenting what each side had said and stating which side had the truth on that point and why. After finishing all the points, he said, "The decision of this court is that Suru Tashi is to hand over all the land and houses to Samdeling Monastery. For using the property of the monastery after his tenure was over until the present, the ex-treasurer is a violator of the law and will be punished. For the use of this land during this period, he will be fined.

"For Suru Tashi, compensation due to the monastery to repay their loss of income is ——, and punishment payment is the amount of ——."

Then the clerk put the name of the court and the Tibetan date at the bottom of the document. The district officer instructed the clerk to put a *chuyik* on the back of the document at the bottom, writing twice the sentence "I will not violate this decision in the future" and leaving spaces for both sides to sign. Then the district officer instructed the clerk to make several copies of the decision.

On the decision day, Suru Tashi came to the court with his son as guarantor, and on the monastery side the monks' representative and four monk officers came. A person acting as guarantor for either party to a dispute had to be a responsible, sensible, and respected member of the community. If a party brought an ordinary person to court as a guarantor, he would be scolded by the judge. The district officer read the full decision document in front of both parties from the beginning to the end, point by point. The clerk handed Suru Tashi's copy to the monastery representative and the monastery's copy to Suru Tashi.

The district officer said, "What do you think about this decision?" [Neither party indicated that it could answer with their opinions at that moment.]

"You may keep these documents for five days. Read through them carefully and decide whether you are satisfied. If you are dissatisfied, you should come with a petition to this court. In this petition, you must write these words: 'Your final decision may be true, but regarding this point I am dissatisfied. Therefore, I request that our case be sent to a higher court.'

"I will take your petition and this decision and send them to the governor, who will review them himself or send them to the Cabinet. The Cabinet usually does not investigate a case itself but gives it to another office in Lhasa. Sometimes, the Cabinet goes through all the documents to see whether the petition and decision were done honestly. If they find any lies or evidence of disrespectful behavior, they send the case back to the governor or a neighboring district officer with orders to reinvestigate.

"Return here in five days with the document I have given you and your decision. If you are both satisfied, then you should tell me."

After five days, both parties returned with their guarantors to court and stated that they accepted the decision. They brought with them the money for compensation, punishment, and court costs. Both of them also brought presents to the caretaker of the courtroom. In this case, the court costs were assessed equally because both parties had created a disruption during a peaceful period in our country.

The parties paid the money they owed by giving it to the court clerk, who checked the amounts. The copies of the decision were exchanged, and both sides placed their seals on the *chuyik* of each copy under the statement that they would not violate this decision in the future, and their guarantors did likewise. The court clerk stamped the documents with the district officer's seal, folded them, and handed one to each party. The court clerk then paid the compensation payment to the monastery. Both sides then exchanged white ceremonial scarves by placing them on the neck of the other. Following this, they said to each other, "From now on, we shall be as relatives." This made the two parties equal again. Then the district officer said, "Take your documents with you. From now on, no one should fight in the future."

At this point, everyone went home. Actually, the monastery won the case completely. They got a new treasurer and all they asked for in their petition, and they had to pay only a little. So this was the famous property case of the Samdeling Monastery in the Kyidong district.

Exegesis

This is a particularly rich description of formal government procedure with its delineation of the questioning, the wording of the decision document, and the role of guarantors. It also points to the exact moment when this situation became a formal legal case requiring such a procedure: the moment the monks' written petition was accepted by the district officer, who had previously remained essentially passive. An accepted point-by-point petition was thus the key to initiating an official court ritual.

By setting out each objection point by point and requiring exact responses,

Tibetan legal questioning allowed for a detailed later examination of the process and exceptions to single items in a decision. This style requires clarity and precision. The focusing of the issues is due to the presentation or limitation by the parties, *not* to skeletonization by the court itself.

Several important aspects of Tibetan legal cosmology are set out clearly in this case. The later stages of the trial demonstrate that "weaker" parties were allowed representatives in court to "speak for them," a practice that became more formalized in the major cities but never resulted in the formation of a distinct profession. Parties were informed of the costs before the decision and allowed time to look at the judgment, a step intended—as was the entire process—to ensure the agreement of all parties to the decision.[8] The back of the document was signed by both parties and their guarantors under the *chuyik,* rendering it in effect a contract between the two that had been structured by the state. Finally, they had to reharmonize themselves to one another and the cosmos by a "getting together ceremony" consisting of the exchange of scarves and friendly words.

This case can be understood as resulting from a breach of etiquette on the part of the central monastery in Lhasa. Suru Tashi, an important and powerful person in his local community, was unceremoniously replaced and then ordered to assume a position subordinate to his replacement. Acceptance of such an order would surely have reduced his stature in the community, and yet the basis of his legal argument, that he now owned the lands of the monastery, was unclear. The district officer showed discretion in accepting his counterarguments at face value and thereby validated Suru Tashi's claim to poor treatment. Balancing community power relations was one of the district officer's roles, particularly the constant tension between the monasteries and powerful families which erupted into disputes on every level of Tibetan society. With an essentially static quantity of social and political prizes to be divided between two key social factions, deftness was required on the part of good government officials in coordinating transitions in powerful positions, such as the office of the monastic treasurer in this case.

PART FOUR

Reports from
the Central Bureaucracy

Introduction

Nor will it do to dismiss as irrelevant the cosmological cast of commonly held ideas about bureaucracy, with their evocation of fate and chance, of innate personal as well as national character, of blame and accountability.
—Michael Herzfeld, *The Social Production of Indifference*

To contextualize the Tibetan cosmology of law within the bureaucracy of the capital city, Part Four travels to the political center of the Plateau to watch the practice of law within the offices and courts of the central administration.

Bureaucratic practice has not been a focus of research in anthropology or comparative law since the inception of those disciplines. From the anthropological perspective, bureaucracies are primarily modern, rational, nonlocal structures having little to do with an understanding of how local knowledge is constructed. An anthropologist does fieldwork, according to the canons of the discipline, in local villages among "native peoples." If the fieldworker encounters bureaucracy, it is in tracking the path of a local person who takes a complaint to a local court. Yet neither studies in ethnicity and cultural boundaries[1] nor even the more recent considerations of colonialism and the rise of nationalism[2] have looked seriously at the bureaucratic local. Only a few recent American studies of local courts by legal anthropologists have begun to ask about the local bureaucratic practice of law.[3]

Comparative law approaches bureaucracies from the other direction, as formal institutions of the nation-state. Comparing courts and administrative offices, arranged in pyramid-shaped diagrams with sets of interrelated boxes, students of comparative law discover that the German Federal Constitutional Court does not have exactly the same functions or appeals process as the U.S. Supreme Court. Constitutions, statutes, legislative processes, judicial discretion—these are generally the subjects of comparison.[4] Not surprisingly, the two perspectives, anthropological and comparative, have had little impact on each other.

Following Max Weber, sociologists have been looking at bureaucracies for a much longer time. For them, bureaucracies are institutions or organizations that have their own culture, rules, roles, ecology, and demography. But sociologists look at how bureaucracies function, whether or not they are responsive or efficient; they study

Plate 42. The Potala of Lhasa, former Winter Palace of the Dalai Lama, viewed from the southwest. The long dark line below is a procession. 1920–21. (Pitt Rivers Museum, University of Oxford)

bureaucracies less often for the social production of local knowledge and local practice. Moreover, they understand the bureaucratic state as a fundamentally modern phenomenon connected to the growth of capitalism, industrialization, and secularization. In the view of most social scientists, the civic-territorial state model emerged only in the eighteenth century in Western Europe;[5] premodern agricultural societies are not thought to have the cultural cohesion, stratification, or technological base to produce a modern bureaucracy.[6]

Part Four situates bureaucracy, in Michael Herzfeld's words, "within the same framework as the smaller-scale societies traditionally studied by anthropologists."[7] It sets out to "study up" the bureaucratic local, the workings of the Tibetan state bureaucracy, in layered, ethnographic detail. In so doing, it follows Herzfeld and Mary Douglas in rejecting the assumed importance of size, sociocultural complexity, and modernity for assessing social organization.[8] Modern Western bureaucracies are neither more rational than nor superior to the "medieval" bureaucracy of Tibet; both have involved equal amounts of belief and reason in transacting daily affairs; both have operated through legal cosmologies encoded in language, myth, and social boundaries.

These chapters focus on the practice of law in the capital city of Tibet in the 1940s

Plate 43. Stairs leading up to the Potala. 1986.

and 1950s.[9] What constituted a legal problem for a Tibetan living in the capital? Did law operate on the same series of levels in the city as in the countryside? What were the quotidian workings of the bureaucracy? What aspects of the cosmology of law informed this practice? Who were the actors, and what were their strategies and resources?

Chapter 20 sets the scene by describing the world of Lhasa in the 1940s, how daily affairs were transacted, how a former policeman went about his work, and how legal cases flowed through the upper three levels of the bureaucracy. Each subsequent chapter reports from a different locality. Chapter 21 describes the City Court of Lhasa and illustrates its functions with the case of a stabbing in a local tavern. Chapter 22 presents the spheres of responsibility of the Municipal Office and reconstructs the 1958–59 Case of the Smelly Toilet—the longest and most interesting case in the book—from the statements of several participants. Finally, Chapter 23 details the operation of the High Court of Tibet—illustrated by a case of murder from the district of Kyidong—and presents aspects of the substantive law of murder in Tibet, including forms of punishment and the influence of social categories on victim compensation.[10]

CHAPTER TWENTY

The World of Lhasa

[Under the peaceful reign of the Fifth Dalai Lama] even an old woman carrying gold
as heavy as a sheep's head can safely travel to India and to the central part of Tibet
to press her forehead against the famous statues of the Buddha [in Lhasa] . . . to
pray in her own manner and to make an offering of her wealth to the Buddha.
—Ganden Podrang Code of the Dalai Lamas

Built on a vast alluvial plain ringed by low brown mountains, the city of Lhasa was
crowned with an immense fortress palace, a hilltop beacon to all who entered.
Under shimmering golden roofs, the Potala, the Winter Palace of the Dalai Lamas,
looked out through the eyes of a hundred windows upon the town and plain below.
This city was the core of the nation, the seat of the ruler, the home of the incarnate
divine head of state; it was the site of the oldest and most sacred temples and images,
the oldest medical college, the largest and most famous monasteries of the ruling
sect of Tibetan Buddhism, the most renowned schools, the most magnificent and
ancient ceremonies, and many of the most ostentatious houses of the nobility. It was
the wealthiest financial and trading center on the Plateau and the locus of the entire
bureaucratic administration of the government. This was Lhasa, the "place of the
gods," the center of the Plateau, the core of the mandala.

For most Tibetans, a pilgrimage to Lhasa to see the great religious sights was a
dream, a far-off goal to be accomplished sometime in their present or future life-
times. It was a journey of exceeding merit to a city with the most sacred images. The
greatest merit was achieved by pilgrims who made the entire journey to Lhasa in
full-body prostrations, moving like inchworms across the hundreds of miles from
their homes, in constant supplication to the deities. In Lhasa itself, the great and
lesser ring roads were filled at all times of the year with walking and prostrating
pilgrims, monks, and laypersons chanting and reciting prayers and mantras as they
circumambulated the shrines. In the center of this high, flat tableland, Lhasa beat like
a religious pulse.[1]

A story is told by Tibetans about the devotion of the pilgrims who visited Lhasa.

One day, the Fifth Dalai Lama looked down from the roof of the Potala Palace and saw
among the pilgrims an old man who was walking and chanting on the Lingkor, the greater

Plate 44. The golden roofs of the Potala decorated and embossed with mantras and good luck symbols. Until 1959, the use of the golden spires on a roof (there are two in this photograph) was limited by law. 1986.

ring road around Lhasa. Above the head of this old man floated the image of a female deity, the Green Tara. Seeing this, His Holiness called the man; when he came into the Dalai Lama's presence, the pilgrim prostrated many times. Finally, the Dalai Lama said to him, "What prayer do you say that makes the Green Tara appear above you?" With that, the man repeated his mantra. Then the Fifth Dalai Lama said, "But that is not correct! The correct mantra for Tara is OM TARE TUTTARE TURE SVAHO!" The man thanked His Holiness profusely, prostrated several more times, and left to do his chanting correctly. When the Dalai Lama looked down again from the Potala, he saw that the Green Tara no longer floated above the man's head. And so it was that the Dalai Lama realized what had happened. He called the man back and this time said, "Whatever your mantra was, repeat it as you did before." For it was the man's devotion, not his correctness, that gave him merit.

Lhasa was a city of enormous wealth by Tibetan standards. Over hundreds of years, gifts to the images, to the living deity of the state, to the monasteries, and to the oracles—as well as taxes and revenues collected by the government—had resulted in splendid religious buildings. Metalworkers from Tibet and Nepal, jewel-cutters, stone-carvers, wood-carvers, and tailors had produced elaborate silk appliqué banners, giant carved wooden altars, hundreds of silver urns filled with burning butter, and huge statues encrusted with jewels and precious metals. Religious devotion had brought an enormous accumulation of wealth to the centers of worship, particularly the Jokhang, the central temple in the Cathedral Complex and home of the most famous statue of the Buddha (see Plate 15).

Plate 45. A view southeast from the roof of the Potala showing the river in the far distance, the road, and on the left the eastern area of the city surrounding the Cathedral Complex. 1920–21. (Pitt Rivers Museum, University of Oxford)

Lhasa was also the city of learning and knowledge, famous for its renowned scholars of Tibetan Buddhism. Pressed into the faces of the hills surrounding the valley were three of the largest monasteries in the world: Drepung said traditionally to have over 7,700 monks; Sera, with 5,500; and Ganden, with 3,300.[2] Each was a center of religious education in which scholar monks trained until the age of thirty by memorizing thousands of pages of text, which were then used as the basis for debates and examinations. Most of the famous secular training schools for both lay and monastic government officials were in Lhasa as well.

A story was told of a young monk from Mili, in the Khams region far to the east, who had the fervent desire but not the money to go to Lhasa to train at a great monastery:

His family was of middling status. While in Khams, he had begged to go to Lhasa for many years to train to be a *geshe,* but it was a difficult journey—often people coming from Khams did not even ride horses because there were so many high passes that horses could not cross—and his family had no money to send him.

After waiting a few years, the monk started out for Lhasa accompanied by his friends. In the middle of their journey they came to a snowy mountain that they had to cross. As the monk was ill from lack of food by this time and couldn't walk from pains in his bare feet, his friends decided to leave him there with only a little roasted barley and some meat. The monk became very unhappy. But slowly, he got up and began to climb the mountain. By nine o'clock at night he could no longer move, and so he slept that night where he fell, in a heap of snow. At midnight he awoke to see a mule near him on the pass. Slipping down near it, he touched the animal and found that it did not move. Then he got on the mule and said to it, "Let's move." He fell asleep on the mule, and it kept walking all night.

When he finally awoke he saw a big temple filled with thousands of monks, some of whom came up to him during their tea break and offered him tea and noodle soup. He tried to wake up, thinking that this must be a dream. Then he realized that he was indeed at Ganden Monastery. The prefect of the monastery, the Songtsen Chenmo, came out to the monk on the mule and asked him where he was from. He replied that he had come from the Khams Mili area and had fallen asleep the previous night on a mountain pass several hundred miles to the east. And so he joined Ganden Monastery for his training.

This monk stayed in Ganden Monastery for the rest of his life and later became the "Ganden Throneholder" [the supreme head of the monastery, one of the highest posts in Tibet]. This is true history.

Daily Life in Lhasa

Family servants awoke first in the houses of Lhasa, rising to start the fires in the hearths after doing their own early morning prayers next to their beds. Cocks crowed and dogs barked early in the morning. One member of the household might be up on the roof or out in the courtyard roasting fresh barley to make *tsampa* flour, while another began the long task of heating the water and then churning the tea into a frothy mixture for the early meal.[3]

Beds in most houses were converted into daytime couches by folding the comforters into a backrest against the wall; the rug that served as a cover for the mattress was never moved. The butter or oil lamps and incense on the altar were lit for morning prayers and prostrations, and juniper branches might be burned on the roof in the morning on special religious days. Animals and small children were fed from the kitchen; garbage was thrown out into the central courtyard; and the day's tasks began in earnest.

Street peddlers (such as the meat-bread sellers), shoemakers, and itinerant merchants began to set up their makeshift stalls on the city streets; they laid out their wares on blankets or overturned wooden boxes, shaded from the sun by white cotton cloths held up by poles. On their way to work some clerks stopped at shops that served thinly cut boiled meat with chili and sauce. Other shops sold a tasty dish made of radishes and carrots. Storekeepers beginning the business day opened their wooden storefront doors and began to rearrange their goods. From early morning, porters and sellers passed by with their loads of vegetables, meat, and grain for the large outdoor market in the center of town. Monks, one by one and in clumps, scurried by on their way to early ceremonies in colleges and temples. Most stalls and stores stayed open until seven o'clock in the evening; a few parts of the market and the taverns remained open until late at night.

Traditionally, the fifteenth and thirtieth days of each Tibetan month—the days of Buddhist ceremonies and meatless meals—were free days with little work required, but after the Thirteenth Dalai Lama's stay in India to avoid the Chinese armies (1910–12), weekly Saturday holidays were declared in Lhasa, and the other free days

Plate 46. Restaurant booths at a festival, selling breads, cakes, biscuits, and fruit. 1920–21. (Pitt Rivers Museum, University of Oxford)

were canceled.[4] Government officials then had Saturday off, but several Lhasa businessmen stated that they kept to the old lunar calendar because it was auspicious for dharma. For big festivals such as the New Year, government offices and most shops were shut for several days at a time.

Every dialect of Tibetan could be heard in the streets of Lhasa, from the far eastern *khamgé* (*khams skad*) to the far western languages of Ladakh and Zanskar. Nepalese businessmen conversed in Nepali, Hindi, and Tibetan. Rural dialectical variations of Tibetan with rude imperatives and staccato commands mingled with the more intonated and honorific Lhasa speech, which was a marker for place, education, and refinement. No one was more condescending about correct pronunciation and education than natives of the capital city. Similarly, as in any major city, nonresidents were derided as dimwitted and foolish, uncultured and ill-spoken; Lhasa stories of the buffoonery of provincial people were profuse and endlessly repeated. Here is one such story as told by a former Lhasa native:

> One time, a Tsangpa man came to Lhasa and stayed in the big grassland outside the city meant for grazing the cattle and horses of people in the city. He was a messenger from Tsang. A hoe was lying on the ground in the grassland. The man walked through the area without seeing the hoe and put his shoe on it. As he stepped, it flew up into the air, the reflection from the blade shone in his eyes, and then it hit him on the leg.
>
> After this, the man from Tsang remained a few more days in Lhasa. By then the hoe was rusty from the rainy season. To one of his friends from Tsang he said, "In the grassland,

there is a child of the sun that has fallen there." He said this because of the shiny hoe. "I went to see him and he hit me on the leg," the man from Tsang continued. "Now, the child of the sun has changed his color because of the rainy season, and when I went back to see him, I decided to avoid him and walked around."

This is what this man from Tsang said! When we hear things like this, we cannot help but talk of the stupidity of the people from Tsang!

In this city of some 60,000 people,[5] trading ventures involving contracts for goods carried over vast distances from other areas of Tibet, China, central Asia, India, Nepal, and Kashmir had been common since the early Empire period of the eighth century.[6] Except for the special product monopolies granted by the government to specific traders or trading partnerships, all commodities were unrestricted for commercial intercourse and available to Tibetans of any social level who had sufficient capital to take part in local or long-distance ventures. Many Lhasa families had at least one brother in a monastery and one or more in trade, as these were two important avenues for increasing the education, the wealth, and thereby the power of the household. Lhasa's markets were filled in the 1940s with matches, glasses, cloth, guns, shoes, and boxes from India; luxury items such as comforters, brocade silks, thread, carved furniture, and special tea from China; and produce and other goods from throughout Tibet.

Transactions for these goods were arranged through the Tibetan equivalents of oral and written contracts, loans, bailments, consignments, deeds of sale, and commercial paper. Tibetans employed several different forms of guarantorship and partnership, many of which were recorded in documents, record books, and receipt books kept in stalls and shops throughout the city. Disputes over these transactions, when they arose, were handled by local craft or ethnic associations, neighborhood block headmen, stewards of noble families, lamas, and the local district courts and offices.

Occasionally, convicts sentenced to wear iron fetters or the large wooden neck ring called a *go* (*sgo*) could be seen begging at the edge of the market. Near the outside steps of the City Court with its large law poles was the site of the public whipping of prisoners, an act considered extremely inauspicious to witness. Other evidences of the operation of law in the city were the huge edicts posted on walls near government offices, such as the annually distributed Mountain Valley Decree, with its list of prohibited activities and guidelines for moral action. Accompanied by retinues of servants, judges and officials traveled daily through the city on their way to their offices, and the police in special uniforms patrolled the streets for security.

How safe a city was Lhasa? According to one older former resident,

there were some thieves and robbers in Lhasa, but the streets were quite safe at night, and this was because the judges were very strict. At seven o'clock most people went home to their houses because the shops and stalls closed. I rarely went out at night. A few bazaars and markets and of course the taverns stayed open quite late, sometimes up to even eleven or twelve o'clock.

There were some thieves and robbers and a few pickpockets in the city. During the big festivals and ceremonies such as Mon Lam, following the New Year, pickpockets were active. A few small boys of about ten years, called *thipdek pa* (*thib breg pa*), would take scissors and cut open any front robe pockets that looked full as people were rushing to a ceremony.

Plate 47. A crowded street in Lhasa during a festival day. 1920–21. (Pitt Rivers Museum, University of Oxford)

There were *chang* (*chang*) shops [beer shops or taverns] all over town. There was no tax on them or on the eating houses, and they made the beer right on the premises. A tavern owner was responsible for crimes committed in his tavern, and even if a crime occurred outside his door, a *chang* seller had to pay some penalty. Usually sellers sent drunks out of their beer houses quickly.

When someone was murdered in a tavern, until the case was reported, no one would even touch the body. Then related persons and the court staff would come to check out how many times he was stabbed and make out a report called a "see report," *korton* (*skor don*). For this kind of case, the *chang* seller, his landlord, and the murderer would all be punished. If the murderer was not caught, the tavern owner was primarily responsible for victim compensation payments. Because of these laws in Lhasa, we had few problems with the taverns.

In all Tibet, there were some very famous prostitutes. Usually they were in the *chang* shops, and people came to ask for them there. The prostitutes were usually under thirty years of age; they would dance in the tavern and then take a man to their home or to a back room in the shop with a vacant bed. In some small *chang* shops there were old unmarried women who had good reputations with the prostitutes; one of them could take a man to the prostitute and then get money for doing so. Although prostitution was illegal, police did not arrest these women; they called them "our friends." But if a young girl without experience was encouraged to do this, her parents could file a case against the prostitution solicitor in court. I have seen such cases.

Also, we had some electric lighting. In 1910 the Dalai Lama went to India, and upon his return he sent some younger Tibetans to England for study. One of these fellows studied electrical engineering through high school and a higher degree so that when he came back he could set up the electricity board. After that, the Potala, rich houses, some of the buildings, and streets had electricity at night. Still, people did not think it was dangerous to walk the streets at night until after the Chinese came.

Police

In the first half of this century there were three different types of police in Lhasa and a few of the other larger cities. The original policemen from "olden times" were called the *korcakpa* (*skor 'chag pa*). They each wore a belted Tibetan robe, a round yellow hat, a copper or gold hoop in one ear, and a short whip in their belts as they patrolled the streets in pairs. One Tibetan reported that they had started with the reign of the Great Fifth Dalai Lama and continued only until 1906, when they were replaced by Chinese-style police; others claimed that all three kinds of police coexisted in Lhasa at various times. *Korcakpa* police officers were connected to the court system and took most of their arrests to the Lhasa City Court for arraignment and trial. One Tibetan reported that over twenty of these police worked exclusively for the court, escorting the judges to work, moving prisoners, bringing in new cases, and carrying out punishment.

A second kind of policemen called the *thuvin* were established sometime during the early part of this century under instruction from the Chinese (one source cited their tenure as from 1906 to 1924). Said to have been clothed in Chinese dress and trained in physical punishment techniques by the Lhasa representative of the Chinese government, they were unsuccessful as an enforcement institution and did not last long, according to several reports.

The third kind, the *polisi* (*po li si*), were organized by the Thirteenth Dalai Lama after his return from India in 1912 (another source said 1924) as a patrolling police force. Dressed in the British style with formal blue uniforms, hats, and whistles, they carried long sticks holstered in leather cases on their belts. A Tibetan who had been living in India returned to train them at the request of the Dalai Lama.[7]

Even after the reforms of the Thirteenth Dalai Lama, the police and the army continued to have the same general forms of recruitment, military ranks, land ownership, housing (although in separate areas), food, and basic training. In many instances they also had the same essential role: maintaining internal peace. The Thirteenth Dalai Lama tried to open recruitment to the general public, upgrade both the army and the police, and separate the functions of the two into specific external and internal duties. Most Tibetans acknowledged that the results of his attempt were mixed at best. After several political scandals, the old style of police and army prevailed.

Police Headquarters in Lhasa were located in the *thom dzig khang* (*khrom gzigs khang*) area north of the Cathedral Complex in a large facility able to house up to three hundred officers plus a mess, a tailor shop, and other amenities. Approximately two hundred more officers lived in other parts of the city, often with their families. Police officers came from all different parts of Tibet and were recruited from families who, in the words of one Tibetan, "gave someone to the police in each generation instead of paying a regular tax on their land." Thus, a father would serve as a full-time watchman for the capital city, followed by one of his sons or even a third member of the household, such as a servant, to fulfill a tax requirement.

A former police officer who is currently a refugee in India told of his experiences on duty in Lhasa:

A policeman's basic duty was to patrol the streets of Lhasa. There were separate guard posts, like little houses, throughout the city, and when a change of shift occurred, the new police on duty marched in a group like soldiers to each of the guard posts and replaced the old shifts one by one. The change of police was every two hours or so in the day and less frequently at night, perhaps every three or four hours. The guard houses were placed in the four directions of the city streets.

The police arrested people on the street rarely, but if they did, it was for offenses like a person urinating or defecating in the street, throwing lots of garbage in the streets, drunkards making problems for others in the streets, shepherds or others who had let their sheep, horses, or other animals wander, and thieves or robbers stealing from the shops. If there was a problem like this, we went over to the persons and talked and advised them. After talking, if they left or took their animals away, then nothing was done. If they would not listen, then a policeman might hit them with their wooden sticks or even take them into the Police Headquarters.

Generally, if a policeman on the street met with a person who was not insane or drunk, and that person did an unusual or even illegal act in front of the policeman, the policeman would stop him. He would talk to the man and find out why he was doing it this way, but he did not ask him to stop what he was doing unless it was clearly wrong. Then we would check for two or three days to see if it continued, but we did not respond at that moment. If a man did something unusual today but he was all right tomorrow, then we said that yesterday he had a problem and didn't feel all right, but now he was fine. If his behavior went on for several days, then maybe we would do something about it.

There were more problems around the beershops on the side streets of Lhasa, of course. One night when I was not working, I saw a fight that took place between two drunk men on the road outside a beer house. One lunged out to stab the other and they fought. The stabber was arrested by the police, who came when they heard the commotion. The policeman took the stabber by the arm strongly and marched him to the police station.

We didn't usually tie people with rope or put fetters on their feet when they were arrested. If we had to tie them, there were several different styles of tying. Some put the hands in back and tied them; others put the hands in front.

I went with the other policeman to the station, and once we got there with the stabber, they reported what happened. In this case, it was not a very serious offense, so they punished him a bit at the police headquarters and let the stabber go.

If the police arrested someone on a small offense [against another], both persons were brought to the office and then asked who did it and whose mistake it was. If the act was done by the man who stabbed and he confessed to it, he was punished and freed. If there was a disagreement between the victim and the stabber or the policeman and the stabber or victim, then they didn't know whom to punish, and it could not be resolved easily. They would question a bit more and try to see if he confessed or if there was an agreement on what happened. If there was still no agreement, the stabber was kept for the night, and the case was written up for the Lhasa City Court. Almost all the cases that came to the police house went to this court.

The police in Lhasa were not harsh. We did not whip any of the people arrested. The public was never whipped in the police station, but they might be beaten with a stick if the offense was light before they were let go. The officers themselves got whipped if they committed any offense when they were on duty or if they made a mistake. A criminal who was picked up for a small offense and brought to the police station might be hit with the long bamboo sticks of the police, almost a yard and a half long, if he was rowdy or if the police knew that he had done the offense and wanted to prevent him from doing it again. But they did not whip or give heavy punishments, because this was allowed only on orders from the court.

There was no difference in the way that a rich or poor person was treated when standing before the government courts. The difference was that if the son of a rich man was found drunk and in a fight on the streets, he usually had servants who took care of him and kept him from ever going to court at all.

Besides patrolling, there were other duties; some police worked in the courts as their assignment for the day and had to move prisoners or carry out the punishments of the court for that day. The Lhasa City Court and the Zhol Court also punished by giving people big wooden collars or iron chains or fetters to walk around with, which were put on by the police.

There were all different sizes and physiques in these policemen in Lhasa. Some were very big and had a good physique; others did not. If a policeman was very small, he had several other police help him to hold on to the man he was arresting. The police were quite brave—this was an important characteristic. Sometimes these big criminals they arrested were not very brave at all.

A good policeman was one who performed his duties well, was brave and honest, and did not do actions that were contrary to religion. Police cannot always be religious, because they have to use the rules and regulations of the country; these two should be differentiated. It is said in the army and also among policemen that when a person does a bad thing, you should be a tiger toward him to catch him; once he is arrested, you should treat him like a son, your child.

In general, I would say that the police in Lhasa had a very good life. They spent a lot of their time playing cards during the festivals and were very happy.

The Central Government

By the twentieth century the three upper levels of the central government (those above the district and governors' offices) were operating in a tight series of referral and advisement loops. The top layer of the government included, at various times, the Office of His Holiness the Dalai Lama, the Office of the Regent, the Office of the Lord Chamberlain, the Office of the Prime Ministers, *silon* (*srid blon*), and the National Assembly.

The second level comprised the Cabinet, on the secular side, and the Ecclesiastical Office, on the religious side, acting as central clearinghouses for all legal cases flowing in and out of the government. Below the Cabinet, on the third level, were support departments for handling specific administrative affairs. The four original functions of the government, as outlined by the Seventh Dalai Lama, had shifted in importance by 1900; the Cabinet was on the second level of the government, and the other three—the Revenue Office, High Court, and Storage Office were on the third level.[8]

All secular legal petitions from the provincial governors and district officers—unsettled disputes in which the parties had refused to agree to the decision, cases of murder or other very serious crimes, appeals from parties who felt that their local government official was not dealing with them fairly, legal matters addressed to the Dalai Lama—arrived at the Cabinet Office in Lhasa. Located on the second floor in the south side of the outer building of the Cathedral Complex, in the 1940s the interconnected rooms of the Cabinet housed five senior cabinet ministers called *kalons* (*bka' blon*), one deputy minister called a *katsab* (*bka' tshab*), one head clerk called a *kadrung* (*bka' drung*), three assistant clerks called *kadron* (*bka' mgron*), three lower clerks called *letsenpa* (*las tshan pa*), and many attendants.[9]

The floor plan of the Cabinet offices, or *kashag* (*bka' shag*), in Figure 14 was drawn under the instruction of a former government official who had worked his way up to the position of head Cabinet clerk. The main room, situated at the extreme west, held the ceremonial altar and a throne for the Dalai Lama; the senior Cabinet ministers were seated along the walls and under the windows. This was the area where the Cabinet ministers, who were among the most powerful and high-ranking officials in the nation, entertained petitions and discussed issues of major and minor legal and political import. Adjoining the main room to the north was the altar room for the protective deities, which doubled as storage space. In the large room east of the main room sat the head clerk and his assistants, waiting to receive, handle, and copy petitions, which were then placed in the document file racks. Hanging on either side of the door to designate the division between these inner three rooms and the outer waiting rooms were the symbols of national authority, the tiger skin–wrapped *bochak*.

A Tibetan who had served as a legal representative in Lhasa in the 1950s explained how a legal petitioner would approach this office:

> I have handled a legal case with the Kashag myself. You approach the Cabinet ministers through one of their four attendants in the outer rooms first. You wait outside the inner rooms where the bodyguards of the Cabinet members sit. When an attendant comes out into the waiting room, you offer a white scarf and your petition letter to him near the entrance to the inner rooms.
>
> Hanging on either side of the lintel to that door to the inner rooms are *bochak,* which are posts [cylinders] about [eight inches] in diameter and [a yard] high filled with cotton, I think, and wrapped in a leopard [or tiger] skin. If the Cabinet was too busy, they used to tie these two together at the bottom to restrict entrance.
>
> The most important seat in the first inner room was occupied by the head clerk and the rest by assistant clerks or attendants who screened all the information and people coming into the inner offices.

At the third or department level, all offices of the government were technically available for referral of legal cases, but only a few appeared to have been used for that purpose, according to my interviews and collected cases. Some secular government offices could be approached directly with legal petitions as well as through referral

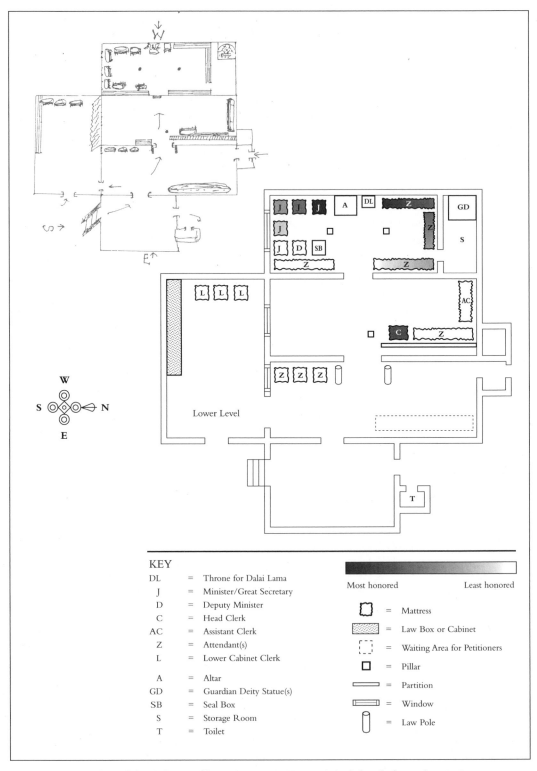

KEY

DL	=	Throne for Dalai Lama
J	=	Minister/Great Secretary
D	=	Deputy Minister
C	=	Head Clerk
AC	=	Assistant Clerk
Z	=	Attendant(s)
L	=	Lower Cabinet Clerk
A	=	Altar
GD	=	Guardian Deity Statue(s)
SB	=	Seal Box
S	=	Storage Room
T	=	Toilet

Most honored   Least honored

	=	Mattress
	=	Law Box or Cabinet
	=	Waiting Area for Petitioners
	=	Pillar
	=	Partition
	=	Window
	=	Law Pole

Figure 14. Floor plan of the Cabinet offices circa 1950. Top: original sketch from description by former Tibetan official (drawing done by Karma Gyatso). Bottom: schematic based on the sketch (not to scale).

from the Cabinet; among these were the Office of the Army, the Storage Office, the Agricultural Office, and the Armory. Departments that took cases only by referral from the Cabinet included the Revenue Office, the High Court, the New Investigation Office, the Grain Tax Office, the General Foreign Office, and the Foreign Office for Nepalese. (This list, based on collected cases, is incomplete, but it is unlikely that many legal cases were referred elsewhere.) Two departmental offices only mentioned here but very important to the overall function of the legal process were the Office of the Army and the New Investigation Office. The latter was established—probably in the 1940s—for the express purpose of consolidating and expediting the legal cases coming into the central government.[10] According to a former Tibetan official, in the 1950s it had two senior officials, two junior officials (one monk and one lay), and twenty-five staff. Disputes referred by the Cabinet to the New Investigation Office (which could be of any type but were usually the more serious noncriminal complaints) were investigated by staff members in teams of two, after which they all met to present their cases and decide them.

The Flow of Cases

The Cabinet was the access point for the majority of secular legal cases coming into any of the upper three legal levels of the government. Once received by the Cabinet, a case was referred out to one of the administrative departments for consideration. This pattern, evident from a careful reconstruction of the paths of cases through the bureaucracy, was confirmed by several Tibetans who had worked as clerks, one of whom explained:

Actually, Lhasa was filled with many, many different courts because all the government departments could be courts. First, all petitions to the government went to the Cabinet. From the Cabinet, they were sent to a department, depending on the subject matter of the dispute and how busy the department was with the load of cases it was considering. Small private disputes, of course, went directly to the three local Lhasa courts, the Lhasa City Court, the Zhol Court, or the Municipal Office. From these local courts, a decision might also be appealed to the Cabinet.

Generally, the Cabinet did not decide any cases, but if a dispute was very subtle, [the ministers] drafted a decision document and presented it to the regent or His Holiness for approval. Some of the central government offices you could go to directly, and some you could go to only through the Cabinet.

By controlling the inflow, outflow, and referral of the majority of legal cases and administrative matters for the entire central government, the Cabinet consolidated information and power in one unit. Indeed, previous students of Tibetan political science have not adequately considered its role: its impact on the operation of the government, its flexibility, and its place in the balance of powers.

Although the Cabinet itself sat as an occasional court for certain cases—particularly those of a more political nature—it was more often the central locus in the flow of legal matters. Judicial review for the average case did not begin until it reached the assigned department. A case sent to the Cabinet (see Figure 15) was forwarded either

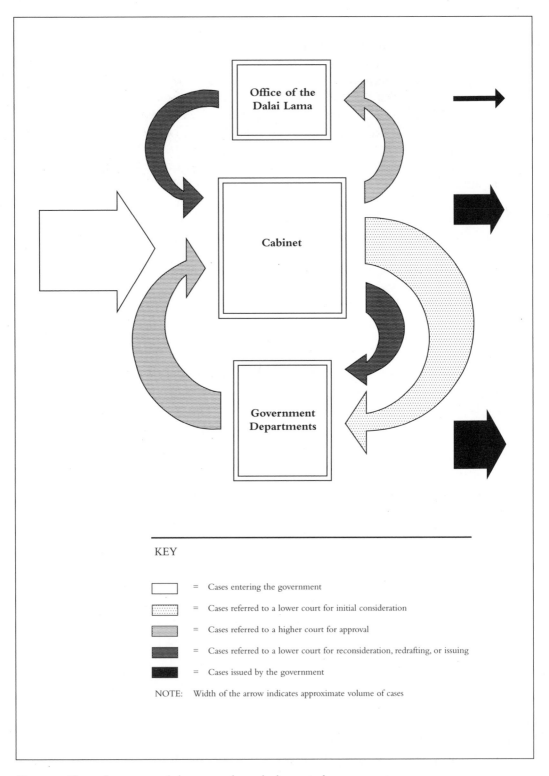

Figure 15. Flow of nonmonastic law cases through the central government.

to the ecclesiastical side or to the most appropriate secular office with instructions for its consideration. For example, murder cases were referred to the High Court. When the High Court had completed its investigation and written a decision, this document was returned to the Cabinet for review. Tibetans said that this part of the process might take anywhere from one month to one year. If the Cabinet disapproved of the judicial decision, another loop of the review occurred.

Once approved by the Cabinet, the decision document was either issued by the Cabinet, sent back to the department to be issued, or moved on to the Office of the Dalai Lama. Rarely, a response was written and issued directly from the Office of His Holiness; more commonly, the document was returned to the Cabinet without the seal of the upper office but with decisions on options or suggestions for a new review, or it was returned *with* a seal and instructions to issue the decision as approved. If unapproved, the entire process began anew with a fresh look by the Cabinet and the High Court (or other department) and new decision documents. Once all the required offices, including the Office of His Holiness, had seen and approved the document, it was typically sent back to the department for final copying, filing, and disposition. It was then the duty of the departmental office to see to the particulars of the case, such as the punishment or release of a prisoner, and to issue copies of the final document to all the significant parties, retaining one copy for the department's own records.

It should be noted that the referential terms for a document changed within the legal process, depending on what office it was issued from and was proceeding to, in accordance with the shifts in honorifics in the Tibetan language (a fact that can cause immense initial consternation for the uninformed interviewer!). A document was referred to less honorifically as it passed to a higher level, and more honorifically as it returned. For example, a letter, memorandum, or interdepartmental correspondence called a *kogya* (*bkod rgya*) when it entered the process received the honorific marker *ka* (*bka'*) when it was issued from or approved by the Cabinet or the Office of the Dalai Lama, thus becoming *kagya* (*bka' brgya*). Likewise, a final legal decision, called a *cétsam* (*bcad mtshams*), became a *kacé*. An order or edict issued directly by the Cabinet or the Office of His Holiness was called, in the honorific, a *kashok* (*bka' shog*); a general term for such an edict was *dantsik* (*gtan tshigs*). Thus, a department would refer to its own document with a lower term until it had been seen by a higher office; once approved at an upper level, the document carried the more honorific term, even if first issued at the lower level. In this way, the terms for documents maintained the hierarchy of legal levels in the offices of the central government in Lhasa.

CHAPTER TWENTY-ONE

The City Court of Lhasa

Arguments start with just a word and grow into a fight.
Though hundreds may die in fighting, at the end, it comes to conciliation.
A tree about to fall blames the wind,
A person who lacks a good complexion blames the blood.
It's not good to fight because it takes time and spoils your wealth.
—Neudong Law Code

In Lhasa the middle ring, Barkor, was a large roadway of cobblestones that surrounded the Cathedral Complex, dividing the city's most sacred and official sector
from its commerce and housing. The name implies an intermediate walkway for
circumambulating a holy shrine with one's right shoulder toward the object, a ritual
of reverence in Buddhism for reciting prayers and gaining merit. Though pilgrims
could be seen there at all times of the day, it was in the early evening of the average
day that the cobbled street filled with the regular population of Lhasa—shopkeepers,
tavern owners, sellers, policemen, farmers, servants, and monks—walking clockwise around the Cathedral Complex. Some of them were engaged in conversation,
some had children on their backs, others carried packs on their way home. Most
held a rosary in the left hand and walked alone, chanting a favorite mantra, or string
of syllables, to evoke a god or goddess: "OM MANI PE ME HUM" or "OM TARE TUTTARE
TURE SVAHO."[1] It was a meditative and mesmerizing activity; the group became a
moving stream of voices gaining its own momentum. As night fell, its numbers
dwindled; most people turned homeward, while the serious pilgrims remained.

Depending on the time of year, the morning hours on this middle walkway saw
merchants, traveling salespersons, visiting pilgrims, farmers from outside the city,
and nomads in season with their carcasses, skins, and hardened cheese to sell. At the
busy times of year the streets were jammed; during an intervening lull, almost
empty. Household merchants filled many of the doorways, their rooms opening like
stalls directly to the street; peripatetic merchants set out their collection of wares on
blankets in the street. There were tavern owners and textile sellers, butter and flour
suppliers, sellers of religious articles and books, shoemakers sitting in their chairs
sewing soles on boots, leathermakers and craftworkers of all kinds plying their

Plate 48. Merchant stalls on either side and a chorten at the end of a side street in Lhasa. 1920–21. (Pitt Rivers Museum, University of Oxford)

trades and offering their wares on the roadway. During the windy season the doors of shops and black-edged windows of the floors above were closed against the dust clouds swirling through the streets. Ringing the edges of the walkway were the three-storied, many-windowed homes of the old families of Lhasa, the Shakapas, the Tsarongs, the Surkhangs. At the front stoop of some of these houses and entrances to inner courtyards, huge black mastiffs were chained, barking at travelers on the roadway.

The City Court of Lhasa

Pressed against the outer north wall of the Cathedral Complex and opening to the middle walkway was a tall edifice called the *nangtse shak* (*snang rtse shag*). No one really knew why it was called this, but some guessed that it was named for a family that had owned it hundreds of years before.[2]

It was an imposing three-storied building in the style of a Tibetan fortress but with whitewashed sides sloping back at an angle from the street. Its south wall abutted the north wall of the Cathedral Complex; its north and west walls were largely blank, with only small, high windows; but on the side facing east a large set of steep central stairs led to the second floor, where a magnificent painted entrance-way framed a huge wooden door with a central iron ring. Hanging from large iron

Plate 49. Market stalls and sellers on the Barkor in front of the Lhasa City Court. 1986.

rings on either side of the door were two long, spiral-painted posts of wood, the law poles, which—together with the public whippings and other punishments executed on the right side of the large stone staircase—told even passersby from out of town that this was a court. Indeed, this was the famous Lhasa City Court.

It is uncertain whether or not this was the first court to be established in the capital city. One Tibetan-Chinese dictionary states that the building is very old, perhaps even dating from the early Empire period and was used as the court for the local government during that time.[3] Accounts of Lhasa from the mid-seventeenth century, however, make little mention of the City Court. The structure could have been a family home in the early period and converted into a court later on. Given the propensity for appropriate cardinal placement in Tibetan cosmology, it is possible to speculate that this building was chosen for its position on the north wall, but outside of the Cathedral Complex, to indicate that it was connected but external to the central

Plate 50. The front (east face) of the former Lhasa City Court with its large stone staircase leading to the second floor. There is a hook on the right door jamb from which a law pole used to hang. The shops on either side of the stairs are modern. 1986.

government's legal concerns. It shares no common hallways, entrances, or facilities with the larger building.

From the beamed threshold of the main doorway on the second floor a low entranceway opened into a small atrium with rooms ahead to the right and ladderlike stairs on the far left leading up to the next floor. Given the thickness of the exterior walls, the inside of the building felt (and feels even today) surprisingly small, with low ceilings and that atmosphere of density common to structures built by ancient Tibetan techniques. The entrance area and the rooms around it were small and cramped; there were no windows either to the outside or onto the atrium. Tibetans said these were waiting rooms, storage rooms, cells for less serious criminals, and temporary holding areas for prisoners awaiting a hearing.

Through a door to the left of the entranceway, a staircase led down to the ground floor.[4] On that level and perhaps below it was the famous *nangtse shak* prison, reported to be a windowless area with separate cells that held a variety of short-term and long-term prisoners. Many Tibetans who have never resided in Lhasa understand the term Nangtse shak to mean "the place of the famous prison."

Climbing the wooden ladder staircase at the far end of the atrium to the third floor, one reached a horseshoe-shaped balcony and a set of rooms surrounding the

Plate 51. View of the third floor of the former Lhasa City Court, taken from the roof of the building. The monk and visitors are standing at one end of the horseshoe-shaped balcony near the ladder staircase from the floor below. The former waiting rooms, storerooms, and courtrooms are both behind the visitors and (not visible) to the right. 1986.

atrium.[5] This was the courtroom floor; most of the rooms were small and white-washed, with scrolled decorations on the pillars and crossbeams. Apparently the two rooms on the northern wall were used for trying cases; Tibetans have described judicial proceedings taking place in both, although the judges sat in only one room at a time. It is probable that the closed room in the corner was the usual court and that the open room with large windows facing out to the verandah was used for special trials when the public could view the proceedings. On the eastern wall were three smaller rooms with some decorations and windows that looked out over the Barkor. These were used as storerooms, space for the secretaries, and also possibly as waiting rooms for petitioners, witnesses, and visitors, as were the small rooms on the west wall.

The territorial jurisdiction of the City Court was the eastern section of Lhasa proper, and in this sense it was truly and only a direct-access district court; it did not take cases from outside the city, nor did it take many on referral from the central government. The western boundary of its jurisdiction was determined by the Turquoise Roof Bridge, which divided the city in half. Some Tibetans spoke of taking many different sorts of criminal and civil cases to the City Court, but in the minds of most lay Tibetans living both inside and outside Lhasa, this was primarily a criminal court and a prison for the eastern half of the city.

A Tibetan who had acted as a representative for others and had gone almost daily to the Lhasa City Court in the 1940s described the procedure involved:

> You go up the outside stone stairs to the second floor and then take the stairs inside to the third floor. The whole [balcony of the] third floor is open to the sky [through the atrium]. There is a waiting room near the stairs, and people also wait on the verandah. A caretaker of the court comes to you and asks you about your case. He will take your papers and go to the judges, the *mipon* (*mi dpon*). Only one person is allowed in to see the *mipon* at a time. Besides the three caretakers, there are also two *shipchopa* (*zhib dpyod pa*), who are the personal secretaries or bodyguards of the judges, the two *dunyik* (*drung yig*), who are the clerks of the court, and the *korcakpa,* the police who come in every day to handle the prisoners in the court. The police change every day, about twenty serving at a time in the City Court.
>
> When you are called by name from the waiting room, you go in to bow, present your petition to the *mipon,* and say what you have to say. I always go into the room in the northwest corner. Sitting on mattresses in the far corner, one facing east and one facing south, with low tables before them, the *mipon* always number two. Petitioners stand before them to show their respect. You may never sit. If you start to give a statement, they will call the secretaries, who then come in through the same door, pull out their mattresses, and sit anywhere, ready to take down what you say. There are small windows on two of the walls for light, and in the winter large brass charcoal braziers burn in the rooms. There are no storage boxes or other furniture in this room.
>
> The court opens around nine o'clock—there is no lunch break or any other break; tea is brought in from the outside in the afternoon—and it usually stops around four o'clock. Sometimes the court goes much longer, however.

The Case of the Lhasa Tavern Lady

Many cases were taken to the City Court of Lhasa during the 1940s by the legal representative for the area of Sakya, a man described by others as "knowledgeable about doing the law."[6] In recounting this case, he presented the layout and legal process of the City Court in rich detail:

> In the eastern part of Lhasa there was a well-known tavern run by a tavern lady, and late one night there arose a bad quarrel in the tavern between two drunk men. Both started a fistfight, then pulled out knives and stabbed each other inside the tavern. This is a serious sort of case that cannot be decided internally [at home]. This incident had to be reported by the watchman for that block of houses to the City Court. Every block watchman and the local police were responsible to see that cases like this were reported to the City Court. If the two men had stabbed each other but there was no bloodshed, then the watchman could have settled the case by himself.

After the fight, the tavern was shut down and sealed off by the court. A caretaker of the court came to seal the house. He took a rope and tied up the doors and the windows. Then he covered each knot with wax and stamped it with the seal of the court.

All the tavern lady's possessions were inside the tavern, including an altar with silver pots, and lots of cash from all the beer sales. Now the husband of the tavern lady was afraid that all their valuable possessions and money would be confiscated by the court or stolen, and so he went that night to the tavern. He broke the seal on the window and took their valuables out. Then he went to the same caretaker of the court, who was his friend, and bribed him with only a little money to reseal the tavern window, saying that he had only taken out some of their own possessions. The caretaker took the money and went and resealed the house. The judge never found out about this part of the case.

The woman who owned the tavern was a subject of the principality of Sakya, so she came to see me as the Sakya representative and asked me to help. The tavern lady knew that she was responsible for the people who came to drink in her tavern, that they should not have been allowed to fight, and that she owed all the payments for problems occurring in her tavern. In Tibet there was no tax on taverns or their owners or on beer sellers, but they had to fight cases in court because they were responsible for the people drinking. This is why she came to see me.

Because I took her case, the next morning I went first to the home of one of the *mipon*, judge of the Nangtse shak. Presenting a white scarf but no money or presents to the judge when I was received, I told him that an incident had occurred the previous night and that the tavern lady had had a very difficult time stopping this fight. I said that she belonged to the district of Sakya, which made her a special citizen, and that she should not be whipped for this case. I went that morning because I knew that it was important to go right away to the judge, because these kinds of cases are decided very quickly in one or two days.

On the following day, I went into the City Court and waited to be heard in the crowded waiting room upstairs. When the case was called, I entered the courtroom, bowed, presented myself to the judges, and asked only that the woman not be whipped, stating that she couldn't do anything to stop the two men from fighting, although she had tried very hard. One of the judges replied that she was the one who was responsible for preventing any problems in her tavern. The judges in the court then said that they would proceed with the case, and so I left.

In the court that day after my appearance, first, the court called the tavern lady and asked her to give a statement of what had happened. She spoke to the court by herself. There were two judges in the court, and their secretaries took down her statement as she said it. The judges asked her many questions, such as "What was the reason for the fighting?" and "Why didn't you stop the fighting?" Then the *shuwa* (*zhu ba*), petition or statement, was written from what she had presented.

Then the two men were called, one at a time. I do not know if they had help or representatives. They gave their own statements, and then they were asked questions from the tavern lady's petition and had to give answers. Then the judges decided and gave a final decision right then, which was copied in a long paper giving the facts of the case and the final punishment. The secretary called the woman and the men to listen as he read the decision, then passed out copies to the three of them. She got a copy of the decision and had to pay court costs of one rupee and one white scarf, and so did each of the men.

At this time, a first payment court cost of one rupee was very cheap; it was not a costly payment. Each person had to pay this, the tavern lady and the two sides to the fight.

The court costs in the Nangtse shak were split up this way: The first payment amount is cut in eight parts, and all eight parts go to the court. This was one rupee for this case. Then one fourth, or two parts of the original payment, is given to the two secretaries. Then for the court caretaker, one fourth of the secretaries' payment, or one-half of one part, is given. Therefore, each person paid a total of ten and one-half parts to the court [or approximately one and a third rupees]. This is how payment was made by each person to the court.

For the two men who stabbed, there were additional punishments and compensation payments: the victim of the [first] stabbing was given something by the stabber as injury compensation, and the [first] stabber was ordered to be whipped by the court. This was done outside the courthouse near the bottom of the stairs at a place used for whipping publicly.

After this decision, the tavern lady was very pleased, and she called me to her house and offered me beer. But I don't drink.

Exegesis

One of the most interesting aspects of this case is the liability of a tavern owner for the actions of her patrons. The doctrine of social responsibility in Tibet dictated that everyone concerned—the watchman, police, tavern owner, and parties to the incident—had a duty to report the occurrence to the court immediately. Women who owned and managed their own property were liable for it; the tavern owner went immediately to find someone influential to help her out. We are not told what gifts or money exchanged hands initially, if any, between the tavern owner and the narrator. To deflect the humiliation of physical punishment, the tavern lady chose someone who was versed in legal procedures and "spoke well." But all parties to this dispute were responsible; there was no zero-sum solution. Both men made several payments to redress the injury to each other and the community, and the first to stab was publicly whipped to impress on both the criminal and the public the illegality of such behavior.

The legal representative in this case made a preliminary visit to the judge at home, without the offer of an elaborate gift, to plead mitigating circumstances. This is an important example of the legal ritual of visiting a judge at home; in this instance it did not involve bribing and operated (almost as an appearance of counsel does in American courts) to let the judge know that the woman had a champion of some distinction who would speak for her. Both here and in court, however, he appeared only for the purpose of requesting mitigation of physical punishment; she herself presented the circumstances of the case. It is likely that his social power as the representative of Sakya, a Vatican-like religious state, influenced the decision.

This is the only case collected that described adequately the process of sealing up the scene of the crime, although several other cases refer to such practices. The law codes describe sealing up parts of the body after an ordeal (for example, hands that have been put in boiling oil are wrapped up and sealed). Finally, the narrator gives a wonderfully detailed discussion of the accounting and payment of court costs, an elaborate subject described at great length in some law codes.[7]

CHAPTER TWENTY-TWO

The Municipal Office of Lhasa

Explanation of the attributes of judges and conciliators necessary to decide a case according to the law:
The three qualities of agreement:

1. He must keep all points and reasons in his mind.
2. He should remove doubts and confusions promptly.
3. He should listen to pleadings with patience.

The four qualities of affection:

1. He should not announce a decision forcefully if one side does not agree.
2. He must not be biased by those near to him.
3. He should decide the case in the most suitable way.
4. He should consult with unbiased, learned people.

—Neudong Law Code

The name *lhasa nyertsang (lha sa gnyer tshang)* means "storehouse for Lhasa City." By the mid-twentieth century, however, storage was only one of the many tasks assigned to the Municipal Office of Lhasa, which had evolved into an administrative office handling everything from disputes occurring inside the Cathedral Complex to problems with sewage disposal in the city. Historically, like most Tibetan government offices, it had acquired a patchwork of duties and responsibilities, not all of which were connected to municipal affairs. Jurisdiction over lawsuits involving Muslims was just one example.

The Municipal Office occupied a series of rooms located inside the administration building of the Cathedral Complex in the southwest corner. Its location on the south side indicated, in the mandalic architecture of the building, its primarily administrative function. In 1957 the office was staffed by four officials of the fifth rank—two monk and two lay—one secretary, and eight clerks called *nyertsang nangtsen (gnyer tshang nang tshan)*. Much of their daily activity, according to officials who worked in this office during the 1940s and 1950s, concerned noncriminal legal cases, but they had multiple other responsibilities as well:

- collecting taxes in the Cathedral Complex area, particularly from the private homes inside the Barkor;
- serving as treasurer for the building;
- supplying many of the necessities of the government offices in the building;
- supervising the Muslims in Lhasa, collecting their personal taxes, also called *mibog* (*mi bogs*) and keeping records of all taxes, births, and deaths among Muslims;
- supervising the municipal regulations of Lhasa City in compliance with the "House Book," *khangdeb* (*khang deb*) which covered new construction (house design, the height of buildings, whitewashing), water use and control (well water, public and internal toilets, gutters, drainage, sewage), garbage removal and dumps, and road access;
- validating and filing copies of house leases, subleases, assignments (the general term is *gangya*), and deeds of sale of buildings, *khang gya* (*khang rgya*), as required;
- regulating the use of roof ornaments, *gyaltsen* (*rgyal mtshan*) (which were limited to houses that had a copy of the Buddhist canon, temples of protective deities, monasteries, or homes of families of the Dalai Lamas), and the display, burning, and replacement of prayer flags in the city;
- overseeing the use, maintenance, and repair of the Jokhang and other temples in the city.

The law cases that the Municipal Office could address as a court were expected, generally, to be noncriminal and related to its duties, particularly disputes between private parties concerning business transactions, land, inheritance, and other civil or municipal matters. The jurisdictional range of the office, however, was geographically limited. It comprised: first, all cases (criminal and otherwise, unless assigned to another office by the Cabinet) that occurred within the confines of the Cathedral Complex itself—that is, within the middle ring walkway—including legal suits from old private families with homes in the southern quadrant; second, all civil cases, particularly those involving land and property, that concerned subject matters located inside the Lingkor (the outer ring walkway of the city) and east of the Turquoise Roof Bridge or outside the outer ring but adjacent to the city on its eastern boundary; and third, all civil cases concerning Muslim Tibetans.

The Case of the Smelly Toilet

One case brought to the Municipal Office of Lhasa in 1958 is perhaps the most interesting of all those I collected. It became a very famous lawsuit over the months of its duration, and several of the participants—judge, parties, and clerks—were available as sources. What follows is a narrative compiled from all these recollections, interspersed with verbatim extracts from the version of the only participant who agreed to be quoted directly.

There was, in Lhasa City, an old enclosed courtyard surrounded by houses. It had a small entrance from the main road, which was congested with daily activities and

Plate 52. The entry to an old enclosed Lhasa courtyard surrounded by houses. 1986.

traffic from the surrounding twenty households; there was a large well and some toilets. In 1957 the Ganden Monastery outside of Lhasa had purchased one of the houses on the courtyard as a hostel for its monks to use when visiting the city to attend special rituals, carry out monastic business, or undergo religious training. A newer house abutting the hostel was rented by an influential Lhasa family, and a dispute arose between the monastic hostel and this house.

The monks of the hostel used a toilet in the courtyard which drained through a partially open sewer passing the family's house; as one member of the family stated, "It was very smelly and very dirty." So this family in the dwelling known as House Three (Family Three) stated that they wanted to seal up the area of the monks' toilet, extend their house, and clean out the drain with the help of the monks. Receiving no response or cooperation over several months, Family Three took its arguments to the Municipal Office in Lhasa, first visiting an older judge at home and then filing a complaint petition in court. Initially, the judge remained unsympathetic; then he stated that he was in favor of the petition of Family Three. The monks in the hostel were duly informed that they would have to make amends or move. Returning to the monastery to report the problem, a monk from the hostel presented the situation and the opinion of the judge, after which the monastic community determined to take action. A senior monk and two junior monks of Ganden Monastery were appointed to fight the case in Lhasa and were asked to begin that day. In the words of the senior monk:

So from the monastery, three of us went. I was senior and two junior monks also went. When we reached the courtyard in Lhasa, we talked to the caretaker of the hostel, who told us he had had a lot of law experience because of ill will toward former monks in our house.

He scolded us and said, "To fight a dispute is not easy. It will take a very long time, last as long as the hostel." But luckily he liked me. At that time, I told him the other problems were past; as to the new situation, we should work together to solve it. But the old man repeated that it was not easy, and I felt afraid.

I went to visit another old man in the city about the problem, and he said to me, "Whoever fights a case should have eighteen knots on his neck [meaning great experience], so you have made a great mistake in coming." This old man advised me to make the hostel caretaker my friend "because he knows a lot."

So I returned to the hostel and asked the caretaker to please support and help us. At first, he found it difficult to accept; then he finally joined us. But the caretaker gave me one condition: he would help, but he would not accept any punishment that might fall on us. So we agreed to take all the responsibility and to do all the work at the court ourselves. He stipulated that if he ever spoke in court or to other people in words not discussed beforehand at our meetings at night, then he would take punishment.

All four of us—the two younger monks, the caretaker, and I—went to court the next day. The two other monks didn't like to talk much but said, "We are ready to fight, but we have no ideas." So all the responsibility fell on me.

When we were in the Municipal Court, it was obvious that the judges weren't listening to our side. There were two judge officials, one a layman and one a monk, in the court. One other monk official was home sick. It seemed that the lay official was an unbiased person who had not made up his mind, so we were determined to say nothing more in court and go to that judge's home privately at night.

When we first went to his home, we gave him the following presents: one high-quality white silk scarf and seventy-five silver coins, *sung* [*srang*]. At that time, the judge scolded us and said that we were violating the rules of the city, had not fought the dispute correctly, did not clean the drainage, did not keep our toilet door closed, and our monks spoke harshly to Family Three. The judge pointed out all these faults to us, but our conclusion later was that he wanted to favor the other side, and the amount we had given was not enough.

Again, we returned to see him at his home with more money—100 silver *sung*—but he talked the same way a second time. Then a third time with 150 silver *sung*.

So we stopped going to his house.

We knew that we had the truth in this case, and our caretaker told us that those with the truth should not have to pay very much. The judge was angry when we stopped coming to his home. It seemed to us that the whole office was against us. Our robes were of low quality, and our house caretaker looked very slovenly, so maybe they thought, "These people can't fight the case; they don't know what they are doing."

The technique used by the monks after this was to discuss everything at night before their appearance in court the next day, planning strategies and words with the caretaker. They did not hire a person to write out their petitions but presented their case orally at each appearance, and the court clerks recorded what they said. According to the agreement between the monks and the caretaker, any new questions from the other side or the judge were not to be responded to immediately in court but discussed first at home.

For one month the case continued in this fashion, with Family Three and the monks appearing at separate interviews before the court almost fifteen times. Meanwhile, Family Three decided to go ahead with construction of a wall to close off the toilet in the courtyard, even though the officials had forbidden new construction until the case was done. The monks determined to stall the case because this was a violation. The senior monk continued:

> So after one month, the office said they would issue a final decision document and told us to come. . . .
>
> The judge said that we should sign *before* reading the decision. But the caretaker knew that the legal way was to read it first; we requested to read it first and then sign. We also asked to have a copy of the document, which was the honest, legal way also. In the document the court stated that they had decided to close our toilet door permanently, that Family Three could extend their walls, and that we were to help them clean out the drainage. There was even a new idea in this decision: that the water gutters of the hostel should not drain down into the courtyard.
>
> After reading this and seeing their actions, we became very angry in court and asked three questions of the judge: First, if we close the toilet, what are we to do? All Lhasa houses are required to have a toilet, so the court must provide us with a toilet. Second, all rainwater falls naturally from the upper story. Where does the court suggest it should be drained? Three, if we have to work to clean drainage, the city of Lhasa drainage is near us, and they should be asked to help also.
>
> So we did not return the document but kept it and did not sign it. The judge said in court, "We will talk again." But we became more brave because we knew that this decision was not the truth, that they were not acting honestly and we did not have to agree.

Another month of court appearances ensued; at some both parties were present, and at others they were called alternately. Family Three, although pressing forward with the courtyard construction, began to worry about their position as the monks continued to postpone a decision, stating on some occasions that they had to return to their monastery for advice, at other times that they had to discuss it among themselves. At one point the judge forbade the hostel caretaker even to come to court, but this produced more stalling by the monks, who continued not to agree to the decision.

At the end of the second month the judge issued a new decision that reduced demands on the monks: the toilet had to be closed permanently, and Family Three could extend their house into the courtyard, but nothing was included about the water runoff or the drainage. Trying to solve the dispute, Family Three said they would sign this decision document when it was presented to both parties in court, but the monks again refused, stating that the judge was not making a truthful decision and that they had determined to fight the case in an upper court. The judge said they could not do that but should take the case into conciliation proceedings outside of court with one of the staff of the Municipal Office.

Plate 53. The quarters of the Dalai Lama at Ganden Monastery while he was taking his *geshe* examinations. The Case of the Smelly Toilet was adjourned for several months so that the monks could attend these examinations at their home monastery. 1920–21. (Pitt Rivers Museum, University of Oxford)

At the conciliation, the monks proposed that Family Three should build a wall blocking off the toilet area but should not extend their house, because that would interfere with the drainage. The conciliator agreed to this solution and presented it to Family Three, but they would not accept it, citing their need for more rooms.

As it was the time for higher-degree examinations in the monastery, and His Holiness the Dalai Lama was to be tested for the *geshe* degree, the monks then left Lhasa for two months. Before departing, they drafted (but did not present) long petition letters to the Cabinet, explaining the entire case and the many improper rulings and procedures of the court.

One night during the two months of the monks' absence from Lhasa, Family Three constructed the entire wall. The caretaker sent the monks a message that the wall had been built, that there was now "nothing left to do." He also suggested that when they returned, they should bring with them twenty or thirty *thutob (mthu stobs)*, or tough monks—often the kitchen or manual workers in the monasteries "who do not take an interest in philosophy"—to stay in the hostel. So the next day the three monks left for Lhasa with fifteen or sixteen *thutob* and arrived to find that the foundation had already been set for House Three's new rooms in the courtyard. They approached the workers and said, "You are not allowed to do this!" But the workers, saying nothing, continued with the building. The monks then retired to the hostel and slept a full night.

The next day the monk representatives went into court to find that a rotation of officials had taken place; the old judge had been replaced by a new young monk officer who was very intelligent and assiduous. Presenting their side again to the court, the senior monk repeated the whole history of the case, listing their particular points of argument: first, that the hostel had been constructed earlier than the house of Family Three; second, that the hostel could not legally close its toilet entirely; and third, that there was no place for drainage if a wall was built or House Three extended. He concluded by asking, "Why are you allowing them to construct?" With this, the new officer agreed to investigate the courtyard himself that evening. The senior monk remembered his visit:

> The new monk officer was happy with my explanation, and when he came to the courtyard that evening, he measured all the construction areas, the building, and the drainage and wrote all this down. Then he ordered the workers on the construction of the extension not to continue and told Family Three of his decision. The hostel caretaker listened to all this and was pleased, saying to me afterward, "We now might win with this man."
>
> At the same time, we continued to prepare our petition to the Cabinet. It contained very harsh language about the actions of the Municipal Court and requested a formal suit against the office itself.
>
> After the monk officer left, Family Three members armed themselves with pistols. We saw that they and their workers had decided to fight. From our side, one young lay boy aimed a gun back at a window on the other side, and the *thutob* armed themselves with stones, as did the other two monk representatives. I became very nervous and thought that this was not a good course.
>
> Immediately, I went secretly to the old caretaker and said to him, "We must do something now!" He said to me, "What new method do you suggest? Perhaps we should try a new way. Tomorrow, if they continue, we will go to the roof of the house and jump over to the house of Family Three, take off their inside ladders, then close the front door so no one can get out, and then I will run and report this to the police."
>
> So I agreed with him. It was a restless night.
>
> The next day I awoke early and went with our petition letter to the Cabinet (which was then meeting in the Summer Palace of the Dalai Lama). At nine o'clock, three of our people went out on the roof of the houses, while the work crew of Family Three began construction again.

While the senior monk was away, one of the other two monk representatives asked the crew twice not to continue in their endeavors, but the workmen would not respond. Telling the caretaker that Family Three would no longer listen, the monks went up onto the roof and took away the ladders between the roofs of the house to prevent movement between the rooftops; meanwhile, the caretaker blocked the hostel's front door from the outside to keep the *thutob* inside. Then the caretaker went to the police. Crying the whole time, he said there was nothing else to be done, and that the police must come and take care of it.

Initially, the police sent one officer and a few staff members back with the caretaker to investigate but found that the parties would not discuss the issues. Family Three told the police that they had waited many months for a decision from the court but none came, and so they had gone ahead with the construction. With this, the police went back to their office and returned with over one hundred fully armed

Plate 54. The section of the city of Lhasa in which the Case of the Smelly Toilet took place, showing the flat roofs on which the police stood. The Cathedral Complex is in the background. 1920–21. (Pitt Rivers Museum, University of Oxford)

officers, who stood on the roofs of all the buildings and surrounded both houses. The construction workers were dismissed at gunpoint. When the senior monk returned in the afternoon,

the dispute was still not decided. The police were in full force, and they came up to me. "You can now open the door of your house, for you will assuredly win your case," they said.

The caretaker responded, "Please don't open the house, for the monks are very mad and they will come out and hurt the other people." So the police suggested that I open the door and go inside to control the monks. I said, "I can control them. I did not collect monks here to demonstrate our power but for protection. We were helpless in this case. You should tell the other family to follow the regulations of the city."

After this, I opened the door and went inside. The monks were all armed with stones and were ready to fight with large knives as well, so I ordered them all into their rooms and said to put their knives away.

Then I came out and invited the police into our house and introduced the monks, saying, "We have no weapons in our hands. We came here to fight, but the other side will win unfairly because they have guns." The caretaker also talked and said that he had tried his best and that we had the truth.

The police then stood near the door to our house and asked me to sign a paper they had made right then; it was a document stating that from now on we would not fight, and the police would take full responsibility to win our case for us in court. They told us, "Even in spite of police, this family does not listen. They are violators, and we will take responsibility to win it for you." I signed and the police signed, and the police kept the document.

So everyone in Lhasa found out about this case; the news spread like fire in the town.

At this point, the new monk officer from the court arrived with some of his staff, filling the courtyard even further. The new officer proceeded to tell the monks in front of the police that they had the truth but should not create any problems with the *thutob* and should proceed to contest the case systematically in court. By that time, said the senior monk,

we knew we would win, so I told him, "We will not fight this case in your office because you have issued three final documents, all in favor of the other side, and you have not decided honestly. Now we will fight in the Cabinet, and your office should send a petition to them. You are a new officer and didn't know much about the old case; this is true."

So he said, "You are right, you were helpless, and I am new, but I will conciliate the case and try to settle it. Please don't file in the Cabinet." So I replied, "We have nothing to say to you. You can't conciliate for us because previous conciliations did not work. We are helpless to fight in the Municipal Office. So you just keep quiet, and we will fight those other two officers in your office who have not been honest."

The police officers then said to the young monk officer, "Their case has taken a long time, and the court was not honest, so now your office should decide the case honestly, or we can't take responsibility for fighting or killing." And the monk officer again requested that we allow him to be a conciliator and not go to the Cabinet. Finally, we accepted.

Then, the monk officer said, "I will be honest, I will come to your place, and you will not have to come to the court. I know I can settle it in a few days." And he added, "Come to court one time to withdraw the case; then I will conciliate the case." Then he left the courtyard. I didn't have much belief in him, but I thought that we must always accept conciliators.

The situation remained at this high pitch for a few more days. The monks visited a Cabinet secretary at home and explained the entire case, much to the dismay of the secretary, who exclaimed, "How could this happen?" Turning to the caretaker, he went on, "You did well and you have the truth." Then he turned to the senior monk and said, "You did well and you have the truth. Tomorrow I will write a letter to the office. We have your petition and you need not worry. We have appointed a new monk officer who is very honest, and we hope he will conciliate your dispute. There is no need to worry. Any fighting or killing would be very serious."

After this, the monk and caretaker went to the home of a judge of the Lhasa City Court, who had already heard about the case, to explain their side. His comments were that the police had acted very fairly, that the monks could be assured of winning, and that he would talk to other officials on their behalf. With this, the senior monk and caretaker returned to their hostel very happy with the support they had received.

Meanwhile, Family Three had also been visiting various government officials at home but had received only cordial greetings and no indications of support. They felt that the tide of the case had turned against them, even though they had been treated unfairly with so much stalling.

The next morning, both parties went back to the Municipal Office, where a copy of the petition before the Cabinet and three letters about the case had been received that morning. The Cabinet letter stated that the case had not been properly investigated and demanded that it be decided honestly or the entire office would be reviewed. A letter from the Cabinet secretary repeated this advice, and a letter from a Lhasa City Court judge said that this case was under his jurisdiction and should be sent to him for decision if it could not be decided honestly in the Municipal Office. The senior monk continued:

We were there one hour while they discussed among themselves. They told us to go home, that they would withdraw the case from the court for conciliation that evening. One clerk in the office had a good relationship with us, and he came near me to whisper that we would now win.

That evening we went to our house. Our opponent in the courtyard had nothing to say. Then the young monk officer came, and we discussed it again with him. At that time, I said, "You are the decision-maker and we will come to your house from now on." So he returned to his house.

The next day, when we went to see him at his house, I presented four points: First, our house is our own—but their house is only a rental, and they should be asked to show their rent document. This was a new point, and he accepted it. Second, they have used guns. Third, their guns must be collected before we can proceed. Fourth, we will say or do nothing until they are disarmed.

We then said nothing for three days. At our next meeting, the monk officer said, "Please now fight the real dispute." But we said, "We will not go to the root dispute until they have disarmed."

On the fourth day I went to the monk officer's house and stressed the same things. The monk officer took a large photo of His Holiness the Dalai Lama which was hanging behind him and put it in front of me. He said, "I have represented Tibet in China for a while, and although I am young, I have already served many years in the government. Please look at the face of His Holiness and try to think of a better way. You are a learned scholar and a monk. Please try a new way." I looked at the photo and tears fell from my eyes. I began to talk of the real root dispute, and on that day we made the plan of his deciding the case in full. Then I returned to the hostel.

With this, the monk officer began to compose the final decision document, *thama (khra ma)*, for the parties. After a complete rendition of the facts of the case and the four months of disputing, it made seven major points.

First, the family could not extend its house "even the size of a needle," for there was no room in the courtyard; second, the monks of the hostel had to keep the door to their toilet closed after use to reduce the smell; third, the Municipal Office would be in charge of cleaning the drainage system now and would repeat this in one year; fourth, Family Three would be responsible for part of the payment for the cleaning; fifth, the hostel would pay fifty silver *sung* for the cleaning; sixth, the monks themselves would not have to do any of the drain cleaning; and seventh, the water pipes on the roofs did not have to be changed.

This was then presented in oral form to Family Three and to me.

So Family Three had to say yes. The monk officer showed me the draft and asked if it was right. I said, "Yes, all is good, but for us to pay fifty silver *sung* is not right and will be the root of more fighting."

He agreed, saying it was not too high an amount but too low and therefore a problem because Family Three would later ask for people to come and clean it. "Okay," he said, "we will omit it. This year you pay five hundred silver *sung*." I said, "No, but we will continue to pay the regular fees for the water pipes." The monk officer said, "If you will please agree, I will pay the five hundred silver *sung*." Then I said, "We should not have to pay it because it is not fair, but if we must pay it, we will."

Now the monk officer became very happy because we had accepted his document. He said, "At first, I was very afraid, but now you have agreed, and we can decide the dispute in one day. I am glad I can decide this; it has become a very famous case in Lhasa. I will pay the five hundred *sung*. I will prepare all those documents, from the prostrations [the beginning section] on, by my own hand. On the top of the document will be the Cabinet seal, which I will get right away." He said this although everyone knows that it takes a very long time to get that seal. With this, all our business was finished.

At this point in the case, the monks and the caretaker returned home to find the twenty families of the courtyard waiting on the outside roadway to receive them with food. As part of "getting together," the process of reharmonizing after the dispute, the three monks went with white silk scarves, tea, and bread to Family Three to present their gifts and make the following statement, as reported by the senior monk:

"We have both fought for the sake of our houses, not for individuals. We have both used harsh words and created strife. Now it is over. Let us be patient and friends in the future."

I gave one silk scarf and fifty silver *sung* to use for offerings. From their side they said, "For us it is all meaningless. We have nothing to say because we have made a large mistake."

This case became very famous in Lhasa because so many monks and policemen were involved. The final decision was very thick, over five sheets glued together because they had to explain the whole case from the beginning.

Then Family Three pulled down all the new constructions. The monk officer came, and we then checked together whether they had extended the wall. They also had to pull down part of the wall near the toilet. Now people there have a new saying: "When construction is already done, if you can then pull the wall down, that is efficacy in fighting the case!"

The court costs were seven gold *sung* from each side to the Municipal Office for withdrawal, but there were no payments to the secretary or other staff members, because the case was settled out of court by a conciliator. After the decision the monks and the caretaker paid final visits to the Cabinet secretary and others, who subsequently advised them that it had all been decided well and honestly and that they should not create any new disputes in the future. None of the parties recounted having heard of any punishment given the former Municipal Office judge who had first heard the case, though one stated that he had been issued a serious warning by the Cabinet.

The senior monk came to some very interesting conclusions as a result of this case:

In one way it was very helpful to me because I learned something about the law and about judges in Tibet. Some of the judges were honest and some were dishonest. In Lhasa the officers were not as able to be dishonest, because the Cabinet and other offices were there always watching them. Outside Lhasa, it was easier to be dishonest.

After that, whenever I stayed in Lhasa, I circumambulated the Lingkor saying *manis*

[mantra prayers] but actually thinking of the dispute. All the time I thought of it. So I thought to myself, "From start to finish, we are accumulating mental afflictions and non-virtuous actions, and if we die now, we are dying through hatred and anger." So then I learned the nonvirtuous actions of fighting, but I did not show sadness to my friends.

Then I went back to my monastery. I explained the whole case in a meeting to the monastic community, concluding, "We fought and won due to the caretaker. So in future, our hostel in Lhasa should care for and support him. We should not fight such disputes anymore because it contradicts the Buddha's religion. I will not fight again, even if someone cuts my limbs. If any dispute arises in future and I am appointed, I will resign from the hostel." I spoke loudly and then I wept. The monks replied that instead of weeping, we should be glad we won. They promised not to ask me again to fight a lawsuit.

Two months later we lost our country to the Chinese. I met that new monk officer in Assam as we were all fleeing the Chinese armies, and he said to me, "Now what is the result of the big dispute?"

The opponent from Family Three also fled to India, and we are now good friends.

Exegesis

This detailed case rewards the reader with myriad insights into the Tibetan cosmology of law. Ultimately, the case was understood by the main narrator as having turned when the minds of the participants recognized inner morality. The cause of the dispute was the afflicted mental views of the actors, their greed, anger, pride, and hatred. Throughout the case the six root afflictions and the secondary afflictions (particularly belligerence, resentment, and deceit) motivated the actions of the parties. Upon seeing the photo of the Dalai Lama, the senior monk was brought up against the standard of the Buddha, who disciplined himself through moral thoughts and actions. Recognizing the comparison as well as his own devotion to the charismatic leader, the monk began to cry. Thus, it was the personal conscience of the main narrator, resonating with the ideal of the Buddha through the image of the Dalai Lama, that led to the ultimate settlement. Conscience, not force or formality, was the instrumentality.

While afflicted mental states produced the conflict, the consequences to the city and cosmos from the conflict also became an important aspect of the story. At the end of the case, the minds of the participants had been calmed, restitution was made, and the community and natural order were rebalanced through an exchange of scarves. This ritual of reconciliation and consensus, the "getting together ceremony" (which happened even before the final decision document was signed) was initiated by the "twenty families of the courtyard waiting on the outside roadway to receive them with food." Both sides made statements of regret and reconciliation, and the winner presented a gift of money to the loser. Everyone recognized responsibility for creating the disturbance; everyone went through a process of expiation. By the end of the case, Family Three as well as the monks had come to the realization that their actions would have karmic results. As the senior monk stated, legal disputes "contradict the Buddha's religion."

Then, as if to show the true nature of reality, within two months most of the key participants had left their homes and fled Tibet entirely; nothing remained of the disagreement. When the two refugees met in India, the former monk officer said, "Now what is the result of the big dispute?" This was a direct reference to the illusory nature of reality. They had expended great emotion, time, and energy on material possessions in this world, only to have them eliminated entirely and rendered unimportant a short while later. All the parties to the former dispute became friends and worked together in India.

Also highlighted in this case is Tibetan legal time. It was not considered unusual to halt the proceedings entirely for two months so that the monks could attend an important ceremony. None of the judges or conciliators asked when a particular action occurred. The fact that Family Three's initial request to the monks and even their petition to the Municipal Office were ignored for months did not become a key issue in the decision.

The power bases of various social groups are amply displayed in this protracted fight: the vast strength of the monasteries surrounding Lhasa, the political clout of the nobles and wealthy families, the brutish actions of the monk thugs and the awkward police. Initially functioning as instruments for a powerful party, the court and conciliator were rendered powerless without agreement from what proved to be an equally powerful opponent. Along the way it became plain that bribery had its pitfalls, the meaning of "truth" and "honesty" was contested, motivations were continually imputed, officials were fortuitously rotated out of office, and proof and cause were tied up in the factoring of the argument. In the process, different types of legal knowledge were refracted through an old man who had experienced many cases and used legal proverbs and phrases correctly, a monk who knew monastic debate, a monk officer fresh from training who was not presumed to be biased in favor of the monastery, and a noble family that presumed personalized legal authority. At each stage in the argument the questions at issue were factored, and new but related issues were brought into the factoring.

Formal court procedure alternated with several different judge-at-home procedures and the efforts of conciliators before a final solution was obtained, demonstrating the remarkably fluid movement of cases between different forms of Tibetan legal ritual. Two different decisions were made by the Municipal Office, but the monks refused to accept them because they were "not the truth." Indeed, the fact that they "did not have to agree" made them feel "brave." After that, several other forums were used: conciliation proceedings that resulted in a third unacceptable decision; petitions to a higher court, the Cabinet; the police, who proffered documents allowing them to be the official representative; withdrawal of the case from the Municipal Office to a second conciliation; visits to a city court judge and Cabinet judges at home; a possible visit to the Cabinet by the conciliator to receive its official seal; and finally, after the decision, visits to the homes of several officials to discuss the results.

Throughout, the actors were making strategic decisions at each point: whether to use oral or written petitions, whether or not to answer questions directly in court, or to allow a judge to violate ritual procedure by demanding signature before the reading of a petition, or to employ the physical power of the *thutob,* or to allow a final decision document with a payment so low (fifty silver *sung*) that the winner is worried it will cause more fighting. Ultimately, a conciliation, not a court, was the actual locus for the effectual completion of the case. And the conciliator "acted as a neighbor" by paying the increased punishment charges himself—a gesture of great Buddhist merit.

Finally, this richly detailed Case of the Smelly Toilet amply demonstrates that formal legal proceedings were very much in operation in Tibet right up to the military takeover by the Chinese army in 1959.

CHAPTER TWENTY-THREE

The High Court of Tibet

You must cultivate a good mental attitude. Regarding law, if you first cultivate a good mind, then it is all right to punish a very bad criminal because you have determined to help change the criminal or to teach a lesson to the public. A good mind is the root of one's own happiness and the nation's benefit. If a person does a bad action with a bad mind, others may follow it. A judge should [always] control those actions with a good mental attitude.

—Former Tibetan Official

To get to the *sherkhang* or *shertim khang* (*gsher khrims khang*), the High Court of Tibet, a petitioner or witness entered the Cathedral Complex through the main door on the west side (see Figure 5), walked along the inner ring (Nangkor) past the Jokhang, climbed stone and then ladder stairs to the open walkway on the second floor of the administration building, and proceeded eastward along the north side of the walkway to the last entrance on the left. The six-foot-high doorway in the white plastered wall was outlined in traditional Tibetan black paint and covered with a multicolored valance cloth. On either side hung the "law sticks," thick wooden poles decorated with spiral bands of black-brown and white, suspended from metal rings beside the door. Prisoners waiting to be heard, witnesses, and other petitioners sat and stood to the left of the doorway along with some of the sweepers, waiting for the business of the day to begin.

The Sherkhang, operating much like any other office within the government, was open every day except ritual holidays. A contingent of sweepers, five to eight persons, and a caretaker were charged with maintaining the smooth operation of the office and its various activities. With the early morning awakening of those who slept on the premises and the arrival of others from their homes the work of the day began. Bedrolls were rolled up, the door to the court was opened, the offices were swept out, and the morning tea was prepared. The clerks of the High Court, called *sherdrung* (*gsher drung*), arrived ahead of the judges and prepared the day's business. They pulled out case files, prepared chalkboard, paper, and ink, finished work left from the day before, and received letters and documents sent from other departments of the government.

Plate 55. The western entrance to the Cathedral Complex, showing sun awning and decorated pillars. 1920–21. (Pitt Rivers Museum, University of Oxford)

The judges, *sherpang* (*gsher dpang*), arrived at the court between nine and eleven o'clock and stayed without a break until five or six. The daily routine was hardly rigid. If there was no business or if the judges had duties elsewhere during the day, they did not come to the court; a judge would send a private servant to inform the clerks of his whereabouts for the day, and the petitioners at the court were duly informed of his absence.

The Court and Its Functions

The High Court consisted of a series of rooms on three levels along the north wall of the second floor of the administration building (Figure 16). Over three hundred years old, the building—similar to all early Tibetan architecture—had thick wooden-beam and plaster walls with some masonry, flat roofs, primarily small and windowless rooms, larger reception rooms with painted wooden columns and beams, low doorways, a single entranceway to each suite of offices, and ladders for staircases between levels.

Immediately to the left as one entered the court was a small room. Two Tibetans indicated that it had been used to store equipment for the Sherkhang and as the living

Plate 56. The door to the former High Court of Tibet on the second floor of the Cathedral Complex building. 1986.

quarters for the court caretaker; a third Tibetan stated that it was a separate office. In 1986, it was being used as a dormitory room for a monk.

A ladder on the north wall led to the back hallway on the upper level. This room contained several storage boxes; one of these was filled with white woolen robes to be worn by prisoners brought to court. Other boxes contained ropes, carpets, rugs, and various supplies for the office. All persons attending court had to pass through this low, dark back hallway before reaching the large front room.[1]

Here the general darkness of the High Court's premises was relieved by light from a break in the ceiling, which covered only half the front room, and from one window to the open-air walkway outside, which looked across to the walls of the Jokhang Temple.

In general, the rooms of the court were described by those who had visited there in the late 1940s and 1950s as simple, functional, and undecorated, with no religious symbols or objects. During working hours, no heaters or lights were used, which

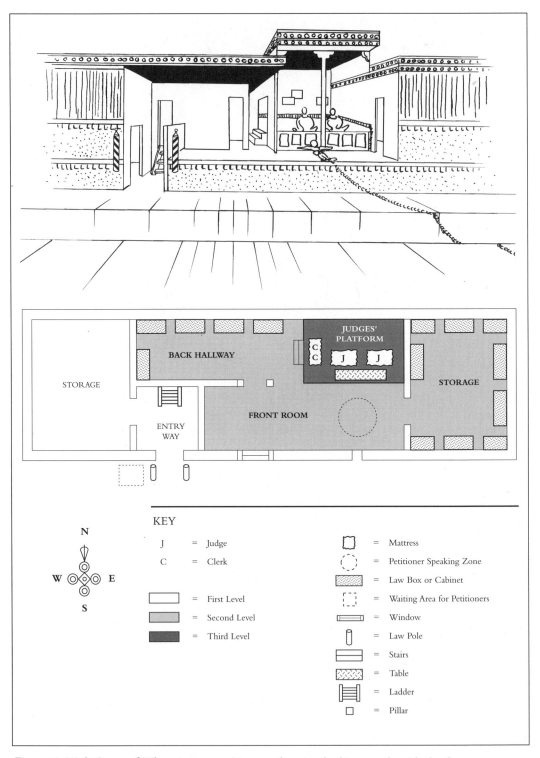

Figure 16. High Court of Tibet circa 1950. Top: an elevation looking north with the front wall of the court cut away. The prisoner before the court is tied to a rope that extends across the inner ring walkway to the "stone cat" or "the lion" on the wall of the Jokhang. Bottom: floor plan of the High Court.

must have made winter mornings particularly harsh for the clerks and judges. One judge said that he liked the main room because the sun could shine in from the south in the winter and warm their mattresses.

A raised platform approximately nine by five feet, extending along the north wall of the main room, was the most important area of the court. A three-foot-high wooden partition and two support pillars separated it from the reception area, and the ceiling above it was much higher than that in any of the other rooms. On the platform at least two judges were generally seated on separate high mattresses, facing out across the wooden screen. Behind them, edicts and lists were posted on the walls within the boundaries of a painted frame of three stripes, black, white, and red. A long, low table pushed up against the screen in front of the judges was filled with the business of the day: law files, ink pots, bamboo pens, knives to sharpen the pens, teacups, and books. On the pillar supporting the southwestern corner of the platform hung the whips used in the court. The two clerks were seated on a long, lower mattress to the judges' right, near the steps to the platform; they faced inward toward the judges, with no table in front of them, as they were expected to write their documents against the palm of the left hand supported by the left knee. Though his authority in decision-making was equal to the lower-ranking judge, the highest-ranking *sherpang* had the position of honor between the lower judge and the clerks. The clerks rose as either judge entered the room and only sat down again after both judges had seated themselves.

Beyond the raised platform a storage room contained large wooden chests filled with law documents, files, and record books. In sacks on the floor were articles of evidence for crimes and the possessions of murderers; these had been seized, bagged, and sealed by the local authorities before being sent to Lhasa. Taxes collected from the oracles and bolts of tweed cloth to be given to the oracles (see below) were also stored in this room, as were ornament lists and books stating what ornaments should be bought for which statues in the Jokhang. On the walls were posted lists and notices; documents and rolled-up files tied together in long strings hung from wooden pillars; an old prayer wheel and a pile of offering scarves sat on one of the boxes. Legend has it that the famous "truth stick" was also kept in this room: it was said that if the stick hit the head of a liar, he would fall mute, but if it struck a truthful man, it would enable him to speak eloquently.

Both historically and among Tibetans today, the Sherkhang was most famous for handling murder cases and for being the last and highest court of appeals in Tibet. In actuality, however, it performed a melange of activities throughout the year. It was responsible for hearing legal cases at the rate of two to three a day (five to six hundred a year, by the estimate of one former judge), including those referred from the Cabinet; the physical punishment of criminals; the storage of documents, valuables, and evidence; keeping accounts for donors of ornaments to grace statues in the Jokhang; tax collection and distribution; attendance on certain oracles; and any other duty assigned by the Cabinet or the Dalai Lama.

One of the most intriguing of the extralegal duties was attendance on the State Oracle of Tibet, who was located in the Nechung Monastery approximately ten miles northwest of Lhasa. Once a month, on an appointed day of offering, members of the High Court went to visit the oracle, taking with them a series of presents—an

Plate 57. The judges' platform in the High Court of Tibet. Note the screen in front, the posted edicts behind them, the whips hanging from the post on the left, and the small area at top right indicating that the front section of the room has no ceiling. c. 1920. (Bell Collection, Mss Eur F 80/284, P71(b), Oriental and India Office Collections, The British Library)

envelope containing gold, white offering scarves, tea, and beer—which were stipulated in a faded list posted on the wall of the court. After riding the ten miles on horseback, they entered the monastery, prostrated to the oracle, and presented the prescribed items.

This ancient practice was based on the connection between law and divination. Like most people in Tibet, criminals wanted advice about the best day to perform an act. A person who proposed to commit a robbery, for example, would seek the guidance of an oracle and, in the process, reveal his plan. The Nechung Oracle, remembering dates, persons, and schemes, would act as a conduit by relating proposed crimes and their perpetrators to the court officials during their appointed visits. The judges who recounted making such visits during the 1940s reported receiving little information about crimes, however, leaving some question as to whether the oracle had lost his role as a conduit.

In addition to these monthly visits, the staff of the High Court collected taxes in the form of silver from the Nechung Oracle and from other oracles in Lhasa, which was then converted into tweed cloth and given back to the oracles on an appointed day. The reason for this complex exchange system was unknown to the judges who had served in the 1940s.

Another duty of the court was keeping the "ornaments lists," in either posted or

Plate 58. The judges' platform of the former High Court of Tibet. Monks are now living in these rooms. The front screen is missing, and the doorway to the storage room on the right is covered by a cloth. 1986.

book form, for each of the sacred images in the Jokhang. When an individual or group came forward to make a religious offering of jewels, or money to buy jewelry, to adorn a statue, the High Court staff looked up the exact requirements for that image and noted the form and amount of the offering, then forwarded the request to make an offering to the Cabinet.

Finally, general investigation requests for records, stored items, or reviews of legal cases were sent to the Sherkhang by the Cabinet on subjects presumed appropriate for its consideration, including the transaction of important noncriminal cases.

The Beginning of a Case of Murder

Murder, *sogcho* (*gsod gcod*), unlike most other criminal acts in Tibet, could not be conciliated or handled on the local level—unless it was committed in an area separately incorporated into the Tibetan nation, such as the Kingdom of Nangchen in the northeast, or a provincial unit that had semiautonomous jurisdiction, such as Chamdo. A murder that occurred anywhere else in the country had to be referred to the central government for final disposition. From the Cabinet the case would be sent to the Sherkhang (or, if it concerned a military officer, to the Office of the Army). The procedures outlined here have been put together from several actual cases of murder, with alternatives noted, in order to illustrate every aspect of the review process.[2]

The story begins in the southwestern part of central Tibet, near the city of Kyidong, close to the Tibet-Nepal border.

When in the mid-1940s in a small village outside Kyidong an incident of theft and subsequent murder occurred, it was the responsibility of the local people to report it immediately to the local government authority, the district office.[3] Liability for a murder in Tibet lies as easily with those who do not report the crime as with the murderer, and therefore notices came immediately from both the victim's family and other people in the form of written petitions. The district officer then sent out a personal representative to investigate. As the alleged murderer in this case was the head of a household, his family members were interrogated in their homes, and several written statements were taken. Evidence of the crime, particularly the murder weapon and other articles, were put into sealed sacks by the investigator and taken back with the suspect, whose hands were tied with a rope, to the district office. In other cases, weapons and valuables as well were either seized by the investigators or placed in one room of the house and sealed off to secure the assets of the murderer for future payments.

At this point, with the murderer identified through two or three separate written petitions and a government investigation, Tibetans referred to the suspect as either "the red-handed man," *lakmarpa* (*lag dmar pa*)—a literal translation of the word for murderer—or as "the prisoner," *tsonpa* (*btson pa*). These terms imply the imposition of guilt in a way the English terms "defendant" and "alleged murderer" do not. In all but one of my collected murder cases, little doubt was expressed by any Tibetan about the identity of the murderer or the guilt of the arrested man.[4]

When the prisoner arrived at the central office of the district, he was either placed in a locked holding room or presented to the district officer and whipped immediately. It should be noted that physical punishment in criminal cases was often spread throughout the legal process and administered at several different points, instead of occurring all at once at the end of the case. A district officer following correct procedure would then send a notice to the Cabinet in Lhasa that he had a murder case on his hands. Next, he conducted his own investigation by taking statements from the investigator who did the initial work (sending out more officials, if necessary, to probe further); talking to the suspect himself; interviewing witnesses to the crime; examining the weapon and other articles of evidence; and entertaining the numerous petitions and requests brought on behalf of the criminal, the victim, and their families.

After this initial stage, he was expected to write out a complete description of the incident, in formal legal document style, giving the results of his investigation, the physical punishment that had been given, payments that should be made, and his conclusion about the case. The district officer would likely follow formal procedure strictly in a case of murder, since the victim's family could pursue its own claims against the murderer, and there were serious sanctions for irregularities by a district court. If the district officer did not follow a thorough investigation and decision process, his actions were viewed by the upper court as preliminary rather than conclusive.

From the district office of Kyidong, the documents were then forwarded for review to the next administrative level, the governor's office in Upper To. From there, documents and additional letters were forwarded to the overgovernor in Shigatse and then to the Cabinet. Within a month or two, a messenger arrived from the Cabinet with a letter authorizing him to collect the criminal and return to Lhasa. Unless the suspect was considered difficult or vicious, he was not tied with a rope during the journey. Letters from the district officer and the governor, the sacks of evidence, and the criminal's possessions were all piled on the backs of animals to accompany the messenger and the prisoner on their trip to Lhasa.

In many instances, the family or relations of the victim also went to the capital city to make their claims for compensation. By visiting officials at home, as well as making formal appearances in court, the victim's family endeavored to influence the decision through all available means. The use of official-at-home and other legal rituals concomitant with the formal procedure could occur in any case where persons other than the criminal wanted to affect the decision of the government. Persons the court would consider hearing in this role included the accused's relatives, his employer or landlord, a monk or lama close to the family, a person of influence known to either family, the owner of the house or land where the incident took place, relatives or friends of the victim, the employer or landlord of the victim, and members of the community or association where the incident took place. A suspect who had no strong family ties, or who had been seized without the knowledge of his community, or who lacked financial resources might pass through the system without any such intervention, either for or against him.

Petitioners trying to affect the court's decision or an official at home, or both, typically explained that they were concerned with one of the following aspects of the case: the actual facts of the incident; the character of the participants; the compensation to be received by the victim's family, employer, landlord, or others; the offering payments for monastery rituals; or the physical punishment of the criminal.

A concerned family arriving in Lhasa would find lodgings and then take one or more of the following tacks. First, they would approach someone knowledgeable about the court system, explain their needs and desires, and request the aid of that person with the understanding that some form of payment might be involved. Or they might go directly to a person of influence in Lhasa with whom they had connections—such as an important family that owned an estate in the area of the crime—and request intervention. Further, they might explain the situation to others indirectly concerned with the decision process—such as the clerks, the sweepers, or the wives of judges—and ask advice or assistance. Many would go directly to the house of the judge, present gifts, relate their story, and seek his intervention. These four avenues could be pursued individually, sequentially, or in any combination within the obvious limitations of time and finances.

The aim of the petitioners was either to affect the court procedure itself or to resolve the case through the ritual of visiting an official at home. Such petitioning served several functions. It allowed a person with little knowledge of the law system or someone from the countryside to be heard sympathetically. It sometimes resulted in the uncovering of facts and evidence which, by reason of a government investigator's incompetence or bad practices, had not been included in the formal record. Finally, it gave an advantage to persons who were very persistent, financially well off, or socially acceptable—thereby reinforcing the existing social system.

At the High Court the clerks were the first to receive the report from the Cabinet clerks that a messenger and a new criminal had arrived from the southwestern province. The referral letter plus all the documentation from the district officer and the governor came in a file to the High Court, with instructions to pick up the sacks of evidence and possessions. The letter stated that the sweepers from the Cabinet had taken the man to the lower-level prison at the Lhasa City Court for holding. While there, he was considered under the jurisdiction of the Sherkhang and was placed, neither fettered nor tied, alone in a locked room.

In the morning, the High Court judges arrived separately, each wearing a long earring in his left ear, a round official hat over hair tied in a knot, and the distinguishing judicial attire—an outer red robe with a lining of blue or gray along the collar and no waist sash. Some judges kept their red robes in court; some wore them to and from their homes every day. Underneath the robe, a judge wore typical official dress—a Tibetan or a Western-style shirt, his own full-length robe, and standard handmade leather boots in white, black, and gray. As they entered the courtroom, the clerks, bent at the waist in greeting, rose and made way for the judges, who climbed the two sets of steps, walked over the clerks' mattress on the platform, and took their seats on the higher mattresses in the center. Everyone else sat down after the judges were seated, and then business commenced.

A list of cases for the day was read to the judges, including the document announcing the arrival of the murder suspect from Kyidong. One of the judges ordered that he be brought to court in the afternoon. An hour or so later a sweeper was dispatched by the clerks to the Lhasa City Court to bring the prisoner. As the court handled two or three cases every day, no case occupied more than three hours of the court's schedule in any one day. By noon, the criminal had been brought up to the door of the High Court, where he waited on the open walkway with a sweeper as his guard. More than an hour later, he was called.

Before seeing the prisoner, the judges read all the reports in the file—from the initial recorded statements of the investigators and the lists of the descriptions of the weapons, evidence, and possessions to the full statement of the district officer and the corroborating letter of the governor. The "red-handed man" from Kyidong was then brought in and placed in front of the judges' platform.

After making sure of his identity, the judges commonly requested an "initial whipping" (see Chapter 24). Redressed in a white prisoner's robe from one of the boxes in the entryway, the prisoner was placed prostrate on the floor with his head facing the judges' platform; if necessary, his feet were tied with a rope that passed out through a small drain hole in the wall near his feet to the outside walkway, where sweepers secured it. Taking down the whips from the pillar at the end of the platform, two other sweepers stood on either side of him to administer the blows, alternately moving their arms back over their heads and then down onto the prisoner's thighs and buttocks.

Legend had it that when visiting the Sherkhang, "one should never look to the stone cat or to the lion." Many Tibetans could repeat this ancient proverb, but only a

Plate 59. The wall of the Jokhang Temple across from the High Court, showing the stone cat in the foreground and another stone loop in the background. 1986.

few recognized its reference to the stone loops that still exist on the walls of the Jokhang, directly across from the High Court.[5] These were said to be used to secure the rope from a criminal's feet, which was passed out the drain hole, across the open walkway and courtyard to the walls of the temple, and through the loops—one shaped like a feline, the other now a worn circle—before being tied securely. To look on those two stone loops was considered very bad luck—the import of the proverb. None of the Tibetans narrating cases of murder heard in the High Court had seen this tying procedure themselves, however; several said it had happened "in old times."

As to the first whipping, one judge explained that the criminal was beaten initially because he had committed a murder, and the beating itself constituted part of the punishment for that offense. There was little if any doubt in the judge's mind that the court was dealing with an individual who had been justly accused. Although they said that they felt great shame in watching a whipping, former judges repeated that it was necessary to impress upon the criminal that he should not repeat these actions in the future. After the whipping the murderer was untied and immediately returned to his jail cell below the Lhasa City Court, where he remained for up to one month before being recalled.

Following the removal of the prisoner, analysis of the case continued in court. The bags of evidence and the criminal's possessions were checked against the lists sent from the district office, then resealed, marked, and put back in storage by the clerks or sweepers. Each of the factors and circumstances of the case as set out in the report was reviewed out loud by the judges: (1) who the participants were; (2) what their jobs in the community were; (3) what exactly happened; (4) who was injured first and how seriously; (5) whether any other person was injured; (6) where the murder had happened and when; (7) how and why it had happened (root and immediate cause); (8) what instruments were used; (9) who had witnessed the crime or any other important event related to it; (10) what investigation had been done by the local, district, and provincial authorities; (11) what other petitions or petitioners were waiting to speak about this case; (12) which relative, landlord, or temple was waiting for compensation; (13) what physical punishment had already been administered and what was suggested; and (14) what court payments had been or should be made. The clerks took notes—simultaneously writing the same thing—as the judges made comments about the documents and noted these points. If a sweeper volunteered the information that the criminal had been sent to this court before, he was ordered to bring out the previous file. A clerk would be sent to bring out a piece of evidence or an old case file on any crime committed by a related family in the same locality.

After concluding the review of documents and evidence, the judges asked the sweeper to bring in the petitioners related to this case, who were all waiting on the walkway outside the courtroom door. Called before the judges one at a time, they presented their statements orally or stood while their written petitions were read. To record an oral petition, the clerks prepared a document giving the substance of the speech and then read it to the petitioner, who, if in agreement, stamped and validated it. In this fashion the court received, one after another, the members of the family of the criminal and the victim, influential persons, representatives, and anyone else with a claim to knowledge or compensation in the case. If any of these statements brought up new issues, the criminal himself would be brought back to court for questioning.

While sifting and reexamining the evidence, the judges were looking for truth in the form of factual consonance. If the criminal persisted in claiming his innocence in spite of all the evidence against him, the court would continue to investigate his case while holding him in jail because "truth could not be reached." This might also involve repeated whippings (called "the questioning whip") each time he returned to court.

In one murder case related by a Tibetan from the province of Dedge in the east, the criminal continued to deny his guilt. His family brought petitions to the High Court repeatedly and tried to petition the Cabinet weekly in Lhasa. As no new evidence was ever produced, he was held for a long time because, in the view of the judges, truth through factual consonance was never achieved between the criminal's story and that of the other witnesses. In the opinion of former judges, a case could not move forward until reinvestigation and reexamination of the different stories of a murder resulted in factual consonance. If they did not, an oath-taking procedure—if accepted by all the parties—was a clear possibility.

Compensation

Even in the most clear-cut murder case in Tibet, many other questions of harmony and disharmony, victim compensation, and funeral payments arose and were the focus of much of the court's deliberation. As early as the seventh century, the administrative records, royal decrees, and legal documents of the Tibetan Empire contained rules about monetary compensation for the act of murder. The law codes of the fifteenth and the sixteenth centuries substantially elaborated these ideas, and the Dalai Lama codes in the mid-seventeenth century established general laws of compensation which remained basically unchanged until the Chinese took over the administration of Tibet in 1959. In the section on murder the ranked scheme of nine levels correlated the victim's social role with a monetary (*tong*) payment of 5 to 200 *sung* (see Figure 7 in Chapter 9).[6]

This prescribed fee owed for a male Tibetan's life was not the whole story, however. Unlike the wergild system of Teutonic times, in which the money paid to the victim's relatives rendered the offender relatively free from other payments, punishments, and acts of revenge, the Tibetans' practice reflected a much more complex view of how society should regain its balance following a murder. They saw multiple possible victims of a socially violent act: the spouse of the deceased, the children, the employer or lord, the local temple or monastery, and the community. To correct the disadvantaged positions of these five persons or groups, the law codes listed additional payments that could be calculated from the *tong* amount: "heart-press" payments for the tears and loss to the spouse; food for the children; replacement of the bloody clothing and mattress of the corpse; "merit payments" in cash, grain, and butter to the family for funerary rites, also called "income for the corpse"; payments to the local temple for religious rituals; "getting together" costs for a ceremony in which the opposing sides indicated that they had forgiven and forgotten, thereby bringing the community back to a peaceful state; and court costs for the trial proceedings. The murderer and the victim's family, whose members were considered parties to the trial proceedings, were consulted with respect to these assessments, and required to sign the court decision indicating their mutual consent to the amount of the *tong* and the various other payments.

Who could make a claim for a *tong* payment or related compensation, and who paid? The murder cases collected demonstrate that although the victim's immediate family was the usual recipient of the *tong* money, other relatives, employers, landlords, and even members of the victim's community could also petition for a share.

In the general instance, the murderer himself paid the entire sum owed. It was his initial and primary responsibility, and the government was entitled to seize his household goods and other valuables for this purpose. If the murderer was destitute, his extended family or his employer or landlord might be pressured for payment. This practice extended the net of social responsibility well beyond the single individual—as did the Tibetan solution to the situation in which the murderer was not apprehended or discovered. In Lhasa the owner of the property on which an unsolved murder had occurred was held responsible for the payment of the *tong* in full.[7] Tibetans have commented to me that this made them very wary of bad actions by their relatives or of having dangerous or drunk people around their houses who might create trouble resulting in legal responsibility. Even though they could easily claim compensation for an act of intersocietal violence, they were also responsible for such acts on the part of others, and several Tibetans declared that they thought this extended responsibility kept violent acts in their society to a minimum.

Clearly, Tibetans viewed the range of harm resulting from an act of murder, which violated the first prohibition of the Buddha, to be very wide. It caused problems with the gods, within the community, and for the family or employer or landlord of the victim, all of whom could claim compensation in the form of *tong* or related payments.

Furthermore, according to the Tibetan view, in addition to paying these funerary, restitution, and other costs, the murderer still deserved both physical punishment and rehabilitation. The payments compensated the community and the victim's family, but it was necessary to ensure that the criminal would not repeat the act. Tibetan judges cited as a primary consideration in their decision-making the need to impress upon the defendant the folly of repetition. In the absence of mitigating factors, most murderers were whipped again in court at the conclusion of the case ("the leaving whip") and often given some other temporary form of Tibetan punishment as well, such as wearing leg irons, serving more jail time, or performing labor on someone else's land for a specified period.

In short, according to official thinking, feuds and violence were minimized if a wide number of people were potentially responsible for the crime, the victims were satisfactorily compensated, and the perpetrator himself was punished physically and, if possible, rehabilitated.

The Conclusion of the Case

Once the *tong* level was decided, other compensations fixed, the source of the money secured, the physical punishments determined, the criminal questioned, all parties heard, and the judges satisfied that factual consonance had been reached, the final decision document was drafted by the clerks of the High Court. The decision document in a murder case took a standard form that encompassed, first, a formal introduction with the address of the person to whom the document was being sent, religious prostration words, and a statement of the authority of the Dalai Lama and the national laws. Second, a central section gave the facts of the case in the order in which they were brought to the court's attention and the court's decision on each point. The third or decision section stated that after thorough investigation the court had found the accused to be or not to be guilty, or that there was some guilt on both sides. This section also listed the required compensations as figured from the *tong* level, other punishments, and court costs. Fourth, a closure section cautioned that these actions must not be repeated in the future, and concluded with the name of the issuing authority, date, and seal of the office. Finally, in a signature section, or *chuyik,* at the bottom or on the back of the document, the criminal, his guarantors, other parties, and their guarantors signed the decision to indicate their agreement.

Several copies of the approved document were made, and all the concerned parties (if they were still in Lhasa) were called to the court to hear the decision read. Payments were then requested and dispersed, and the finished copies of the decision were dated, stamped with the seal of the High Court, and distributed to the parties. If the case was important enough to be issued from the Dalai Lama's Office or the Cabinet (see Figure 15, Chapter 20), the documents were sent to that office for application of its seal. The copy to remain in the Sherkhang was put in a large cloth file with the other pertinent documents. Envelope makers were called in if copies also had to go to the original district officer or governor.

Finally, a sweeper or government messenger was called to receive a copy of the decision and an administrative letter relaying instructions about the prisoner. In the case of "the red-handed man" from Kyidong, this referral letter and the prisoner were sent to a district officer in an area quite distant from his own. To promote his rehabilitation, the man was made the owner of a newly cultivated piece of land with tax responsibility for three years.

Excursus: The Ecclesiastical Office

Looking south through the large front windows of the immense fortresslike Potala, the Ecclesiastical Office, *tse yiktsang* (*rtse yig tshang*), occupied two rooms with high ceilings in the Dalai Lama's administrative palace (though during the summer it moved, with the Dalai Lama, to quarters in the Summer Palace). As the highest office for religious affairs other than the Private Office of His Holiness, the *yiktsang* was equal in status to the highest secular office, the Cabinet. Four Great Monk Secretaries presided over the myriad ecclesiastical concerns of the country; thousands of monks, hundreds of monasteries, and religious festivals, revenue, and legal disputes from every part of Tibet were under the jurisdiction of this office.

A door from the hallway led into the large, rectangular main room at its northeast corner. Against the walls on all but the windowed side were wooden storage cabinets, *yigam* (*yig sgam*), for letters and documents, stacked floor to ceiling. Each double-doored, locked unit was approximately three by four feet. One bank of these cabinets did not reach quite to the ceiling; on top was a small altar with statues and a photo of the Dalai Lama. The room had no other adornments. Two sets of windows, stretching along the southern wall and looking out over the valley to the meandering Kicchu River and mountains beyond, gave the room its light and some heat from the sun.

Sitting on a mattress against the wall between the two southern windows was the office caretaker, the *yiktsang nyerpa* (*yig tshang gnyer pa*), working at his small table. He had an official rank but wore no special robes, and he commonly stayed at his post through many years of changes in staff. The caretaker handled the daily maintenance and operations of the office: opening its doors in the morning, storing and using the various keys, keeping some accounts and office records, and receiving any petitions or documents. As a consequence, he was the gatekeeper and monitor of all official business, and few visitors underestimated his significance.

In front of the storage cabinets along the west wall sat the four Great Monk Secretaries, *dunyik chemo* (*drung yig chen mo*), on four higher mattresses (Figure 17). They wore no official hats or earrings for their daily work and resembled other monk officials in dress. The senior secretary sat farthest from the windows, and the most junior sat closest; each had a table between his mattress and the next to hold reference documents. They did all their writing against their knees, facing north so that light from the windows came over their right shoulders. Appointed to the office by the Dalai Lama and serving at his will, these men had rotated in and out of several official positions before becoming Great Monk Secretaries and had reached at least the third level of official rank. They were quite rightly considered important men and capable of rendering real service to His Holiness.

In front of the storage cabinets along the north wall of the room was a long continuous mat on which sat the rest of the office staff: usually fifteen clerks in a row, elbow to elbow, facing into the room. Eleven were taken from the ranks of lower-level monk officials; four were trainees. There were no secular officials in this office. The eleven monk officers, *laykatse dunyik* (*las ka rtse drung yig*), had varied duties: some drafted letters; others copied office documents; some retrieved or refiled documents, took notes, and ran errands for the secretaries; others managed the storeroom next door or organized office business. The row of clerks proceeded from most senior, nearest the senior secretary, to most junior.

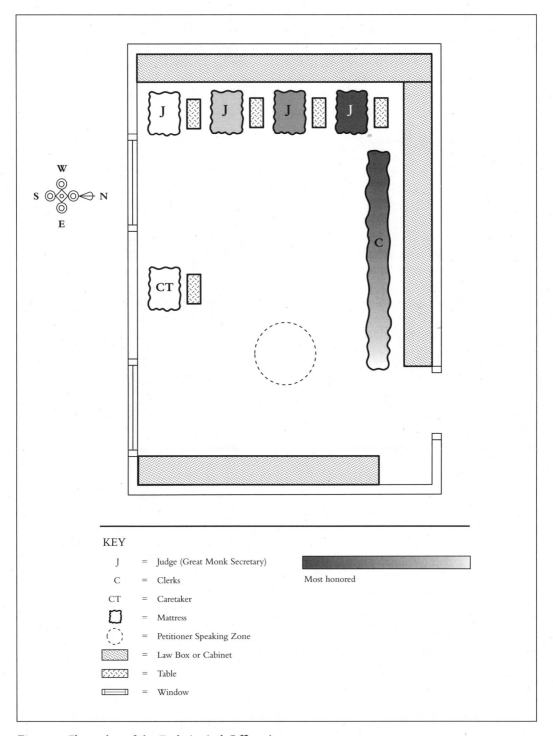

Figure 17. Floor plan of the Ecclesiastical Office circa 1950.

Closest to the door on the mat were the four monk trainees, who ranged in age from fourteen to twenty. To have the privilege of training in one of the highest offices in the land, these students had had to undergo a special *yiktsang* entrance examination that covered Tibetan handwriting, language, and mathematics. Once chosen, they served for approximately four years, receiving instruction from various members of the staff and each monitored by a senior monk official or a Great Monk Secretary. This office was considered an excellent place to practice letter writing and other basic clerical skills, and one of the most prestigious avenues to future advancement. After completing his training, the monk trainee had to pass an examination for entrance into government service. At that point, he was given the lowest-level monk officer rank and had to wait (for what could be a rather long period) for a government appointment.

To reach the office to present a petition, a layperson or monk had to go first to the Zhol section of Lhasa, a mile from the center of the city, and then climb several hundred high stone steps zig-zagging back and forth across the front of the hill on which the enormous palace stood. And once inside the Potala, one could easily get lost in the labyrinth of hallways, ladder stairs to different floors, elegant chapels, and endlessly connecting rooms.

Upon reaching the Ecclesiastical Office, the petitioner stood near the door and waited. The petition or application for an important case brought to this office, as well as the person presenting the petition, was not called a *shuwa*, as in a typical legal case, but a *nyenshu* (*snyan zhu*). Upon seeing a visitor, the office caretaker got up from his mat and went to the door. The petitioner then presented the document with the words, "Please give this to the Head of the Office," and went on to explain the gist of the petition.

The caretaker, bowing deeply, presented the document to the senior Great Monk Secretary, who, unless more important work was pressing, read it through and then passed it to the next secretary, and so on, until all four had seen it. The caretaker bowed again from the waist and either returned to his seat or went to tell the petitioner when to expect a response.

Both civil and criminal law cases, *kachu*, arrived at the *yiktsang,* including problems concerning individual monks and disputes between monks or between a monk and another person; disputes inside a monastery or between a monastery and another party; problems occurring or concerning tenants on a monastic estate or between a monastic and a private estate tenant; and disputes concerning the staff of the *yiktsang* itself. (A staff member, a relative of a staff member, or a former staff member could bring a law case; as might be expected, the system of allowing present and former staff members and their relatives to use the office as a forum for dispute settlement greatly increased access to it for lay and nongovernmental persons.)

The range of subject matters, according to most Tibetans, was very broad. As a former clerk said, "Actually we decided all types of quarrels: land disputes, family quarrels, monastery disputes, distribution of monk funds." Nor was the size of the lawsuit a bar, although a small dispute would be decided by only one or two of the Great Monk Secretaries, whereas a large dispute had to be decided by all four secretaries *en banc*.

Once the document had been read, the applicant was either called in at that time or summoned at a later date. For the interview, the petitioner was brought into the center of the large main room and told to remain standing, facing the full row of Great Monk Secretaries. One of these, acting as a judge, began by asking the petitioner to relate his or her story in full.

If land ownership papers, *dantsik*, or agreement documents, *gangya*, were important to the case, or if other persons had been witnesses or could give testimony, *pang po* (*dpang po*), these documents or names were presented during the initial speech. Petitioners were also expected to produce, if so requested, the relevant physical evidence or "articles of verification," *rato ngopo* (*ra sprod dngos po*), such as the actual knife used in a stabbing incident or a sample of articles that had been stolen.

Next came questioning by the judges, following the petition point by point as in secular courts. Each secretary asked many questions, and the answers were noted down by one of the clerks. Although the other clerks and students were expected to be attending to their own work, they could all hear the entire proceeding. This was, in a sense, another part of their general training: observing and learning the techniques and rhetoric used for law case settlement. The stance, attitude, sincerity, method of speech, and deftness of rhetoric of the speaker were noted silently by all the staff and commented on in private; these attributes were sure to affect the judges' opinion of the testimony. At the end of the questioning the applicant was excused, and a time was set to interview the person against whom the complaint had been brought.

The applicant's opponent, the *katé* (*kha gtad*), called to give his or her own report of the situation and present any relevant documents, was greeted at the doorway by the caretaker. After the response petition had been reviewed by one of the Great Monk Secretaries, the opponent came before the judges to give a statement. (As in most Tibetan courts, if the petitioner, the opponent, or a witness came to the *yiktsang* without a written petition, a clerk would record the statement and read it back; once the speaker was satisfied with it, this document was signed and thereafter treated as a formal written petition to the court.)

If more than one opponent was named in the original petition, all those named could be summoned at the same time; in some instances, they even stood together for questioning, though more commonly, each speaker was called individually. The opponents were required to answer each point in the original petition as well as explain their own position to the satisfaction of the judges. A *timsopa,* a person who advised others on how to pursue a case, was not allowed in the *yiktsang* except to represent a person who could not appear.

After the petitioner, the opponent, and perhaps some witnesses had each spoken once in court, the petitioner was recalled (this process and the documents resulting from it were called the answering petition, *shulen* [*zhu lan*]). A case lasted as long as was necessary to ask and answer all the points in the petitions. If it was a difficult one, both sides were called back several times and their responses and disagreements constantly compared until the two agreed to approximately the same story. As in the secular courts, the judges sought factual consonance.

If a large disparity between versions persisted after an extensive period of time, the judges might either employ a legal device such as a test or oath (see Chapter 11) or take the unusual step of calling both sides into court together and questioning each in the other's presence.

When the four Great Monk Secretaries decided that no further consonance of the facts would be achieved and it was time to resolve the case, they took out all the documents that had been presented, the notes taken by the clerk from the various speakers' statements, and the physical evidence, and they made comparisons. Before a decision could be issued, all the secretaries had to agree.

Once an agreement had been reached, a paper was drafted by the clerk, using the formal style of a decision document. Its introductory section began, "In the land of the snows" and went on to describe the government of the Dalai Lama and the benevolent deities of the state. The middle section detailed the entire legal procedure: original petition, opponent's response, and all the documents, statements, and pieces of evidence in chronological order with their points enumerated. In the final section the secretaries stated that they had made a thorough investigation of all the evidence, gave their decision as to the guilt of the sides and the required resolution, and usually concluded with the phrase "and in the future you should not repeat these things."

Former clerks from the Ecclesiastical Court stated that there were two reasons for being very careful in issuing a decision: first, so that the Dalai Lama would approve of it as honest and truthful, and second, so that the two sides to the decision would agree with it. A small percentage of important decision documents requiring review went directly to the Office of the Dalai Lama, which received requests for review from so many government offices and individuals that this part of the process could be lengthy. All decisions by the office of the Dalai Lama were binding on the lower office; that is, an approved document remained as drafted, but any suggested changes were automatically made.

Once the decision was complete and approved, three identical copies were prepared by the office clerks and the two parties summoned to receive and review a copy. If either party was dubious about the decision or wanted to ponder its contents, a future time was set for them to reappear and give their opinions. If they both agreed to it there in the office, the secretaries proceeded to the final step. Both parties were asked to sign the *chuyik,* which in the style of this office was placed at the very bottom of the front of the document. It included the sanction determined by the office, such as "within such and such a month of the Tibetan year, the *nyenshu* pays to the *katé* [this amount] of money." Both parties had to agree specifically to this and stamp the document with their seals in front of the Great Monk Secretaries and each other. With the final stamp of the office, the legal procedure of the *yiktsang* was concluded.

After the parties left the main room with their decision documents in hand, the clerk responsible for the case rose to file away the third or office copy of the decision. Finding the appropriate cabinet by the letter of the Tibetan alphabet on the door, the clerk opened the lock with a key from the caretaker. Glued to the inside of the cabinet door was a more detailed index of the individual files or papers stored there. He placed the copy of the decision in the cabinet, added its name to the index, locked the cabinet, returned the key, and went back to his regular work. The case was complete.

PART FIVE

Crimes and Officials

Introduction

To draw an analogy, one might be outside somewhere and, as long as one is not
paying special attention but is simply sitting there with a wandering mind, day-
dreaming about this and that, one would not necessarily notice if many cars or
people pass back and forth. One would not especially notice, or even know, whether
or not a lot of traffic passed by because one would not be concerned. But if, . . . another day on the same spot, one really paid attention to the number of people and
cars passing by, one would notice a great deal of traffic. One might conclude,
"There is a lot more traffic today than before," whereas, in fact, there is not. At this
time, instead of being oblivious, one is being aware.
> —Geshe Ngawang Dhargyey, *A Commentary on the Kalacakra Tantra*

One of the basic tasks of a study of legal cosmology is to collect and present material
from as many angles and in as many different forms and voices as possible. Multiple
refractions from multiple vantage points, each added to the next, begin to create an
awareness of the space that law occupies in another society. In the process, our
assumptions about law in that society are gradually displayed, questioned, and ultimately displaced by new material. Much as in a kaleidoscope, a series of changing
phases, events, and pictures continuously resolves into patterns and pictures and
then moves again. Each new refraction gives us new information; each momentarily
frozen kaleidoscopic image tells us a little bit more, moves us one step away from
being oblivious, one step closer to being aware.

Parts Three and Four, focused first on the country side and then on the capital,
contextualizing legal concepts, rituals, language, and symbols in the actual practice
of law. Part Five takes a more holistic approach. Chapter 24's presentation of
Tibetan criminal jurisprudence, through verbatim quotation from laypersons, officials, and the law codes, emphasizes the connections and interrelations between the
core concepts that motivated petitioners, influenced judges' decisions, and determined popular responses. What may seem from the Western perspective to be a
regime of severe physical punishments is placed within the jurisprudential and practical confines of the Tibetan viewpoint. Chapter 25 is the narrative autobiography of

a high-ranking official. The anecdotes he relates, the joys and fears he experiences, the jobs he is assigned, his devotion to the Dalai Lama—each aspect of his story provides a new refraction of the Tibetan cosmology of law. In many ways, this story of a Tibetan official in the first half of the twentieth century, though anecdotal and idiosyncratic, may be the most relevatory chapter in the book.

CHAPTER TWENTY-FOUR

Crime and Punishment in Tibet

Just as the branches of the thorn tree are burned in the fire,
so the troublemaker should be arrested and tied up.
Just as clouds bring rain to all the land to produce good crops,
so indeed will good law and order bring well-being to the people.
—Ganden Podrang Code of the Dalai Lamas

Many Tibetans will state that criminal offenses were infrequent in Buddhist Tibet, a fact they attribute to various causes from religious devotion to strict punishment for offenses. There are no figures on the actual number of crimes or criminal arrests, and there were too few government bureaucrats with even minimal arrest and detention capabilities spread throughout the Plateau to have had much effect on extensive crime. One area of exception was banditry and robbery on the trade routes, which most Tibetans believed to be significant. Robbers were the subject of many myths and tales of adventure told by Tibetans with a mixture of humor, curiosity, and awe.[1] One example:

There was a famous old man who used to steal, not because he was poor but as a hobby, and he did it all through his life. One night, when he went out with a group of boys, they saw an encampment of merchants with huge bricks of pressed tea piled into an area so large that the travelers had all made their beds on it. The old man said, "I will go and make a disturbance to awake them and when I do, all of you should steal the tea." So he left, and with a rope he made two tight loops over the feet of one merchant and started to drag him away. The man awoke and began shouting, which caused all the others to come stumbling to his aid. Then the boys went in and stole the tea bricks, and they all got away.

Because government punishments such as whipping were viewed as harsh by many Tibetans, the great majority sought the leniency and flexibility of internal settlement forums for the resolution of all of their disputes, even those involving crimes. A plethora of possible legal sanctions—such as ostracism, damage clauses, refusal of aid, fines, and shaming—were available in internal as well as governmental forums, and local, nongovernment decision-makers were thought more likely to find solutions that would work within the community, rectify the individual's behavior, and not create disharmony. As one former legal representative stated: "All Tibetans try very hard to avoid disputes, even over crimes, and do anything they can to stay out of court. Before they go into formal government courts, they will talk with their relatives, neighbors, and friends nearest to them. If a lama can come to conciliate, he will advise them to stop fighting." This approach placed a great emphasis on the significance of good opinion and position within the community, and consensus and agreement between parties to disputes.

Still, although internal settlement rituals occurred far more frequently and were arguably more significant then court trials, certain serious crimes—referred to by some Tibetans as "black crimes" and by others as "stealing-a-horse, killing-a-man offenses"[2]—were not generally permitted to be handled on the local level but had to be reported to the central government through the district officer.[3] These were commonly listed as poisoning, murder, treason, arson, theft (including burglary and robbery of significantly valuable articles), rioting, severe injury to another, and significant sorcery or black magic.

Tibet was quite typical of various Asian governments at the turn of the century in the types and severity of traditional physical punishment to which it could sentence the perpetrators of serious crimes. The law code of the Ch'ing dynasty of China, in operation until 1911, listed five degrees of punishment (basically unchanged in format since the T'ang Code of the seventh century): striking with lesser bamboo four to twenty times; striking with larger bamboo twenty to forty times; banishment from one to three years after sixty to one hundred blows; perpetual banishment with forced labor after one hundred blows; and death by strangulation, decapitation, or slicing of the body.[4] Early Vietnamese law, such as the Lê code, also outlined severe physical punishments.[5] Nomadic and central Asian law codes stressed payment in fines and, in certain instances, *le droit du taillon*—"blood revenge"—for both murder and mutilations.[6] Traditional Mongolian law, much of which dates from the great Jasagh (Yasa) law code of Chinggis (Genghis) Khan in 1206, had punishment by fines for both murder and theft, as well as death, flogging, and exile (but not mutilation).[7] All these resemble certain of the provisions in the Tibetan law codes in force in the early twentieth century.

Tibetan criminal jurisprudence, which first appeared in administrative documents in the eighth century, evolved over the next twelve centuries into a core of five concepts to be considered: (1) the uniqueness of each case; (2) "what is suitable for punishment"; (3) considerations of karma; (4) the correct purposes of punishment; and (5) the correct types of punishment. These five concepts, which are scattered throughout the law codes, were often mentioned by both former officials and laypersons who had had some experience with criminal proceedings.[8]

The Uniqueness of Each Case

Tibetan courts saw most criminal cases as unique, *shen dang mida wa* (*gzhan dang mi 'dra ba*), and relied on the factoring of the pertinent criteria of that case for its disposition. A former legal representative explained:

The most important thing is always the correct factors for investigating, and the judge is expected to know them. A thief will have an opponent who has submitted a petition with evidence, and it is with reference to this petition and its evidence that questions are then asked by the judge. The judge is limited to the points brought up in the petition; if the petitioner has evidence, the judge will ask the thief the specific points. If he accepts the points and begs the pardon of the court and petitioner, the case is over, and the decision will be written. If the thief does not accept or agree, the judge will say, "You had better think this all over carefully. I have proof before me of the fact that you did this." He will then be asked again, and if he still does not agree, he may be whipped for lying.

In the mind of the judge, the thief is more of a criminal or more guilty if he is lying than for the fact of the theft. If the thief and the other side bring up other factors in court, the judge is then not limited only to the original petition but to all of the points brought up. The judge will look to the evidence of these factors as well.

Usually the judge says to the thief as to evidence that the thief has presented about another person who did the crime, "If he stole articles from your mother before," which is a factor in the case, "then why didn't you then inform the court of the theft?"

As to the question of stealing, whether or not it is allowed, the judge will say, "Is anyone ever allowed to steal?" The thief replies, "It is not allowed." Then the judge says, "If it is not allowed, then what is your reason for stealing?" In this way, they question back and forth about the factors of the case.

Although each type of offense was considered to be the product of its own detailed factors, some general factors were pertinent in most criminal cases:

- the seriousness of the crime;
- any injury occurring during the crime—to one or both parties—and its severity;
- the circumstances of the crime, such as location, time of year, the presence of a mob;
- the position—social category, occupation, gender, age, rank, record of previous crimes, and wealth—of both the victim and the accused;
- the level, quality, and type of evidence;
- any mitigating factors—such as a self-defense or a good character reference from an influential friend ("looking to the face of a high person")—which might allow for relaxation of punishment;
- the mental state of the accused, including motivation and intent;
- competency (dependent on age and mental ability);
- root cause and immediate cause; and
- the general placement of fault.

Suitable Punishment

A former Tibetan administrative assistant compared my explanation of American ideas with Tibetan views of "what is suitable for punishment," *jidar opa donggo shing* (*ji ltar 'os pa gtong dgos shing*): "In Tibet, it is not like it is for you; your action fits a particular section of the law code, and then you are assigned a particular punishment level. Any type of punishment could be awarded for any type of crime in Tibet, depending on the factors involved, such as the size of the crime." Tibetan law, he continued,

did not have a fixed punishment connected to an offense. The law codes list all the bad crimes and then all the bad punishments, but it is up to the judge to decide the level and seriousness of the crime and of the punishment. No specific punishment of a specific offense.

For example, I know a case in which one person poisoned another. The poisoner was guilty, but he claimed that he was sent by another to do it. The judge then made a very clear investigation of this. If this is discovered to be true, the real culprit is punished. For a case of poisoning, the judge must look at who and where the offense was done, where the poison was made, and who was involved in the manufacture. Then the person who started it should be punished.

The reason for not specifying crime with punishment is that each infraction must be investigated individually in Tibet. This is a method, a process, and not a specific rule. The law codes, for example, are describing a process or method for people and judges only. This is different from the Buddhist Vinaya, where the rules and infractions and punishments are all spelled out; when you look for an infraction in the Vinaya, you find the rules very specific and detailed in their relation to the vows of the Bodhisattvas. In this way, the law codes are not like the Vinaya.

Unlike most other law codes such as the fifteenth-century Lê code of Vietnam—which specifies, for example, that "whoever trespasses through the residential palace gates shall be punished by decapitation"[9]—Tibetan law codes contain only a few passages that directly correlate specific infractions with specific punishments. In American legal terminology, the Tibetans lacked a detailed statutory guideline for criminal sentencing. Instead, their law codes listed the factors appropriate for consideration—the circumstances, actors, and level of each crime; punishment was then expected to be adjusted to these factors at the discretion of the decision-maker. This does not mean that there was no community consensus among local populations and trained officials as to what sorts of punishments were just and appropriate, given specific factors. Tibetans would often state that a particular punishment was too harsh or too lenient in the presence of certain factors. Nevertheless, since each case was unique, the range of possible punishments was wide.

This aspect of Tibetan criminal law is very distinctive; it lacks the linear connection between particular infractions and punishments, commonly graded as to severity and importance, which characterizes many other criminal legal systems. Even in systems that do codify such correlations, however, latitude in sentencing (according to mitigating and aggravating factors or special consideration for special people) and wide ranges of possible terms of imprisonment often result in de facto discretionary sentences. The results of the Tibetan system, therefore, were arguably not all that different from those of systems in which the punishment is "mandatorily" fixed. But because the Tibetan system posits the uniqueness of individual cases as an initial principle, whereas other systems do not, the expression of this latitude takes the place of an enumeration of crimes and punishments in the Tibetan law codes: "Punish according to the circumstances of the crime,"[10] and "[The criminal] should be punished according to whatever is suitable."[11]

Karma and Future Life

It was relevant to bring up issues of karma, *lay,* an important part of the Tibetan legal cosmology, during a criminal trial. Tibetans often commented that the judge and accuser used phrases such as "You are not now thinking of the effects of karmic action—consider this!"

Karma entered the legal process in at least four ways. First, it was part of the argumentation in court. Second, punishment administered by officials was expected to be oriented toward improving the criminal's future life; thus, a punishment that allowed the person to remain in this world but encouraged the practice of dharma for the rest of her or his life was definitely preferable to a death sentence because it would result in a higher, rather than a lower, karmic rebirth. Third, karmic consequences were used as a rationalization in cases in which one or more of the parties could not be punished. Fourth, a judge's motivation in sentencing had to be correct if he was to avoid taking on the negative karmic aspects of his action. Observations from former judges illustrate their mental attitude while administering a punishment:

> Whatever punishment is given, it is due to the karma of the criminal, and I think of this and hope that he will become a better person.

> I felt great shame when I watched a whipping in court, and often I tried not to watch. Still, I knew that it must be done because the man had done a murder, and this is a most heinous crime.

The Correct Purposes of Punishment

To a Tibetan, the general purpose of punishment was to restore the community, the victim, and the gods to a position of balance; it was a holistic view that took into account the degree and type of harm that had been generated by the incident, as determined in the factoring process. The economic payments demanded from defendants and distributed to the victims and their employers, relatives, and local temples were part of the attempt to rectify the possible social harm caused by the crime and to ensure a retention of balance in the future.

The specific purposes of punishment were to impress upon criminals the grievousness of their acts, to ensure that they would remain mindful not to repeat their ill deeds, and to impress upon the public at large the evil of criminal behavior. According to the law codes, the first of these purposes, impressing the defendant, could be best accomplished through arrest, confinement, physical punishment, and enforced labor "for the sake of recollecting in the future whatever bad actions have been done."[12] For the second, "to promote mindfulness to inhibit future [bad actions], one must pay a fine in court called *chepa* [*chad pa*] for this kind of punishment."[13]

To achieve the third purpose, impressing the population, "it is necessary to stop the increase of bad actions through whatever showy means, such as beating the drum of law and blowing the big horn, to call all the people for reading the legal decision and giving a speech."[14] In addition, whips, stocks, and other equipment were hung in plain view from the doors of courts; convicted criminals might be freed but sentenced to wear fetters or wooden collars for all to see; notices were published of a criminal's activities; and some whippings and other punishments were done publicly.

The Correct Types of Punishment

The majority of criminal sentences in Tibet prior to 1959 involved economic, physical, and labor punishments, with the emphasis of both the law codes and the cases on the imposition of economic sanctions.

One of the most distinguishing features of Tibetan criminal cases was the system of payments called *tong*, the nine-part ranking of monetary sums that equated the level of compensation with the social and economic status of the victim of a crime.[15] Once the amount of the *tong* was determined, it became the central figure from which other payments could be calculated. The Case of the Murdered Monks, told by the *timsopa* who handled the case in court in Lhasa, demonstrates both the layperson's knowledge of the *tong* system and its actual operation.

> Every year in the same month, almost a thousand monks traveled west from their home monastery in Khams to Ngor Monastery in central Tibet to receive teachings from the Sakyas. When they came this long distance, they begged food and clothing along the way from the people in the districts. One year I heard that a man and his friends became very angry at the monks and killed two of them. This was a very terrible happening.
>
> Now the person who had killed the monks was a member of the Tibetan army, and so the local community sent a petition to the Cabinet, and the case was sent by the Cabinet to the Office of the Army. So the man was brought to that office in Lhasa, and he was whipped with the "initial whip" by the guards of that office.
>
> Then two women who had known the murdered monks well and were from their home village came to me and asked that I go into court for them. I said that I had nothing to appeal to the court for. They asked me to appeal to the court for the *tong* payment. For one ordinary monk, the compensation is nine *dotsé* (*rdo tshad*), so for two monks it was eighteen *dotsé*.[16] If the monks have robbed or fought, then the amount of the *tong* payment is reduced. So, in response to the request of these women, I said that I would petition the court office for them.
>
> So I went to the office and found that there were two army chiefs acting as judges in this case. One was of Cabinet minister rank, and the other was of the next lower rank. Instead of carrying a written petition with me, I just went to the office and made the request orally. After I presented the entire oral petition, the judges told me they would consider the claim of the women and said that I should return when the case was decided.

Later, I was called to the court. The secretary brought the final decision document outside and read it in front of the waiting room to the court. I was then given a notice to come back the day after tomorrow.

On that day, the secretary of the court again read the decision and explained the court costs section and the victim compensation of the *tong* and all the many other payments required. Then the secretary asked all sides of the dispute to sign the decision document, including the murderer (the army man) and me. So, at the bottom of the document, the murderer and I both signed and sealed the document. Then the secretary turned to the murderer and asked him for the *tong* payment.

He offered it, and the secretary took the money from the murderer and handed it to me. Then from this payment of eighteen *dotsé* the secretary subtracted the court costs and the ink fees for the secretaries and handed the rest to me. There were three copies made of the document, and I received one. After that I left, so I did not find out what other punishments were given to the murderer.

Then I went to see the two women who had asked me to represent them. I gave them all the remaining money, and later they used it all for the funeral rites and for other religious rituals for the future lives of the monks. I took an account from these women of what they had spent and the offerings they made and sent the receipts for this to their home district. Usually, the *tong* payment goes to the relatives, but this time the only people who knew the monks and claimed it were these two women, so it went to them. That was the end of the case.

In contrast to economic penalties—which compensated the victim, restored balance, and steered the criminal from recidivism by promoting mindfulness—the two functions of physical punishment were to impress the offender with the seriousness of the crime and the public with the dangers of criminal activity. To this end, most physical punishment was meant to be short-lived, painful, and exoteric. Tibetan government policy dictated that physical punishment could be administered only on the actual person of the criminal and only by the order of a government official— that is to say, not on other members of his family or household and not by a nongovernmental person. From the comments and stories of Tibetans, it would appear that the former dictate was followed but that the latter was not; individuals other than government officials did at times administer physical punishments.

Although whipping was not considered traditionally Tibetan, nor is it mentioned in the law codes, by the twentieth century it was the most typical form of physical punishment. The general term for "whip" included at least three different instruments, ranked according to the severity of their results.

For the lightest of punishments, a *korcak* (*skor 'chag*) was used, a foot-long stick of wood with three or four hand-sized leaves of leather bound to one end by a rope. This whip was traditionally used on the face. The accused was expected to puff out his cheeks as hard as he could; then the leather leaves of the *korcak* were whacked against them. Several Tibetans remembered having been dealt this punishment for infractions in school, and, as the word used to designate this whip is part of the word for police, *korcakpa,* some stated that the police carried it as well. Tibetans said that it hurt only a little bit; to cause real damage, this whip had to be beaten very strongly many times against the cheek, which was not the usual practice.

Most punishments were rendered with the *tachak* (*rta lcag*), which had a twenty-four- to thirty-inch handle of flexible wood such as bamboo, about an inch and a half in diameter, to which three braided leather thongs of up to four feet were attached—either bound with a rope or tied through an end hole (three are hanging from a pillar at the far left in plate 57). It was this whip that was used at three different points in a criminal trial: (1) for an "initial whipping" called a *jorchak* (*'byor lcag*), when a prisoner was first received by the authorities; (2) for a "questioning whipping" called a *dichak* (*dri lchags*), when a criminal in custody returned to court for further examination; and (3) for a "departing whipping" called a *thonchak* (*thon lcag*), when the final physical punishment determined by the court was administered.[17]

The whip capable of the greatest damage was the *ponpo wengyuk* (*dpon po dbang rgyug*), a hard stick of two feet or more in length with a handle. One former judge of the High Court said that this whip was chiefly decorative. Few Tibetans had any knowledge of its secular use, though it is very similar in style to the rigid-handled whips to which leather thongs could be attached, said to be carried by the *géko* (*dge skos*), the police sergeants of the monasteries.[18]

Some written sources speak of whippings occurring in a "flogging place" or on a "flogging board." According to Tibetans, whippings were administered at or near the courthouses, often in public. A Lhasa resident who frequented the area outside Lhasa City Court described

an open space right in the front to the right of the stairs to the Nangtse shak where the whippings were done. It was very public, in front of all the people, because it was thought that they received a very strong lesson not to act like this when they saw the punishment. It was done the same way in the Sherkhang, the court inside the Cathedral Complex itself.

The person is laid flat on the ground with his face down, wearing regular clothes. Sometimes they give him prison clothes, which are white cloth robes; sometimes his skin is bare. No one ties him down, but if he complains, then one of the police will hold him down. Two police or guards whip him from either side alternately with leather thong whips on the area of his bottom and thighs. Sometimes when you went by the court this was going on. It was said that if you watch it, you will have bad fortune.

Whipping was the general method employed by district officers, governors, and courts throughout Tibet for physical punishment, and stories of it were repeatedly told by both official and lay Tibetans. Mitigation of whippings was possible if pleaded as a separate issue immediately before the government officer, especially if the particular officer did not like to use the whip, or if a monk or other person of influence requested that it not be administered for a specific reason such as the sex, age, health, or special circumstances of the accused.[19] There seems to have been little doubt in the minds of most officials as to the guilt of persons who were actually apprehended after investigation, a fact that justified even an initial whipping. Only rarely, in the opinion of both lay and official Tibetans, was the man initially brought into custody and whipped later found to be innocent.[20]

Other physical punishments can be divided into two categories: those considered traditional in Tibet, and those introduced by outsiders such as the British and the Chinese. Evidence cited by Tibetans for this distinction included the foreign-

Plate 60. Convicts in stocks and their guards in the Zhol prison. 1920–21. (Pitt Rivers Museum, University of Oxford)

sounding names applied to the instruments used in the latter and the lack of reference to such punishments in either the law codes, historical records, or oral history.

Among methods considered traditionally Tibetan were fetters and stocks; the law codes use the term "heavy wooden fetters" several times.[21] Pictures and recounted cases indicate that prisoners thought capable of fleeing were put in foot or hand stocks while in prison. Convicted criminals might be sentenced to wear iron foot and hand fetters or chains of various weights, either for a specified number of years or for life. Fetters of various kinds were also used in conjunction with various other punishments.

Also recorded in the ancient law codes—although few Tibetans I talked with reported having seen them carried out—were *kidam* (*khyi dam*), stamping the word meaning "dog," on the forehead with a hot iron; *kotum* (*ko btums*), sealing a criminal in a fresh animal skin and leaving it to dry, then throwing the body in the river; and *gyansar kurwa* (*gyang sar bskyur ba*), throwing a criminal off a high precipice.

Talion (*lex talionis*) was obviously rare by the twentieth century and reserved for the punishment of the most onerous offenses. The Dalai Lama law code of 1650 lists "big crimes done during times of peace"—"killing a lama, killing a headman, robbing a monk, stealing from the king's storehouse, disgracing officials, giving poison, causing injury through mantras, killing a relative, 'killing a man, stealing a horse offenses,' robbing, the death of a man pursuing a thief, using a dangerous weapon, rioting by mob, attacking high officials, and revolting against the government"—and then continues:

> In short, so that anyone will see these illegal actions [to be wrong]:
> From the body of the criminal,
> take out the eyes,
> cut the Achilles tendon,
> cut off the tongue,
> cut off the hands,
> throw [the criminal] from a high mountain or into the river,
> execute the death sentence, and so forth.
> Depending on the size of the crime,
> the punishment [should be cut] from his body with a knife or scissors,
> to strongly admonish [all persons] in the future.[22]

Few Tibetans had seen such severe penalties exacted, but a former monk official related a firsthand observation of this kind of punishment done publicly:

> When I worked for the governor of Khams in Chamdo city, they used to send an army man as a messenger for official deliveries. He was equipped with both a short and a long rifle on his journeys, and he rode alone on his horse. During my tenure, one of these messengers was killed by robbers who wanted his weapons.
>
> So an investigation committee was formed to catch these notorious robbers, and having determined the identity of the killers, the governor ordered the army to catch them. Some were caught and others weren't. Three men and their two wives who acted as assistants were caught. As a monk official, I was not allowed to have anything to do with this sort of punishment, so it was left to the lay official in the office. The final punishment determined was that the three men should have their legs cut off from the knee down, and this was written in the document.
>
> Then the head of the local monastery and some of its lamas came to request of the governor that this punishment not be given, and they talked about the long life of the Dalai Lama. So the punishment was reduced to cutting one heel tendon and slitting one ear of each of the men.
>
> The punishment was done in the capital city. First a group of army men marched in and brought the criminals. Then a representative of the government spoke and scolded the criminals for their crimes in front of all the people. The criminals were brought to him and had to kneel down before him; he continued his scolding, saying that the criminals should have been given the death sentence or had their leg cut off, but lamas had intervened, so that only a section of flesh would be cut from the leg.
>
> Then, the criminals were taken to a separate place not far away at the edge of the city and surrounded by army men, so that it was difficult for commoners to see. A five-gun salute was fired. The heel tendons of the men were cut, and then the blood was sealed with an iron rod dipped in hot oil. The criminals never cried, but all the women [watching] did. After this, as the criminals lay down on the ground, all the people brought them offerings of food, blankets, clothes, and money to demonstrate their forgiveness of them now that they had been punished, and their compassion for the criminals' suffering. That foot would be entirely useless to them from then on and their punishment was completed.

One punishment device that was quite common in twentieth-century Tibet but considered a Chinese import, because of its prevalence in China, was the wooden neck cangue (*go*). When employed as a short-term punishment, the *go* was large, heavy, and square and carried a printed notice of the defendant's crime. It was worn around the village or city during the day for a prescribed period of time to denounce and humiliate the criminal publicly. When employed as a long-term or lifetime punishment, it was usually round, smaller, lighter, and sometimes used in conjunction with iron hand or foot fetters.[23]

After the economic fines had been paid and the criminal had received a whipping or other physical punishment, the final decision of the court could include further provisions intended to achieve the miscreant's rehabilitation, promote mindfulness, or inhibit recidivism. Among other possibilities, the law code suggests, "A labor punishment . . . should be given according to the circumstances."[24] The labor punishments described in recorded cases usually required that the defendant either move to an area distant from his home and farm a new plot of land for several years, while paying the taxes to the government; move to a distant area to work land for a private family that needed help; or return to his home area but work under supervision for his family or a former landlord.

Incarceration other than during trial was not imposed in most of Tibet because of the lack of facilities and staff. The larger cities did maintain either a locked room or a prison capable of housing prisoners for longer periods of time, at their own or their families' expense for clothing and food. In Lhasa, both the City Court and the Zhol Court had famous prisons: the *zhol lékhung* was reported to have a holding capacity of thirty to fifty men at a time, and the Nangtse shak prison had two separate holding rooms on the first floor and a large windowless room in the basement.[25] Imprisonment was not a preferred option, however, and is not mentioned as such in the law codes, although secondary sources do mention the confinement of high-ranking persons for extensive periods as a punishment after trial.[26]

Still other post-trial punishments mentioned in interviews or cases were ostracism by the accused's community or town, publication of a criminal offense in a document or edict, reduction of rank for an official, and loss of occupational status.

CHAPTER TWENTY-FIVE

The Life History of Kungola Thubten Sangye

Even an ordinary person
will automatically become
a person of good moral character,
through the virtue and merit
of his service to the government.
—Ganden Podrang Code
of the Dalai Lamas

In some two years' worth of daily discussions and interviews over a four-year period, Kungola Thubten Sangye—a monk official in the former Tibetan government who subsequently worked for the government-in-exile of the Dalai Lama in India—related anecdotes and tales that I have translated and put together in chronological order to form a life history. Kungola never imparted his autobiography in sequenced units; indeed, he strenuously objected to the idea that his life might be important or interesting and requested that I write about the Thirteenth Dalai Lama instead. Nevertheless, I present his story here, in his voice, because it says so much about the cosmology of law in Tibet. Or perhaps this is nothing more than a belated eulogy. So be it.[1]

Birth and Childhood

I was born in the Gongkar area, just south of Lhasa on the river. The name given to me at my birth was Ngawang Norbu. My father's name was Kyerab Tharchin. Our family name was Nesar, and it was the name given to the small farm in our area of which my father was the landlord. His father had been a small farmer in the area before him.

My mother's name was Lhawang Chonzom, and she was a daughter of one of the tenants on his family farm. My mother's father's name was Khangser Lhoma, which means "new house in the south."

Plate 61. Kungola Thubten Sangye working on the law codes at the Library of Tibetan Works and Archives in Dharamsala, India. 1983.

My father's job was confined entirely to the affairs of the farm and tenants. The house I grew up in had twenty servants for the family, and the farm had about ten tenant-farming households. The servants had no land themselves but were paid wages by my father and had their own families and houses on the property. This place of Nesar had been owned by an aristocrat named Chungchor Wangdu before it became our land. He was a governor in western Tibet, a high official, and had this land as part of his government allotment. It seems that Chungchor Wangdu's brother had built a big house in our area of Nesar and consequently had a lot of debts to be paid to the government for financing the house. My father was friendly with Chungchor Wangdu and was to be appointed as owner of the farm if he would assume the debt of the house. I think this is how we acquired the farmland.

My birth date was the Tibetan Year of the Water Rat, which is the Western year of 1910. I was an ordinary little boy, always playing around the farm until the age of six. Someone who saw me would have thought that I was just a little village boy, wrapped in woolen cloth, and not new clothes at all. I lost my mother when I was very young; I could hardly walk when she died. There is only a faint memory of going upstairs to her room and not being allowed to go in because she was seriously ill. So I was brought up by my auntie, Somola. Auntie acted as a mother would, and I remember sleeping with her in her bed and reaching for her breasts to drink, but there was no milk. She did not become the wife of my father however; for some years he was away from the house while my aunt and I stayed in my mother's house. I remember that my maternal grandmother was also very nice.

In my father's house there was an uncle named Tenzin Dhondrup. He had his own house, which was large like a big building in a city, but it was not in good shape. Then my father started sharing my uncle's wife with him, and they all lived in my father's house. This wife had come from Lhasa and her name was Dolma Tsering. A while after this my uncle died; it happened when I was nine or so. He fell very sick and died. Then I started staying with my father in his house but visiting my mother's house often. When my uncle died, Dolma Tsering stayed with my father as his wife.

In my mother's house there was my auntie Somola, named Tsering Palden, and my grandmother, who was called Sonam Dolma. It was a nice house, and there were some servants there to help them. Actually, my aunt did have a little daughter, but no one knew who the father was because he never stayed afterward. I can remember my auntie and grandmother quarreling and my grandmother saying in a very loud voice, "I don't have to stay here and I don't have to look after this Ngawang Norbu!" It was not long after this that I went to stay with my father in his house again.

The First Tutor and School

At seven years of age I started learning at home under a tutor whose name I just don't recall. The man looked like a monk in layman's clothes, and he taught me the alphabet and writing and other things. He came from outside the farm. My father was very careful to observe the traditions of astrology as to where in the house the teacher should sit and where I should face and the times of the class. Every aspect of the teaching was regulated so that it would be auspicious and correct. The teacher came only once a week. I learned the alphabet, pronunciation, and a couple of different writing styles in the cursive script in these lessons, and so they felt that I was good at learning. I was never beaten with a stick in class, but there was a lot of homework.

At eight, I remember, it was decided that I should be instructed in the formal "head" script, and so I was sent to the Dechen Chokhor Gonpa, a monastery of the Kagyu sect up in the hills behind our farm. I went there for about three or four months and was tutored by the ex-abbot of the monastery. The ex-abbot was a meditator in the tradition of the great teacher of Naropa, Naru Chudrug. The younger brother of the ex-abbot was the head chanter of the monastery, and so I stayed with him in his house while I learned the script. There was another student with me, so we both learned it together, and it went rather quickly. While I stayed there, I saw that all the young monks sat on the roofs of the monastery memorizing and reciting their texts. I felt very jealous because I knew only a few of the root mantras, which I had learned at home, like the root mantra of Manjushri. I was very inquisitive and wanted to know what they were saying before and after all the mantras as well, so I sat and listened and learned it for myself. Then later I went to my teacher and said, "I know something more than what you have taught me" and I recited it exactly. I found it very easy. The teacher said to me, "You are a good boy. Keep it up!"

It became cold, and in the winter of my eighth year I went back to my farm to stay. The Manjushri stanzas that I had learned I found later were not common in Lhasa or throughout Tibet; they were ancient and had come from India.

The next year I was sent to join the government school in our area of Gongkar district. It was about three miles from my house and in the eastern part of the district. The district had been divided in half, into eastern and western districts, each with its own officer to administer it. The school was in the eastern half, and I was put in a hostel in the western half, which was still close by. The school was in the old fortress house of the district office, and it was a very big place. Previously, there had been a teacher appointed by the government who came specially to teach the students in the area. When I went there, the eastern district officer was our teacher. He was very good in calligraphy and language, and his name was Nyima Dorje.

On the tenth and thirtieth day of each month we were given vacations from school, and someone came from my farm to pick me up. I went home and then was brought back the next day for school again. I remember that one summer day I went on my own, walking, and I had to wade through a river to get home. Farmers from our land began shouting at me from the other side that I should not cross, that I should wait. There was a big commotion, but I just kept going because I wanted to be home.

My father was a highly respected man in the area, and this made me a little privileged in the government school. I had a close relationship with the teacher, who was the district officer of the eastern side. Sometimes he hit me and got very angry, and other times he praised me. I remember crying for help to the teacher's wife one of these times. To her husband she said, "If you don't act right in the future, you will get beaten instead of the boy." The teacher was very reserved and serious with his students, and he didn't laugh at all.

Schooling in Lhasa and the Summer Palace

After two years at the district school, when I was eleven years old, I went to Lhasa for more education. I was sent to the Kyere School and stayed in the house of a man with whom my family had a relationship, an attendant of the Thirteenth Dalai Lama. This attendant worked in the Potala but stayed in his own house in Lhasa. Since I had come from a village school, there was a strict admission test; they found my writing style to be slightly different, and so I had to go through a short writing class to relearn the style of my letters. In a year, which was considered very fast, I got to write on paper in a book instead of on the wooden board we all used for learning.

I received a letter announcing the death of my grandmother while I was at that school. Once, I tried to separate two students who were quarreling, and instead they began to beat me up. I had to take leave of school for several days after that, as I had been hit so badly on the right side of my head.

When I was thirteen, I joined the Chensel School, which was on the grounds of the Summer Palace of His Holiness the Dalai Lama. My friend Gelong was also at the school. We stayed within the compound of the palace grounds with our teacher all the time. Although the entire business of the palace surrounded the life and work of His Holiness the Dalai Lama, we didn't think about him, Gyalwa Rinpoche,[2] at all except perhaps with awe, fear, and special respect. His Holiness the Dalai Lama was very fond of gardening, and whenever he went out to the garden, he would sow the seeds and ask the students to help. We all ran here and there with tools and water as he guided us. Even if the class was in session, we would run from class to help him. Also, sometimes he visited the school and our hostel. Once, when he was in the school, he saw our whip and said to us, "It is good to get punished when you are young, then you will appreciate it when you are older." At a ceremony when I was fourteen, he gave me my new name, Thubten Sangye. After that I was no longer Ngawang Norbu.

One of our teachers had an excellent hand. He told me that I had to work hard because I had come from a village; he said it would be "hard to be as good as Kesang [another teacher] or me." But my tenure there proved very fruitful, and I tried hard to improve my handwriting style. By the time I was fourteen or fifteen I was able to write quite well and had a very high standard of Tibetan, much higher even than they teach now. Grammar at the Summer Palace was taught by Geshe Sherab Gyatso. We learned a lot. He was very conscious of his students and he would say to us, "You must be good!" which meant that we should keep up his reputation. Spelling was very hard with him, and he had us just memorize most of the spellings, such as the Lekshe Jowang [text]. He always gave us a lucid explanation, quite laboriously, word for word. These special tuitions were an hour a day, and we were given a lot of homework to do besides that.

I stayed at the Summer Palace until I was eighteen years of age. My teacher advised against my going to the Winter Palace school for training because, he said, it was too much discipline and not as good an education. When I was at the Summer Palace, I remember missing my classes in the school in Lhasa because it had had an open atmosphere with lots of students playing and laughing; in the Summer Palace there were two teachers, and both of them were quite strict.

We sometimes saw some of the foreigners who visited His Holiness, like the Political Officer of Sikkim and the British Political Officer named Charles Bell. Also, I remember Colonel MacDonald and Mr. Rosemayer. When the change of the Viceroys occurred in India, a person came to Tibet with letters and presents. The Political Officers always gave guns and rifles as presents to attendants and officers because the Tibetans were very fond of them. I remember a present to His Holiness of a sofa set and something called a spring bed, which went up and down. The order

Plate 62. Main entrance to the Summer Palace of the Dalai Lama showing the guards at the gates and the prayer poles. 1920–21. (Pitt Rivers Museum, University of Oxford)

went out for the sofa set to be covered in yellow brocade so that the Dalai Lama could sit on it. I was fifteen or sixteen then. A special horse was also brought up by the British Officer, a huge horse, as a present. Also, when I was fifteen I became a monk, but I never lived in a monastery or took full vows.

Appointment to the Government

When I was eighteen, my official papers were sent to the Ecclesiastical Office. Appointments in the government were an involved process; a person had to have connections and to lobby somewhat. It was much tougher to get a good appointment from my training in the Summer Palace than it was for students in the Winter Palace school. First, we all were given a test paper with different script styles. We made three samples that were then sent with white scarves of the best kind to three different teachers, His Holiness, the prime minister, and the head of the Ecclesiastical Office.

During that year when I was eighteen, just before I became an officer, I took lessons from Chune Lama Rinpoche, whose proper name was Ngawang Lobsang. He taught me certain religious texts. I also got teachings from Trata Rinpoche, who was the tutor to His Holiness and later a regent.

When one applied to be a government officer, first, the school evaluated all the students and made its own selection. Then its list was sent to the Office of His Holiness, and only the top one or two students got appointments. But there are four different times of selection during the year: the New Year, the Mon Lam Festival that follows it, Getar (around March third), and then Ganden Gamchu. And so at nineteen I received my first appointment in the Iron Horse Year, the Western year of 1930. My appointment was to the Office of His Holiness in the Summer Palace to be a government secretary.

Before I reported to work, I took two months off. I went to see my father in Gongkar, who was ill at the time. He was living in a small house on a hill, sitting all day and meditating. I stayed with him for three days. My father could not even stand up or move. He asked me to give him my hand, and he held my hand while he said this to me:

"I have left you no share of the property because I have given all my property to your sister, who has children. I like you, so do not be distressed. I always pray for your happy life, and I made many offerings in Lhasa and have given all your share to the Three Jewels of Religion as an offering. After I go, make no trouble for your sister. I have asked your stepmother to make an offering in Lhasa when I die, and you should assist her."

This was his final will. After two more days I left, and he passed away. So after his death my stepmother made offerings in many places, at the Cathedral Complex in Lhasa, Samye Monastery, Tashilungpo Monastery in Gyantse, and other monasteries. After joining the government office, I also made 1,000 offerings in my father's name at each of these places, including the Podrang Monastery and the Tangdrug Monastery, which was constructed by the Tibetan queen of the first historic king in the seventh century and has since been destroyed.

No one thought that I had been disinherited from my paternal inheritance. We didn't have much paternal inheritance in our family, really; for the land and the peasants of our land, we owed a big rent and tax to maintain them. By then I was a monk, and monks cannot inherit. So I made 1,000 offerings and for this I also had to arrange 1,000 butter lamps, 1,000 incense sticks, and so forth. At a later date, I also offered 10,000 butter lamps.

Then I went to the Office of the Dalai Lama, called the "Inner House," to begin my first appointment. For the next three years I was a clerk, dealing with all the people who came visiting and all the correspondence coming to that office, until 1933, when His Holiness the Dalai Lama died. In that office I didn't deal directly with law cases, but many legal documents came into the office.

I remember a man who was sent out from our office as a governor and was brought back to Lhasa because of his bad deeds. His miscarriage of justice was brought to His Holiness's attention through an open appeal when he was traveling from the Summer Palace to the Cathedral Complex. The man had cheated the people badly and was brought back to Lhasa and punished with a wooden collar around his neck. As a student, I also saw another man punished in Lhasa outside of the Lhasa City Court in a cage with his head through a hole at the top, though his feet could touch the ground. Lashings of prisoners and criminals took place in the same area, in front of the court near the steps. I saw it only sometimes. On very rare occasions the severed limbs of very bad criminals would be displayed in front of the

Lhasa or other police station. This happened in one case involving a soldier who killed a member of the police guard, and so the head of the army, Tsarong, ordered this as the punishment.

Administrator of a Monastery

After the death of the Thirteenth Dalai Lama in 1933, I was reassigned to a new government monastery, established by the Thirteenth Dalai Lama, called Ganden Rabgye. It was in the Kurab Namgyal district, Lhoka region, two days by horse from Nangdzong. My responsibilities were to administer the monastery and collect the revenues from the nomads in the area. The produce collected was used to feed the monks and pay for my own necessities. This area was famous for its butter, good barley, and meat. I stayed there for one year until I was reassigned. In this new monastery area there were a hundred monks, five hundred tenant farmers connected to the monastic lands, many nomads, and other government farmers. It was a very good monastery, and many visiting lamas taught there. At the termination of my stay the community of monks called me to the temple and did a long-life ceremony for me while I sat next to the abbot. In this way I came to know that I was loved by the monks as an administrator.

Then a letter from the Cabinet arrived at the monastery and I was informed that I had been promoted, effective immediately, and reassigned to the Chinese delegation. This was not a favor to me because in those days it was considered very bad to be sent out of the country, as it would ruin your health and be very difficult. After returning to Lhasa I prostrated many times in front of Reting Rinpoche, who was the regent of the country as we awaited the incarnation of the Fourteenth Dalai Lama. I requested not to go. He responded to me: "I have heard that China is good. I may even come along. All you have to do is send a telegram to me if you want to come back, and you will be relieved of your duties." So I responded: "All right, I will go if you want me to go."

Only three of us were actually sent. I was appointed as the junior member, and both of my senior companions died in China, so health was a real problem for us! I think that one of them died because of bad tea. He didn't like the Chinese black tea in the morning, and so he always made his own tea with sweet milk that he often used to keep in a tin. I think that the milk went bad and this caused his death, but I don't know.

The Delegation to China

We left for China in the wintertime at the end of the Wood Pig Year, or 1935, when I was twenty-five, and I stayed for four years in China until the Earth Hare Year, 1939. We were stationed in Nanking, which was the capital of China then. I will not tell stories of China now, for it would take too long.[3]

When we learned of the discovery and enthronement of the new Dalai Lama, preparations were made to return to Tibet. Before the delegation left, the three

Tibetan officials were invited to a large banquet by Chiang Kai-shek. One of the
senior members, Kenchung, was already ill at that point, and he died very soon after
that. I found out that the other senior member died just after I reached Lhasa. At the
banquet, Chiang Kai-shek came up to me and shook my hand and said, "You are
quite young, so you should come back to China!" When he said that, I thought to
myself, "I will never become someone great like Mao Zedong or Chiang Kai-shek."
I compared the way Chiang Kai-shek walked to that of the Thirteenth Dalai Lama,
and then I thought that the Chinese people and their country were very unfortunate
and lacking in merit.

We arrived back from China in the winter of 1939, when I was twenty-nine years
old. I had come by ship, accompanying a high official named Wu Chung-hsui, who
was part of the Chinese delegation to the enthronement of the new Dalai Lama. The
Chinese delegation traveled in three ways, depending on the rank of the officials
going to the ceremony. The most important officials flew from Chungking to Hong
Kong to Calcutta. The second-level officials, such as the man I was accompanying,
went from Chungking to Hong Kong by air, then from Hong Kong to Calcutta by
sea. The third group went across land by bus to northern Burma, by train to
Rangoon, and by sea to Calcutta. From Calcutta, we all traveled to Lhasa.

It was the middle of winter in Tibet when we arrived. The enthronement was
scheduled for after the New Year Losar Festival in 1940, the Iron Dragon Year. I
went again to the Regent Reting Rinpoche and appealed to be free of my service,
even though the term of my fifth year was not over. I did not want to return to
China. I had learned that now both of the senior officials in China were dead. Others
advised me to return because I was young and knew the language well.

I had decided not to come back to China, even before I left, and so had appointed a
servant of the second officer to take care of the office and all the business. This later
proved quite useful, and he did a good job. When I went to ask the regent to relieve
me, he granted my request. So I was relieved informally, but I still had to wait and
go through formal channels. After my resignation from the job was accepted formally, the regent issued instructions to look for a replacement.

Assignment to the Eastern Provinces

Within the year, I was promoted to the fourth rank and sent to be one of the two
junior officials under the overgovernor of Chamdo, whose name was Kungo
Nangchung. The overgovernor had Cabinet-level rank. I was the monk junior
officer, called a *kenchung* (*mkhan chung*), and my companion, named Sugupa, was the
lay officer, called a *rimshi* (*rim bzhi*). Reting Rinpoche, the regent, had arranged the
appointment. I traveled far to the east to get to my new post in the town of Changra.
We were in charge of more than nineteen districts altogether.[4]

My duties were to administer the area. Many people came to me in this position
with their legal cases because in this area it was said, "We will go to the Changra
kenchung, and he will do justice." I don't remember all the minor cases that I had to
solve. I do remember that I was forced to dismiss several of the local heads of areas,
because we required good and honest people, and the local people would bring suit

against them. These legal cases were difficult. Of course, in very minor cases, there were no documents. When it was necessary because of the size of the case, we prepared documents, approved them, and had them signed by the government and parties.

Although there was no law code provided in our office at that place, I had my own copy from my father, and I used it in my office in Changra. Actually, I had two of them. The one I used was a good copy of the standard code for government officials during the time of the Thirteenth Dalai Lama; it was the Ganden Podrang Code of Thirteen Sections. It stated in my copy that this was the same as that used in the High Court, the Sherkhang, in Lhasa. Although this was the standard text, many other texts were preserved through the centuries in families throughout Tibet. Officials in the government all knew that there was a standard code and that when they were sent out to a district, they must know the code. If they had no experience in administration, then they wouldn't know much about it. Some people took an interest in the law codes and some didn't. When I later asked about the code in the Sherkhang, I was told that the original was no longer there, only a copy. The original had been removed to the Cabinet Office. Tradition was that the Desi Rinpoche Sangye Gyatsho, the regent of the Fifth Dalai Lama, had personally presented the original to the High Court. It was supposed to be passed down to each new Sherkhang judge and explained, but I don't know if this was done. I also heard that an extra section was added to the code by the Sherkhang, but I do not know what this is.

We received the Mountain Valley Decree, *rilung tsatsik,* every year in our area to be posted for all of the people to see and hear the laws of the land. It had one section that prohibited the killing of wild animals, for the job of the hunter is very sinful. I heard a true story about this in Changra.

Near my house at that time, in an area called Tsam Kawa, there was a lot of grassland with beautiful hills, and a kind of deer called the *lawa* (*gla ba*) was prevalent there. I was told that one hunter was killing these deer with the help of a bamboo trap. One day he came to the trap and found that it had been thrown in another place, and he wondered who had done this. He set the trap again and again found that it had been moved. This happened several times. So he decided to hide and watch the place to see who was doing this. The place where he had set the trap was very rocky, and carved into the rock was an image of the manifestation of the Buddha called Chenresi. No one knew whether the image had just appeared on the rock or a man had carved it by hand. As the hunter kept looking, he saw the Chenresi come out of the rock and go and pull the trap and put it in another place. Immediately, he sprang from where he was hiding and ran to the mountain to look at the image on the rock. It was the same. Right then he confessed his sins from hunting and began to engage in the practice of dharma. He did not hunt ever again.

My overgovernor was replaced by a high-ranking official named Yuthok. World War II was now in full swing, and in 1942 I was transferred from my office to a new post, that of the Supply Office of the eastern area in Chamdo. It was considered a good post with a lot of responsibility, and I spent three years there. Basically, my job was to collect revenues locally and get money from Lhasa, which I then used to distribute supplies to the military in the area, as well as to the overgovernor and his staff. There were over 5,000 military officers and soldiers for whom I had to provide wages, supplies, clothes, and so forth. I was the head of the supply house, and many considered this position to be that of a second overgovernor.

I did this job for three years. My income was good, and I didn't have to deal with many legal problems or disputes, such as fights or law cases—only supplies. But I foresaw many problems in the area I was working in. After a few years I could see that the Chinese were constantly pushing in, and there were going to be many difficulties providing supplies. Also, when I was appointed to fourth rank, many people were surprised because it was such a high rank, even for a person from a noble family, and I was not from such a family. I didn't like it that many people were surprised. Before deciding what to do next, I went to attend a lama of the area known for his prophecy and divination. After introducing myself and presenting white scarves and a present, I mentioned my fear and attitudes, told him my thoughts about the low supplies and difficulties with recruitment. He was an incarnation of an omniscient one, and the god Chenresi was revealed to him in meditation. The lama agreed to do a *mo,* or divination, for me. After he did it, he said to me, "We will have a totally different kind of war, but it will not be now. So the resignation is up to you." So I decided to resign what was considered by everyone to be a very privileged post. But the incursion of the Chinese happened during the time of my successor, who lost everything.

But I lost some of my good fortune in this place as well. I had owned for a long time a *yeshe norbu* (*yid bzhin nor bu*), a kind of wish-fulfilling gem that comes from the ocean. Mine was like a paperweight in shape and heaviness. *Yeshe norbu* is also a common word and a name in many texts. My stone came from Mount Kailash near Lake Manosowar, and it was green and red and very smooth. During the war between China and Japan I left it in Khams. When I had that stone, I always had a good amount of money. With a real *yeshe norbu,* if you pray to it, whatever your wishes are, they are fulfilled. This was the way it was in ancient times, but later on we have not seen this kind of stone.

In the Main Administration in Lhasa

I returned to Lhasa in 1945 and was posted for the next thirteen years in the capital city. First, I was posted to the government Auditor's Office, located above the Revenue Office, in the Cathedral Complex. Orders for this reassignment were made even before I left my post in Khams, so I had only a couple of months off before I began this job. I was still a *rimshi,* a fourth-rank official, which is the highest level that I ever obtained, for I was given no further promotions.

In the Auditor's Office there were three officials: a general secretary with the fourth rank who was our senior, me, and then a lay official named Nga Pho, who came from a famous Tibetan family. Under us were three or four secretaries to write correspondence and keep records. We could get extra help any time we wanted it from the Accounting Office. Most people considered this office a stepping-stone to the Cabinet. I was very regular in my attendance at the office, but the other two went to other places and other offices on assignment. This made me the *kungshu:* that is, the one who was sitting in and watching the office. After two years I was

Plate 63. An English letter and a Tibetan letter. 1920–21. (Pitt Rivers Museum, University of Oxford)

given an outside duty as well to attend to the Foreign Office, because the senior officer there was ill and later died. After a while a third-rank official named Kungo Liu Shar was appointed to the Foreign Office, and so my position there disappeared.

I can remember thinking that Tibetans were sometimes foolish in foreign affairs. When I was a child, I heard the story of Colonel Younghusband, the British military man who came into Tibet just before I was born. Before he came, Younghusband first sent a letter to the Tibetan government. It was looked at by several people in the government and commented on. Then it was decided that it should be returned to him with no reply. The British government received it back and thought that there had been no one to translate the letter, so they sent it again with a translation. But this time when it was received in Tibet, it was not even opened and was immediately sent back again. Then our government sent an army to protect the border, and after that the British started an expedition. It seems to me that the Tibetan government should have checked the letter and given the correct reply. This was a mistake!

While I lived in Lhasa I had a house of my own with servants to take care of me. I also had a very good dog at that time, a big black Tibetan dog that I tied outside the door during the day. There were many beggars in Lhasa, and this dog stopped them from coming into the house all the time. At night I freed the dog inside the house, and he always bounded up the stairs. He would come into my room and lick my cheeks. Then I would ask the servants to take him outside to the courtyard and feed him. At night, when the doors to the house were closed, he slept on the roof of the house, which was flat. Years later some beggars gave my dog poison, and he died.

In Tibet, rooms and houses have good and bad fortunes. If people die or get sick in a room, we believe that these are not good rooms, and we should shift to a new place. People used to say that my house in Lhasa was very lucky, and I was very happy the whole time I lived there. I began to study dharma in that house; I studied the rituals of Tantra completely there. People told me the house was lucky because a former Ganden throneholder, one of the highest members of the clergy in Tibet, used to live there.

In 1948 I was moved to another office in the Cathedral Complex called the Storage Office, *lachak dzokhang (bla phyag mdzod khang)*. Much of the revenue and income from all of Tibet went to the Storage Office: money, butter, tea, and every other kind of product except for grain, which was recorded and kept elsewhere. I stayed in that office for ten years. Every person in that office was in the fourth rank, including the well-known Kungo Taring. In 1950, when His Holiness escaped for the first time because of the Chinese invasion, I went with him as a private secretary and storage officer. Upon our return I stayed in Lhasa, working in the central Storage Office.

Assignment to Phari

In my forty-eighth year I was reassigned as the governor of an area in the south called Phari, famous because the town of Phari lies on the major trading and access route from India. It was considered an excellent post full of advantage, because the governor of Phari always received many visitors and presents. While I was in that position, people used to come to see me at home a lot; it was very common. They usually came to see me with their legal and other problems first at home, and then discussed it later in the office. I can remember that many monks came to visit me, asking for better salaries. People never came empty-handed when they came to see me, for it is traditional to come with a present.

I visited Lhasa during my tenure in Phari and found it very tense. Then I returned to Phari, and within two months I had to leave. The Chinese came in to take over the country completely. I came out at the same time that His Holiness did, but like many Tibetans, I tried to go through Bhutan. The Bhutanese turned all of us back and wouldn't let us through, so I headed out the second time for Assam in eastern India. I entered India in Japaiguri district and made it to the Katihar railroad station. We were all put in a settlement camp in Buxalama and then moved later to be near His Holiness in Mussoorie.

Since then I have been in India, serving His Holiness the Fourteenth Dalai Lama.

Conclusion

Like the moon that rises from the bountiful ocean,
spreading the white light of nectar to destroy the darkness,
so truthful petitions arise from the king's law,
spreading the rays of truth to destroy all falsehood.
So it is said.

—Ganden Podrang Code of the Dalai Lamas

A few days before I left Dharamsala for the final time in the late fall of 1986, Kungola Thubten Sangye arrived before I did at the office where we worked every morning and began, with his usual laborious lumbering, to climb the steps. I met him on the second flight and stayed behind him, taking the steps one at a time after him.

"I had a dream last night," he said and stopped to look down at me. "I had a dream last night that I was reborn in America." I didn't respond. He continued looking at me and said, "In my dream, I was born to an American woman." He turned to continue up the steps. "We must finish early today because I have many more mantras to complete in preparation."

On the morning of my departure, men came to carry my trunks of research notes down to the bus for the long journey back to New Delhi. John, my husband, had left several months earlier to get back to his work at Berkeley. Over the course of that last week I had attended several *momo* dinners, thanked everyone repeatedly, and said goodbye. Most of the possessions I had collected over the previous three years had been distributed to assorted friends, the wife of an assistant, the monk next door. I closed up the small room where we had lived, locked it, and walked down the steps, past the workrooms and living quarters of the Library of Tibetan Works and Archives. Hurrying across the plaza in my long skirt and long-sleeved shirt, my hair in a bun, I thought of all the problems to be faced in New Delhi shipping the trunks and the loud Indian music blaring from the speakers on the new buses.

As I turned the corner, I saw Kungola. He had been waiting for me most of the morning. I stopped short and then approached. He clasped both my hands between his hands and bowed his head. I bowed my head and held it down in deference until after he spoke. "The outside needs to know about these things we have talked about," Kungola said.

Plate 64. Mani stones at Kema Monastery. Such stones were often whitewashed or painted to emphasize the mantras carved in relief. Each spoken or carved mantra is an act of karmic merit in preparing for one's next rebirth. 1942–43. (Ilya Tolstoy, Library, The Academy of Natural Sciences of Philadelphia)

My eyes filled with tears as I responded, "I will bring a book back to show you." Fumbling with some packages he had under his arm, Kungola took from its newspaper wrapping a white silk scarf and put it around my neck as he said, "It is very important that people know about these matters, so you must work hard. I will die before you come back." Unwrapping another package in his hands, Tibetan style, he let each of the pieces of cloth fall away while he held it in his palm. As the last triangle of cloth dropped, it revealed several pages of the religious text he had been reciting over the last weeks. "Take these with you." He rewrapped the pages, folding each triangle in toward the center and then tying a long cloth tail around and around the final package. I bowed again and took it with me as I turned to go down the hill. I didn't stop crying until we reached the halfway point on the bus at Chandigarh.

A few years later a friend, Warren Smith, was traveling to Dharamsala, and I asked if he would carry copies of my preliminary manuscript with him to present to the Dalai Lama and several others. When he came to my little research office (then at Harvard), I brought out several copies of the manuscript, a few presents, and some letters. Warren protested strenuously about the bulk. "I was planning on traveling light," he laughed. "Write down who these go to, will you?"

He called several months later after he returned, and we met for lunch. On the way to the restaurant, Warren said, "Rebecca, one of the people on your list, Thubten Sangye, died the month before I got there. I gave the book to Tashi Tsering and told him to keep it in the library."

I have often wondered, while standing in my black suit before a sea of future lawyers, what Thubten Sangye would think of me now. He would watch me do the ritual verbal dance of an American law professor and notice my erect body posture, my authoritative gestures, and the way I walk back and forth in front of the chalkboard. It seems certain that he would be surprised at the big, bright room and the number and gender of the students, but he would probably not comment on these things.

The lessons of Thubten Sangye present a puzzle. From the perspective of comparative law, the Tibetans had a secular state system with hierarchically arranged courts administered by judges and clerks. They used logical analysis, followed procedures, recorded decisions in documents, and used long-established law codes. On the other hand, their legal system was so thoroughly Buddhist that none of the typical maxims any American law professor—indeed, any comparativist—would apply to a bureaucratic legal system apply to Tibet. This is the conundrum that confronts me when I look at the picture of Thubten Sangye which hangs above my desk. I am left, after considering the Tibetan legal system, with several different kinds of questions and a range of implications about legal systems in general.

(1) Buddhism has both radical particularity and cosmological integration as the basis of its world-view. This means that the Tibetan legal system treated individuals both as entirely unique—not comparable to one another—and as entirely integrated, part of the same cosmic system. Tibetans used dichotomies and dialectical argumentation, along with mysticism and many other techniques, as tools to deal with a system of radical particular integration. But their different starting point brings into question the use of Western dualistic analysis and models for analyzing legal systems such as Tibet's and perhaps other legal systems as well. Omnipresent dualisms—good/bad, nature/culture, primitive/modern, religious/secular, right/left, scholastic/scientific, faith/reason, public/private—permeate the investigation, modeling, and presentation of Western material on legal systems. If most of our conceptual tools are based in a dualistic form of thinking, from logic to symbolic analysis, from categorization to normative evaluation, we will move first to separate and categorize, and then to label as good or bad.

My questions, then: How are we to analyze a system that has radical particularity, does not prioritize dualistic thinking, and uses several different types of reasoning at the same time? What happens if we do not make the dualistic move of separating off other societies in terms of complexity and modernity?

(2) Tibetans believed that their legal system was permeated with the moral requirements of the Buddha and that the self-regulation of each individual's mind was the key to all social systems. This is a radically particular view. Although it created difficulties in the effort to adduce internal motivations and mental states from external behavior (a problem recognized by many legal systems, including our own), still they remained certain of the location and source of morality. The Buddha was an immutable standard of right behavior, the source of legitimation. Hundreds of tales of his decisions in untoward circumstances formed an image for Tibetans of the

absolutely correct moral actor. A social system was good to the extent that the actors within the system were examining themselves with respect to this standard, reflecting on their own motivations, thinking of present and future lives, and working to reduce their mental afflictions. Punishment was meant to promote a return to inner morality.

Such an analysis of morality raises some fundamental questions about the location of morality and the separation of law and morality in both Western and East Asian jurisprudence. Is our analysis of law and its relationship to morality only more dualistic thinking? What happens when members of a social system are not operating on inner morality and need only fulfill external behavioral requirements? Is *mens rea,* guilty intent, similar to inner morality? Are the eternal standards of the Buddha similar to other universally applied sets of moral norms? What does all this mean for legal socialization within societies?

(3) From the Tibetan example it is apparent that some legal systems and decision-making processes result in *neither* general rule formation and application *nor* the regular use of case precedent. They are particularistic (if one can avoid the negative connotation of that word). The importance of legal recording and remembering, of legal replicating and reproducing in a society has to do with understandings of the nature of law, of procedure, of concepts of time, personhood, and conflict. In Tibet, procedure and predictability meant factoring, and factoring did not require following or forming rules, using or setting precedent. Since the Buddha's life and path provided a constant immutable standard, the universal application of a rule to demonstrate legitimacy was unnecessary.

Or would we just call the stories and standards of the Buddha "rules"? If we analyzed legal systems as non-rule-forming and lacking in precedent, would they look any different? What does this say about our idea of equality? How does Tibet affect our theoretical and comparative models of law systems?

(4) Tibetans followed not rules but factors in the law; they used sets of factors related to each circumstance to determine the unique situation of the individual involved. The law codes are filled with factors to be considered in a variety of circumstances, together with hortatory admonitions, precatory advice, and ancient sayings. The Tibetan understanding of legal factoring is related to Buddhist logic, rationality, and reasoning. The purpose of logic in Buddhism is to transcend the individual perspective and, through study and debate, to understand the tenets of the Buddha's path. Reasoning leads to an enlightened view, and an enlightened view is compassionate toward all sentient beings. In short, faith and reason, logic and compassion are all integrated. Logic and rationality within such a system do not mean rule formation, the use of precedent, the logic of consequence or of antecedence.

Perhaps, though, the operation of this system of legal logic isn't really so different from ours. Is the use of precedents a process of rationalization? Is logic another way of saying "the way we think about things"?

(5) For many, the most interesting and unusual aspect of the Tibetan system is its lack of finality and closure. Cases could be reopened right after they were decided,

even when the parties had both agreed to the judge or conciliator's decision. Tibetans considered this one of the best aspects of their system: they were free to disagree until they felt that the dispute had been correctly decided. Judicial decisions had no finality in the way we understand finality; calming the mind and reaching real harmony were necessary before a dispute could actually be over. In Buddhism, this continuing freedom to disagree is part of the infinite potential of the mind to change and choose. At law, it resulted in the nonexclusiveness of forums, a lack of closure of cases, and also a great flexibility in choosing the kind and level of forum and the type of legal procedure to be followed.

For many American lawyers, such a system seems incomprehensible. But is it really? Do our concepts of closure correlate with the reality of our system? To what extent are our doctrines of closure—*stare decisis* and *res judicata*—related to other ideas about stability and predictability in society?

(6) According to Western legal philosophy, the state's ability to punish is one of the most important attributes of a bureaucratic legal system. The Tibetan legal structure had too few government bureaucrats and police to operate in that way on the Plateau. Local sanctions such as ostracism, shaming, loss of prestige due to fighting, loss of religious merit, loss of social prestige, financial loss, and the discomfort of delay were undoubtedly more important than official sentencing. A state bureaucracy without significant ability to punish is a conundrum in our terms, but the Tibetan example proffers universal procedure and local sanction as a large part of the political glue binding a country together, rather than the state's sanctioning power.

Consensus too took a form different from the consensus-building of Japan or majoritarian consent in America. In Tibet, it meant that individuals must actually consent, even in some criminal cases, to every part of the process—from the choice of forum, authority, and procedure to the decision and the penalties imposed. Without consent, the legal process did not function. This is radically particular consent. The consent of each individual to every part of each case comprised the consent of the society. In America we label such a system normatively as weak and see its government as incapable of enforcing the law. Buddhists saw it as the only solution within their religion and the only way to ensure real consent and personal freedom.

We presume that allowing consent in every part of a legal system would cause the system to fail. Why is that? Don't we also have universal procedure and weak judicial enforcement in several parts of *our* system?

(7) The nature of the relationship between religion and law in Tibet appears to have been much more complex than the simple religious/secular split we employ in the West. All laws in Tibet were understood as religious, but there were two types: religious law for religious practitioners, and religious law for laypersons. There were also, in a sense, two types of secular law in that law for religious institutions passed through the ecclesiastical side of the government, and law for laypersons was administered by the district courts and the Cabinet. But religion permeated the secular legal system in the form of Buddhist standards, logic, factoring, jurisprudential concepts, and reality shifts that moved an argument into otherworldly reasoning. In the West, the religious perspective is often characterized as dogmatic and destructive

of the democratic conversation. In the Tibetan refugee community today, Tibetans are not interested in democracy without a charismatic religious figure to guide them.

Why dichotomize religious law and secular law? Why do some scholars presume that religion stops the conversation?

(8) Fairness in Tibet meant using Buddhist moral tenets and logic, legal factoring, and the law codes to investigate every aspect that was presented in a case. The judge or conciliator then fashioned a suitable solution that had to be agreed to by all parties. Factoring each situation uniquely was regarded as logical, compassionate, fair, and legitimated by the law codes. Truth, a multivalent term in Tibet, was first the consensus of two parties to a similar view of what happened, not the sparks from clashing sides. Truth was also the ideal and separate standard of the Buddha. Another notion of truth—well-experienced, honest judges conducting cases with proper formal procedural steps resulting in decisions agreeable to the parties—was closer to American ideas of justice and due process. A final understanding of truth, internal truth and morality, we would perhaps label personal honesty.

Some of these notions of fairness and honesty in Tibet seem to have been directly related to procedure. To what degree is this true of other systems? How is fairness connected to religion? Or does "fairness" in most societies just mean "doing what is expected"?

Final Thoughts on the Cosmology of Law

As a way of understanding these various issues, I have suggested viewing Tibetan law through the interpretive framework of a kaleidoscopic cosmology. This is a fundamentally different starting point for an analysis of law, one that decenters and destabilizes as it coheres and integrates. Derived from the rich source of Buddhist philosophy, Tibetan legal cosmology is based in assumptions about the world as simultaneously both wholly interconnected and completely particular. Everything is in a constant state of flux, impermanence, and cyclical regeneration.

The framework of cosmology is a larger claim than that of legal culture or legal system. In the Tibetan case, legal concepts and practices are not independent units operating in a separate, autonomous unit designated as "the legal system." Neither are they the particular province of a professionalized group, nor a specific set of rules and forums. Instead, they are understood to be entirely connected to and derived from the Tibetan Buddhist world view of the integrated All-One mandala. The framework of legal cosmology is therefore entirely connected to its cultural base, to the interpenetration of culture with law and the embeddedness of law in culture.

Narratives have been the road to unfolding the legal cosmology of the Tibetans. They are the primary presentation form in the book because Tibetans spoke about law in the form of stories with exegeses. But we can hear stories only when we already know the range of possible meanings, the correct formats, and their possible interpretive contexts. Stories can "say something" to us only when we already know what is going on and what we might expect to hear. Rather than oppositional tools to surprise and arrest the reader, narratives here speak in the voice and tone of a

Tibetan, evoke the mundanity of daily life in Tibet. From verbatim cases to detailed descriptions and autobiographies, from local hail protection rituals to hearings in the central bureaucracy, each narrative is layered on the last, reconstituted by the next.

This presentation of the Golden Yoke of Tibet will, I hope, be followed by other versions to contest and deepen our insights into this rich treasurehouse of material, this "bountiful ocean" of Tibetan legal cosmology. Studying with Kungola Thubten Sangye and sharing this material have brought me full circle to think more deeply about our own unacknowledged assumptions and the possibly contingent nature of what we assume to be essential in *our* cosmology of law.

Notes

Introduction

1. Sonam is not the real name of the monk. Few real names are used in this text.

2. GP:816–23.

3. A *khel*—pronounced "kay" in many areas—is a measurement equivalent to approximately 30 pounds, according to several Tibetans I spoke with. One author, however, has claimed that it is equivalent to 271 pounds (Norbu 1974).

4. Michael Herzfeld (1992) does a wonderful job of explaining the problems and purposes of using the term "Western."

5. For Thubten Sangye's partial life history, see Chapter 25. "Kungola" is a title of respect (much like "sir"): *ku* is an honorific prefix; *la* is an honorific suffix; *ngo* means "face" or "presence."

6. I spent five months in India and Nepal in 1981 and returned to the United States to do more studying and some interviewing. Between September 1983 and November 1986 I was in Nepal, India, and Tibet except for two breaks: one to study classical Tibetan literature with Geshe Sopa in Madison, Wisconsin, for a short time, and four months in Oxford and London looking at early twentieth-century documents on Tibet. Between 1987 and 1994 I also interviewed Tibetans in the United States.

7. Weber 1958:289. Tibetans, perhaps more than any other culture, have been subjects of Edward Said's orientalism, rendered exotic and totally "Other" ("Land of Snows," Shangri-la) and therefore irrelevant. See Said 1978; Asad 1973, 1986; Fabian 1983. Recently, Tibetan scholars such as Don Lopez (1994) have begun to question and write about the dynamics of orientalism operating in Tibetan studies.

8. Berger 1967.

9. Goldstein 1989; Hoffmann 1975.

10. Petech 1973.

11. Shakabpa 1967; Walt van Praag 1987.

12. Snellgrove and Richardson 1980; Stein 1972.

13. Goldstein 1973.

14. Norbu 1974.

15. Gombo 1978.

16. Rahul 1969.

17. See, e.g., Grunfeld 1987.

18. Davis 1975, 1987; Ginzburg 1980, 1983, 1991; Ladurie 1979.

19. Haley 1985; see also Bodde and Morris 1967. The literature in this area is immense. See the work of William Alford, David Buxbaum, Jerome Cohen, James Feinerman, Dan F. Henderson, Philip A. Kuhn, Joseph Needham, R. P. Peerenboom, Benjamin I. Schwartz, Hugh Scogin, Helen Siu, and Karen Turner.

20. Ch'en 1979:84–85; cf. Johnson 1979.

21. Friedman (1970) has stated that looking at legal culture allows one to see "those values and attitudes in society which determine what structures are used and why; which rules work and which do not and why." The term is most commonly used in the literature, however, to describe what it is that lawyers, judges, and petitioners do and think. Here the problem is that even when you know *what* these actors do, you still don't know much about *how* or *why* they do it or *where* their ideas come from.

In recent years, the term "culture" has become a suspect category for anthropologists; see Clifford 1986, 1988. It is used in this book as a shorthand term for the range of possible contestable practices and actions that make up what Tibetans understand to be their collective world (Geertz 1966).

22. Legal anthropologists have addressed this aspect of the larger frame of legal issues with various terms: "invisible realities" (Malinowski 1959 [1926]); "the wider conceptual framework" (Collier 1973); "the coherent cultural assumptions manifest in the judicial domain" (Moore 1986); "intersubjective assumptions" (Rosen 1989); "conceptions of order" (Greenhouse 1986); "legal consciousness" (Merry 1990; Starr 1992); "cultural logic" (Comaroff and Roberts 1981); "cultural paradigms" (Conley and O'Barr 1990); "clusters of ideology" (Nader 1990); and "the moral and legal frameworks that emerge from particular narratives of trouble" (Yngvesson 1993).

23. See Luhmann 1985; Teubner 1988, 1993.

24. Comaroff and Comaroff 1992.

Chapter 1

1. The Sino-Tibetan family of languages had its origin in the desert region of the Huang Ho River more than 5,000 years ago. Its three major branches are the Sinitic languages, Burmese, and the Bodic languages spoken in southern China, Tibet, the Himalayas, Burma, Bangladesh, and Assam. Tibetan, a Bodic language, is monosyllabic; it has five vowels, twenty-six consonants, an ablaut verb system, tones, and a subject-object-verb word order; it is highly contextual and metaphorical; and it includes three levels of honorific vocabulary used according to the person being addressed—all characteristics of Sino-Tibetan languages in general.

2. Formal kinship terminology in the southern region distinguishes between patrilateral and matrilateral at the second ascending generation, is bifurcate collateral at the first ascending generation, and shows a typical Hawaiian generational pattern at ego's generation level. In practice, this results in a strong bias toward distinguishing between a person's matrilateral and patrilateral kin for the purposes of inheritance by ego from the first or second ascending

generation. Concomitantly, at ego's generational level, there is only a distinction by sex; in American terminology, this means using the terms "brother" and "sister" for all relatives in one's generational level, including cousins. Interviews with Tibetans indicated that their ego generation terminology was conducive to the easy unity of fluid polyandrous and polygynous households and that terminological use varied greatly by region. For more on marriage patterns and contracts, see the excursus following this chapter.

3. Traditionally, training was available in the five major disciplines (science of the mind, medicine, art, logic, and metaphysics) and the five minor disciplines (poetry, prosody, drama, astronomy, and prose writing).

4. Beckwith 1977:89.

5. The best account of the process of incarnation is from the memoirs of the Fourteenth Dalai Lama himself: "But in the year of the Water Bird, that is, in 1933, Thubten Gyatso departed from this world and as the news spread through Tibet, the people were desolate. . . . With the passing of the Thirteenth Dalai Lama, the search began at once for his reincarnation, for each Dalai Lama is a reincarnation of his predecessor [while] the first was an incarnation of Chenresi, the Buddha of Mercy.

"First, the Regent had to be appointed by the National Assembly to govern the country until the new reincarnation could be found and grow to maturity. Then in accordance with the time-honored customs and traditions, the state oracles and learned lamas were consulted as a first step towards finding out where the reincarnation had appeared. Curious cloud formations were seen in the northeast from Lhasa. It was recalled that after the Dalai Lama died, his body was placed seated on a throne [and] the face had turned towards the east. And on a wooden pillar on the northeastern side of the shrine where his body sat, a great star-shaped fungus suddenly appeared.

"Next, in 1935, the Tibetan Wood Pig Year, the Regent went to the sacred lake of Lhamoi Latso in Chokhorgyal about ninety miles southeast of Lhasa. The people of Tibet believe that visions of the future can be seen in the waters of this lake. Several days were spent in prayer and meditation and then the Regent saw the vision of three Tibetan letters—Ah, Ka and Ma—followed by a picture of a monastery with roofs of jade green and gold and a house with turquoise tiles. A detailed description of these visions was written down and kept a strict secret. In the following year, high lamas and dignitaries carrying the secrets of the visions were sent out to all parts of Tibet to search for the place which the Regent had seen in the waters. [One party of the several sent out traveled to a village in the east called Takster and found a monastery and house of this description, the names of which began with the foregoing letters.]

"Their leader asked if the family living in the house had any children and was told that they had a boy who was nearly two years old. [The members of the party, including the head monk of Sera monastery, went into the house disguised as traders.] There they found the baby of the family and the moment the little boy saw the lama, he went to him and wanted to sit in his lap. The lama was disguised in a cloak which was lined with lambskin but round his neck he was wearing a rosary which had belonged to the Thirteenth Dalai Lama. The little boy seemed to recognize the rosary and he asked to be given it. The lama promised to give it to him if he could guess who he was and the boy replied that he was Sera-aga, which meant in the local dialect, "a lama of Sera." The lama asked who the "Master" [of the party] was and the boy gave the name Losang. He also knew the name of the real servant, which was Amdo Kesang. . . . All the party stayed in the house for the night and early next morning when they were making ready to leave, the boy got out of his bed and insisted that he wanted to go with them. I was that boy" (Dalai Lama 1962).

Following this initial trip, a large party of dignitaries was sent to the small peasant house in

Takster, and the boy was presented with many objects and their exact duplicates to determine whether he could recognize the previous possessions of the Dalai Lama. He passed this and several other tests. Two years later, after other signs, lamas, and oracles had been consulted, official permission was granted to bring the young boy to Lhasa. Once installed there, the new Dalai Lama was given monastic training to the level of *geshe* before he assumed full political powers at his majority.

6. Snellgrove and Richardson 1980:170, 182.

Chapter 2

1. There appear to be at least four separate parts to the code, some added much later than the time of the original king. The information in the text on the early law codes is primarily abstracted from an article by the late Geza Uray (1972). I was also fortunate to see a translation of a portion of this early code by Terry Ellington (1984) of the University of Washington.

2. Self-aggrandizing introductions became a standard for the later codes; appropriate words of Buddhist prostration and several paragraphs giving some history and the name of a "humble compiler" were included as well. This earliest code retains the simple format of a statement that the king did these acts.

3. Uray 1972.

4. Several Tibetans claimed that the sixteen moral principles were actually written during the fourteenth century, however. See also French 1987, 1995; Richardson 1989, 1990.

5. Tucci 1949.

6. Cassinelli and Ekvall 1969.

7. Michael 1982; Uray 1972; Snellgrove and Richardson 1980; Tucci 1949.

8. It is even questionable whether Changchub Gyalsen actually wrote a new law code. The codes usually cited as his appear to date not from his reign but from that of the fourth, fifth, or sixth king of the Phamogru dynasty, although they may have been based on one written during the time of this first Phamogru king. In any case, the first hundred-year dynasty of the Three Kingdoms period was an active time for innovation in legal drafting and compilation.

9. Several versions of this text are available. In particular, this passage refers to *zin bris kyi bod rgyal sne'i gdong pa'i khrims yig zhal bce bco lnga pa* (n.d.); see also *Tibetan Legal Materials* 1985:15–35.

10. Following the style of the early codes, these attributes are arranged in numerical sets such as the "Five Types of Speech": (1) "black-eyed speech"; (2) "evil speech," which comes in eight forms; (3) "glorious speech," which comes in twenty-five forms; (4) "sharp-response speech"; and (5) "high victorious speech," including "the four great causes," "the four great symbols," and "the four great qualities" that distinguish an excellent party to a suit (ND:17–51). These passages have a pleasing lyrical rhythm and straightforwardness. Although the style of writing is at times elliptical, at times discursive, there is much to be learned about the social customs and legal practices of Tibet in the fourteenth century from these enumerations and proverbs.

11. ND:34–51.

12. E.g., the murder section (ND:108–98 and Br:1–11) gives a history of the law of murder; the social classes that distinguish the victim compensation payments (these categories were already present in the Empire period); exceptions in the case of the killing of a woman or killing by a child; murder during a theft; murder by mob or multiple persons; attempted murder; payments in land instead of money or goods; mitigation in payments; merit payments for the purification of the dead body; payments in the case of cremation and for

religious ceremonies; numerous categories of allowances to be paid to all the relatives; reductions resulting from payment; and the form the payments can take.

13. E.g., one version of the Tsang code states that the king appointed a compiler (referred to in rather humble terms as "the donkey with a leopard skin on its back") because there was no legal system in central Tibet, and each region had its own rules. This scholar collected many ancient law books, legal texts kept by a lama, and oral statements of law from an old man (or men); he observed the laws of the different regions of Tibet, Hor, Mongolia, Bhutan, and Monpa and received the word of the Tsang kings on law. From these multifarious sources, the compiler then assembled, compared, and categorized the legal rules into sixteen sections.

14. Although the actual rules elucidated in this compilation most likely predate the time of King Karma Tenkyong Wangpo, this cannot at present be proved.

15. The four optional sections are (1) the "Brave Tiger" and "Fearful Fox" (on military administration); (2) "Rules for Officers"; (3) "Barbarians on the Border"; and (4) "The Other Side of the Pass."

Chapter 3

1. See the excursus following this chapter.

2. In Tibetan, *chusi neden (chos srid gnyis ldan)* or *chusi netrel (chos srid gnyis 'brel)*.

3. There are two types of extant Dalai Lama law codes. One states that it was written by a local governor under the guidance of the first regent, Sonam Choephel, and the Mongolian benefactor of the Fifth, Gushri Khan (who was called in the codes by his Tibetan name, Tenzin Chogyal); the other was written only a few years later by the fifth regent, who is also credited with a work titled "Twenty-One Rules for the Government Officer" (see French 1995).

4. Tucci (1949:37) states: "The Phagmogru's [Neudong] code prevailed and, after being revised by the Fifth Dalai Lama and the *sde srid, sangs rgyas rgya mtsho,* is still used in Tibet." Some other scholars have followed his lead; however, the Tsang—not the Neudong—code is the real template.

5. The Thirteenth Dalai Lama did have an Army Code of Rules written in the early 1920s.

6. *Ganden (dga' ldan),* literally "joyful, blissful," is used to name several things. Among these are a paradise in the Buddhist cosmos, and one of the three great Gelukpa sect monasteries in the Lhasa Valley, founded by the reformer Tsongkhapa. In the phrase Ganden Podrang ("palace or castle of Ganden"), it is also the name of the government of Tibet under the Dalai Lamas.

7. All these topics and many others are contained in the code. It is not merely a criminal code, though its criminal sections are substantial. Although it is divided neatly into sections titled by subject, it is not a tightly organized document. In some parts, whole paragraphs are lifted intact from the Tsang code and inserted into the body of the text, though they may not be in sequence. As an important compilation of the legal rules, customary practices, and administrative requirements, it influenced the entire Himalayan region for several centuries.

8. For a chart of the various ranks and the positions associated with them in the Tibetan government, see Goldstein 1989:13.

9. For an explanation of Tibetan "estates," see the excursus following Chapter 9.

10. Chapters 17 and 18 discuss the legal processes on a small and a large estate of the nobility.

11. Frazer describes this period in Lhasa at length in *The Golden Bough* (1922:662–65),

treating one of the final ceremonies as an example of the periodic expulsion of evils in the material vehicle of a scapegoat.

12. See French 1990b, reviewing Walt van Praag 1987.

13. Goldstein (1989:815–16) has argued that "the monasteries worked in the government to prevent modernization," and were "ultimately responsible for its military backwardness" in the face of Chinese invasion. He also faults the constant infighting of the nobility for the "demise of the Lamaist state."

14. For the numerous versions of these events from many different vantage points, see, e.g., Avedon 1984; Goldstein 1989; Norbu 1986; Walt van Praag 1987.

15. See International Commission of Jurists 1959.

16. On the current situation of Tibetan refugees and the Tibetan government-in-exile, see French 1991; for more concise ethnographic material, see French 1990a and 1994.

17. For a discussion of this distinction, see Shain 1991.

18. Personal communication; see also Dhondup 1994.

19. For an excellent review of the ideas and literature on diasporas in general, see Clifford 1994.

Introduction to Part Two

1. See Tambiah 1970:35.

2. With multiple coexisting temporal patterns rather than rigid linear time as in the West, the sequencing of facts is often less important in Tibetan trials, and a larger range of facts uncoupled from their temporal markers can be introduced.

3. "The cosmos," says David Holmberg (1989:114), "never resolves into a final totalizing image, for each practitioner approaches it from a distinct position, focuses on certain members of the pantheon and establishes particular relations between humans."

4. Legal anthropologists have noted that this can take the form of a "normative repertoire" presented in "paradigms of argument" (Comaroff and Roberts 1981), "clusters of ideology" relating to norms (Nader 1990), or even a discussion of the normative nature of engaging in conflict at all (Greenhouse 1986).

5. See Rosen 1984.

6. The use of the "reasonable man" as a legal universal has been argued heatedly by legal anthropologists Paul Bohannan (1957) and Max Gluckman (1973).

7. The language and discourse of disputing, an important part of legal ethnography (see Brenneis 1988; Conley and O'Barr 1990) is presented only briefly in Part Two. Parts Three, Four, and Five have extensive verbatim examples of legal language.

8. The jurisprudence of truth, presented in Chapter 12, concerns the set of concepts that an individual member of the culture uses in thinking about things legal. One aspect of this is "legal consciousness," the "consciousness that law can provide appropriate aid for the difficulty at hand" (Merry 1990:37); another is "the intersubjective assumptions" (Rosen 1989) through which a person reasons out a legal issue.

Chapter 4

1. The Sanskrit term is *parikalpita*.

2. The Sanskrit is *paritantra*.

3. The Sanskrit is *parinispanna*.

4. Geertz 1973:119–20.

5. For a more extended discussion of karma and crime, see Chapter 24.

6. Bodhisattvas are individuals on the path to enlightenment who are committed to the altruistic aspiration of full enlightenment for all sentient beings.

7. In their fundamental constructions, these ideas are quite similar to new theories of fuzzy logic and of mental consciousness, which reject bivalence or dualism as a fundamental principle. Fuzzy logic, a new kind of mathematical logic, starts from the premise that most categories are mental constructions and per se indeterminate, uncertain. Distinctive binary contrasts don't exist; understanding is positional; category boundaries are fuzzy (see Kosko 1993). John Searle (1992) begins the task of redefining the consciousness of the mind by rejecting conceptual mind/body dualism and focusing on positionality within a "background" of capacities and circumstances. These and other recent works resonate with the Tibetan understanding of reality and the mind. See also Lakoff 1973.

Chapter 5

1. In Tibetan, these six realms—which correspond to the six types of rebirth—are called respectively *lha (lha), lama yin (lha ma yin), me (mi), tundo (dud 'gro), yidak (yi dwags),* and *nelwapa (dmyal ba pa).*

2. For other anthropological considerations of time, see Fabian 1983; Geertz 1966; and an excellent recent work, Hoskins 1993.

3. For an example of such a hiatus, see the Case of the Smelly Toilet in Chapter 22.

4. Carol Greenhouse (1986) has written about the negative conceptualization of conflict which, in one group of Southern Baptists, led to an inability to engage in legal conflict.

Chapter 6

1. Other Tibetan words used to indicate this complex are *lo (blo),* mind-cognition; *yi (yid),* mind-consciousness; *nying (snying),* mind-compassion; *sampa (bsam pa),* mind-thinking; and *shay (shes),* mind-wisdom.

2. Ts:336.

3. GP:278, 294, 799, 800, 801, 1294.

4. Rosen (1984:47–56) has a very interesting discussion of intention in a Muslim community. See also Rosen 1985, and several essays in Lopez 1988 on the concept of intention in Buddhism, which parallel the ideas presented here.

5. GP:911–17. For a discussion of women and children with respect to this issue, see Chapter 14.

6. See Asad 1993.

7. See Comaroff and Roberts 1981.

8. Br:337–39.

9. Br:340–54; see also Chapter 11.

10. Benpa Topgyal related these sixteen to me in 1993. Each of the many versions I collected in Tibetan in Nepal, India, and Tibet had different numbering and some differences in substantive content. See also Michael 1982.

Chapter 7

1. The Tibetan for "do not kill" is *shay sogcho pong way tim chéso (shes srog gcod spong ba'i khrims bcas so);* see LS:2–3.

There is an enormous amount of material on myths as they relate to various fields—comparative religion, classics, biblical studies, anthropology, folklore, psychology—but very little on myths in the field of law. See generally Doty 1986; Dundes 1984; Eliade 1960, 1963. In law, see Engel 1993; Fitzpatrick 1992.

2. Doty 1986:11.

3. This discussion of myth elides the distinctions between types of myths and also between myth, legend, and folktale. See, among others, Dundes 1984.

4. The viewpoint here is that there *is* myth in the modern world but that our myths posit law as nonmythic. Lasch (1978), following Nietzsche, has argued that in the modern world religion and myth have given way to law and finally social therapy, that legitimation is no longer through mythic authority but through submission to the reality of facts. The process Eliade (1963:111) calls "demythicization"—a myth being "emptied of religious meaning and becom[ing] a legend or a nursery tale"—is not part of the Tibetan point of view and, arguably, not of ours either.

5. The Tibetan terms are *logu (lo rgyus)*, royal accounts and military narratives; *gyalrab (rgyal rabs)*, genealogies of kings, clans, incarnations; *chojung (chos 'byung)*, origins of religious schools; *namthar (rnam thar)*, biographies of saints; *dalok ('das log)*, stories of the return of the dead; *dungtam (sgrung gtam)*, legends; *shay (bshad)*, "explanations"; *mang (smrang)*, "expositions"; and *pay (dpe)*, archetypes in a ritual exorcism. This list does not include stories about gods and several other categories. The literature in this area is vast; see Haarh 1969; Karmey 1975; Stein 1971; Tucci 1949.

6. Stone (1979) has defined narratives as "the organization of material in a chronologically sequential order and the focusing of the content into a single coherent style." An emphasis on narrative has returned, Stone argues, because of a disillusionment with materialism and economic models of explanation, the rise of the importance of the notion of culture, the decline of intellectual commitment among Western intellectuals, and the continuing indeterminancy that has resulted in a poor record for the quantification theorists. He goes on to outline the problems of such a narrative approach in history: for example, the difficulty of distinguishing the normal from the eccentric, and the question of interpretation.

7. As such, narrative is a key technique for feminist and critical race theorists. See, e.g., the Rodrigo Chronicles of Richard Delgado, discussing law and economics (1993a) and love and laissez-faire economics (1993b).

8. See Bennett and Feldman 1981; Jackson 1988; Mumby 1993.

9. Comaroff and Roberts 1981; Rosen 1984.

10. For some recent examples by legal anthropologists, see Merry 1990; Yngvesson 1993.

11. I heard parts of this myth in Nepal (see also Karmey 1975). Note that it encodes two typical aspects of Tibetan law: inheritance by the female of a lesser share, and playing dice.

12. *Tsugla khang (gtsug lag khang)* is the general term for a temple or hall of worship in a large monastery. It is used in reference both to the chief temple of Lhasa, the Jokhang, and to the entire complex of buildings surrounding it—a complex that other authors have called the Cathedral of Lhasa, the Central Temple, and the Cathedral Complex, among other names. I use the terms *tsugla khang* and "Cathedral Complex" interchangeably to mean the collection of buildings surrounding the Jokhang, inside the middle walkway.

13. It is reasonable to assume that government offices took their respective places within this outer building sometime during the eighteenth century, perhaps before or during the reign of the Seventh Dalai Lama, because the Fifth's written "Guide to the Jokhang" does not include a discussion of offices at the cardinal points, and the myth credits the Seventh with this plan.

14. The *tsikhang lékung (rtsis khang las khungs)*.

15. The *lachak dzokhang (bla phyag mdzod khang)*.

16. The *sherkhang (gsher khang)*.

17. The quadratic orientation around a central deity is also corroborated by the location of the respective offices according to Zasak Taring (1980 and personal communication), who was a Tibetan official in the first part of the century.

18. In 1985 the monk caretaker of the *tsugla khang* repeated the mythic story to me and was able to point out each of these rooms within the outer building, though most of them were either shut or being used as dormitories for monks.

19. Retchung n.d. (my translation).

20. LS:5–6. The Tibetan is *shaypa dzun pangné denpar maway tim chéso (shes pas rdzun spangs nas bden par smra ba'i khrims bcas so)*.

21. LS:7–8. The Tibetan is *shaypa thama panté mi dzawa dumpay tim chéso (shes pas phra ma spangs te mi mdza' ba bsdum pa'i khrims bcas so)*. For the rest of these mythic legal stories see the excursus following this chapter.

Chapter 8

1. Frake 1969.

2. Michel Foucault (1976, 1980) outlines the ways in which social discourses constitute social practices. Many of the discourses he describes are related to professionalized realms.

3. Louis Althusser (1971) and Fredric Jameson (1981) are just two of the scholars who have stimulated interest in this aspect of discourse.

4. Br:337–39.

5. The use of these terms is not restricted to the "judge" when he is "in court"; if one went to see a judge outside of court about a case, he was still referred to as a "judge." A Tibetan calls this going to see the "judge at home."

6. For copious renditions of political proverbs and songs used during the first half of the twentieth century, see Goldstein 1982, 1989.

7. For a more extensive review of this topic, see French 1995.

8. See also Cabezón 1994; Perdue 1992; Sierksma 1964.

9. The best two works on this aspect of Tibetan culture are Beyer 1978; Nebesky-Wojkowitz 1975.

10. See Malinowski 1954, 1965; Tambiah 1985, 1990.

11. For a neutralized, philosophical, and nonmagical description of this process, see esp. Austin 1962 and Searle 1969.

Chapter 9

1. This word in several permutations occurs very commonly in the law codes.

2. See Chapter 8 for some concepts of magical power and law.

3. In the sense of physical strength, this term was applied to the fighting monks called *thutob (mthu stobs)*, who often tried to enforce the law through their own physical prowess; see the Case of the Smelly Toilet in Chapter 22.

4. See esp. Deleuze and Guattari 1977; Foucault 1976, 1979, 1980.

5. Scholars throughout the history of social science have identified various aspects of power. Austin Turk (1976) outlined five basic types—physical, political, ideological, economic, and diversionary (or power to influence), to which Lazarus-Black (1994) has added "familiary" (citing Bourdieu 1977) and discretionary (citing Comaroff and Roberts 1981).

6. Religious, mystical, spiritual power and its relation to other types constitute an area of research that is much neglected in studies of Tibet; see Beyer 1978.

7. Anthony Giddens (1979, 1993) has stressed a duality of power conceptualized as the capability of an agent and a property of the collectivity as evidenced in social institutions.

8. These ideas were originally presented in Felstiner et al. 1981.

9. When I ask this question, I am referring particularly to the work of Raymond Williams and of John and Jean Comaroff (1992) in positing the hegemonic as what a member of a society takes for granted as true and how this is reflected in that person's ideology or articulated system of meaning abstracted from his or her world view. This view of power is very useful for a study of Tibet. Explicating Tibet within this framework would require first knowing fully the legal cosmology (this book begins this project) and then investigating how hegemonic power worked. Melvyn Goldstein has begun this second task in his enormous work on Tibet's demise (1989).

10. Not addressed here are myriad other Tibetan understandings of power, such as Buddhist virtue, charisma, mystical force, black magic, humility, purity of essence, the power of the mind, power places such as pilgrimage spots, and physical presence.

11. This pattern follows the Indian model of the *chakras* of the body.

12. These are the upper and lower levels of the nobility described to me repeatedly by Tibetans. Petech (1973:19) lists three classes of aristocrats, *yab gzhis, sde dpon,* and *sku drag.* Goldstein (1989:6) states that there was "a small group of about 30 higher status families" called *mda dpon mi drag* and "120 to 170 lower or 'common' aristocratic families."

13. In Tibetan, there are various words for ownership. In general, an owner is a *dagpo (bdag po);* a property owner can be referred to as an "owner of property," a "landholder," or even a "householder." Property for which there was an owner was referred to as "held by an owner," *dagzung (bdag bzung).* A peasant who held his land directly from the government was called a "government landholder." Landholding peasants whose land was covered by an intermediate title (see the Excursus following this chapter) were referred to as "peasants on an estate," with the further refinement of "peasants on a monastic estate" and "peasants on a private estate." Holders of intermediate titles were referred to simply as "government officers" or "estate owners," *shika dagpo (gzhis ka'i bdag po),* or by some term of honorific address such as "gentleman" or "honorable sir."

Everyone was a "subject of the government," *ngasab (mnga' zhabs)* or *ngabang (mnga' 'bangs),* often synonymous with the general term for a taxpayer, *tel tokan (khral sprod mkhan).* A person who labored in the fields for a living and resided in an agricultural village but did not own land or pay taxes was referred to as a "little smoke"; those who paid taxes to the government were referred to by their status or occupations (see French 1990a for more Tibetan terminology).

14. *Labrang* were the corporate holdings, real property, and other assets of incarnate lamas.

15. Ellington 1984.

16. The codes state that placement in these categories was based on criteria in this order: family lineage; birth; rank; occupation; financial power; government office; and stigmatized (outcaste) attribute.

17. See the Excursus following this chapter.

18. The difference between direct-access and referral courts is detailed in Chapter 13.

19. There may have been additional jurisdictional bases for foreigners (one might expect the Chinese citizens in Lhasa, for example, to have had special access to the Amban, their representative there), but no others came to light in my interviews.

20. See the Excursus following Chapter 23.

21. This entire area of legal disputes inside and between Tibetan religious institutions is a fruitful area for further research.

1. A conciliation or *bardum*—also called *nangdum (nang 'dum)*—was defined as (1) a compromise by the mutual concession of the parties, *bardum chépa (bar 'dum byed pa)*, (2) arranged by a conciliator, *barmi* or *bardum pa* or *bardum dong ken (bar 'dum gtong mkhan)*, (3) who helped the parties come to an agreement, *pentsun thunpa (phan tshun mthun pa)* or *tsopa dumdik chépa (rtsod pa 'dum 'grig byed pa)*, (4) in a place of conciliation, *dumsa ('dum sa)*, (5) often resulting in a conciliation agreement document, *dumyik* or *baryik (bar yig)* or *dumtha ('dum khra)*, (6) which was, like its judicial counterpart, signed by the conciliator and both parties to the dispute. (Examples of these proceedings are detailed in Part Three.)

2. ND:267–71.

3. ND:278–79.

4. The Case of the Smelly Toilet in Chapter 22 is a good example of this point.

5. A controversy, *kachu*, was (1) formulated into a petition, *shuwa (zhu ba)*, and (2) taken to a court, *timkhang* or *timsa*, (3) to be decided, *timtagché (khrims thag bcad)* or *thakcho nangwa (thag gcod gnang ba)* or *thakché pa (thag bcad pa)*, (4) by an official who could give out punishments, *tsara (rtsa ra)*, and (5) issue a judicial decree, *thama (khra ma)* or *chéyik (bcad yig)* or *chétha (bcad khra)* or *timki yikcha (khrims kyi yig cha)*.

6. The terminology for many of these steps was also specialized; see French 1990a.

Chapter 11

1. Bartlett 1986:164; see also Hyams 1980.

2. The work of Michael Lambek (1988, 1993) and others on oracular speech and its use in social settings is particularly relevant here.

3. GP:885–88.

4. *Bonpo* is an ancient religious tradition in Tibet–thought by some scholars to be of Kashmiri origin–which has absorbed many Buddhist ideas and traditions. The Dharma Protectors, also known as *dharmapalas*, are a class of deities who protect the teachings of the Buddha. They appear in male and female forms and have both wrathful and worldly countenances.

5. For the Tibetan proverbs and terminology in this section, see French 1990a:511–22.

6. GP:281.

7. ND:417–25.

Chapter 12

1. Chapter 24 covers many of the same issues with specific reference to Tibetan concepts of criminal jurisprudence.

2. Robert Ekvall (1973:14–16) uses the term *rgyu 'bras*, cause-effect, to signify the Tibetan "dialectic of the correlation of contradiction. . . . As a concept having two degrees of meaning or levels—fairness and justice—it is at the apex of a semantic triangle . . . [and] stands for: fairness in the marketplace, value stated or questioned, and price asked for or given; fairness in social relations—decisions made or concessions granted in problems of inheritance, marriage, divorce, assignment of role, cognizance of status fitness, recognition of need, deference to self image and much else." He notes that all aspects of conciliation proceedings and decisions were subject to being scrutinized as "having justice or not." This sounds very close to the ideas of

honesty and truthfulness expressed in this chapter. Perhaps the general range of meaning is the same, but the words employed are different because Ekvall's field experience was almost entirely in the far northeast among nomadic pastoralists; see Ekvall 1968.

3. GP:838–39.

4. Martin Shapiro (1981) and other legal scholars following his lead have long argued that the conventional American prototype of courts ignores the importance of mediation and consent integral to these forums. Many of Shapiro's points about lack of sanctions, disputants choosing to go to court, and the desire for factual certainty apply to Tibet. He states that "a major function of courts in many societies is to assist in holding the countryside" (1981:23); I would have to substitute either "legal rituals" or "legal cosmology" for the term "courts" in the case of Tibet. Shapiro's discussion of law in Imperial China presents a nice comparison to the material in this book.

5. Laura Nader (1990) has argued that we need to look at the mechanisms that promote harmony as thoroughly as those that result in conflict.

6. GP:786.

7. These ideas are reiterated in the area of criminal law in Chapter 24.

8. GP:1167, 1098.

9. The six aspects or stages to enlightenment, with their botanical metaphors intact, were given as factors of analysis by Tibetans of religious bent: (1) the primary cause, or seed; (2) the basis, or soil; (3) the secondary cause, metaphorically understood as water and sunlight; (4) the method, or daily watering of the plant; (5) the result, or green shoot; and (6) the activity, or growth of the plant. See French 1990a.

10. The Tibetan for physical evidence is *ngo po thog ne khung kel* (*dnos po'i thog nas khungs skyel*), and for oral evidence is *nag thok khung kel* (*nag thog khungs skyel*).

11. See Dewey 1924; Rosen 1989. For a good review of the Anglo-American history and philosophy of precedent (and the problems it entails), see essays in L. Goldstein (1987).

12. Usually, only an old clerk would be able to recall whether the petitioners had been in court before, or whether the court had decided a very similar previous case.

13. Compare the Tibetan notion with a critique of the American idea of equality by Peter Weston (1982:596), who points out that the American form is "an empty form having no substantive content of its own."

Chapter 13

1. See the Excursus following this chapter for the use of these furnishings. See also French 1990a.

2. For an extended description of this court, see Chapter 23.

Chapter 14

1. See Ehrlich 1936; Gierke 1957.

2. A recent example is Robert C. Ellickson (1993:7), who restates a very old idea: "Large segments of life are conducted beyond the shadow of the law. Informal norms, not legal rules, mainly shape relations among students and coworkers, business dealings and international affairs." See also Ellickson 1991.

3. See Weber 1954, 1964; Llewellyn and Hoebel 1941.

4. See Pospisil 1971; see also Middleton 1966. It is important to note that each legal level

may be defined differently and need not even be a "level" in the hierarchical sense: one subgroup level may be culturally defined, the next economically defined, and so forth; also, differing hierarchies of subgroup legal levels can coexist within the same larger unit. Modern legal systems too often have variant and yet coexisting hierarchies of legal levels based on territory and occupation.

5. Moore 1982, 1986:329.

6. Pierre Schlag (1990a, 1990b, 1991) has suggested that another way of understanding this is to think in terms of varying subjects and frames.

7. Thurman 1984:146.

8. See the essays in Carrithers et al. 1985 on the category of the person.

9. In Tibetan, *lokel ba (blo 'khel ba)* or *lokel po (blos 'khel po).*

10. GP:896–901. Similar language is used in Ts:441–46, as shown in this chapter's epigraph.

11. See GP:902–16.

12. See M'Naughton's Case, 8 English Rep. 718 (1943).

13. For the ecclesiastical wing of the government, see the Excursus following Chapter 23.

14. Ts:336 (see Chapter 6 for greater detail).

15. One bachelor official told this story of his servants: "I had seven servants in Lhasa. I never beat my good servants, for it was best to listen to them. I had a servant who was much older than me who drank. One day, he got very drunk, and he talked to me, scolding me, saying "Kungola [honorable sir], you should look to what each servant is doing!" This was very impolite, but I did nothing to this servant because he was older.

"It happens that owners do hit their servants sometimes; they hit them with a stick or with their fist, or they slap them. Servants never hit back. If the servant doesn't do the work, the owner gets mad and hits him. I have seen some owners throw all the food served on a tray back at the servant saying, 'Why have you made such bad food?'

"Dharma tells us that we should not do this, but it did happen. I have even struck my servants. I sent one servant to give a message to a person; he wandered in the marketplace looking at goods for hours and never came home. Finally, when he came home and had not delivered the message, I asked, 'Why did you take so long?' and I hit him."

16. One Tibetan told the story of a family separation case involving a highly influential and important family from an area just outside Lhasa. The family unsuccessfully tried conciliation and other techniques at the household level, and finally a government representative was called in. When he decreed that the family should split into its two warring halves with each part receiving exactly half of all the possessions, the mother of the family on one side and the dissenting daughter-in-law on the other carried the decision to a ridiculous degree by cutting in half every piece of silk, every painting, every piece of jewelry, and even every pot, so that each side would have its share. Observers considered this a valid but absurd method of carrying out the official's decision.

17. A well-educated elderly Tibetan explained it in this way: "We always tried to avoid going to sue (in a government court) unless the person is hot tempered or sharp tongued. It is very important to be a good neighbor, we say 'it is better [that it be done by] our neighbor although an enemy, than our relative who stays far away.' Neighbors are very important; they will try to solve problems, even judge and give advice. Some good neighbors will offer their money and jewelry to solve a dispute."

18. Among the nomadic tribes of Nangchen, a large territory four hundred miles northeast of Lhasa, the headman of one community stated that he was the first to seek a resolution of a fight between two men. He traveled from one tent to the other, talking and presenting explanations, questions, and solutions to each side in turn, and in this way a dispute between two tentholds was resolved. If he had not been able to decide it, the case could have gone up to

the local leader and possibly even have traveled through the three levels of princes over these local leaders and finally to the king, who was incorporated into the Tibetan government at the rank of governor.

19. Nebesky-Wojkowitz (1975:155–56) reports that the blacksmiths of Lhasa also had an association, called *dupelpa ('dod dpal pa),* which was controlled by the government and held an annual festive meeting known as the *yarkyi (dbyar skyid).*

20. That they handled many of their own internal conflicts seems clear, however, from interview information: references by outsiders to the associations in Tibet, and references to handling internal problems themselves by both refugee association members and Tibetans living on the Plateau. In Dharamsala, India, the current residence of the Dalai Lama, the "U-Tsang Association" (named after the two central regions of Tibet from which its members migrated) handles many different activities, from soliciting money for the performance of rituals in the local temple and coordinating the funeral expenses and cremation of Tibetan refugees without immediate family, to arranging numerous social activities for the community.

21. This case is all the more interesting because so few of the cases I collected made an issue of ethnicity.

Chapter 15

1. Spiro (1982:203) has also used this term to describe the Buddhist symbolic world of Burma.

2. The best introduction into this work is through Eco 1979; Morris 1931; Peirce 1980; Saussure 1959; Silverstein 1975.

3. Semioticians talk about aspects of this relationship such as the *designatum,* that which the sign refers to; the *denotatum,* the object of reference if it actually exists; the *interpretant,* the sign created in the mind of the receiver, etc.

4. See Lévi-Strauss 1963, 1976.

5. See esp. the original work of Mary Douglas (1970) and Victor Turner (1967).

6. See Lakoff 1987.

7. Geertz 1973:89. He defined culture, and an aspect of culture such as a legal system, as "an historically transmitted pattern of meanings embodied in symbols, a system of inherited conceptions expressed in symbolic forms by means of which men communicate, perpetuate and develop their knowledge about and attitudes toward life." These ideas, according to Geertz, are a fusion of the phenomenology of Husserl, the sociology of Weber, and the emphasis on "meaning" of Alfred Schütz.

8. There are, of course, several different approaches to symbolism in addition to the structuralism of Lévi-Strauss and the interpretive symbolism of Geertz. See, e.g., Schneider 1976; Skorupski 1976; and Sperber 1975.

9. Lévy-Bruhl 1985 (originally published in 1910).

10. Evans-Pritchard (1937) began by critiquing Lévy-Bruhl's work with data from the Azande of West Africa by showing that types of explanation vary within a society depending on the context and may have an internal rationality or consistency of their own, based on a particular cultural framework. See also Horton and Finnegan 1973; Kuhn 1962; Tambiah 1985, 1990. The arguments of Alasdair MacIntyre, Steven Lukes, and Charles Taylor as well are presented in Hollis and Lukes 1982; Overing 1985; and Wilson 1979.

11. This section was helped by discussions with the art historian Kristen Van Ausdall. Western medievalists use the term "scholasticism" to describe the form of rationalistic thought that prevailed alongside mystical cosmological thinking in the Middle Ages. Scholasticism,

even the work of Saint Thomas Aquinas, is understood to be in some sense a rudimentary, dogmatic, non-scientific form of premodern thought.

12. Cabezón (1994:15) has argued that scholasticism is a useful cross-cultural category for religious studies.

13. See Teubner 1988, 1993. Steve Smith and I have discussed these points; see Smith 1991a, 1991b.

14. Sahlins 1976.

15. See Le Goff 1988, e.g. 91.

16. See Schwartz 1985, esp. chaps. 6, 9; also Allan 1991; Needham 1956; and Pereenboom 1993.

17. Luhrmann (1989:352–56) similarly calls for more detailed ethnography in this area and comments that the rationality debate falsely assumes "the existence of clear-cut, coherent beliefs."

18. Tucci 1970:vii.

19. Aung-Thwin 1991; Christie 1986; Marr and Millner 1986; Wolters 1982. For a more general discussion, see also Arjomand 1993 and Ishii 1986.

20. See Goldstein 1971c, 1989; Samuel 1982.

21. Geertz 1987.

22. For a description of one such ceremony, including an exorcism, see French 1990a.

23. This was the configuration in a section of the Kalacakra Tantra ritual initiation I attended in Bodhgaya, India, in the mid-1980s. See also Dhargyey 1985; and Sopa et al. 1985.

24. Tucci 1970:23–25.

25. David Gellner (1992:191) is describing the mandala model with respect to early Malla Nepal, its capital city, and its Newar Buddhist inhabitants.

26. Comaroff 1985:6.

27. In Tibetan, *lhai naljor (lha'i rnal 'byor)*.

28. Beyer 1978:379. I commonly encountered rituals evoking Tara during my fieldwork; one was conducted in my own house in 1986 with wording very similar to that quoted by Beyer.

29. Taring 1984.

30. The huge Potala, the Winter Palace, in conjunction with the Summer Palace, *norbulinka (nor bu gling ka),* located outside Lhasa's outer ring to the far west, operated as a separate and distinct legal unit under the direction of the Office of the Dalai Lama.

Chapter 16

1. Privately owned land was measured in *kung (rkang);* the equivalent measure for estate land was *don (don)*. One *kung* or one *don* equaled five *khel* of grain.

2. This process took place every year, with the headman and representatives rotating annually but the members of the monasteries remaining the same.

Chapter 17

1. Under the Thirteenth Dalai Lama (1876–1933), the social rank categories of officials were relaxed slightly through His Holiness's practice of rewarding government rank on the basis of merit. The Thirteenth was a modernizer and attempted to institute reforms, especially after his brief exile in India (1910–12), where he learned about British administrative, legal,

and educational practices. Thus, by the second and third decade of the twentieth century, it was possible for a well-educated, efficient, and diligent government official, monastic or lay, to rise to the fourth rank without either *depon* or *midak* background and to acquire an estate in return for his service. Likewise, a son from one of these upper levels of families could lose official status if he did not perform his functions well.

2. Since a *khel* of seed was about thirty pounds, some 21,000 pounds could be sown on this farm. Tibetans measured a field by the amount of seed that could be strewn and grown on it: that is, by its ability to produce grain rather than by size. Thus, a very fertile ten-*khel* field could be a few acres, while a very infertile ten-*khel* field could be many acres.

3. The Excursus following Chapter 9 explains Tibetan land ownership and estate holding.

4. This part of the narrative is corroborated in the secondary literature. In the early 1920s the Phala estate near Gyantse comprised "over 1,400 farms as well as 13 grazing grounds, each supporting 15 to 20 families of graziers," according to Charles Bell (1924), then the British Consul in Lhasa. An estimated "20,000 sheep altogether" were "grazed in scattered grazing grounds" around the estate. It was an immense operation, involving thousands of Tibetan peasants organized into villages, each with its headman, all managed by a staff operating out of the estate house. Most of the supplies necessary for the maintenance of this virtual province were produced either in rooms and workshops at the main house or in the peasant households and then brought to the main house as taxes.

5. Tucci (1956) describes the landmarks cited by this Tibetan narrator.

6. Unfortunately, no accurate copy of this edict was available in any of the libraries, Tibetan or Western, or from any Tibetan as far as I was able to discover. Apparently related closely to the original edicts for the Tibetan law codes, it would be a mine of information and might help explain the average Tibetans' understanding of the laws of the country, since the annual reading was one of their major interactions with law.

7. These extracts from this "lecture" are quoted verbatim from the key narrator of this incident. For Tibetan words, see French 1990.

8. For more information on taxation, see the Excursus following this chapter.

Chapter 18

1. See the Excursus following Chapter 3.

2. Tibetans estimated that in the 1940s, five *tolas* of gold equaled fifty grams of gold dust. Taxes paid to the central government from the twenty-seven regions amounted to more than 1,000 kilos (2,205 pounds) of butter a year, by the narrator's estimate, and 50,000 kilos (over 55 tons) of barley. Some of the butter went to supply the local monasteries, and the rest was sent to Lhasa, where it was split between Ganden Monastery and the Storage Office of the central government. Both the butter and the barley were first stored on the estate and then transported on estate animals to the Neudong district office in the northern part of the Yarlung Valley. From there they went to the district office of Samye, home of the most famous and most ancient monastery in all of Tibet. Taxes were sent to the central government only once or twice a year, depending on need and request.

3. GP:1095–99; 1136–40; 1144–47.

4. See the Excursus following Chapter 14 for more on inheritance of land.

Chapter 19

1. Many of these headquarters were located at the sites of ancient centers of administration, *dzong,* meaning "fortress" or "castle," and had district officers called *dzong pon.* Districts

included several townships and were the first administrative level of the central government bureaucracy (see Chapter 14).

2. The Pitt Rivers Museum at Oxford has kindly made the journals of Charles Bell, the British representative in Lhasa in the 1920s, available to scholars. This passage, no. 60 in a section headed "Tibetan Random Notes" (Bell n.d.), appears to be quite similar in content to the Mountain Valley Decrees sent out annually. I have inserted Bell's original footnotes in brackets. The translation Bell quoted was probably done by a member of the Phala family; I do not have the original Tibetan.

3. See the Excursus following Chapter 13.

4. Figure 13 includes a sketch drawn by a member of the district office staff from 1944 to 1946.

5. The word *dékhel,* denoting a local measurement, combines the terms *dé,* a small bowl measurement, and *khel,* a unit of grain. Another possible Tibetan spelling is *bre khyad.* See the Excursus following Chapter 18.

6. See the Excursus on taxation, following Chapter 17.

7. During his tenure, there were associations of farmers who collected grain, of persons who managed religious ceremonies, of women who collected money for the fasting rituals at the temple every eighth and fifteenth of the month, and a very ancient association of townspeople who practiced and performed the local folk dances and songs and also arranged weddings and festivals. These local associations did not settle their own disputes as those in Lhasa did.

8. See the Excursus on court costs following Chapter 10.

Introduction to Part Four

1. The literature on ethnicity is enormous. For one of the original introductory works, see Barth 1969.

2. On nationalism, see Anderson 1983; E. Gellner 1983; Kohn 1967.

3. See Conley and O'Barr 1990; Merry 1990; Yngvesson 1993.

4. There are several wonderful exceptions. See Damaska 1968; Vagts 1990.

5. See A. Smith 1986, 1988; E. Weber 1979.

6. See E. Gellner 1983.

7. Herzfeld 1992:13.

8. See Douglas 1986; Herzfeld 1987, 1992.

9. The accounts of these offices and courts as they operated before 1959 are based on four sources of information: older maps and accounts; my own visits to these rooms in the 1980s; individuals who formerly functioned as clerks, officials, and caretakers; and laypersons who had visited the offices when they were in operation.

10. The Excursus following Chapter 23 presents equivalent material from the ecclesiastical perspective by detailing the operation of the Ecclesiastical Office, the highest court for the monastic bureaucracy.

Chapter 20

1. For the organization and geography of the city, see Chapters 7, 14, and 15; for its history, see Chapter 3.

2. The Tibetan for Drepung, is *'bras spungs;* Sera, *se rwa;* and Ganden, *dga' ldan.* Tucci (1956:102) says the numbers are 7,700 for Drepung, 6,600 for Sera, and 3,300 for Ganden.

3. The description in this section combines my own observation of Tibetan daily activities

during three years in India, Nepal, and Tibet with the extensive comments of Tibetans on their lives in pre-1959 Lhasa. Every one of the described activities still takes place daily in the city.

4. Bell (1924:109) details the Thirteenth Dalai Lama's sojourn in India and corroborates the changes in Lhasa afterward.

5. The accuracy of this figure, arrived at after discussions with many Tibetans, is questionable, since estimates of population in Tibet are notoriously variant.

6. Beckwith 1977.

7. Hugh Richardson writes that a Sikkimese Police Officer named Sirdar Bahadur Legs ldan lags established the polisi. "In my day, the police were hardly in evidence and were a rather ragged, virtually useless body." (Letter to the author).

8. The Ecclesiastical Office, which had its own loop of review with the offices above it, worked with a few closely related offices rather than a set of departments below it. Legal cases could come to it directly or through a simple ecclesiastical channel of appeal leading from the local level of a satellite monastery to its major monastery or provincial authority and then on to the Ecclesiastical Office. See the Excursus following Chapter 23.

9. See French 1990a for additional Tibetan terminology.

10. Though most sources said this office was started in the 1940s, two said it was initiated during the Reting regency in the 1930s; a third dated it in 1952 during the enthronement of the Fourteenth Dalai Lama.

Chapter 21

1. These are, respectively, the mantra to invoke Chenresi (also called Avalokitesvara), the god of compassion, and Tara, goddess of compassion.

2. Other, conflicting spellings of this name include *nang tse shag, nang rtse shag, nag tse shag,* and *snang rtse shar.* It was conjectured by some that "hundreds of years ago" a man named *snang rtse ba* had lived there and that the building was therefore called his residence, or *snang rtse shag.*

3. In *bod rgya tshig mdzod chen mo* (a 1985 Tibetan-Chinese dictionary published in Beijing), s.v. *snang rtse shag.*

4. This door was locked and sealed shut when I was there in 1986.

5. It is not clear whether in earlier times there was only a wooden ladder (as there is today) or an inside staircase connecting the two floors.

6. As a separate administrative area in Tibet, Sakya had its own representative in Lhasa.

7. See the Excursus on court costs, following Chapter 10.

Chapter 23

1. This back hallway was a dark and unlit area in 1986; however, there is some question as to whether or not the wall now standing between it and the front room was there before 1959; only one of the diagrams drawn by former judges or petitioners included it. On the other hand, the wall and doorway appear very old and worn, in keeping with the rest of the courtroom.

2. I collected some fifteen cases of murder heard by the High Court, but narrators did not always know the conclusion, the final decision contents, or the compensation payment.

3. Kyidong and its district office are described in Chapter 19.

4. Except for the death of two females by poisoning, all the other murder cases I collected involved both a male perpetrator and a male victim.

5. The stone rings visible on the wall of the Jokhang in 1986 were obviously very old, but it is unclear whether the plainer one was the "lion" or whether there is another stone carving resembling a lion, perhaps on the floor below the cat.

6. GP:607–54. The ninefold ranking system for monetary compensation first appeared in the documents of the early Empire period of the eighth century. There were many known contacts with the Chinese at that time, and it is possible that this system was influenced by the T'ang law code (619–906 A.D.). The available early Tibetan fragments on law, however, match social rankings to monetary payments, not to the T'ang code's five punishment levels (light stick, heavy stick, penal servitude, life exile, and death penalty). Moreover, the ninefold ranking system of the T'ang categorized only officials within the administration, not the entire population as the Tibetan fragments do. Certainly, the Tibetan term *tong*—which has many meanings, including "a thousand" and "empty, vacant"—presents another interesting question. See Johnson 1979, and Chapter 24.

7. The case of Tashi and Dorje in Chapter 14 illustrates this point.

Chapter 24

1. Robbery, theft, burglary, and their subdivisions were the subject matter of one section of all Tibetan law codes (see Ts:116ff. for an example) and were extensively detailed in the Vinaya.

2. For the Tibetan terminology, see French 1990a.

3. Exceptions to this requirement did occur: offenses in these categories which were hushed up completely, those known only to one person who did not reveal them, and those committed in areas where the local people traditionally handled these crimes themselves or areas that were considered separately incorporated.

4. There were also "supplemental punishments": wearing the cangue or wooden collar (weighing from thirty-two to forty-five English pounds) for a "fixed number of days, months, or years"; having the name of the offense tattooed on the forearm or face; whipping, as an addition to or substitute for blows with the stick; torture, such as "twisting the ears, slapping or beating, making the prisoner kneel on a chain, or squeezing the fingers or ankles with wooden compressors"; and after decapitation, the exposure of the head in a public spot (Bodde and Morris 1967:95–98).

5. These included light-stick penalties in five degrees from ten to fifty strokes; heavy-stick penalties in five degrees from sixty to one hundred strokes; penal servitude in three degrees; characters tattooed on the neck and face; the use of iron chains; exile in three degrees; and the death penalty in three degrees of slicing, strangulation, and decapitation (see Nguyen and Tai 1987). Later Vietnamese codes copied the Ch'ing code directly.

6. The criminal law of the Kirghiz, as compiled in 1876, listed death (singly or with near relatives), the severing of a limb, freezing in water, whipping, flogging with rods, degrading punishments, deprivation of property, monetary and property fines, banishment from the community, and compulsory service in lieu of a fine or debt (see Riasanovsky 1965b).

7. See Jagchid and Hyer 1979; Krueger 1972; Riasanovsky 1965b.

8. Many of the legal concepts described in Chapter 12 applied also in the criminal sphere, including agreement and consensus. Judges continued criminal cases until factual consonance was reached, because the victim, the victim's relatives, the defendant, and other parties to the crime were required to indicate by signing the final decision document that they agreed to the

punishments and costs. Questions unexplored here but equally interesting are external influences on these Tibetan concepts and, reciprocally, the influence of these concepts on punishment in the rest of Asia.

9. Nguyen and Tai 1987.

10. Ts:167.

11. Ts:168.

12. GP:338.

13. GP:343–45.

14. GP:332–36.

15. The nine-part social ranking system was presented in Chapter 9 and detailed with reference to murder in Chapter 23.

16. In 1934, one *dotsé* was reported by Kungola Phala to be approximately equivalent to a British pound sterling (Bell n.d.); other sources cite it as equivalent to four pounds of silver bullion.

17. The number of times the questioning whipping and the departing whipping were administered and the number of strokes each time were discretionary, determined by the court. Both were said by several persons to be much more serious than the initial whipping and capable of causing wounds.

18. There is a photograph of this rigid-handled whip in the India Office Library in London as part of the Sir Charles Bell Prints and Drawing Collection, Number J-245, and an example of it in silver in the Oxford Museum.

19. See the Case of the Tavern Lady, Chapter 21.

20. What should be done in such a circumstance is described by an eminent Tibetan noble named Kungola Phala, quoted in the records of Sir Charles Bell (n.d.): "If the accused is found innocent after two or three floggings, the person who falsely accused him, besides being himself punished, has to compensate the innocent accused, the amount of compensation depending on the amount of (physical) punishment that has been inflicted on the innocent man. Suppose two or three floggings have been inflicted, he may have to compensate the accused to the extent of two or three *dotsé* (i.e., two or three pounds sterling)."

21. For the Tibetan equivalents, see French 1990a.

22. GP:146b–51.

23. Other nontraditional devices involved (1) garrotting cages in which the criminal was suspended, which three separate sources reported having seen in front of the Lhasa City Court in the 1940s; and (2) a finger presser pictured in the Bell photograph collection in the Oriental and India Office, British Library.

24. GP:305.

25. This second prison is described in Chapter 21.

26. Goldstein 1989; Stoddard 1985.

Chapter 25

1. For more information about our relationship and his importance to this work, see the Introduction. For considerations of this particularly Western form of composition, "the biography," which imposes Western concepts of time, materialism, sequencing, self-hood, agency, form, and rationality on what is in this case a collection of anecdotes and illustrations not intended for that purpose, see Olney 1980; on the problem of idiosyncrasy, see Comaroff and Comaroff 1992; Ginzburg 1980, 1993; and Stone 1979.

2. "Rinpoche" is a title, meaning "precious jewel," often added to the name of an honored teacher.

3. Kungola has written a memoir on his time in China during these years (Sangye n.d.).

4. These districts, Kungola said, included "Magam, Tsokhang, Sanga, Korcho, Tsang nes, the eastern half of Dedge from the Dri Chu river, Pa Shu, Tri Yab, Chamdo, Lhatok, Dema, Riuche, Shunto, Tardzong, Lhodzong, Poto Dzong, Pome Yeon Dzong, Pocho Dzong, and some in the north of mixed jurisdiction. Of these, Dedge, Pa Shu, Tri Yab, Chamdo, and Lhatok didn't have undergovernors because each one had a local king or lama-king who ran the area as a princely state. They were all under government jurisdiction, of course, and responsible to our office."

Bibliography

Tibetan Sources on Law

Bod kyi khrims yig chen mo zhal lce bcu drug gi 'grel pa bzhugs so. Law Code of the Tsang King in sixteen sections. Thimpu, Bhutan: Kunsang Topgyel and Mani Dorji (Class II Shop No. 3).

"Bras ljongs bstan bsrung rnam rgyal gyis sde srid sangs rgyas rgya mtshor khrims skor dogs gcod shu ba." Legal questions addressed to the Fifth Dalai Lama by the Second King of Sikkim. Manuscript acquired in Tibet.

"Dmag khrims gsar bzo yong ba zhes." Army Law Code. Manuscript acquired in Tibet; appears to have been produced (hand printed with wooden blocks) in the twentieth century, perhaps as late as 1950.

"rGyal khrims gser." Law code of the Tsang King in eleven sections. Manuscript Ta.5 13548, Library of Tibetan Works and Archives, Dharamsala, India.

"Khrims 'degs kyi ang rims bshugs so." List of court cost payments. In *Tibetan Legal Materials.* Ballimaran, Delhi, India: Dorjee Tsering at M. M. Offset Press, 1985.

"Khrims yig bzhugs pa." Law Code of the Ganden Podrang in thirteen sections. Manuscript Ta.5 13547, (seventeenth-century), Library of Tibetan Works and Archives, Dharamsala, India.

"Khrims yig chen mo dang zhal lce bcu drug pa sogs bzhugs." Law Code of the Tsang King in sixteen sections. Manuscript Ta.5 13544, Library of Tibetan Works and Archives, Dharamsala, India.

"Khrims yig dang gzhan dag nye mkho sna tshogs bzhugs." Possibly an edict of the Tsang King Karma Tenkyong. Manuscript Ta.5 13545, Library of Tibetan Works and Archives, Dharamsala, India.

"Khrims yig zhal lce 13 dang 15 bcas le tshan gnyis yod / zhus dag lan gnyis song." Law Codes of the Tsang King in thirteen and sixteen sections. Manuscript acquired from P. Richardus, Von Meinen Collection, Leiden Museum, Holland.

"Khrims yig zhal lce bcu gsum bzhugs so." Law Code of the Tsang King in thirteen sections. Manuscript Ta.5 13549, Library of Tibetan Works and Archives, Dharamsala, India.

"sKu rgyal lam." List of court cost payments. Manuscript Ta.5 7015, Library of Tibetan Works and Archives, Dharamsala, India.

Library of Tibetan Works and Archives Documents. Collection of more than 150 original Tibetan documents on law and administration. Microfilmed by Jampa Samten, 1986.

"Po pho brang bsam 'grub rtse nas sngon gyi chos rgyal mes dbon gyi bka' khrims." Law Code of the Tsang King, with edicts. Handwritten, handsewn book, acquired from a native of Kyidong, Tibet.

Sangye, Thubten. "Handwritten Law Code Notes." Manuscript in author's collection.

Tibetan Legal Materials. 1985. Collection of texts in Tibetan on the legal and administrative structure of Tibet from a manuscript preserved in the Library of Tibetan Works and Archives. LTWA Publication. Ballimaran, Delhi, India: Dorjee Tsering, M. M. Offset Press.

"gTshang pa rgyal po'i khrims yig zhal lce bcu gsum pa." Law Code of the Tsang King in thirteen sections. Manuscript Ta.5 13546, Library of Tibetan Works and Archives, Dharamsala, India.

"Zin bris kyi bod rgyal sne'i gdong pa'i khrims yig zhal bce bco lnga pa." Law Code of the Neudong King in fifteen sections. Manuscript Ta.5 13550, Library of Tibetan Works and Archives, Dharamsala, India.

Additional Tibetan Sources

Dalai Lama V. N.d. *sKu gsung thugs gsar bzengs rin po che'i mchod rdzas khang bzang gi dkar chag dang tham pud deb khrims yig gi 'go rgyangs sde bzi'is go 'phar phye ba'i skal bzang.* Reproduced from Lhasa prints in the library of Tsepon W. D. Shakapa. New Delhi, India: T. Tsepal Taikang, Jayyed Press.

"Phags pa shes rab kyi pha rol tu phyin pa'i snying po'i mdo / shes rab snying po bzhugs so." The Sacred Sutra of the Heart of Perfection of Wisdom. Manuscript.

Retchung. N.d. *"Mi la ras pa'i rnam thar."* Life story of the famous Tibetan saint Milarapa, 1040–1123. Manuscript.

Sangpo, Khetsun. N.d. *Biographical Dictionary of Tibet and Tibetan Buddhism.* Dharamsala, India: Library of Tibetan Works and Archives.

Sangye, Thubten. N.d. *Rgya nag nan cing don gcod mi 'gro theng gnyis pa'i lo rgyus.* Memoir of Thubten Sangye's years in China as a representative of Tibet. Library of Congress Foreign Books Collection; and Library of Tibetan Works and Archives, Dharamsala, India.

Shakabpa, Tsepon. 1982. *Lta ldan rwa sa 'phrul snang gtsug lag khang gi dkar chag.* Guide to the Central Temple of Lhasa. Kalimpong, India: Tsepon Shakabpa.

Other Sources

Abel, Richard. 1973. "A Comparative Theory of Dispute Institutions in Society." *Law and Society Review* 8:217–347.

Allan, Sarah. 1991. *The Shape of the Turtle: Myth, Art, and Cosmos in Early China.* Albany: State University of New York Press.

Allen, N. J. 1979. "Fourfold Classification of Society in the Himalayas." In *Himalayan Anthropology: The Indo-Tibetan Interface,* ed. James Fisher. The Hague: Mouton.

Althusser, Louis. 1971. *Lenin and Philosophy, and Other Essays.* Trans. Ben Brewster. New York: Monthly Review Press.

Anderson, Benedict R. 1983. *Imagined Communities: Reflections on the Origin and Spread of Nationalism.* London: New Left Books.

Andress, Joel M. 1966. *Culture and Habitat in the Central Himalayas.* Ann Arbor, Mich.: University Microfilms.

Aris, Michael. 1979. *Bhutan: The Early History of a Himalayan Kingdom.* Warminster, Eng.: Aris & Phillips.

Aris, Michael, and Aung San Suu Kyi, eds. 1979. *Tibetan Studies in Honour of Hugh Richardson: Proceedings of the International Seminar on Tibetan Studies.* Warminster, Eng.: Aris & Phillips.

Arjomand, Said A., ed. 1993. *The Political Dimensions of Religion.* Albany: State University of New York Press.

Asad, Talal. 1973. "Two European Images of Non-European Rule." In *Anthropology and the Colonial Encounter,* ed. Talal Asad. London: Athlone Press.

——. 1986. "The Concept of Cultural Translation in British Social Anthropology." In *Writing Culture: The Poetics and Politics of Ethnography,* ed. James Clifford and George Marcus. Berkeley: University of California Press.

——. 1993. *Genealogies of Religion: Discipline and Reasons of Power in Christianity and Islam.* Baltimore: Johns Hopkins University Press.

Aung-Thwin, Michael. 1991. "Spirals in Early Southeast Asian and Burmese History." *Journal of Interdisciplinary History* 21:575–602.

Austin, John L. 1962. *How to Do Things with Words.* Oxford: Oxford University Press.

Avedon, John F. 1984. *In Exile from the Land of Snows.* New York: Knopf.

Aziz, Barbara N. 1978. *Tibetan Frontier Families: Reflections of Three Generations from Ding-ri.* Durham, N.C.: Carolina Academic Press.

Bacot, Jacques. 1940. *Documents de Touen-houang relatifs a l'histoire du Tibet.* Paris: P. Guenther.

Barth, Frederik. 1964. "Capital, Investment and the Social Structure of a Pastoral Nomadic Group in South Persia." In *Capital, Savings, and Credit in Peasant Societies: Studies from Asia, Oceania, the Caribbean, and Middle America,* ed. Raymond W. Firth and B. S. Yamey. Chicago: Aldine.

——, ed. 1969. *Ethnic Groups and Ethnic Boundaries.* Boston: Little, Brown.

——. 1987. *Cosmologies in the Making: A Generative Approach to Cultural Variation in Inner New Guinea.* Cambridge: Cambridge University Press.

Bartlett, Robert. 1986. *Trial by Fire and Water: The Medieval Judicial Ordeal.* Oxford: Clarendon Press.

Beckwith, Christopher I. 1977. "Tibet and the Early Medieval Florissance in Eurasia: A Preliminary Note on the Economic History of the Tibetan Empire." *Central Asiatic Journal* 21:89–104.

——. 1987. *The Tibetan Empire in Central Asia: A History of the Struggle for Great Power among Tibetans, Turks, Arabs, and Chinese during the Early Middle Ages.* Princeton: Princeton University Press.

Bell, Charles A. 1924. *Tibet, Past and Present.* Oxford: Clarendon Press.

——. 1928. *The People of Tibet.* Oxford: Clarendon Press.

——. 1931. *The Religion of Tibet.* Oxford: Clarendon Press.

——. 1946. *Portrait of the Dalai Lama.* London: Collins.

——. N.d. Unpublished records and diaries of Charles Bell, including "Tibetan Random Notes." Pitt Rivers Museum, University of Oxford.

Bennett, W. Lance, and Martha S. Feldman. 1981. *Reconstructing Reality in the Courtroom: Justice and Judgment in American Culture*. New Brunswick, N.J.: Rutgers University Press.

Berger, Peter L. 1967. *The Sacred Canopy: Elements of a Sociological Theory of Religion*. Garden City, N.Y.: Doubleday.

Berreman, Gerald D. 1975. "Himalayan Polyandry and the Domestic Cycle." *American Ethnology* 2:127–38.

———. 1978. "Ecology, Demography, and Domestic Strategies in the Western Himalayas." *Journal of Anthropological Research* 34:326–68.

Beyer, Stephen V. 1978. *The Cult of Tara: Magic and Ritual in Tibet*. Berkeley: University of California Press.

Bhagvat, Durga N. 1939. *Early Buddhist Jurisprudence*. Poona, India: Oriental Book Agency.

Bira, S. 1977. "A Sixteenth Century Mongol Code." Trans. Sh. Rashidonduk and V. Veit. In *Zentralasiatische Studien*. Weisbaden: Kommissionsverlag Otta Harrassowitz.

Bloch, Marc L. B. 1963. *Feudal Society*. Trans. L. A. Manyon. Chicago: University of Chicago Press.

Blondeau, A. 1972. "Les Religions du Tibet." In *Encyclopédie de la Pléiade: Histoire des Religiones III*. Paris: Encyclopédie de la Pléiade.

Bodde, Derk, and Clarence Morris. 1967. *Law in Imperial China: Exemplified by 190 Ch'ing Dynasty Cases*. Philadelphia: University of Pennsylvania Press.

Bogoslovskii, Vasilii A. 1972. *Essai sur l'histoire du peuple tibetain; ou, La naissance d'une société de classes*. Paris: C. Klincksieck.

Bohannan, Paul J. 1957. *Justice and Judgment among the Tiv*. Oxford: Oxford University Press.

Bourdieu, Pierre. 1977. *Outline of a Theory of Practice*. Trans. Richard Nice. Cambridge: Cambridge University Press.

———. 1984. *Distinction: A Social Critique of the Judgment of Taste*. Trans. Richard Nice. Cambridge: Cambridge University Press.

Braudel, Fernand. 1972. *The Mediterranean and the Mediterranean World in the Age of Philip II*. Trans. Sian Reynolds. New York: Harper & Row.

———. 1973. *Capitalism and Material Life: 1400–1800*. Trans. Miriam Kochan. New York: Harper & Row.

———. 1980. "History and the Social Sciences: The *Longue Durée*." In *On History*, trans. Sarah Matthews. Chicago: University of Chicago Press.

———. 1982. *The Wheels of Commerce*. Trans. Sian Reynolds. New York: Harper & Row.

Brenneis, Donald L. 1988. "Language and Disputing." *Annual Review of Anthropology* 17:221–37.

Brenneis, Donald L., and Fred R. Myers, eds. 1984. *Dangerous Words: Language and Politics in the Pacific*. New York: New York University Press.

Burman, Sandra B., and Barbara E. Harrel-Bond, eds. 1979. *The Imposition of Law*. New York: Academic Press.

Buxbaum, David C., ed. 1978. *Chinese Family Law and Social Change in Historical and Comparative Perspective*. Seattle: University of Washington Press.

Cabezón, José I. 1994. *Buddhism and Language: A Study of Indo-Tibetan Scholasticism*. Albany: State University of New York Press.

Carrasco-Pizana, Pedro. 1959. *Land and Policy in Tibet*. Seattle: University of Washington Press.

Carrithers, Michael, et al. 1985. *The Category of the Person: Anthropology, Philosophy, History*. Cambridge: Cambridge University Press.

Cassinelli, C. W., and Robert B. Ekvall. 1969. *A Tibetan Principality: The Political System of Sa sKya*. Ithaca: Cornell University Press.

Cech, Krystyna. 1988. "A Bonpo bCa'-yig: The Rules of the sMan-ri Monastery." In *Tibetan Studies,* ed. Helga Uebach and Jampa L. Panglung. Munich: Kommission fur Zentralasiatische Studien, Bayerische Akademie der Wissenschaften.

Chang, Wejen, ed. and trans. 1990. "Readings in Chinese Legal Thought." Unpublished collection of translated works. East Asian Legal Studies Center, Harvard Law School.

Chattopadhyaya, Alaka. 1981. *Atisa and Tibet: Life and Works of Dipamkara Srijnana in Relation to the History and Religion of Tibet.* Trans. Lama Chimpa. Calcutta: Asiatic Society.

Chaudhuri, Sibadas. 1971. *Bibliography of Tibetan Studies: Being a Record of Printed Publications Mainly in European Languages.* Calcutta: Asiatic Society.

Ch'en, Paul Heng-chao. 1979. *Chinese Legal Tradition under the Mongols: The Code of 1291 as Reconstructed.* Princeton: Princeton University Press.

Christie, Jan W. 1986. "Negara, Mandala, and the Despotic State: Images of Early Java." In *Southeast Asia in the Ninth to Fourteenth Centuries,* ed. David G. Marr and A. C. Millner. Singapore: Institute of Southeast Asian Studies; Canberra: Research School of Pacific Studies, Australian National University.

Clifford, James. 1988. *The Predicament of Culture: Twentieth-Century Ethnography, Literature, and Art.* Cambridge, Mass.: Harvard University Press.

———. 1994. "Diasporas." *Cultural Anthropology* 9:302–38.

Clifford, James, and George E. Marcus, eds. 1986. *Writing Culture: The Poetics and Politics of Ethnography.* Berkeley: University of California Press.

Collier, Jane F. 1973. *Law and Social Change in Zinacantan.* Stanford, Calif.: Stanford University Press.

Comaroff, Jean. 1985. *Body of Power, Spirit of Resistance: The Culture and History of a South African People.* Chicago: University of Chicago Press.

Comaroff, John L., and Jean Comaroff. 1992. *Ethnography and the Historical Imagination.* Boulder, Colo.: Westview Press.

Comaroff, John L., and Simon Roberts. 1981. *Rules and Processes: The Cultural Logic of Dispute in an African Context.* Chicago: University of Chicago Press.

Conklin, Harold C. 1962. "Lexicographical Treatment of Folk Taxonomies." *International Journal of American Linguistics* 28(pt. 4):119–41.

———. 1972. *Folk Classification: A Topically Arranged Bibliography of Contemporary and Background References Through 1971.* New Haven: Department of Anthropology, Yale University.

Conley, John M., and William M. O'Barr. 1990. *Rules versus Relationship: The Ethnography of Legal Discourse.* Chicago: University of Chicago Press.

Conze, Edward. 1975. *Buddhism: Its Essence and Development.* New York: Harper Colophon.

Coulborn, Rushton. 1956. *Feudalism in History.* Princeton: Princeton University Press.

Crook, John A. 1967. *Law and Life of Rome.* London: Thames & Hudson.

Dalai Lama XIV [Bstan-dzin-rgya-mtsho]. 1962. *My Land and My People.* New York: McGraw-Hill.

Damaška, Mirjan R. 1968. "A Continental Lawyer in an American Law School: Trials and Tribulations of Adjustment." *University of Pennsylvania Law Review* 116:1363–78.

———. 1986. *The Faces of Justice and State Authority: A Comparative Approach to the Legal Process.* New Haven: Yale University Press.

Dargyay, Eva K. 1982. *Tibetan Village Communities: Structure and Change.* Warminster, Eng.: Aris & Phillips.

Davis, Natalie Z. 1975. *Society and Culture in Early Modern France: Eight Essays.* Stanford, Calif.: Stanford University Press.

———. 1987. *Fiction in the Archives: Pardon Tales and Their Tellers in Sixteenth-century France.* Stanford, Calif.: Stanford University Press.

Deleuze, Gilles, and Félix Guattari. 1977. *Anti-Oedipus: Capitalism and Schizophrenia.* Trans. Robert Hurley et al. New York: Viking Press.

——. 1994. *What Is Philosophy?* Trans. Hugh Tomlinson and Graham Burchell. New York: Columbia University Press.

Delgado, Richard. 1993a. "Rodrigo's Second Chronicle: The Economics and Politics of Race." *Michigan Law Review* 91:1183–1203.

——. 1993b. "Rodrigo's Third Chronicle: Care, Competition, and the Redemptive Tragedy of Race." *California Law Review* 81:387–415.

Dewey, John. 1924. "Logical Method and Law." *Cornell Law Quarterly* 10:17–27.

Dhargyey, Geshe Ngawang. 1982. *An Anthology of Well-Spoken Advice on the Graded Paths of the Mind.* Dharamsala, India: Library of Tibetan Works and Archives.

——. 1985. *A Commentary on the Kalacakra Tantra.* Dharamsala, India: Library of Tibetan Works and Archives.

Dhondup, K. 1994. "Dharamsala Revisited: Shangrila or Sarajevo?" *Tibetan Review,* July, pp. 14–20.

Doty, William G. 1986. *Mythography: The Study of Myths and Rituals.* University: University of Alabama Press.

Douglas, Lawrence, and Austin Sarat. 1994. "(De)Mythologizing Jurisprudence: Speaking the 'Truth' about the 'Myth.'" *Law and Social Inquiry* 19:523–41.

Douglas, Mary. 1970. *Natural Symbols: Explorations in Cosmology.* New York: Pantheon.

——. 1986. *How Institutions Think.* Syracuse, N.Y.: Syracuse University Press.

Downs, James F. 1964. "Livestock and Social Mobility." *American Anthropologist* 66:1115–19.

——. 1964. "Tibetan Symposium: Introduction." *American Anthropologist* 66:1096–99.

Dundes, Alan, ed. 1984. *Sacred Narrative: Readings in the Theory of Myth.* Berkeley: University of California Press.

Eco, Umberto. 1979. *A Theory of Semiotics.* Bloomington: Indiana University Press.

Ehrlich, Eugen. 1936. *Fundamental Principles of the Sociology of Law.* Trans. Walter E. Moll. Cambridge, Mass.: Harvard University Press.

Ekvall, Robert B. 1961. "The Nomadic Pattern of Living among the Tibetans as Preparation for War." *American Anthropologist* 63:1250–63.

——. 1963. "Some Aspects of Divination in Tibetan Society." *Ethnology* 2:31–39.

——. 1964a. "Law and the Individual among the Tibetan Nomads." *American Anthropologist* 66:1110–15.

——. 1964b. "Peace and War among the Tibetan Nomads." *American Anthropologist* 66:1119–48.

——. 1968. *Fields on the Hoof: Nexus of Tibetan Nomadic Pastoralism.* New York: Holt, Rinehart & Winston.

——. 1973. "Correlation of Contradictions: A Tibetan Semantic Device." Paper given at the Ninth International Congress of Anthropological and Ethnological Sciences, Chicago.

Eliade, Mircea. 1960. *Myths, Dreams and Mysteries: The Encounter between Contemporary Faiths and Archaic Realities.* Trans. Philip Mairet. New York: Harper & Row.

——. 1963. *Myth and Reality.* Trans. Willard R. Trask. New York: Harper & Row.

Ellickson, Robert C. 1991. *Order without Law: How Neighbors Settle Disputes.* Cambridge, Mass.: Harvard University Press.

——. 1993. "How Professors Preempt Copyright Law." *Yale Law Report,* Fall, p. 7.

Ellington, Terry J. 1980. "Tibetan Monastic Constitutions: The bCa' Yig." Paper presented at the Ninth Wisconsin South Asia Conference, Madison, Wis., November 8.

——. 1984. Unpublished translation of Tun-huang documents. University of Washington, Seattle.

Engel, David M. 1978. *Code and Custom in a Thai Provincial Court: The Interaction of Formal and Informal Systems of Justice.* Tucson: University of Arizona Press.

———. 1993. "Origin Myths: Narratives of Authority, Resistance, Disability, and Law." *Law and Society Review* 27:785–826.

Epstein, Arnold L. 1967. "The Case Method in the Field of Law." In *The Craft of Social Anthropology,* ed. Arnold L. Epstein. London: Tavistock.

Evans-Pritchard, Edward E. 1937. *Witchcraft, Oracles, and Magic among the Azande.* Oxford: Clarendon Press.

Fabian, Johannes. 1983. *Time and the Other: How Anthropology Makes Its Object.* New York: Columbia University Press.

Fallers, Lloyd A. 1969. *Law without Precedent: Legal Ideas in Action in the Courts of Colonial Busoga.* Chicago: University of Chicago Press.

Felstiner, William F., et al. 1981. "The Emergence and Transformation of Disputes: Naming, Blaming, and Claiming . . ." *Law and Society Review* 15:631–54.

Ferrari, Alfonsa. 1958. *mK'yen brTse's Guide to the Holy Places of Central Tibet.* Rome: Instituto Italiano per il Medio.

Filippo de Filippi, ed. 1937. *An Account of Tibet: The Travels of Ippolito Desideri of Pistoia, S.J., 1712–1727.* London: Routledge.

Fisher, James F. 1986. *Trans-Himalayan Traders: Economy, Society and Culture in Northwest Nepal.* Berkeley: University of California Press.

Fitzpatrick, Peter. 1992. *The Mythology of Modern Law.* New York: Routledge, Chapman & Hall.

Foucault, Michel. 1976. *The Archeology of Knowledge.* Trans. A. M. Sheridan Smith. New York: Harper & Row.

———. 1979. *Discipline and Punish: The Birth of the Prison.* Trans. Alan Sheridan. New York: Vintage.

———. 1980. *The History of Sexuality.* Trans. Robert Hurley. New York: Vintage.

Frake, Charles O. 1969. "Struck by Speech: The Yakan Concept of Litigation." In *Law in Culture and Society,* ed. Laura Nader. Chicago: Aldine.

Frazer, James G. 1922. *The Golden Bough: A Study in Magic and Religion.* New York: Macmillan.

French, Rebecca R. 1987. "The Law and Codes of the Dalai Lamas: Their Origin, Style, and Use in Tibet and the Other Himalayan Kingdoms." In *Himalayas at a Crossroads: Portrait of a Changing World,* ed. Deepak Shimkhada. Pasadena, Calif.: Pacific Asian Museum Press.

———. 1990a. "The Golden Yoke." Ph.D. diss., Yale University.

———. 1990b. Review of *The Status of Tibet: History Rights, and Prospects in International Law,* by Michael C. van Walt van Praag. *American Journal of International Law* 84:996–99.

———. 1991. "The New Snow Lion: The Tibetan Government-in-Exile in India." In *Governments-in-Exile in Contemporary World Politics,* ed. Yossi Shain. New York: Routledge.

———. 1994. "Tibetans." In *Encyclopedia of World Cultures,* vol. 6, *Russia/Eurasia and China,* ed. David Levinson. Boston: G. K. Hall.

———. 1995. "Tibetan Legal Literature: The Law Codes of the dGa' ldan pho brang." In *Tibetan Literature: Essays in Honor of Geshe Sopa,* ed. José Cabézon and Roger Jackson. Ithaca, N.Y.: Snow Lion Press.

Fricke, Thomas E. 1986. *Himalayan Households: Tamang Demography and Domestic Processes.* Ann Arbor, Mich.: UMI Research Press.

Friedman, Lawrence M. 1970. "Legal Culture and Social Development." *Law and Social Science* 4:29–44.

——. 1977. *Law and Society: An Introduction*. Englewood Cliffs, N.J.: Prentice-Hall.

Furer-Haimendorf, Christoph von. 1975. *Himalayan Traders*. New York: St. Martin's Press.

Gazetter of Sikhim. 1894. "Sikkim Laws." In *The Gazetter of Sikhim*. Calcutta: Gazetteer of Sikhim Press.

Geertz, Clifford. 1966. *Person, Time and Conduct in Bali: An Essay in Cultural Analysis*. New Haven: Yale University Press.

——. 1973. *The Interpretation of Cultures: Selected Essays*. New York: Basic Books.

——. 1983. *Local Knowledge: Further Essays in Interpretive Anthropology*. New York: Basic Books.

——. 1987. *Negara: The Theatre State in Nineteenth-Century Bali*. Princeton: Princeton University Press.

——. 1988. *Works and Lives: The Anthropologist as Author*. Stanford, Calif.: Stanford University Press.

Gellner, David N. 1992. *Monk, Householder, and Tantric Priest: Newar Buddhism and Its Hierarchy of Ritual*. Cambridge: Cambridge University Press.

Gellner, Ernest. 1973. "Scale and Nation." *Philosophy of the Social Sciences* 3:1–17.

——. 1974. *Legitimation of Belief*. London: Cambridge University Press.

——. 1983. *Nations and Nationalism*. Oxford: Basil Blackwell.

——. 1992. *Postmodernism, Reason, and Religion*. London: Routledge.

Giddens, Anthony. 1979. *Central Problems in Social Theory: Action, Structure and Contradiction in Social Analysis*. Berkeley: University of California Press.

——. 1993. *New Rules of Sociological Method: A Positive Critique of Interpretive Sociologies*. Stanford, Calif.: Stanford University Press.

Gierke, Otto von. 1957. *Natural Law and the Theory of Society, 1500 to 1800*. Trans. Ernest Barker. Boston: Beacon Press.

Gilissen, John, ed. 1963. *Introduction bibliographique à l'histoire du droit et a l'ethnologie juridique*. Brussels: Université Libre de Bruxelles.

Ginzburg, Carlo. 1980. *The Cheese and the Worms: The Cosmos of a Sixteenth Century Miller*. Trans. John and Anne Tedeschi. Baltimore: Johns Hopkins University Press.

——. 1983. *The Night Battles: Witchcraft and Agrarian Cults in the Sixteenth and Seventeenth Centuries*. Trans. John and Anne Tedeschi. Baltimore: Johns Hopkins University Press.

——. 1989. *Clues, Myths and the Historical Method*. Trans. John and Anne Tedeschi. Baltimore: Johns Hopkins University Press.

——. 1991. *Ecstasies: Deciphering the Witches' Sabbath*. Trans. Raymond Rosenthal. New York: Penguin.

——. 1993. "Microhistory: Two or Three Things That I Know about It." *Critical Inquiry*, Fall, pp. 10–35.

Gluckman, Max. 1955. *The Judicial Process among the Barotse of Northern Rhodesia*. Manchester, Eng.: Manchester University Press.

——. 1965. *Politics, Law, and Ritual in Tribal Society*. Oxford: Basil Blackwell.

——. 1973. *Custom and Conflict in Africa*. New York: Barnes & Noble.

Goldstein, Laurence, ed. 1987. *Precedent in Law*. New York: Oxford University Press.

Goldstein, Melvyn C. 1968. *An Anthropological Study of the Tibetan Political System*. Ann Arbor, Mich.: University Microfilms.

——. 1971a. "The Balance between Centralization and Decentralization in the Traditional Tibetan Political System." *Central Asiatic Journal* 15:170–82.

——. 1971b. "Serfdom and Mobility: An Examination of the Institution of 'Human Lease' in Traditional Tibetan Society." *Journal of Asian Studies* 30:521–34.

——. 1971c. "Taxation and the Structure of a Tibetan Village." *Central Asiatic Journal* 15:1–27.

——. 1973. "The Circulation of Estates in Tibet: Reincarnation, Land and Politics." *Journal of Asian Studies* 32:445–55.

——. 1978. "Adjudication and Partition in the Tibetan Stem Family." In *Chinese Family Law and Social Change in Historical and Comparative Perspective,* ed. David C. Buxbaum. Seattle: University of Washington Press.

——. 1982. "Lhasa Street Songs: Political and Social Satire in Traditional Tibet." *Tibet Journal* 7:56–57.

——. 1989. *A History of Modern Tibet, 1913–1951: The Demise of the Lamaist State.* Berkeley: University of California Press.

Gombo, Ugen. 1978. "The Traditional Tibetan Economy: An Overview Analysis from a Socio-Anthropological Perspective." *Tibetan Review* 13:18–22.

Gordon, Antoinette K. 1959. *The Iconography of Tibetan Lamaism.* Rutland, Vt.: Tuttle.

Greenhouse, Carol J. 1986. *Praying for Justice: Faith, Order and Community in an American Town.* Ithaca: Cornell University Press.

Grunfeld, A. Tom. 1987. *The Making of Modern Tibet.* London: Zed Books.

Guenther, Herbert V. 1977. *Tibetan Buddhism in Western Perspective: Collected Articles of Herbert V. Guenther.* Emeryville, Calif.: Dharma.

Guenther, Herbert V., and Leslie S. Kawamura, eds. 1975. *Mind in Buddhist Psychology.* Emeryville, Calif.: Dharma.

Gulliver, Phillip H. 1963. *Social Control in an African Society: A Study of the Arusha, Agricultural Masai of Northern Tanganyika.* Boston: Boston University Press.

——. 1969. "Dispute Settlement without Courts: The Ndendeuli of Southern Tanzania." In *Law in Culture and Society,* ed. Laura Nader. Chicago: Aldine.

——. 1979. *Disputes and Negotiations: A Cross-Cultural Perspective.* New York: Academic Press.

Haarh, Erik. 1969. *The Yar-lun Dynasty: A Study with Particular Regard to the Contribution by Myths and Legends to the History of Ancient Tibet and the Origin and Nature of Its Kings.* Copenhagen: G. E. C. Gad's Forlag.

Haley, John O., comp. 1985. "Readings on the Legal Orders of Northeast Asia." Unpublished collection. Harvard Law School.

——, ed. 1988. *Law and Society in Contemporary Japan: American Perspectives.* Dubuque, Iowa: Kendall/Hunt.

——. 1991. *Authority without Power: Law and the Japanese Paradox.* New York: Oxford University Press.

Hamnett, Ian. 1977. *Social Anthropology and Law.* London: Academic Press.

Hari, Anna M. 1980. *An Investigation of the Tones of Lhasa Tibetan.* Huntington Beach, Calif.: Summer Institute of Linguistics.

Hart, Herbert L. A. 1961. *The Concept of Law.* Oxford: Clarendon Press.

Hart, Herbert L. A., and Tony Honore. 1985. *Causation in the Law.* Oxford: Clarendon Press.

Hayden, Robert M. 1987. "Turn-Taking, Overlap and the Task at Hand: Ordering Speaking Turns in Legal Settings." *American Ethnologist* 14:251–70.

Hedin, Sven. 1909. *Trans-Himalaya: Discoveries and Adventures in Tibet.* London: Macmillan.

Henderson, Daniel. 1964. "Settlement of Homicide Disputes in Sakya (Tibet)." *American Anthropologist* 66:1099–1105.

Herzfeld, Michael. 1987. *Anthropology through the Looking Glass: Critical Ethnography in the Margins of Europe.* Cambridge: Cambridge University Press.

——. 1992. *The Social Production of Indifference: Exploring the Symbolic Roots of Western Bureaucracy.* Chicago: University of Chicago Press.

Hoffmann, Helmut H. R. 1970. "Tibetan Historiography and the Approach of the Tibetans to History." *Journal of Asian History* 4:169–77.

———. 1975. *Tibet: A Handbook*. Bloomington: Research Center for the Language Sciences, Indiana University.

Hollis, Martin, and Steven Lukes, eds. 1982. *Rationality and Relativism*. Cambridge, Mass.: MIT Press.

Holmberg, David H. 1989. *Order in Paradox: Myth, Ritual, and Exchange among Nepal's Tamang*. Ithaca: Cornell University Press.

Hooker, M. B. 1975. *Legal Pluralism: An Introduction to Colonial and Neo-Colonial Laws*. Oxford: Clarendon Press.

Hopkins, Jeffrey. 1983. *Meditation on Emptiness*. London: Wisdom.

Horton, Robin, and Ruth Finnegan, eds. 1973. *Modes of Thought: Essays on Thinking in Western and Non-Western Societies*. London: Faber & Faber.

Hoskins, Janet. 1993. *The Play of Time: Kodi Perspectives on Calendars, History, and Exchange*. Berkeley: University of California Press.

Humphreys, Caroline. 1978. "Pastoral Nomadism in Mongolia." *Development and Change* 9:133–60.

Hyams, Paul R. 1980. *Kings, Lords, and Peasants in Medieval England: The Common Law of Villeinage in the Twelfth and Thirteenth Centuries*. Oxford: Clarendon Press.

International Commission of Jurists. 1959. *The Question of Tibet and the Rule of Law*. Geneva: International Commission of Jurists.

Ishii, Yoneo. 1986. *Sangha, State, and Society: Thai Buddhism in History*. Trans. Peter Hawkes. Honolulu: University of Hawaii Press.

Jackson, Bernard S. 1988. *Law, Fact, and Narrative Coherence*. London: Deborah Charles.

Jagchid, Sechin, and Paul Hyer. 1979. *Mongolia's Culture and Society*. Boulder, Colo.: Westview Press.

Jameson, Frederic. 1981. *The Political Unconscious: Narrative as a Socially Symbolic Act*. Ithaca: Cornell University Press.

Jaschke, Heinrich A. 1954. *Tibetan Grammar: Supplement of Readings with Vocabulary*. New York: Frederick Ungar.

Jest, Corneille. 1978. "Tibetan Communities of the High Valleys of Nepal: Life in an Exceptional Environment and Economy." In *Himalayan Anthropology: The Indo-Tibetan Interface*, ed. James F. Fisher. The Hague: Mouton.

Johnson, Wallace. 1979. *The T'ang Code*, vol. 1, *General Principles*. Princeton: Princeton University Press.

Just, Peter. 1986. "Let the Evidence Fit the Crime: Evidence, Law, and 'Sociological Truth' among the Dou Donggo." *American Ethnologist* 13:43–61.

———. 1990. "Dead Goats and Broken Betrothals: Liability and Equity in Dou Donggo Law." *American Ethnologist* 17:75–89.

Karmey, Samten. 1975. "A General Introduction to the History and Doctrines of Bon." In *Memoirs of the Research Department of the Toyo Bunko*. Tokyo: Toyo Bunko.

Koch, Klaus-Friedrich. 1974. *War and Peace in Jalemo: The Management of Conflict in Highland New Guinea*. Cambridge, Mass.: Harvard University Press.

Kohn, Hans. 1967. *The Idea of Nationalism* (1944). New York: Collier-Macmillan.

Kosko, Bart. 1993. *Fuzzy Thinking: The New Science of Fuzzy Logic*. New York: Hyperion.

Krader, Lawrence. 1963. *Social Organization of the Mongol-Turkic Pastoral Nomads*. Bloomington: Indiana University Press.

Krueger, John R. 1972. "New Materials on Oriat Law and History." *Central Asiatic Journal* 16:194–205.

Kuhn, Thomas S. 1962. *The Structure of Scientific Revolutions*. Chicago: University of Chicago Press.

Ladurie, Emmanuel Le Roy. 1979. *Montaillou: The Promised Land of Error.* Trans. Barbara Bray. New York: Vintage Books.

Lakoff, George. 1973. "Hedges: A Study of Meaning Criteria and the Logic of Fuzzy Concepts." *Journal of Philosophical Logic* 2:458–508.

———. 1987. *Women, Fire and Dangerous Things: What Categories Reveal about the Mind.* Chicago: University of Chicago Press.

Lambek, Michael. 1988. "Spirit Possession/Spirit Succession: Aspects of Social Continuity among Malagasy Speakers in Mayotte." *Ethnologist* 7:318–31.

———. 1993. "Cultivating Critical Distance: Oracles and the Politics of Voice." *PoLAR: Political and Legal Anthropology Review* 16:9–18.

Lasch, Christopher. 1978. *Culture of Narcissism: American Life in an Age of Diminishing Expectations.* New York: Norton.

Lattimore, Owen. 1951. *Inner Asian Frontiers of China.* New York: Capitol.

Lazarus-Black, Mindie. 1994. *Legitimate Acts and Illegal Encounters: Law and Society in Antigua and Barbuda.* Washington, D.C.: Smithsonian Institution Press.

Le Goff, Jacques. 1980. *Time, Work, and Culture in the Middle Ages.* Trans. Arthur Goldhammer. Chicago: University of Chicago Press.

———. 1988. *The Medieval Imagination.* Chicago: University of Chicago Press.

Lévi-Strauss, Claude. 1963. *Structural Anthropology.* Vol. 1. Trans. Claire Jacobsen and Brooke G. Schoepf. New York: Basic Books.

———. 1976. *Structural Anthropology.* Vol. 2. Trans. Claire Jacobsen and Brooke G. Schoepf. New York: Basic Books.

Lévy-Bruhl, Lucien. 1973. "Durkheim and the Scientific Revolution." In *Modes of Thought: Essays on Thinking in Western and Non-Western Societies,* ed. Robin Horton and Ruth Finnegan. London: Faber & Faber.

———. 1985. *How Natives Think* (1926). Trans. Lilian A. Clare. Princeton: Princeton University Press.

Li, Shih-yu Yu. 1950. "Tibetan Folk-Law." *Journal of the Royal Asiatic Society* 1950:127–48.

Li, Tieh-Cheng. 1960. *Tibet: Today and Yesterday.* New York: Bookman.

Llewellyn, Karl N., and E. Adamson Hoebel. 1941. *The Cheyenne Way: Conflict and Case Law in Primitive Jurisprudence.* Norman: University of Oklahoma Press.

Lopez, Donald S., ed. 1988. *Buddhist Hermeneutics.* Honolulu: University of Hawaii Press.

———. 1994. "New Age Orientalism: The Case of Tibet." *Tibetan Review,* May, pp. 16–20.

Luhmann, Niklas. 1985. *A Sociological Theory of Law.* Trans. Elizabeth King and Martin Albrow. London: Routledge & Kegan Paul.

Luhrmann, Tanya M. 1989. *Persuasions of the Witch's Craft: Ritual Magic and Witchcraft in Present-Day England.* Cambridge, Mass.: Harvard University Press.

Macfarlane, Alan. 1976. *Resources and Population: A Study of the Gurungs of Nepal.* Cambridge: Cambridge University Press.

Maine, Sir Henry S. 1878. *Ancient Law: Its Connection with the Early History of Society, and Its Relation to Modern Ideas.* London: John Murray.

Malinowski, Bronislaw. 1954. *Magic, Science and Religion, and Other Essays.* Garden City, N.Y.: Doubleday.

———. 1959. *Crime and Custom in Savage Society* (1926). Patterson, N.J.: Littlefield, Adams.

———. 1965. *Coral Gardens and Their Magic,* vol. 1, *Soil Tilling and Agricultural Rites in the Trobriand Islands.* Bloomington: Indiana University Press.

Marcus, George E. 1993. *Perilous States: Conversations on Culture, Politics, and Nation.* Chicago: University of Chicago Press.

Bibliography

Marcus, George E., and Michael M. J. Fischer, eds. 1986. *Anthropology as Cultural Critique: An Experiment in the Human Sciences*. Chicago: University of Chicago Press.

Marr, David G., and A. C. Millner, eds. 1986. *Southeast Asia in the Ninth to Fourteenth Centuries*. Singapore: Institute of Southeast Asian Studies; Canberra: Research School of Pacific Studies, Australian National University.

Meisezahl, R. O. 1973. "Die Handschriften in Den City of Liverpool Museums." *Zentralasiatische Studien* (Weisbaden) 7:221–84.

Merry, Sally E. 1990. *Getting Justice and Getting Even: Legal Consciousness among Working-Class Americans*. Chicago: University of Chicago Press.

Merryman, John H. 1969. *The Civil Law Tradition: An Introduction to the Legal Systems of Western Europe and Latin America*. Stanford, Calif.: Stanford University Press.

Messick, Brinkley M. 1993. *The Calligraphic State: Textual Domination and History in a Muslim Society*. Berkeley: University of California Press.

Michael, Franz. 1982. *Rule by Incarnation: Tibetan Buddhism and Its Role in Society and State*. Boulder, Colo.: Westview Press.

Middleton, John. 1960. *Lugbara Religion: Ritual and Authority among an East African People*. Oxford: Oxford University Press.

———. 1966. "The Resolution of Conflict among the Lugbara of Uganda." In *Political Anthropology*, ed. Marc J. Swartz et al. Chicago: Aldine.

Miller, Beatrice D. 1956. "Ganye and Kidu: Two Formalized Systems of Mutual Aid among the Tibetans." *Southwestern Journal of Anthropology* 12:157–70.

———. 1960. "The Web of Tibetan Monasticism." *Journal of Asian Studies* 20:197–203.

Milsom, Stroud F. C. 1981. *Historical Foundations of Common Law*. London: Butterworths.

Moore, Sally F. 1969. "Law and Anthropology." *Biennial Review of Anthropology: 1969*, pp. 252–300.

———. 1982. *Law as Process: An Anthropological Approach*. London: Routledge & Kegan Paul.

———. 1986. *Social Facts and Fabrications: "Customary" Law on Kilimanjaro, 1880–1980*. Cambridge: Cambridge University Press.

———. 1987. "Explaining the Present: Theoretical Dilemmas in Processual Ethnography." American Ethnological Society Distinguished Lecture, San Antonio, Texas.

Morris, Charles W. 1931. "Foundations of the Theory of Signs." In *Collected Papers*, ed. Charles S. Pierce. Cambridge, Mass.: Harvard University Press.

———. 1946. *Signs, Languages, and Behavior*. New York: Prentice-Hall.

Mumby, Dennis K., ed. 1993. *Narrative and Social Control: Critical Perspectives*. Newbury Park, Calif.: Sage.

Nader, Laura. 1990. *Harmony Ideology: Justice and Control in a Zapotec Mountain Village*. Stanford, Calif.: Stanford University Press.

Nader, Laura, and Duane Metzger. 1963. "Conflict Resolution in Two Mexican Communities." *American Anthropologist* 65:584–92.

Nader, Laura, and Harry F. Todd, eds. 1978. *The Disputing Process: Law in Ten Societies*. New York: Columbia University Press.

Nebesky-Wojkowitz, René de. 1975. *Oracles and Demons of Tibet: The Cult and Iconography of Tibetan Protective Dieties*. Graz, Austria: Akademische Druck- u. Verlagsanstalt.

Needham, Joseph. 1956. *Science and Civilization in China*. Cambridge: Cambridge University Press.

Nguyen, Ngoc Huy, and Ta Van Tai. 1987. *The Lê Code: A Comparative Sino-Vietnamese Legal Study with Historical-Juridical Analysis and Annotations*. Athens: Ohio University Press.

Norbu, Dawa. 1974. *Red Star over Tibet*. London: Collins.

Norbu, Jamyang, ed. 1986. *Warriors of Tibet: The Story of Aten and the Khampas' Fight for the Freedom of Their Country*. London: Wisdom.

Norbu, Thubten J., and Colin M. Turnbull. 1970. *Tibet.* New York: Simon & Schuster.

O'Barr, William M. 1982. *Linguistic Evidence: Language, Power, and Strategy in the Courtroom.* New York: Academic Press.

Obermiller, E. 1932. *History of Buddhism: A Translation of Bu-sTon's Chos-hByung.* Heidelberg: O. Harrassowitz.

Offner, Jerome A. 1983. *Law and Politics in Aztec Texcoco.* Cambridge: Cambridge University Press.

Olney, James, ed. 1980. *Autobiography: Essays Theoretical and Critical.* Princeton: Princeton University Press.

Ortner, Sherry B. 1973. "Sherpa Purity." *American Anthropologist* 75:49–63.

———. 1978. *Sherpas through Their Rituals.* New York: Cambridge University Press.

———. 1984. "Theory in Anthropology since the Sixties." *Comparative Studies in Society and History* 26:126–66.

———. 1989. *High Religion: A Cultural and Political History of Sherpa Buddhism.* Princeton: Princeton University Press.

Overing, Joanna. 1985. *Reason and Morality.* London: Tavistock.

Palakshappa, T. C. 1978. *Tibetans in India: A Case Study of Mundgod Tibetans.* New Delhi: Sterling.

Paul, Robert A. 1977. "The Place of Truth in Sherpa Law and Religion." *Journal of Anthropological Research* 33:167–84.

———. 1982. *The Tibetan Symbolic World.* Chicago: University of Chicago Press.

Pereenboom, Randall P. 1993. *Law and Morality in Ancient China: The Silk Manuscripts of Huang-Lao.* Albany: State University of New York Press.

Peirce, Charles S. 1980. "Logic as Semiotic: The Theory of Signs." In *The Philosophy of Peirce: A Critical Introduction,* ed. Robert Almeder. Oxford: Basil Blackwell.

Pelliot, Paul. 1961. *Histoire ancienne du Tibet.* Paris: Librairie d'Amerique et d'Orient.

Perdue, Daniel E. 1976. *Introductory Debate in Tibetan Buddhism.* Dharamsala, India: Library of Tibetan Works and Archives.

———. 1992. *Debate in Tibetan Buddhism.* Ithaca, N.Y.: Snow Lion Press.

Petech, Luciano. 1972. *China and Tibet in the Early 18th Century: History of the Establishment of the Chinese Protectorate in Tibet.* Leiden: E. J. Brill.

———. 1973. *Aristocracy and Government in Tibet, 1728 to 1959.* Rome: Instituto Italiano per il Medio ed Estremo Oriente.

———. 1977. *The Kingdom of Ladakh: c. 950–1842 A.D.* Rome: Instituto Italiano per il Medio ed Estremo Oriente.

Peter, Prince of Greece and Denmark. 1952. "The Moslems of Central Tibet." *Journal of the Royal Central Asian Society* 39:233–40.

Polanyi, Karl, et al., eds. 1957. *Trade and Market in the Early Empires: Economies in History and Theory.* Glencoe, Ill.: Free Press and Falcon's Wing Press.

Posner, Richard. 1990. *The Problems of Jurisprudence.* Cambridge, Mass.: Harvard University Press.

Pospisil, Leopold J. 1958. *Kapauku Papuans and Their Law.* New Haven: Yale University Press.

———. 1963. *The Kapauku Papuan Economy.* New Haven: Yale University Publications in Anthropology.

———. 1971. *Anthropology of Law: A Comparative Theory.* New York: Harper & Row.

Rabinow, Paul. 1986. "Representations Are Social Facts: Modernity and Post-Modernity in Anthropology." In *Writing Culture: The Poetics and Politics of Ethnography,* ed. James Clifford and George E. Marcus. Berkeley: University of California Press.

Rahul, Ram. 1969. *The Government and Politics of Tibet.* Delhi: Vikas.

Riasanovsky, Valentin A. 1965a. *Customary Law of the Nomadic Tribes of Siberia*. Bloomington: Indiana University Press.

——. 1965b. *Fundamental Principles of Mongol Law*. Bloomington: Indiana University Press.

——. 1979. *Customary Law of the Mongol Tribes*. Westport, Conn.: Hyperion Press.

Richardson, Hugh E. 1954. "A Ninth Century Inscription from Rkon-Po." *Journal of the Royal Asiatic Society* 3/4:157–73.

——. 1957. "A Tibetan Inscription from Rgyal Lha-OKhan; and a Note on Tibetan Chronology from A.D. 841 to A.D. 1042." *Journal of the Royal Asiatic Society* 3/4:57–78.

——. 1962. *A Short History of Tibet*. New York: Dutton.

——. 1964. "A New Inscription of Khri Srong lDe brTsan." *Journal of the Royal Asiatic Society* 1/2:1–13.

——. 1969. "The Inscription at the Tomb of Khro lDe Srong brTsan." *Journal of the Royal Asiatic Society* 1:29–38.

——. 1972. "The rKong-Po Inscription." *Journal of the Royal Asiatic Society* 1:30–39.

——. 1978. "The Sino-Tibetan Treaty Inscription of A.D. 821/823 at LhaSa." *Journal of the Royal Asiatic Society* 2:135–62.

——. 1989. "Early Tibetan Law concerning Dog-bite." *Bulletin of Tibetology*. n.s. 3:5. Gangtok, Sikhim.

——. 1990. "Hunting Accidents in Early Tibet." Unpublished.

Roberts, Simon. 1979. *Order and Dispute: An Introduction to Legal Anthropology*. New York: St. Martin's Press.

Robinson, Richard H., and Willard L. Johnson. 1977. *The Buddhist Religion: A Historical Introduction*. Encino, Calif.: Dickenson.

Rockhill, William W. 1895. *Notes on the Ethnology of Tibet: Based on the Collections in the U.S. National Museum*. Washington, D.C.: Government Printing Office.

Roerich, George N., ed. 1976. *The Blue Annals*. Delhi: Motilal Banarsidass.

Rosen, Lawrence. 1984. *Bargaining for Reality: The Construction of Social Relations in a Muslim Community*. Chicago: Chicago University Press.

——. 1985. "Intentionality and the Concept of the Person." In *Criminal Justice*, ed. J. Roland Pennock and John W. Chapman. New York: New York University Press.

——. 1989. *The Anthropology of Justice: Law as Culture in Islamic Society*. Cambridge: Cambridge University Press.

Rubel, Paula G. 1967. *The Kalmyk Mongols: A Study in Continuity and Change*. Bloomington: Indiana University Press.

Ruegg, David S. 1966. *The Life of Bu ston Rin po che, with the Tibetan Text of the Bu ston rNam thar*. Rome: Instituto Italiano per il Medio ed Estremo Oriente.

Sahlins, Marshall D. 1976. *Culture and Practical Reason*. Chicago: University of Chicago Press.

——. 1981. *Historical Metaphors and Mythical Realities*. Ann Arbor: University of Michigan Press.

Said, Edward W. 1978. *Orientalism*. New York: Pantheon.

——. 1994. *Culture and Imperialism*. New York: Vintage.

Samuel, Geoffrey. 1982. "Tibet as a Stateless Society and Some Islamic Parallels." *Journal of Asian Studies* 41:215–29.

Saussure, Ferdinand de. 1959. *Course in General Linguistics*. Trans. Wade Baskin. New York: Philosophical Library.

Schama, Simon. 1988. *The Embarrassment of Riches: An Interpretation of Dutch Culture in the Golden Age*. Berkeley: University of California Press.

Schlag, Pierre J. 1990a. "'Le hors de texte, c'est moi': The Politics of Form and the Domestication of Deconstruction." *Cardozo Law Review* 11:1631–74.

——. 1990b. "Normative and Nowhere to Go." *Stanford University Law Review* 43:167–91.

——. 1991. "The Problem of the Subject." *Texas Law Review* 69:1627–1743.

Schneider, David J. 1976. "Notes toward a Theory of Culture." In *Meaning in Anthropology.* Albuquerque: University of New Mexico Press.

Schram, Louis. 1954. *The Monguors of the Kansu-Tibetan Frontier.* Philadelphia: American Philosophical Society.

Schuh, Dieter. 1973. *Untersuchungen zur Geschichte der tibetischen Kalenderrechnung.* Wiesbaden: Steiner.

——, ed. 1978. *Urkunden, Erlasse und Sendschreiben aus dem Besitz sikkimeisischer Adelshauser und des Klosters Phodang.* St. Augustin, Germ.: VGH Wissenschaftsverlag.

Schuh, Dieter, and J. K. Phukhang. 1979. *Urkunden und Sendschreiben aus Zentraltibet, Ladakh, und Zanskar.* St. Augustin, Germ.: VGH Wissenschaftsverlag.

Schwartz, Benjamin I. 1985. *The World of Thought in Ancient China.* Cambridge, Mass.: Belknap Press.

Scogin, Hugh T., Jr. 1990. "Between Heaven and Man: Contract and the State in Han Dynasty China." *Southern California Law Review* 63:1325–1404.

Searle, John R. 1969. *Speech Acts: An Essay in the Philosophy of Language.* London: Cambridge University Press.

——. 1992. *The Rediscovery of the Mind.* Cambridge, Mass.: MIT Press.

Shahrani, Nazif M. 1978. "The Retention of Pastoralism among the Kirghiz of the Afghan Pamirs." In *Himalayan Anthropology: The Indo-Tibetan Interface,* ed. James F. Fisher. The Hague: Mouton.

——. 1979. *The Kirghiz and Wakhi of Afghanistan: Adaptation to Closed Frontiers.* Seattle: University of Washington Press.

Shain, Yossi, ed. 1991. *Governments in Exile in Contemporary World Politics.* New York: Routledge.

Shakabpa, Tsepon W. D. 1967. *Tibet: A Political History.* New Haven: Yale University Press.

Shapiro, Martin. 1981. *Courts: A Comparative and Political Analysis.* Chicago: University of Chicago Press.

Shen, Tsung-Lien, and Shen-chi Liu. 1953. *Tibet and the Tibetans.* Stanford, Calif.: Stanford University Press.

Shweder, Richard A., and Robert A. Levine, eds. 1984. *Culture Theory: Essays on Mind, Self, and Emotion.* Cambridge: Cambridge University Press.

Sierksma, K. 1964. "Rtsod-pa: The Monachal Disputation in Tibet." *Indo Iranian Journal* 8:141.

Silverstein, Michael. 1975. "Linguistics and Anthropology." In *Linguistics and Neighboring Disciplines,* ed. Renate Bartsch and Theo Vennemann. New York: American Elsevier.

Sinor, Denis. 1969. *Inner Asia: History, Civilization, Languages: A Syllabus.* Bloomington: Indiana University Press.

Skorupski, John. 1976. *Symbol and Theory: A Philosophical Study of Theories of Religion in Social Anthropology.* Cambridge: Cambridge University Press.

Smith, Anthony D. 1986. *The Ethnic Origins of Nations.* Oxford: Basil Blackwell.

——. 1988. "The Myth of the 'Modern Nation' and the Myths of Nations." *Ethnic and Racial Studies* 11:1–26.

Smith, Gene E. 1969. *University of Washington Tibetan Catalogue.* Seattle: University of Washington.

Smith, Michael G. 1974. *Corporations and Society: The Social Anthropology of Collective Action.* London: Duckworth.

Smith, Steven D. 1987. "Symbols, Perceptions, and Doctrinal Illusions: Establishment Neutrality and the 'No Endorsement' Test." *Michigan Law Review* 86:266–332.

——. 1990. "The Pursuit of Pragmatism." *Yale Law Journal* 100:409–49.

——. 1991a. "Reductionism in Legal Thought." *Columbia Law Review* 91:68–109.

——. 1991b. "The Rise and Fall of Religious Freedom in Constitutional Discourse." *University of Pennsylvania Law Review* 140:149–240.

Snellgrove, David L. 1957. *Buddhist Himalaya: Travels and Studies in Quest of the Origins and Nature of Tibetan Religion*. Oxford: Bruno Cassirer.

——, ed. 1959. *The Hevajra-Tantra: A Critical Study*. London: Oxford University Press.

——. 1966. "For a Sociology of Tibetan Speaking Regions." *Central Asiatic Journal* 11:199-219.

——. 1987. *Indo-Tibetan Buddhism: Indian Buddhists and Their Tibetan Successors*. Boston: Shambala Press.

Snellgrove, David L., and Hugh Richardson. 1980. *A Cultural History of Tibet*. Boulder, Colo.: Prajna Press.

Sopa, Geshe L., et al. 1985. *The Wheel of Time: The Kalachakra in Context*. Madison, Wis.: Deer Park.

Sperber, Dan. 1975. *Rethinking Symbolism*. Trans. Alice L. Morton. Cambridge: Cambridge University Press.

Spiro, Melford E. 1982. *Buddhism and Society: A Great Tradition and Its Burmese Vicissitudes*. Berkeley: University of California Press.

Starr, June. 1992. *Law as Metaphor: From Islamic Courts to the Palace of Justice*. Albany: State University of New York Press.

Starr, June, and Barbara Yngvesson. 1975. "Scarcity and Disputing: Zeroing-in on Compromise Decisions." *American Ethnologist* 2:553–66.

Staunton, George T. 1966. *Ta Tsing Leu Lee: Being the Fundamental Laws, and a Selection from the Supplementary Statutes, of the Penal Code of China*. Taipei, Taiwan: Ch'eng-Wen.

Stcherbatsky, F. Theodore. 1922. *The Central Conception of Buddhism*. London: Royal Asiatic Society.

——. 1962. *Buddist Logic*. New York: Dover.

Stein, Mark A. 1933. *On Ancient Central-Asian Tracks: Brief Narrative of Three Expeditions in Innermost Asia and North-Western China*. London: Macmillan.

Stein, Rolf A. 1971. "Du récit au rituel dans les manuscrits tibétans de Touenhouang." In *Etudes tibetaines, dédiées a la mémoire de Marcelle La Lou*. Paris: Librairie d'Amerique et d'Orient.

——. 1972. *Tibetan Civilization*. Trans. J. E. Stapelton Driver. Stanford, Calif.: Stanford University Press.

——. 1981. *La civilisation tibetaine*. Paris: Sycomore/l'Asiatheque.

Stoddard, Heather. 1985. *Le mediant de l'Amdo*. Paris: Société d'Ethnographie, Nanterre.

Stone, Lawrence. 1979. "The Revival of Narrative: Reflections on a New Old History." *Past and Present* 85:3–24.

——. 1981. *The Past and the Present*. Boston: Routledge & Kegan Paul.

Strayer, Joseph R. 1956. "Feudalism in Western Europe." In *Feudalism in History*, ed. Rushton Coulborn. Princeton: Princeton University Press.

——. 1965. *Feudalism*. Princeton, N.J.: Van Nostrand.

Surkhang, W. G. N.d. "Tax Measurement and Lag 'Don Tax." *Bulletin of Tibetology* 3:15–28.

Tachikawa, Musashi. 1983. *A Catalogue of the United States Library of Congress Collection of Tibetan Literature in Microfiche*. Tokyo: International Institute for Buddhist Studies.

Tai, Ta Van. 1988. *The Vietnamese Tradition of Human Rights*. Berkeley: University of California Press.

Tambiah, Stanley J. 1970. *Buddhism and the Spirit Cults in North-East Thailand*. Cambridge: Cambridge University Press.

——. 1985. *Culture, Thought and Social Action: An Anthropological Perspective*. Cambridge, Mass.: Harvard University Press.

——. 1990. *Magic, Science, Religion, and the Scope of Rationality*. Cambridge: Cambridge University Press.

Taring, Zasak J. 1980. *Lhasa Tsug-Lag Khang gi Sata and Karchag: The Index and Plan of the Lhasa Cathedral in Tibet*. New Delhi: Indraprastha Press.

——. 1984. *Map of Lhasa*. Tokyo: University of Tokyo Press.

Teubner, Gunter. 1984. "Autopoiesis in Law and Society: A Rejoinder to Blankenburg." *Law and Society Review* 18:291–301.

——, ed. 1988. *Autopoietic Law: A New Approach to Law and Society*. Berlin: De Gruyter.

——. 1993. *Law as an Autopoietic System*. Trans. Anne Bankowska and Ruth Adler. Oxford: Blackwell.

Thomas, Lowell, and Lowell Thomas Jr. 1950. "Out of This World: A Journey to Lhasa." *Collier's*, February 11, pp. 13–17, 70.

Thompson, Edward P. 1966. *Making of the English Working Class*. New York: Vintage.

Thurman, Robert A. F. 1976. *The Holy Teaching of Vimalakirti: A Mahayana Scripture*. University Park: Pennsylvania State University Press.

——, ed. 1982. *The Life and Teachings of Tsong-khapa*. Trans. Sherpa Tulku et al. Dharamsala, India: Library of Tibetan Works and Archives.

——. 1984. *Tsong Khapa's Speech of Gold in the Essence of True Eloquence: Reason and Enlightenment in the Central Philosophy of Tibet*. Princeton: Princeton University Press.

Toussaint, Gustave-Charles, ed. 1933. *Le Dict de Padma (Padma Thang Yig)*. Paris: Leroux.

Trubek, David M. 1972. "Max Weber on Law and the Rise of Capitalism." *Wisconsin Law Review* 20:720–53.

——. 1986. "Max Weber's Tragic Modernism and the Study of Law in Society." *Law and Society Review* 20:573–98.

Tsarong, Dundul N. 1983. "A Tibetan Government Official's Life History and Government Responsibilities." Ed. from taped interviews by Beatrice Miller. Paper presented at the Twelfth Annual Conference on South Asia, Madison, Wis., November 4–6.

Tucci, Giuseppe. 1949. *Tibetan Painted Scrolls*. Rome: Libreria dello Stato.

——. 1950. *The Tombs of the Tibetan Kings*. Rome: Instituto Italiano per il Medio ed Estremo Oriente.

——. 1956. *To Lhasa and Beyond: Diary of the Expedition to Tibet in the Year 1948*. Rome: Instituto Poligrafico dello Stato.

——. 1970. *The Theory and Practice of the Mandala: With Special Reference to the Modern Psychology of the Subconscious*. Trans. Alan H. Brodrick. New York: Samuel Weiser.

——. 1980. *The Religions of Tibet*. Trans. Geoffrey Samuel. Berkeley: University of California Press.

Turk, Austin T. 1976. "Law as a Weapon in Social Conflict." *Social Problems* 23:276–91.

Turner, Victor W. 1967. *The Forest of Symbols*. Ithaca: Cornell University Press.

——. 1969. *The Ritual Process: Structure and Anti-Structure*. Ithaca: Cornell University Press.

Unger, Roberto M. 1975. *Knowledge and Politics*. New York: Free Press.

——. 1976. *Law in Modern Society: Toward a Criticism of Social Theory*. New York: Free Press.

Uray, Geza. 1960. "The Four Horns of Tibet according to the Royal Annals." In *Acta Orientalia Academiae Scietarium Hungaricae*. Budapest: Magyar Tudomanyos Akademia.

——. 1972. "The Narrative of Legislation and Organization of the mKhas-Pa'i dGa'-sTon: The Origins of the Traditions concerning Sron-brCan sGam-Po as First Legislator and Organizer of Tibet." In *Acta Orientalia Academiae Scietarium Hungaricae*. Budapest: Magyar Tudomanyos Akademia.

Vagts, Detlev F. 1990. "International Law in the Third Reich." *American Journal of International Law* 84:661–704.

Van der Sprenkel, Sybille. 1962. *Legal Institutions in Manchu China: A Sociological Analysis.* London: Athlone Press.

Van Velsen, J. 1967. "The Extended-Case Method and Situational Analysis." In *The Craft of Social Anthropology,* ed. Arnold L. Epstein. London: Tavistock Press.

Vostrikov, Andrei I. 1970. *Tibetan Historical Literature.* Trans. Harish C. Gupta. Calcutta: Soviet Indology.

Waddell, Laurence A. 1972. *Tibetan Buddhism, with Its Mystic Cults, Symbolism, and Mythology, and in Relation to Indian Buddhism.* New York: Dover.

Wagner, Roy. 1986. *Symbols That Stand for Themselves.* Chicago: University of Chicago Press.

Walt van Praag, Michael C. van. 1987. *The Status of Tibet: History, Rights, and Prospects in International Law.* Boulder, Colo.: Westview Press.

Watson, Alan. 1974. *Legal Transplants: An Approach to Comparative Law.* Charlottesville: University Press of Virginia.

——. 1977. *Society and Legal Change.* Edinburgh: Scottish Academic Press.

Weber, Eugen. 1979. *Peasants into Frenchman: The Modernization of Rural France, 1870–1914.* London: Chatto & Windus.

Weber, Max. 1954. *On Law in Economy and Society.* Trans. Edward Shils and Max Rheinstein. New York: Simon & Schuster.

——. 1958. *The Religion of India: The Sociology of Hinduism and Buddhism.* Trans. and ed. Hans H. Gerth and Don Martindale. Glencoe, Ill.: Free Press.

——. 1964. *The Theory of Social and Economic Organization.* Trans. A. M. Henderson and Talcott Parsons. New York: Free Press.

Weston, Peter. 1982. "The Empty Idea of Equality." *Harvard Law Review* 95:537–96.

Wilson, Bryan R., ed. 1979. *Rationality.* Oxford: Basil Blackwell.

Winch, Peter. 1964. "Understanding a Primitive Society." *American Philosophical Quarterly* 1:307–24.

Wolters, O. W. 1982. *History, Culture, and Religion in Southeast Asian Perspectives.* Singapore: Institute of Southeast Asian Studies.

Wylie, Turrell V. 1959. "A Standard System of Tibetan Transliteration." *Harvard Journal of Asiatic Studies* 22:261–67.

——, ed. 1962. *The Geography of Tibet According to the 'dZam-gling rGyas-bShad.* Rome: Instituto Italiano per il Medio ed Estremo Oriente.

Yamaguchi, M. 1970. *Catalogue of the Toyo Bunko Collection of Tibetan Works on History.* Tokyo: Toyo Bunko.

Yang, Ho-Chin, ed. 1969. *The Annals of Kokonor.* Bloomington: Indiana University Press.

Yngvesson, Barbara. 1993. *Virtuous Citizens, Disruptive Subjects: Order and Complaint in a New England Court.* New York: Routledge.

Younghusband, Francis E. 1910. *India and Tibet: A History of the Relations Which Have Subsisted between the Two Countries from the Time of Warren Hastings to 1910, with a Particular Account of the Mission to Lhasa of 1904.* London: John Murray.

Zunz, Oliver, ed. 1985. *Reliving the Past: The Worlds of Social History.* Chapel Hill: University of North Carolina Press.

Tibetan Word Index

nor (nor), 172
nupa (nus pa), 107
nyanshu (snyan zhu), 308, 310
nyenka (nyen ka), 140
nyertsang nangtsen (gnyer tshang nang tshan),
    277
nying (snying), 355
nyingma pa (rnying ma pa), 30, 35, 197–198

opo ('os po), 115

pa (pha), 27
pang po (dpang po), 309
pashi (pha gzhis), 172
pashul (pha shul), 172
pashul budzin (pha shul bus 'dzin), 172
pay (dpe), 356
pentsun thunpa (phan tshun mthun pa), 138, 359
phamogru (phag mo gru), 42–43, 204, 352
polisi (po li si), 260
ponpo wengyuk (dpon po dbang rgyug), 322
potala (po ta la), 45, 119, 124, 187–190, 235,
    250–251, 253–255, 260, 306, 308, 330, 363
pul (phul), 230

ragyab pa (rags gyab pa), 112, 167
rangdo (rang 'dod), 109
rangnang gi dope (rang snang gi 'dod pas), 109
rato (ra sprod), 144
rato ngopo (ra sprod dngos po), 309
reting (rwa sgreng), 335
rig (rigs), 143
rilung tsatsik (ri klung rtsa tshig), 208, 336
rimshi (rim bzhi), 335, 337
rinpoche (rinpoche), 369
rongtim (rang khrims), 76, 80, 100, 164
rulsubmé (rul sub med), 139–140

sakya pa (sa skya pa), 35, 42
sampa (bsam pa), 143, 355
sem (sems), 75, 76
ser tel (ser khral), 199
shan phab (unknown), 127
shay (bshad), 356
shay (shes), 355
shelkar (shel dkar), 149, 196–199, 201–203, 236
shen dang mida wa (gzhan dang mi 'dra ba), 316
shengi wang (gshan gyi dbang), 62
sherdrung (gsher drung), 291
sherkhang (gsher khang), 291–292, 295, 297,
    300, 305, 322, 336, 357
sherpang (gsher dpang), 292, 295
shertim khang (gsher khrims khang), 291
shi (gzhi), 143
shidu (gzhis sdod), 206
shika dagpo (gzhis ka'i bdag po), 358
shipchopa (zhib dpyod pa), 274
sho (sho), 134
shogu (shog bu), 156
shug (shugs), 108
shulen (zhu lan), 309
shusho (zhu zho), 226
shuwa (zhu ba), 275, 308, 359
shuwa shulen (zhu ba zhu lan), 109
shuway yigay (zhu ba'i yi ge), 226
silon (srid blon), 262

sipa sum (srid pa gsum), 70
sogcho (gsod gcod), 297
somola (sru mo lags), 329
sung (srang), 114, 127, 280, 286–287, 289, 303

tachak (rta lcag), 322
tamkas (tam ka), 234
tanka (thang ka), 112, 132
tel tokan (khral sprod mkhan), 358
thakché pa (thag bcad pa), 359
thakcho nangwa (thag gcod gnang ba), 359
thama (khra ma), 286, 359
thartuk (mthar thug), 143
thipdek pa (thib breg pa), 258
thom dzig khang (khrom gzigs khang), 260
thonchak (thon lcag), 322
thutob (mthu stobs), 282–283, 285, 289, 357
tim (khrims), 100
timchak (khrims lchag), 180–181
timdak (khrims bdag), 100
timdem (khrims gtam), 100
timgam (khrims sgam), 158
timjuk (khrims 'jug), 180–181
timkhang (khrims khang), 100, 359
timki yikcha (khrims kyi yig cha), 359
timme (khrims mi), 225
timpon (khrims dpon), 100
timsa (khrims sa), xvii, 100, 359
timsopa (khrims bzo pa), 225, 309, 320
timtagché (khrims thag bcad), 359
timyik zhalche chu sum zhug so (khrims yig zhal
    lce bcu gsum bzhugs so), xvii
tob (stobs), 107
tsa wa (rtsa ba), 142–143
tsampa (rtsam pa), 4, 5, 256
tsang (gtsang), xvii, 14, 22, 41, 43–46, 53, 112,
    114, 129, 159, 163, 207, 236–237, 257–258
tsangpa (gtsang pa), 257
tsara (rtsa ra), 359
tsasik (rtsa tshig), 43
tse yiktsang (rtse yig tshang), 306
tsikhang lékung (rtsis khang las khungs), 356
tsodag (gtso drag), 237
tsongkhapa (tsong kha pa), 353
tsonpa (btson pa), 298
tsopa (rtsod pa), 102
tsopa dumdik chépa (rtsod pa 'dum 'grig byed
    pa), 359
tsuchung (tshugs chung), 155
tsugla khang (gtsug lag khang), 356–357
tsukug (tshugs 'khyug), 155
tsultim (tshul khrims), 100
tsuring (tshugs ring), 155
tsutun (tshugs thung), 155
tu (mthu), 107
tundo (dud 'gro), 355

uchen (dbu chan), 155
ulak ('u lag), 5
umé (dbu med), 155

wang (dbang), 107
wanglang (unknown), 239

yabmay (yab mes), 172
yabshi (yab gzhis), 110, 358

General Index

Ability, power as (*nupa*), 107
Accounting system, 229–31, 275–76
Adultery, seriousness of, 143
Agreement. *See* Consensus, concept of
Agricultural tax, 215–16
All-One symbol
  Tibetan mandala as, 177–80, 182–85, 346
  Western conceptualization of symbols and,
    175–77
Amdo province, 23, 25, 53, 170
American legal concepts, and Tibetan law, 9, 16–
    17, 57–59. *See also* Jurisprudence; Reasoning
  both parties present for legal proceedings, 109
  closure and finality, 139–40, 213–14, 344–45
  comparative law, 17, 249–52, 343–46
  competency, 161–64
  consent and consensus, 74, 115, 137–38, 202–3,
    224–25, 281, 286–87, 288, 345
  due process, 138
  equality, 109, 344, 360n.13
  evidence, 144–45
  fundamental fairness, 138, 346
  gaps in the law, 16
  indeterminacies, 16
  intention, 76, 77, 355n.4
  logic and rationality, 145, 176–77, 344,
    360n.11
  mens rea, 344
  motivation, 288, 344
  omission/commission distinction, 141–42
  precedent, 9, 145, 344, 360n.11
  predictability, 161
  proximate cause, 142
  reasonableness, 79–80, 354n.6
  religious/secular split, 12–14, 345
  res judicata, 9, 139–40, 213–14, 345
  risk, 140–42
  rule-formation, xii, 16, 67, 344
  sanctioning power of the state, 315–25, 345
  stare decisis, 139–40, 345

time, 72–73, 240, 289
truth, 137–38
veracity and false testimony, 109–10
Animal tax, 216
Appeal procedure, 154
Appellate/lower court distinction, 153–54
Appropriateness, concept of (*opo*), 115, 143, 213
Architecture
  mandala as spatial organizing device in, 177–
    80
  regulations governing roof ornaments and, 278
Asad, Talal, 78
Asian legal systems, Tibetan system compared
  with, 14–16, 316
Associations (*kyiduk dang tsokpa*), 166–69,
    365n.7. *See also* Boundaries
Asura. *See* Demigods
Atisha (eleventh-century scholar), 185, 236
Authority. *See also* Conciliator; Decision-makers;
    Judges
  idea of (*na og*), 115
  symbols of, 180–81, 263

Bah clauses. *See* Contracts
Beckwith, Christopher, 34
Beggars. *See* Outcastes
Bell, Sir Charles, 151, 233, 331, 364n.4, 365n.2
Beyer, Stephen, 186
Bohannan, Paul, 354n.6
Boundaries. *See also* Associations; Central Gov-
    ernment; Community; Competency; Dis-
    trict; Household; Human sentient being;
    Identity; Individual; Legal levels; Township
  cosmology of law defining, 160
  expansion of concept of law, 159
  multivalent legal, in concepts of identities,
    units and levels, 160
Brenneis, Donald, 354n.7
Bribes, 123, 225, 276, 280, 289
Bridegroom (*magpa*), 32, 38

Chinese invasion of Tibet and, 49–50, 237, 339

enthronement of, 334, 335

government-in-exile in Dharamsala, India, 9, 50–52

on process of incarnation, 351n.5

Frake, Charles, 99

Friedman, Lawrence, 350n.21

Frivolous suits, 213

Fuzzy logic, 355n.7

Ganden Monastery, 50, 63, 255–56, 279–82, 339, 353, 364–65
  Case of the Smelly Toilet and, 279–90

Ganden Podrang law codes of the Dalai Lamas, 1, 327, 336
  conciliation in, 4
  on division of family property, 226
  on hierarchy, 109–10
  on internal dispute settlement, 147
  on law and order, 315
  on local practice of law, 195
  magical words in, 104
  on oaths and ordeals, 130–31
  on peacefulness of Tibet, 253
  provisions of, 45–46
  on succession of Dalai Lamas, 69
  on truth, 137
  on truthful petitions, 341

Geertz, Clifford, 62, 176, 362n.7

Gellner, David, 184

Gelukpa period, 45–49

Geography, 21–26

Gierke, Otto von, 159

Ginzburg, Carlo, 15, 85

Goldstein, Melvyn, 14–15, 354n.13, 358n.9

Gongkar (town and district), 6, 170, 196, 327–30, 333

Government, Tibetan. See Central government

Government-in-exile, 9, 10, 50–52. See also Fourteenth Dalai Lama

Government record books (jétha sherpang), 5–7, 118, 158

Governor (chikab), 47, 170–71, 198

Great Monk Secretaries, 306

"Green Rules" (ngotim), 199–202, 203

Greenhouse, Carol, 354n.4, 355n.4

Guarantor, 243, 244

Guenther, Herbert V., 107

Guilt, imposition of, 298, 300–301

Gyantse, city of, 1, 65–66, 113, 178, 196, 207, 333, 364

Hail protection, 197–203, 216

Haley, John, 15

Handcuffs. See Fetters

Heart of Wisdom Sutra, 224

Hells, in Tibetan realms, 70

Herzfeld, Michael, 245, 250

"Hidden sins," 80–81

Hierarchy, concept of, 108–10. See also Social categories and stratification
  honorifics and, 109, 210, 214, 223, 267, 350n.1
  legal procedure and, 109–10, 267
  mandala symbolism and, 179
  spatial format of legal spaces and, 147–53, 202, 203

High Court of Tibet (sherkhang; shertim khang)
  court building of, 292–95
  courtroom floor plan for, 149, 150–51, 294
  functions of, 295–97
  judges platform in, 294, 295, 296, 297
  jurisdiction of, 295
  law code in, 336
  oracles and, 130
  physical access to, 291, 292, 293
  procedures for murder cases in, 297–305
  referral process and, 153–54, 267
  storage of documents and, 158

History
  Annales school, 15, 84
  cultural history, 15, 84
  law codes as, 41–44
  narrative and, 17–18, 84–85, 346

History of Tibet
  Chinese incorporation of Tibet, 49–50
  Gelukpa period of, 45–49
  incorporation of land into Tibet, 53
  law codes as, 41–44
  Phamogru dynasty, 42–43
  Sakya period, 42
  Tibetans in exile (1958 to present), 50–52
  Tsang dynasty, 42–43

Hoebel, E. A., 159

Holmberg, David, 354n.3

Honesty (drungbo), 137, 138, 346

Honorifics, 109, 210, 214, 223, 267, 350n.1

"House Book" (khangdeb), 278

Household (kim tsang)
  as legal level, 164–65
  as legal unit, 26–27, 165–66, 202, 215
  taxes and, 172, 215, 216, 217

Human sentient being. See also Boundaries; Mind
  categories of, and legal competency, 161–64
  notion of, in Tibetan philosophy, 160–61

Identity. See also Boundaries; Individual
  as human sentient being in Tibetan philosophy, 160–61
  legal competency and, 161–64
  relation to boundaries, units and levels, 160

Illusion, notion of. See Reality, illusory nature of

Impermanence, Buddhist doctrine of, 35–36

Income tax, 216

India, Tibetan refugee community in, 9, 10, 50–52, 63, 81, 346

Individual. See also Boundaries; Identity; Mind
  as legal level, 164
  as legal unit, 164–65
  mandala symbolism and, 177, 178, 184–87
  time, rebirth and, 72

Inherent power (tu), 107

Inheritance
  of dependency between peasant and landlord, 215
  general patterns of, 172–73
  intestate, 172–73
  patrilineal, 172
  property distinctions in, 172
  taxes and, 216
  wills and, 91, 173–74, 333

"Initial whipping" (jorchak), 300–302, 322

Story of the Close Friends and, 92
Story of the Two Blacksmiths and, 96
State law (*gyatim*), 100
State Oracle, 48–49, 130, 295–96
Stealing
  as crime, and factoring, 316–17
  Story of the Laughing Thief and, 95
  Story of the Stolen Tea and, 315
Stone, Lawrence, 84–85, 356n.6
Stone cat, 294, 300, *301*
Strength, power of (*tob*), 107
Subject matter, jurisdiction based on, 115, 140,
  239–40, 278, 308, 316
Suffering, 36, 64
Surkhang family, 206, 207, 210, 212, 270
Suru, Tashi, 241–45
Suspects (*lakmarpa; tsonpa*)
  in murder cases, 298
  tying of, 261, 300–301
Symbols. *See also* Mandala
  of legal authority, 180–81
  Western conceptualization of, 175–77

Tambiah, Stanley, 57, 59
Tantric meditation, 186
Tara (deity), 185–87, 224, 254
Tashilungpo (state), *196*, 200, 219, 333
Taverns, 261
  liability of owners of, 259, 274–75, 276
Taxation, 215–17
  annual tax to the central government from
    Lhagyari, 364n.2
  collection of taxes, 170, 216, 239, 278
  delinquent taxes and, 214
  Donkey Tax Case and, 210–13, 214
  estates and, 220
  forms of, 215–16
  land ownership and, 118, 215
  local pattern of, 4–5
  "man tax" and, 215
  measures and, 229–30
  oracles and, 216, 296
  police duty and, 261
  relief from, 217
  responsibility for taxes and, 4–5, 172, 215
  service-labor tax (*ulak*), 5
Ten Nonvirtuous Acts (*mége bacu*), 41, 75, 80–82
  factors and, 143–44
  legal myths and, 83, 91–97
Territory, jurisdiction based on, 115, 274, 278
Theft. *See* Stealing
"Thickness of the case" (*kachu karlo*), 138, 240,
  287
Thirteenth Dalai Lama, 208, 256, 351n.5, 352n.5
  reforms of, 113, 237, 363n.1
  Thubten Sangye and, 330–32, 333
  unexplained illness of, 130
Three Kingdoms, 42
Thurman, Robert, 160–61
Tibet, country of
  Chinese presence in, 25, 49–50, 337, 339
  consequences of Buddhist doctrines for, 36–37
  foreign affairs and, 338
  Gelukpa period in history of, 45–49
  geographic regions of, 21–26, 53
  incorporation of land into, 53

  law codes in history of, 41–44
  mandala as encompassing model in, *178–79*
  map of Tibetan Plateau, *22–23*
  provincial subunits in, 219
  terms for people of, 25–26
Tibetan legal system. *See also* Central govern-
    ment of Tibet; Legal levels; Legal procedure
  Buddha standard and, 79–80, 343–44
  causality in, 142–43
  cosmological categories and, 59–60
  flexibility of, 139–40, 203, 289
  general categories of law in, 100
  illusory nature of reality and, 62–66
  jurisdiction in, 115–17
  kaleidoscopic cosmology of, 16–17, 346–47
  karma and, 63–64
  legal language and, 99–105
  monastic debate and, 102–5
  myth of Milarapa and, 91
  nature of conflict and, 73–74
  necessity of consensus in, 138–39
  negative motivation and, 76–77
  nomadic groups and, 204, 361n.18
  non-decay of an issue or agreement (*rulsubmé*)
    in, 139, 140, 344–45
  notions of time and, 72–73, 240, 289
  other Asian legal systems and, 15–16, 316
  from perspective of comparative law, 343–46
  religious nature of, 12–14, 345–46
  role of myth in, 91–97
  taxation and, 217
  Ten Nonvirtuous Acts and, 80–81, 91–97
  Western works on Tibetan history and, 14–15
Tibetan people (*bopa*)
  diaspora culture and, 50–52
  population in Lhasa, 238
  regional ethnicity among, 25–26
  religion of, 35–37
  social groups among, 26–33
  trading activities of, 33–34
Time, notions of, 72–73, 240, 289
To province, 150, 170, 236, 298
Tong system, 112, *114*, 127–28, 171, 303–4, 320–
  21, 367
Topgyal, Benpa, 81–82
"Tough monks" (*thutob*), 282, 283, 285, 289
Township (*dongkir rimpa*), 169. *See also*
  Boundaries
Trade, 33–34. *See also* Commerce
Transmigration, Buddhist doctrine of, 36
Tribe, as nomadic political unit, 28
Truth (*denpa*)
  as factual consonance, 137, 138–40, 302–3,
    367n.8
  as fairness in procedure, 138, 281, 289, 346
  as personal standard, 138
  Tibetan *vs.* American views of, 137–38
  truthfulness, 137
"Truth stick," 295
Tsang dynasty, 43–44
Tsang law code, 43–44, 353n.7
  compilation of, 353n.13
  on legal competency, 159
  oaths and, 129
  social ranking system in, 114
Tsangpo River, *22*, 25, *196*, 206, 219